WORKSHOPS IN COMPUTING
Series edited by C. J. van Rijsbergen

Springer

Berlin
Heidelberg
New York
Barcelona
Budapest
Hong Kong
London
Milan
Paris
Tokyo

Also in this series

continued on back page...

James Clifford and Alexander Tuzhilin (Eds)

Recent Advances in Temporal Databases

Proceedings of the International
Workshop on Temporal Databases,
Zurich, Switzerland,
17–18 September 1995

Published in collaboration with the
British Computer Society

 Springer

James Clifford, PhD

Alexander Tuzhilin, PhD

Leonard N. Stern School of Business, Information Systems Department, New York University, 44 West 4th Street, Suite 9-170, New York, NY 10012-1126, USA

ISBN-13:978-3-540-19945-8

British Library Cataloguing in Publication Data
Recent Advances in Temporal Databases : Proceedings of the International Workshop on Temporal Databases, Zurich, 17–18 September 1995. – (Workshops in Computing Series)
  I. Clifford, James   II. Tuzhilin, A.A.   III. Series
  005.74
ISBN-13:978-3-540-19945-8   e-ISBN-13:978-1-4471-3033-8
DOI: 10.1007/978-1-4471-3033-8

Library of Congress Cataloging-in-Publication Data
A catalog record for this book is available from the Library of Congress

Typesetting: Camera ready by contributors

34/3830-543210 Printed on acid-free paper

Preface

The International Workshop on Temporal Databases held in Zürich, Switzerland, 17–18 September 1995 brought together researchers from academic and industrial institutions with database practitioners interested in keeping up with the state-of-the-art developments in the management of temporal data. A previous workshop in Arlington, Texas in June 1993 focused on the development of an infrastructure that would spur the development of commercial implementations of many of the generally agreed-upon features of temporal database management that have emerged from the temporal database research community over more than a decade of research. This ARPA/NSF-sponsored Arlington workshop saw the formation of the TSQL2 Language Design Committee, which led to the development of the recently completed TSQL2 Language Specification, and also created a "consensus" glossary of temporal database terminology and a test suite of temporal database queries.

The Zürich workshop was conceived from the outset to be universal in scope and international in participation. The Call for Papers sought to evoke the highest quality and most up-to-date temporal database research from around the world. Mindful of the important work accomplished by the previous workshop, the Call also specifically sought out research papers and panels that would comment and build upon the widely publicized results from Arlington.

These proceedings contain the papers that were selected for presentation at the International Workshop, on Temporal Databases held in Zürich, Switzerland on 17–18 September 1995. This workshop, jointly sponsored by the VLDB Foundation, ARPA, the National Science Foundation, Aalborg University and ETH-Zürich, was held at ETH in Zürich immediately after the 21st annual VLDB Conference. This arrangement was designed to facilitate the widest possible international participation by enabling many participants to combine attendance at both venues.

The Call for Papers attracted 55 research papers and 4 panel proposal submissions from over 16 countries on 5 continents, a clear confirmation of the fact that research in the temporal database area is truly international. Paper selection was handled by a Program Committee consisting of 24 temporal database researchers representing a variety of academic and industrial institutions from 13 countries, using the "double-blind reviewing" method. The 18 papers and 2 panel descriptions that are included in this volume are the result of this selection process.

The topics of the papers covered in this volume range from highly theoretical to experiential reports on how temporal databases are, or can be, used to solve practical, real-world problems. The papers have been organized into the following groups:

- Temporal and Spatio-Temporal Data Models and Design Issues
- Temporal Constraints
- Critical Evaluations of TSQL2
- Alternative Views on Temporal Data Models
- Implementation Issues for Temporal DBMSs
- Potpourri

In addition to the technical papers, brief synopses of two panels which were held at the workshop are included in this volume. The first panel, "The State-of-the-Art in Temporal Data Management: Perspectives from the Research and Financial Applications Communities", addressed the state of the field of temporal data management from two perspectives. In the first part of the panel, members of the research community reported on the state-of-the-art of the infrastructure for temporal DBMS research and implementation. Then, in the second part of the panel, the state-of-the-art in business practices for the management of temporal data was discussed from the perspective of the financial services business sector, one of the largest commercial application areas in need of effective temporal data management. A second panel, "Whither TSQL3?", addressed the design issues that it was felt ought to be central to any TSQL3 proposal for incorporating a temporal dimension into the emerging SQL3 Standard. It also considered the practical issues of an organizational structure that should be put into place in order to have the most impact on commercial DBMS implementations.

Many people helped in putting together this workshop. First of all, the Steering Committee was responsible for shepherding an initial idea from its inception through to the reality of the workshop. The Program Committee, with the help of some external reviewers listed in this volume, carefully reviewed the papers under an extremely tight schedule. The Local Arrangements Chair, Robert Marti of ETH-Zürich, helped to coordinate the planning of the workshop with the VLDB Conference organizers. Thanks are due especially to the workshop sponsors: the VLDB Foundation, ARPA, the National Science Foundation, Aalborg University, and ETH-Zürich. Special thanks are due to Balaji Padmanabhan for his help in the day-to-day management of all of the Program Committee's labors.

Finally, we would like to thank all of the authors who submitted papers for this workshop. It is their work that keeps this field a vibrant and exciting area of database research.

New York City   James Clifford and
September 1995   Alexander Tuzhilin

Workshop Organization

Steering Committee:

Arie Segev (Chair), UC Berkeley and Lawrence Berkeley Lab, USA
James Clifford, New York University, USA
Christian S. Jensen, Aalborg University, Denmark
Tamer Özsu, University of Alberta, Canada
Barbara Pernici, Politecnico di Milano, Italy
Niki Pissinou, University of Southwestern Louisiana, USA
Richard T. Snodgrass, University of Arizona, USA

General Chair:

Christian S. Jensen, Aalborg University, Denmark

Program Chair:

James Clifford, New York University, USA

Program Committee:

Gad Ariav, Tel Aviv University, Israel
Jan Chomicki, Kansas State University, USA
Albert Croker, Bernard M. Baruch College, CUNY, USA
Ramez Elmasri, University of Texas, Arlington, USA
Opher Etzion, Technion, Israel
Shashi K. Gadia, Iowa State University, USA
Fabio Grandi, Università di Bologna, Italy
Matthias Jarke, University of Aachen, Germany
Wolfgang Käfer, Daimler Benz, Germany
T.Y. Cliff Leung, IBM Santa Teresa Lab, USA
David Lomet, DEC Cambridge Research Lab, USA

Nikos A. Lorentzos, Agricultural University of Athens, Greece
Inderpal Singh Mumick, Bell Laboratories, AT&T, USA
Beng-Chin Ooi, National University of Singapore, Singapore
John F. Roddick, University of South Australia, Australia
Colette Rolland, Université de Paris 1, France
Ellen Rose, Massey University, New Zealand
N.L. Sarda, Indian Institute of Technology, Bombay, India
Edward Sciore, Boston College, USA
Abdullah Uz Tansel, Bernard M. Baruch College, CUNY, USA
Babis Theodoulidis, University of Manchester, England
Vassilis J. Tsotras, Polytechnic University, USA
Alexander Tuzhilin, New York University, USA

Finance Chair:

Marianne Baudinet, University of Brussels, Belgium

Registration Chair:

Andreas Steiner, ETH-Zürich, Switzerland

Publicity Chair:

Uffe K. Wiil, Aalborg University, Denmark

Local Arrangements Chair:

Robert Marti, ETH-Zürich, Switzerland

Publications Chair:

Alexander Tuzhilin, New York University, USA

External Reviewers:

Aziz Ait-Braham
Chuanheng Ang
Sonia Bergamaschi
Don Berndt
Paolo Ciaccia
Manolis Koubarakis
Daniel Lieuwen
Mario A. Nascimento
Vaios Papaioannou
S.R. Schwer
C. Souveyet

Contents

V. Implementation Issues for Temporal DBMSs

VI. Potpourri

VII. Panels

I. Temporal and Spatio-Temporal Data Models

Extending Temporal Relational Databases to Deal with Imprecise and Qualitative Temporal Information*

Vittorio Brusoni, Luca Console, Paolo Terenziani

Dip. Informatica, Università di Torino

Corso Svizzera 185 - 10149 Torino (Italy)

E-mail: {brusoni,lconsole,terenz}@di.unito.it

Barbara Pernici

Elettronica e Informazione, Politecnico di Milano

Piazza Leonardo da Vinci 32, 20122 Milano (Italy)

E-mail: pernici@elet.polimi.it

Abstract

In several application domains, there is a need for historical databases supporting also imprecise and qualitative temporal information. We propose a formal theory for handling imprecise and qualitative temporal information in a relational temporal database. In particular, we introduce a relational algebra in which the traditional operators are extended in order to deal with imprecise and qualitative time; we examine the properties of the operators, showing that the algebra we introduce is a consistent extension of the snapshot algebra. Finally, we show how a temporal relational database based on this theory can be built on top of a conventional relational database.

1 Introduction

The limitation to absolute and precise temporal information in temporal databases is restrictive in many domains and thus there is a growing interest for the possibility of dealing with different types of temporal information (consider, e.g., [9, 8, 5, 10]):

Precise absolute times. Several models in the literature are able to deal with precise time as time stamps associated with tuples (or attributes). For example, a pair of dates $\langle d_1, d_2 \rangle$ can be associated with a tuple t to denote that t was valid in the interval of time between d_1 and d_2.

Imprecise absolute times. The starting and the ending points of the intervals in which a tuple is valid can be specified in an imprecise way. In this case, one can represent the fact that a tuple is valid in a period which started between two dates d_1 and d_3 and finished between two dates d_2 and d_4.

Qualitative times. As regards qualitative information, several algebras for temporal reasoning have been developed within the artificial intelligence community (e.g., Allen's interval algebra [1] or Vilain and Kautz's point algebra

---

*This work was partially supported by CNR, under grant no. 94.01878.CT07.

[15]). In such a case only constraints on the relative positions of time intervals (points) can be expressed; for example, one may assert that the validity time of a tuple precedes (or is included) in the validity time of another tuple, without providing any absolute reference for such validity times.

The goal of this paper is to propose an extension of historical relational databases in order to deal with all the types of information listed above. While many approaches to temporal databases deal with queries concerning qualitative temporal relations between validity times, the problem of expressing the validity time of tuples using qualitative relations has been faced only in [5, 11]. Such a possibility, however, is important in many applications. Moreover, we also consider cases where incomplete or no information about the validity time of some tuples is available.

The paper is organized as follows. In Sect.2 we present a relational algebra for historical databases dealing with the types of information mentioned above. Several properties of the operators are discussed showing that the same optimizations applicable in the snapshot case are applicable also in the temporal one. We also discuss equivalence and reduction properties of our temporal algebra showing in such a way that it is a consistent extension of the snapshot algebra. In Sect.3 we introduce the modal operators POSS and NEC to deal with temporal queries and we discuss their properties. In Sect.4, we illustrate temporal functions associated with the algebra. Sect.5 provides examples of queries. In Sect.6 we discuss implementation issues. In particular, since tractability is important in evaluating queries, we isolated a tractable core of temporal information (which can deal with most of the commonly used types of information) and we used LaTeR [2], a manager of (possibly incomplete) qualitative and quantitative temporal information. We then discuss how the model we propose can be implemented by coupling a relational data base management system such as ORACLE with LaTeR. Finally in Sect.7 we evaluate our approach on the basis of the criteria provided in the literature and we compare it with related approaches.

2 The temporal relational model and its temporal algebra

In our approach a temporal database consists of a set of tables and a set TA of temporal assertions concerning the temporal information associated with the tuples in the tables.

2.1 Temporal assertions

Different types of temporal information are considered in TA. In addition to precise and imprecise absolute dates and qualitative times, we also consider metric information such as duration of tuples and delays between tuples.

At least three different problems arise when extending a relational temporal database in order to deal with incomplete, imprecise and/or qualitative temporal information.

- First of all, temporal information cannot be stored as a time stamp associated with tuples. In particular, qualitative relations such as temporal ordering of tuples regard pairs of tuples (e.g., i_1 *before* i_2, specifying that the interval i_1 in which a tuple is valid precedes the interval i_2 in which another tuple – possibly of a different table – is valid). This means that new structures for representing pieces of temporal information have to be introduced. In the following we shall refer to such pieces of information as the table TA of temporal assertions.

- The primitive operators in the relational algebra have to be extended and new operators introduced. This is a major extension since one has to manipulate temporal information which may be partially or even totally unspecified. Since the definition of the operators is significantly different with respect to those in the literature and new operators have to be introduced, the properties of the operators have to be proved.

- Unlike absolute temporal information, qualitative temporal information needs reasoning. Such a reasoning consists of two tasks: (i) checking the consistency of the temporal information and (ii) inferring information about all the intervals given the assertions in TA. For example, the consistency check must detect inconsistent assertions such as i_1 *before* i_2 and i_2 *during* i_1. Furthermore, reasoning must entail i_1 *after* i_3 from the temporal assertions i_1 *during* i_2 and i_3 *before* i_2.

Our approach is completely independent of the language used in order to express the temporal assertions in TA; the only requirement is the existence of an algorithm for performing temporal reasoning and for checking the consistency of a set of assertions. In the examples in the following we shall use the language provided by LaTeR (see [2] for a definition of the language).

Figure 1 provides a set of temporal assertions TA that will be used in the examples in the following: the first assertion specifies that the interval i_1 started on 1/12/92; the third assertion specifies that i_3 started on 1/6/93 and ended on 10/12/93; the fourth assertion is a qualitative one specifying that the intervals i_1 and i_3 meet (i.e., the end of i_1 is equal to the start of i_3); the fifth assertion specifies that i_5 started during i_1; the sixth assertion specifies that i_5 started at least 60 days before the start of i_6.

2.2 Temporal tables

Our model deals with both temporal and snapshot tables. In this paper, for the sake of brevity, we describe only the treatment of temporal tables (the algebraic operators behave as usual on snapshot tables).

The scheme of a temporal table can be divided into two parts: $\langle S, T \rangle$. The *data part S* is a set of data attributes names and corresponds to the scheme of a standard table. The *temporal part T* is a mandatory attribute which represents the valid time of the tuples and ranges in the *domain of the coalesced temporal elements* (intuitively, a set of disjoint time intervals; see the next subsection). Figure 2 contains a set of tables that will be used as examples in the following sections. For example, the scheme of a temporal table MAN (manager) is $\langle \{\text{Man}, \text{Emp}\}, T \rangle$ and a tuple $t \in$ MAN may be such that $t(\text{Man}) = $ 'Mary', $t(\text{Emp}) = $ 'John', and $t^T = \{i_2, i_7\}$, where t^T denotes the temporal part: Mary was the manager of John in the period of time given by the union of the time intervals i_2 and i_7.

2.3 The domain of the coalesced temporal elements

In our model, time is a totally ordered and continuous set of time points denoted by $I\!\!P$. A time interval i is a convex set of time points in $I\!\!P$, denoted by its starting and ending points (respectively i^- and i^+); i.e., all points between i^- and i^+ belong to i. We denote as $I\!\!I$ the domain of the time intervals and as $I\!\!E$ the power set $2^{I\!\!I}$ of $I\!\!I$ (i.e., an element $E \in I\!\!E$ is a set of time intervals). Thus a temporal element $E \in I\!\!E$ can be conceived as a (possibly non-convex) set of time points in $I\!\!P$; such a set is denoted by $ext(E)$.

Definition 1 $ext : I\!\!E \to 2^{I\!\!P}$; $ext(E) = \bigcup_{i \in E} i$

A *coalesced temporal element* E is a set of disjoint time intervals:

Definition 2 $E \in I\!\!E$ is coalesced *if and only if (1)* $\forall i \in E, i \neq \emptyset$ *and (2)* $\forall i_1, i_2 \in E$ *such that* $i_1 \neq i_2$ *we have that* $(i_1^+ < i_2^-)$ *or* $(i_2^+ < i_1^-)$.

Definition 3 $I\!\!E^c$ *is the subset of* $I\!\!E$ *that contains all and only the coalesced time intervals.*

A coalesced temporal element provides a unique representation for $ext(E)$. In fact, the following holds:

Property 1 *Given* $E_1, E_2 \in I\!\!E^c$, $ext(E_1) = ext(E_2)$ *iff* $E_1 = E_2$.

A coalesced temporal element E is the smallest set of intervals $E' \in I\!\!E$ such that $ext(E') = ext(E)$. Moreover, the intervals in a coalesced temporal element E are *maximal*, i.e., the following property holds:

Property 2 *Given* $E \in I\!\!E^c, \forall i \in E, \neg \exists j \in I\!\!I, j \subseteq ext(E),$ *such that* $i \subset j$

Thus, intuitively, E is coalesced if and only if it contains only maximal non-overlapping intervals.

We define three operators on the elements of $I\!\!E^c$: pointed intersection ($\dot{\cap}$), pointed union ($\dot{\cup}$) and pointed negation ($\dot{\neg}$). The definitions are given in terms of union and intersection of time intervals. More precisely:

TA
i_1 SINCE 1/12/92
i_3 SINCE 1/6/93
i_6 SINCE 10/3/93 UNTIL 10/12/93
i_1 MEETS i_3
START(i_5) DURING i_1
START(i_5) ATLEAST 60 DAYS BEFORE START(i_6)
START(i_3) ATLEAST 30 DAYS AFTER END(i_2)
i_4 UNTIL 1/3/93
END(i_6) EQUAL END(i_3)
i_5 MEETS i_6
END(i_2) 30 $-$ 90 DAYS BEFORE START(i_7)
i_2 OVERLAPS i_1

Figure 1: Temporal Assertions

Definition 4 *Given $E_1, E_2 \in \mathbb{E}^c$. $E_1 \dot{\cap} E_2 = \bigcup_{i_1 \in E_1, i_2 \in E_2} (i_1 \cap^{II} i_2)$, where*

$$
i_1 \cap^{II} i_2 = \begin{cases}
\{\langle i_1^-, i_1^+ \rangle\} & \text{if } (i_1^- > i_2^-) \wedge (i_1^+ \leq i_2^+) \\
\{\langle i_2^-, i_1^+ \rangle\} & \text{if } (i_1^- \leq i_2^-) \wedge (i_1^+ \leq i_2^+) \\
\{\langle i_1^-, i_2^+ \rangle\} & \text{if } (i_1^- > i_2^-) \wedge (i_1^+ > i_2^+) \\
\{\langle i_2^-, i_2^+ \rangle\} & \text{if } (i_1^- \leq i_2^-) \wedge (i_1^+ > i_2^+) \\
\emptyset & \text{otherwise}
\end{cases}
$$

The definitions of $\dot{\cup}$ and $\dot{\neg}$ are similar to Definition 4. Intuitively, $E_1 \dot{\cup} E_2$ is equal to the (unique) coalesced temporal element E_3 such that $ext(E_3) = ext(E_1) \cup ext(E_2)$. $\dot{\neg} E$ is equal to the (unique) coalesced temporal element E_1 such that $ext(E_1) = \neg ext(E)$. Starting from $\dot{\cup}$ and $\dot{\neg}$ we define also the difference between temporal elements: $E_1 - E_2 = E_1 \dot{\cap}(\dot{\neg} E_2)$.

Proposition 1 *$\mathbb{E}^c$ with the operations $\dot{\cap}$, $\dot{\cup}$ and $\dot{\neg}$ is a Boolean algebra; in fact, the following properties hold:*

(a) *Closure: $\mathbb{E}^c$ is closed with respect to $\dot{\cap}$, $\dot{\cup}$ and $\dot{\neg}$.*

(b) *Commutativity of $\dot{\cap}, \dot{\cup}$.*

(c) *Associativity of $\dot{\cap}, \dot{\cup}$.*

(d) *Absorption: $E_1 \dot{\cup}(E_1 \dot{\cap} E_2) = E_1$ and $E_1 \dot{\cap}(E_1 \dot{\cup} E_2) = E_1$.*

(e) *Distributivity of $\dot{\cup}$ with respect to $\dot{\cap}$ and vice versa.*

(f) *Existence of neutral elements $0 = \{\}$ and $1 = \{\langle -\infty, +\infty \rangle\}$ such that $E \dot{\cup} 0 = E$ and $E \dot{\cap} 1 = E$.*

(g) *Complementation: $E \dot{\cap} \dot{\neg} E = 0$ and $E \dot{\cup} \dot{\neg} E = 1$*

In practice, the definition of the domain of coalesced temporal elements $\mathbb{E}^c$ and of its operations allows us to represent and to deal with non-convex sets of time points by means of unique sets of maximal convex time intervals.

2.4 Temporal primitive operators

In order to deal with temporal tables, the definition of the snapshot algebraic operators (i.e., $\sigma, \pi, \times, -, \cup$) must be extended for manipulating the temporal part T of the tables.

Selection. Selection selects the tuples whose data part satisfies the condition ϕ (which is a condition on the data part only), regardless of their temporal part. In the following, we denote as $sch(R)$ the schema of the data part of R.

SAL			
Emp	**Sal**	**Tax**	**T**
John	100	10	$\{i_1\}$
Mary	150	15	$\{i_4\}$
John	120	12	$\{i_3\}$

RANK		
Emp	**Rank**	**T**
John	assistant	$\{i_5\}$
John	associate	$\{i_6\}$

MAN		
Man	**Emp**	**T**
Mary	John	$\{i_2, i_7\}$

Figure 2: Temporal tables

$$S = sch(R) = sch(\sigma_\phi(R))$$
$$\sigma_\phi(R) = \{t|t \in R, \phi(t(S))\}$$

Projection. Projection can be used to select data attributes. As regards the temporal part, projection makes the pointed union ($\dot\cup$) of the temporal parts of the tuples whose selected data parts are equal.

$$A \subseteq sch(R)$$
$$sch(\pi_A(R)) = A$$
$$\pi_A(R) = \{s|\exists t \in R, s(A) = t(A), s^T = \dot{\bigcup}_{r \in R, r(A)=t(A)} r^T\}$$

Cartesian product. As regards Cartesian product, the temporal part of the resulting tuples is computed using the *intersection semantics*, i.e., the pointed intersection ($\dot\cap$) of the temporal parts of the original tuples is computed. It is important to notice that the resulting table contains only the tuples whose temporal part is not empty.

$$S_1 = sch(R_1)$$
$$S_2 = sch(R_2)$$
$$sch(R_1 \times R_2) = S_1 \cup S_2$$
$$R_1 \times R_2 = \{\ s|\exists t_1 \in R_1, \exists t_2 \in R_2, s(S_1) = t_1(S_1), s(S_2) = t_2(S_2),$$
$$t_1^T \dot\cap t_2^T \neq \emptyset, s^T = t_1^T \dot\cap t_2^T\}$$

Union. The union operator makes the union of two tables R_1 and R_2 in such a way that, given two tuples $t_1 \in R_1$ and $t_2 \in R_2$ whose data parts are equal, then the temporal part of the resulting tuple is equal to $t_1^T \dot\cup t_2^T$.

$$S = sch(R_1) = sch(R_2)$$
$$sch(R_1 \cup R_2) = S$$
$$R_1 \cup R_2 = \{s| (\ \exists t_1 \in R_1, \exists t_2 \in R_2, t_1(S) = t_2(S),$$
$$s(S) = t_1(S), s^T = t_1^T \dot\cup t_2^T) \vee$$
$$(\exists t_1 \in R_1, \forall t_2 \in R_2, t_1(S) \neq t_2(S), s(S) = t_1(S), s^T = t_1^T) \vee$$
$$(\exists t_2 \in R_2, \forall t_1 \in R_1, t_1(S) \neq t_2(S), s(S) = t_2(S), s^T = t_2^T)\}$$

Difference. The definition of difference $R_1 - R_2$ is similar to the definition of union. In this case, if there are two tuples $t_1 \in R_1$ and $t_2 \in R_2$ such that $t_1(S) = t_2(S)$ then the temporal part of the resulting tuple is given by pointed difference ($\dot-$) between t_1^T and t_2^T.

$$S = sch(R_1) = sch(R_2)$$
$$sch(R_1 - R_2) = S$$
$$R_1 - R_2 = \{s| (\ \exists t_1 \in R_1, \exists t_2 \in R_2, t_1(S) = t_2(S), s(S) = t_1(S),$$
$$t_1^T \dot- t_2^T \neq \emptyset, s^T = t_1^T \dot- t_2^T) \vee$$
$$(\exists t_1 \in R_1, \forall t_2 \in R_2, t_2(S) \neq t_1(S), s(S) = t_1(S), s^T = t_1^T)\}$$

2.5 Properties of the temporal algebra

As pointed out in [12], there are several criteria in order to characterize a temporal algebra. In this section we discuss some important properties of the algebra introduced in the previous subsections.

Equivalence proof. The equivalence proof guarantees that all the queries that are possible when time is not modeled are also possible (and produce analogous results) when time is modeled. In the proof we use the function Transform(R, E) which converts a snapshot relation R into a temporal relation whose tuples have the temporal part equal to E, where E is an arbitrary coalesced temporal element. This and the following proofs are not reported in this paper, for the sake of brevity (see [3] for the proofs).

Definition 5 Transform$(R, E) = \{s | \exists t \in R, s(S) = t(S), s^T = E)\}$ *where R is a snapshot table and $E \in I\!E^c, E \neq \emptyset$.*

Proposition 2 (Equivalence proof) *Let R, R_1 and R_2 be snapshot relations and $E \in I\!E^c, E \neq \emptyset$. The following equivalences hold:*
  (a) Transform$(\sigma_s(R), E) = \sigma(\text{Transform}(R, E))$
  (b) Transform$(\pi_s(R), E) = \pi(\text{Transform}(R, E))$
  (c) Transform$(R_1 \times_s R_2, E) = \text{Transform}(R_1, E) \times \text{Transform}(R_2, E)$
  (d) Transform$(R_1 \cup_s R_2, E) = \text{Transform}(R_1, E) \cup \text{Transform}(R_2, E)$
  (e) Transform$(R_1 -_s R_2, E) = \text{Transform}(R_1, E) - \text{Transform}(R_2, E)$
where $\sigma_s, \pi_s, \times_s, \cup_s$ and $-_s$ denote the snapshot operators.

Reduction proof. The reduction proof guarantees that each temporal operator reduces to the corresponding snapshot operator when time is disregarded. In the proof we use the function Snapshot(R, P), which applies to a temporal relation R and a time point P and gives as result the corresponding snapshot relation at time P.

Definition 6 Snapshot$(R, P) = \{s | \exists t \in R, s(S) = t(S), (ext(s^T) \cap P) \neq \emptyset\}$ *where R is a temporal table and $P \in I\!P$.*

Proposition 3 (Reduction proof) *Let R, R_1 and R_2 be temporal relations and $P \in I\!P$. The following equivalences hold:*
  (a) Snapshot$(\sigma(R), P) = \sigma_s(\text{Snapshot}(R, P))$
  (b) Snapshot$(\pi(R), P) = \pi_s(\text{Snapshot}(R, P))$
  (c) Snapshot$(R_1 \times R_2, P) = \text{Snapshot}(R_1, P) \times_s \text{Snapshot}(R_2, P)$
  (d) Snapshot$(R_1 \cup R_2, P) = \text{Snapshot}(R_1, P) \cup_s \text{Snapshot}(R_2, P)$
  (e) Snapshot$(R_1 - R_2, P) = \text{Snapshot}(R_1, P) -_s \text{Snapshot}(R_2, P)$
where $\sigma_s, \pi_s, \times_s, \cup_s$ and $-_s$ denote the snapshot operators.

Algebraic properties. Our temporal relational algebra satisfies other properties typical of the snapshot algebra. Among the others, we discuss those properties that we consider more important to characterize our model.

(a) It is possible to define the temporal counterpart of the other non-primitive algebraic operators (i.e., $\cap$, Θ-*join* and $\div$) in terms of the five primitive temporal operators introduced above. For example, intersection can be defined as:
$$R_1 \cap R_2 = \pi_S(\sigma_{t(S)=t(S')}(R_1 \times \delta_{S \leftarrow S'}(R_2)))$$
where $sch(R_1) = sch(R_2) = S$, δ is the renaming operator and S' is an arbitrary renaming of S. Such a definition corresponds to the following intuitive notion of intersection:

$$S = sch(R_1) = sch(R_2)$$
$$sch(R_1 \cap R_2) = S$$
$$R_1 \cap R_2 = \{s| \; \exists t_1 \in R_1, \exists t_2 \in R_2, s(S) = t_1(S) = t_2(S),$$
$$t_1^T \dot\cap t_2^T \neq \emptyset, s^T = t_1^T \dot\cap t_2^T\}$$

(b) The operators we introduced indeed define an algebra, i.e., a closed structure that satisfies the typical properties of relational algebras. In particular:

- Cartesian product, union and intersection are commutative and associative.

- Distributivity and absorption hold between union and intersection.

- Cartesian product and intersection can be distributed with respect to the other operators.

(c) A cascade of selections can be combined into a single selection (commutativity of selection follows from this property):

$$\sigma_{\phi_1}(\sigma_{\phi_2}...\sigma_{\phi_n}(R)...) = \sigma_{\phi_1 \wedge ... \wedge \phi_2}(R)$$

(d) A cascade of projections can be combined into a single projection:

$$\pi_{X_1}(\pi_{X_2}...\pi_{X_n}(R)...) = \pi_Y(R)$$

where $X_1, ..., X_n \subseteq sch(R)$ and Y is the largest $Y \subseteq sch(R)$ such that $Y \subseteq X_1, ... , Y \subseteq X_n$.

(e) Projection and selection are mutually commutative.

(f) Projection and selection can be distributed with respect to Cartesian product, union, difference and intersection. For example, the distributivity of projection on union holds:

$$\pi_X(R_1 \cup R_2) = \pi_X(R_1) \cup \pi_X(R_2)$$

where $sch(R_1) = sch(R_2)$ and $X \subseteq sch(R_1)$.

Some remarks are important at this point. First of all, notice that all the properties we introduced above are consequences of the definition of the domain of coalesced temporal elements and of the properties of pointed operations. Furthermore, besides providing a clear semantics for our temporal algebra, most of these properties are also important because they can be used in the optimization strategies in the snapshot algebra. This means that the same optimizations are applicable also in the temporal case.

2.6 Temporal selection and temporal join

In the previous section, we defined the temporal counterpart of snapshot operators. In this section we introduce two operators which are peculiar of the temporal algebra. Temporal selection and temporal join select the intervals in the temporal parts of the tuples which satisfy a unary or binary temporal condition ψ.

Temporal selection. Given a unary temporal condition ψ (e.g., a condition about the temporal location or duration of a time interval), temporal selection is applied to a temporal relation R and recomputes the temporal part t^T of each tuple $t \in R$, in a such a way to maintain, in the resulting temporal part, only the time intervals that satisfy ψ. If the resulting temporal part of a tuple is empty, then the tuple is not part of the resulting table.

$$S = sch(R)$$
$$sch(\hat{\sigma}_\psi(R)) = sch(R)$$
$$\hat{\sigma}_\psi(R) = \{s | \exists t \in R, s(S) = t(S), S(\psi, t^T) \neq \emptyset, s^T = S(\psi, t^T)\}$$

where $S(\psi, E)$ is defined as follow:

$$S(\psi, E) = \{i \in E | \psi(i)\}$$

Left/right temporal join. Temporal join is used to compare tuples of two relations according to a predicate ψ on their temporal part (ψ thus is a binary predicate; e.g., requiring that the time interval associated with a tuple in the first relation must be "before" that associated with a tuple in the second relation). As regards the data part, the result is the concatenation of the data parts of the tuples satisfying the temporal condition. Two temporal join operators have been introduced; they behave differently on the temporal part: left temporal join maintains the time intervals of the first relation which satisfy the temporal condition; right temporal join maintains the time intervals of the second relation which satisfy the condition. For example, left temporal join gives as result the concatenation of the data part of each tuple $t_1 \in R_1$ with each tuple $t_2 \in R_2$, such that the condition ψ holds between at least one of the time intervals $i_1 \in t_1^T$ and at least one of the time intervals $i_2 \in t_2^T$. The temporal part is the set of time intervals $i_1 \in t_1^T$ satisfying the condition.

$$S_1 = sch(R_1), S_2 = sch(R_2)$$
$$sch(R_1 \bullet \Join_\psi R_2) = S_1 \cup S_2$$
$$R_1 \bullet \Join_\psi R_2 = \{s | \ \exists t_1 \in R_1, \exists t_2 \in R_2, s(S_1) = t_1(S_1), s(S_2) = t_2(S_2),$$
$$L(t_1^T, \psi, t_2^T) \neq \emptyset, s^T = L(t_1^T, \psi, t_2^T)\}$$

where $L(t_1^T, \psi, t_2^T)$ is defined as follows:

$$L(t_1^T, \psi, t_2^T) = \{i_1 \in t_1^T | \exists i_2 \in t_2^T, \psi(t_1^T, t_2^T)\}$$

Right temporal join has a similar definition. In this case, the temporal parts of the tuples of the second relation are maintained in the resulting table.

Properties of temporal selection and temporal join. Most of the properties which hold for the other primitive operators do not hold in the case of temporal selection and temporal join, because they select the tuples on the basis of the intervals in the temporal part, which in general are changed by the application of the primitive operators. For example, temporal selection does not distribute with respect to union:

$$\hat{\sigma}_\psi(R_1 \cup R_2) \neq \hat{\sigma}_\psi(R_1) \cup \hat{\sigma}_\psi(R_2)$$

In fact, suppose that the temporal condition ψ requires that the duration is at least 15 days, and that there are two tuples $t_1 \in R_1$ and $t_2 \in R_2$ such that $t_1(S) = t_2(S), t_1^T = \{i_1\}, t_2^T = \{i_2\}$ and i_1 holds between 1/1/91 and 10/1/91 and i_2 holds between 8/1/91 and 17/1/91. Then in $\hat{\sigma}_\psi(R_1 \cup R_2)$ there is a tuple t such that $t(S) = t_1(S) = t_2(S)$ with $t^T = \{i_1 \cup i_2\}$, which satisfies the condition ψ, while in $\hat{\sigma}_\psi(R_1) \cup \hat{\sigma}_\psi(R_2)$ there is not.

Temporal selection and temporal join have the following properties (among the others):

(a) $\hat{\sigma}_{\psi_1}(\hat{\sigma}_{\psi_2}...\hat{\sigma}_{\psi_n}(R)...) = \hat{\sigma}_{\psi_1 \wedge ... \wedge \psi_2}$

(b) $R_1 \bullet \Join_\psi R_2 = R_2 \Join \bullet_{inv(\psi)} R_1$

(c) $(\hat{\sigma}_{\psi_1}(R_1)) \bullet \bowtie_{\psi}(\hat{\sigma}_{\psi_2}(R_2)) = R_1 \bullet \bowtie_{\psi \wedge \psi_1(T.R_1) \wedge \psi_2(T.R_2)} R_2$

(d.1) $\hat{\sigma}_{\psi_1}(R_1 \bullet \bowtie_{\psi} R_2) = \hat{\sigma}_{\psi_1}(R_1) \bullet \bowtie_{\psi} R_2$

(d.2) $\hat{\sigma}_{\psi_1}(R_1 \bowtie_{\psi} \bullet R_2) = R_1 \bullet \bowtie_{\psi} \hat{\sigma}_{\psi_1}(R_2)$

3 Modal selectors

Up to now, we discussed primitive and temporal operators and their properties, without taking explicitly into account the fact that the temporal conditions introduced by these operators have to be evaluated on the basis of a given set of temporal assertions TA. In particular, two different types of temporal conditions have to be considered:

1. *explicit* temporal conditions, introduced by temporal selection and temporal join (e.g., lasting at least 15 days);

2. *implicit* temporal conditions, introduced by the primitive operators. For example, the Cartesian product between $R_A = \{\langle t_A(S_A), t_A^T \rangle\}$ and $R_B = \{\langle t_B(S_B), t_B^T \rangle\}$ gives as result $R_A \times R_B = \{\langle t_A(S_A) \cdot t_B(S_B), t_A^T \dot{\cap} t_B^T \rangle\}$. This means that, for each interval $i \in t_A^T$ and for each $j \in t_B^T$ the intersection $i \cap^{II} j$ must be considered, or, in other words, the implicit condition $i \cap^{II} j \neq \emptyset$ must be checked.

In the following we call *existence condition* for an interval i_k the conjunction of explicit and implicit conditions about i_k and we denote it by $\psi_k(i_k)$.

Existence conditions must be evaluated on the basis of the temporal assertions in TA. However, in our approach, TA may contain imprecise, incomplete and/or qualitative temporal information. Thus, existence conditions can be evaluated in at least two different ways:

- the conditions can be evaluated as necessary ones; in such a case the conditions are satisfied if they necessarily hold given the assertions in TA, or, in other words, if they are entailed by the assertions in TA. The modal operator NEC has been introduced in order to deal with this case.

- the conditions can be evaluated as conditions about possibility; in such a case the conditions are satisfied if they may hold given the assertions in TA, or, in other words, if they are consistent with the assertions in TA. The modal operator POSS has been introduced in order to deal with this case.

NEC operator.
$sch(\text{NEC}(R)) = sch(R)$
$\text{NEC}(R) = \{s | \exists t \in R, s(S) = t(S), \text{MUST}(t^T) \neq \emptyset, s^T = \text{MUST}(t^T)\}$
    MUST is defined as follows:
        $\text{MUST} : I\!E \to I\!E$
        $\text{MUST}(E) = \{i_k | i_k \in E, TA \vdash \psi_k(i_k)\}$

POSS operator.
$sch(\text{POSS}(R)) = sch(R)$
$\text{POSS}(R) = \{s | \exists t \in R, s(S) = t(S), \text{MAY}(t^T) \neq \emptyset, s^T = \text{MAY}(t^T)\}$

MAY is defined as follows

$$\text{MAY} : I\!\!E \to I\!\!E$$
$$\text{MAY}(E) = \{i_k | i_k \in E, (TA \land \psi_k(i_k)) \text{ is consistent}\}$$

MUST and MAY are functions that, given a set of time intervals and a set of temporal assertions TA, select those intervals whose existence conditions are respectively necessary or possible, given TA. These functions are to be provided by the temporal reasoning module. Given $E \in I\!\!E$ and a set of assertions TA, the following properties of MUST and MAY hold:

(a) $E \supseteq \text{MAY}(E) \supseteq \text{MUST}(E)$
(b) $\text{MAY}(\text{MAY}(...\text{MAY}(E)...)) = \text{MAY}(E)$
(c) $\text{MUST}(\text{MUST}(...\text{MUST}(E)...)) = \text{MUST}(E)$
(d) $\text{MAY}(\text{MUST}(E)) = \text{MUST}(\text{MAY}(E)) = \text{MUST}(E)$

3.1 Properties of the modal operators

Given the set of the assertions TA, the NEC and POSS operators are like two selection operators, such that the former is more restrictive than latter. The following properties characterize their semantics.

Definition 7 *Given two temporal tables R_1 and R_2 with the same scheme S, $R_1 \sqsubseteq R_2$ if and only if $\forall t_1 \in R_1 \exists t_2 \in R_2$ such that $t_1(S) = t_2(S)$ and $t_1^T \subseteq t_2^T$.*

Given an instance of a database $\langle \{R_1, R_2, ..., R_n\}, TA \rangle$ and two derived tables A and B, the following properties hold:

(a) $\text{POSS}(R_i) = \text{NEC}(R_i)$ for all base tables $R_1, ..., R_n$. In practice, the intervals given in the temporal part of the tuples in the base tables must exist; in others terms the intervals mentioned in the base tables certainly exist even if their location in time may be partially or totally unspecified.
(b) $\text{POSS}(A) \sqsupseteq \text{NEC}(A)$.
(c) $\text{NEC}(\text{NEC}(...\text{NEC}(A)...)) = \text{NEC}(A)$
(d) $\text{POSS}(\text{POSS}(...\text{POSS}(A)...)) = \text{POSS}(A)$
 NEC and POSS operators satisfy a particular form of distributivity with respect to the others algebraic and temporal operators:
(e.1) $\text{NEC}(\pi_X(A)) = \text{NEC}(\pi_X(\text{NEC}(A)))$
(e.2) $\text{POSS}(\pi_X(A)) = \text{POSS}(\pi_X(\text{POSS}(A)))$
(f.1) $\text{NEC}(\sigma_\phi(A)) = \text{NEC}(\sigma_\phi(\text{NEC}(A)))$
(f.2) $\text{POSS}(\sigma_\phi(A)) = \text{POSS}(\sigma_\phi(\text{POSS}(A)))$
(g.1) $\text{NEC}(A \cup B) = \text{NEC}(\text{NEC}(A) \cup \text{NEC}(B)))$
(g.2) $\text{POSS}(A \cup B) = \text{POSS}(\text{POSS}(A) \cup \text{POSS}(B)))$
(h.1) $\text{NEC}(A \times B) = \text{NEC}(\text{NEC}(A) \times \text{NEC}(B)))$
(h.2) $\text{POSS}(A \times B) = \text{POSS}(\text{POSS}(A) \times \text{POSS}(B)))$
(i.1) $\text{NEC}(A - B) = \text{NEC}(\text{NEC}(A) - \text{NEC}(B)))$
(i.2) $\text{POSS}(A - B) = \text{POSS}(\text{POSS}(A) - \text{POSS}(B)))$
(j.1) $\text{NEC}(\hat{\sigma}_\psi(A)) = \text{NEC}(\hat{\sigma}_\psi(\text{NEC}(A)))$
(j.2) $\text{POSS}(\hat{\sigma}_\psi(A)) = \text{POSS}(\hat{\sigma}_\psi(\text{POSS}(A)))$
(k.1) $\text{NEC}(A \bullet \bowtie_\psi B) = \text{NEC}(\text{NEC}(A) \bullet \bowtie_\psi \text{NEC}(B)))$

(k.2) $\text{POSS}(A \bullet \bowtie_\psi B) = \text{POSS}(\text{POSS}(A) \bullet \bowtie_\psi \text{POSS}(B)))$

Such identities are also important in order to simplify complex expressions for reducing the computational effort during the evaluation. For example, POSS and NEC operators can be distributed on all terms of a complex expression to reduce the number of intervals and tuples maintained in each derived table in the expression; for instance, using (b), (d), (f.1) and (k.1) the following holds:

$$\text{NEC}(\hat{\sigma}_\psi(\text{POSS}(A)) \cup \text{NEC(B)}) = \text{NEC}(\text{NEC}(\hat{\sigma}_\psi(\text{NEC}(A))) \cup \text{NEC(B)})$$

4 Temporal functions and other features of the temporal algebra

In this section, we introduce a set of functions that allows the user to extract pieces of temporal information from the temporal database.

WHEN and LASTING functions. We allow the user to obtain the temporal location and the duration of the intervals associated with the temporal part of the tuples, as obtained after the application of temporal reasoning to TA. To this purpose, we introduce the temporal functions $\mathcal{F}_{\text{WHEN}}$ and $\mathcal{F}_{\text{LASTING}}$.

$S = sch(R)$

$sch(\mathcal{F}_{\text{WHEN}}(R)) = S \cup \{\text{WHEN}\}$

$\mathcal{F}_{\text{WHEN}}(R) = \{s | \exists t \in R, s(S) = t(S), s(\text{WHEN}) = \text{WHEN}(t^T), s^T = t^T\}$

$sch(\mathcal{F}_{\text{LASTING}}(R)) = S \cup \{\text{LASTING}\}$

$\mathcal{F}_{\text{LASTING}}(R) = \{s | \ \exists t \in R, s(S) = t(S), s(\text{LASTING}) = \text{LASTING}(t^T),$
$\qquad\qquad s^T = t^T\}$

where R is a temporal table and WHEN and LASTING are two functions provided by the temporal reasoner. Given a list of time intervals, WHEN returns the list of the temporal locations of the starting and ending points of the intervals; LASTING returns the list of the durations of the intervals.

INT function. Given a temporal table R, the INT function returns a temporal table R' whose tuples contain only one interval in their temporal part. Given a tuple $t \in R$ whose temporal part t^T contains n intervals $\{i_1, ..., i_n\}$, then it is represented in R' by means of $t_1, ..., t_n$ distinct tuples such that $t_1^T = \{i_1\}, ..., t_n^T = \{i_n\}$. In order to make distinct the data part of the tuples $t_1, ..., t_n$, the attribute INT is added to the scheme of R and it is set to a unique different value for each one of the tuples $t_1, ..., t_n$.

$S = sch(R)$

$sch(\mathcal{F}_{\text{INT}}(R)) = S \cup \{\text{INT}\}$

$\mathcal{F}_{\text{INT}}(R) = \{s | \ \exists t \in R, \exists i \in t^T, s(S) = t(S), s(\text{INT}) = \langle \text{unique identifier}\rangle,$
$\qquad\qquad t^T = i\}$

Snapshot tables. Our model can deal also with snapshot tables. The functions Transform and Snapshot are provided in order to obtain the temporal version of a snapshot relation and vice-versa. We also provide a function *Atemporal* which discharges the temporal part of a table R. In this case, the resulting table is a snapshot table which contains all the tuples is R, regardless of their validity time. The primitive operators π, σ, $\times$, $\cup$ and $-$ behave as usual when applied to snapshot tables. On the other hand, if $\times$, $\cup$ or $-$ are applied to a temporal relation T and to a snapshot relation S, the relation S is coerced to the temporal table $Trasform(S, \{i_\infty\})$, where $i_\infty = (-\infty, +\infty)$.

Obviously, temporal selection, temporal join and temporal functions are not defined for snapshot tables.

5 Examples

Let us now consider the temporal database in figure 1 and 2 and let us show some examples of queries.

Ex.1. How long was John assistant or associate? This query can be expressed as follows:

$$\mathcal{F}_{\text{LASTING}}(\text{NEC}(\pi_{\text{Emp}}(\sigma_{\text{Emp}='John' \text{ and } (\text{Rank}='associate' \text{ or } \text{Rank}='assistant')}$$
$$(\text{RANK})))) \quad (1)$$

The resulting table is:

Emp	LASTING	T
John	$334 - 375$ DAYS	$\{i_5 \cup i_6\}$

where 335-375 days is the duration of the time interval $i_5 \cup i_6$ obtained by coalescing i_5 and i_6.

Ex.2 How much was John's salary when Mary was his manager?

The query can be expressed in two different ways, depending on whether one is interested in necessity or possibility.

$$\text{POSS}(\pi_{\text{Sal}}(\sigma_{\text{Emp}='John'}(\text{SAL}) \times \sigma_{\text{Emp}='John' \text{ and } \text{Man}='Mary'}(\text{MAN}))) \quad (2)$$

The resulting table is:

Sal	T
100	$\{i_1 \cap i_2, i_1 \cap i_7\}$
120	$\{i_3 \cap i_7\}$

Notice that, given TA, no intersection is possible between i_3 and i_2, so that the time interval $i_3 \cap i_2$ is not part of the result.

$$\text{NEC}(\pi_{\text{Sal}}(\sigma_{\text{Emp}='John'}(\text{SAL}) \times \sigma_{\text{Emp}='John' \text{ and } \text{Man}='Mary'}(\text{MAN}))) \quad (3)$$

The resulting table is:

Sal	T
100	$\{i_1 \cap i_2\}$
120	$\{i_3 \cap i_7\}$

Notice that, in the case of query about necessity, the time interval $i_1 \cap i_7$ is not part of the result since the fact that i_1 and i_7 intersect is consistent with but is not entailed by TA.

In case one were interested in the temporal location of the time intervals in the resulting table, one could express the query (3) as follows:

$$\mathcal{F}_{\text{WHEN}}(\text{NEC}(\pi_{\text{Sal}}(\sigma_{\text{Emp}='\text{John}'}(\text{SAL}) \times \sigma_{\text{Emp}='\text{John}' \text{ and } \text{Man}='\text{Mary}'}(\text{MAN}))) \qquad (4)$$

The resulting table would be:

Sal	WHEN	T
100	$\langle 1/12/92, 2/12/92 - 2/5/93 \rangle$	$\{i_1 \cap i_2\}$
120	$\langle 1/6/93 - 31/7/93, 10/12/93 \rangle$	$\{i_3 \cap i_7\}$

Ex.3 "How long did John earn more than 50 when he did not have Mary as his manager?"

This query can be expressed as follows:

$$\mathcal{F}_{\text{LASTING}}(\text{NEC}(\pi_{\text{Emp}}(\sigma_{\text{Sal}>50 \text{ and } \text{Emp}='\text{John}'}(\text{SAL}))$$
$$-\pi_{\text{Emp}}(\sigma_{\text{Man}='\text{Mary}' \text{ and } \text{Emp}='\text{John}'}(\text{MAN})))) \qquad (5)$$

The resulting table is the following:

Emp	LASTING	T
John	30-90 DAYS	$i_1 - (i_2 \cup i_7)$

Ex.4 "How much did John's manager earn before John was an associate?"

$$\text{NEC} \quad (\pi_{Sal}(\text{SAL} \bowtie_{\text{Man.MAN}=\text{Emp.SAL}} (\sigma_{\text{Emp}='\text{John}'}(MAN)) \bullet \bowtie_{\text{BEFORE}} (\sigma_{\text{Rank}='\text{associate}' \text{ and } \text{Emp}='\text{John}'}(\text{RANK}))))$$

Sal	T
150	$i_4 \cap i_2$

6 Implementation

In this section we briefly sketch a prototype implementation of the framework presented in the paper. The implementation is based on the co-operation between a DBMS and a temporal reasoner. The advantage of this solution is the availability of traditional DBMS functionalities in addition to time-related features.

It is worth noting that the type of temporal assertions dealt with by the system affects considerably its architecture. In fact, if temporal assertions are also qualitative relations, a temporal reasoner is needed in order to check their consistency and make inferences. In this case, the complexity of the temporal reasoner depends on the type of temporal assertions manipulated by the system.

On the other hand, if the temporal assertions involve only absolute locations, then temporal reasoning is not needed. In this case, in fact, each set of temporal assertions is consistent and the task of inferring the extension of the intervals from TA can be performed trivially.

In our system we have chosen to represent temporal information using the LaTeR high level language [2, 7]; using LaTeR has the advantage of allowing the use of qualitative and quantitative relations yet retaining a polynomial time complexity for correct and complete temporal reasoning; in fact, the complexity of reasoning is $O(N^3)$, where N is the number of the temporal intervals mentioned in the set TA of assertions. LaTeR can deal with locations (precise or imprecise) of intervals, duration (precise or imprecise) of intervals, qualitative relations (limiting to the continuous pointisable ones [16]; notice, however, that this limitation is not too restrictive, since most of the commonly used qualitative constraints are continuous pointisable [14]) and delays between starting and ending points of intervals. Moreover, LaTeR also provides, among the others, the functions MUST MAY, WHEN and LASTING discussed in sections 3 and 4.

The architecture of the system is shown in figure 3. The system is composed of a commercial DBMS (the ORACLE relational system in our implementation) loosely coupled with the LaTeR temporal reasoner through an interface module (IM).

An important aspect of LaTeR is that query evaluation needs only local temporal reasoning and can be thus performed very efficiently; more specifically, queries are answered in time at worst cubic in the number of intervals involved in the query, independently of the total number of intervals mentioned in TA (see [4]). LaTeR also supports an efficient incremental updating of the set of temporal assertions. Such a feature allows the user to insert new temporal assertions and query about them, without the necessity of performing reasoning on the whole set of temporal assertions (which would require cubic time in the number of intervals in TA). In other words, also in this case the answers can be provided by performing local reasoning on the entities involved in the update and the query, providing the very same results that would be obtained by performing non-local reasoning on the whole set of temporal assertions TA. Global reasoning to propagate the update to the whole set of temporal assertions can be performed on demand or off-line, when the session is closed (see [4]).

In addition, in order to perform operations on temporal elements we have extended LaTeR to manipulate unions, intersections, and differences of sets intervals, such as the ones described in Sect.2.

The interface module manages the interaction between ORACLE and LaTeR as well as the interaction with the user. IM provides primitives for creating and deleting temporal (and snapshot) tables and for manipulating tables (update and query operations).

User defined temporal tables are represented in ORACLE by extending standard tables with the temporal attribute T; temporal assertions are managed by ORACLE in the TA table.

Updates concerning temporal information are managed by IM in two steps. First, the new temporal assertions are passed to LaTeR in order to check their consistency and to perform temporal reasoning. Second, if no inconsistency is detected by LaTeR the assertions are passed to ORACLE which stores them.

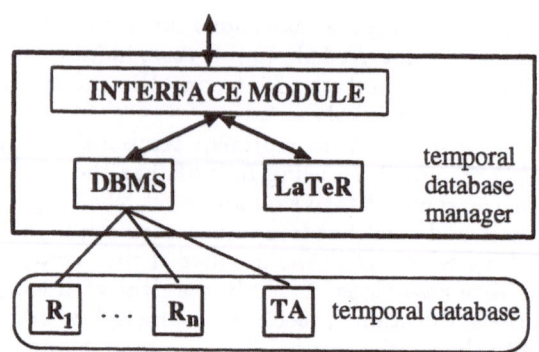

Figure 3: Architecture of the temporal database management system.

IM implements the temporal relational algebra defined in the previous sections by means of a cooperation between ORACLE and LaTeR. More specifically, IM coordinates the work of ORACLE and LaTeR: each expression in the relational algebra is decomposed by IM in a sequence of queries (performed in SQL) to the ORACLE base tables and a sequence of queries to LaTeR. More specifically, the cooperation is based on the interleaving of three different activities:

- IM queries ORACLE in order to build the data part of the tables resulting from a query in the temporal algebra;

- IM builds the expressions corresponding to the temporal elements to be associated with tuples;

- IM queries LaTeR to check the consistency of the resulting expression and to identify possible or necessary tuples to be inserted in the intermediate or result tables.
  The ability of LaTeR to answer queries efficiently is very important in this phase. In particular, it is possible to efficiently remove from the derived tables all the tuples whose temporal expression is inconsistent. In fact, the distributivity of the NEC and POSS operators (and the fact that NEC → POSS) guarantees the correctness of deleting such tuples as soon as possible. Moreover, LaTeR allows us to do that efficiently by performing only local checks.

As an example, let us consider the following query:

$$NEC(\hat{\sigma}_{\text{AFTER}15/5/93}\pi_{\text{Sal}}(\sigma_{\text{Emp}='\text{John}'}(SAL) \times$$
$$\sigma_{\text{Emp}='\text{John}' \text{ and } \text{Man}='\text{Mary}'}(MAN))) \quad (6)$$

The query is evaluated as follows:

- The relevant tuples are extracted from the SAL and MAN tables, by means of the following SQL query:

  SELECT * FROM SAL, MAN
  WHERE SAL.Emp = "John" AND MAN.Emp = "John"
  AND MAN.Man = "Mary"

- IM computes the intermediate temporal table using the result of the query above; T is constructed for each tuple as the intersection of SAL.T and MAN.T. Each intersection is computed by LaTeR (by local propagation) which removes impossible intersections (e.g $i_3 \cap i_2$).

- Projection on the attribute Sal is computed by an SQL query (no changes in the temporal part is performed in this example); after this step, the first table in the example 2 is obtained as a result, as shown in section 5.

- For each interval in the temporal part, IM calls LaTeR to evaluate whether it is necessarily after 15/5/93. Only the interval $i_3 \cap i_7$ satisfies this condition and thus the resulting table is the following:

Sal	T
120	$\{i_3 \cap i_7\}$

Also this test is performed by LaTeR by means of a local propagation, considering only the time intervals explicitly mentioned in the query.

This architecture is particularly suitable for efficient query processing. The computational effort needed to answer a query is given by the effort to answer a relational query (which can be possibly optimized using relational equivalences) plus the overhead given by performing LaTeR query processing. Such an overhead is independent on the dimension of TA and, since it depends on the dimension of the existence condition only, is in general little. Furthermore, since LaTeR provides incremental updating, performances are interesting also during the updating of the database.

7 The temporal relational model and its temporal algebra

In [12], the authors identify 26 criteria for evaluating temporal algebras. Such criterias can be used to classify our temporal algebra with respect to other models presented in literature.

- In our algebra the tuples are time stamped by means of a set of intervals, thus attribute values in a tuple are synchronous (see [13]).

- Our algebra is a consistent extension of the snapshot algebra (Transform proof) and can be reduced to it (Snapshot proof).

- The values of the temporal part of a tuple are not independent of the values of the temporal part of other tuples in the relations of the database, since such values are constrained by the temporal assertions in TA. This issue adds a degree of complexity to the model, but it is an explicit feature which improves the expressivity of the model.

- Non-primitive operators (i.e. $\cap$, Θ-join and $\div$) are defined and they retain the properties of their snapshot counterpart.

- The algebra does not need the use of nulls; furthermore, it can deal with unknown temporal information without using nulls.

- Our algebra is indeed an algebra, which satisfies the basic algebraic equivalences of the snapshot algebra. Furthermore, it supports other equivalences between primitive operators, non-primitive operators and temporal operators.

- Finally, from the definition of the domain of coalesced temporal elements, each relation has an unique representation.

All algebras discussed in [12] consider precise times, usually expressed as dates, i.e., as temporal tags associated with data.

The possibility of dealing with incomplete information has been mainly discussed in the literature by Gadia [9]; Gadia's approach focuses both on incomplete data (outside the scope of the present paper) and on incomplete temporal information.

The main advantage of our approach with respect to Gadia's one is the possibility of dealing with qualitative relations between points and intervals, stating explicitly, for instance, that the end of an interval meets with the start of the another interval.

Indeterminacy has been also proposed in [8], with indeterminate events and intervals, possibly associated with a plausibility function for ordering events. Queries in that approach are computed with a determinate result, with a given confidence level, while our approach is to show incomplete information also in query results.

Incomplete non-temporal information has been studied in the database community and existing approaches can be partially extended to historical databases [6]. For instance, the approach showing results of queries grouping tuples in definite, indefinite and maybe tuples - with a model based semantics for defining the query language - can be extended to the temporal context.

As regards qualitative information, Chaudhuri [5] has been the first to handle relations between times in an historical database. However, Chaudhuri introduces strong limitations on the types of relations between times that can be used.

A recent interesting approach has been proposed by Koubarakis [11], who handles constraints on the extreme points of intervals and between times in general, using both local and global constraints. Koubarakis uses precedence and disjunctive relations between time points, and he does not focus on tractability of temporal reasoning. In Koubarakis's approach, moreover, it is not clear how necessity and possibility queries are answered when qualitative relations are used. In addition, the join operator is based only on a snapshot semantics, so that a comparison of times is not allowed (e.g., "salaries starting after a promotion"), while, in our approach, we can deal naturally with such situations: with (left/right) temporal join, we can select tuples on the basis of a comparison of times associated to a pair of tuples involved in a join operation.

Most of the basic choices in our approach (e.g., associating time with tuples rather than with attributes) are similar to those in Navathe's approach [13], which however does not deal with qualitative and imprecise temporal information (while we did not consider aggregate operators yet).

8 Concluding remarks

In this paper we presented an approach to deal with incomplete, imprecise and qualitative temporal information in historical relational databases. We have defined an extension to relational algebra to handle these types of information, and we proved that the extension we defined for primitive operators maintains the properties valid in the snapshot algebra. We also discussed how a relational database can be transformed into a temporal database using an external temporal reasoning module for inferring temporal information, strictly integrating the extended algebraic approach with the LaTeR time reasoning system. The architecture we propose for the integration is independent of the specific temporal reasoner being adopted; however, the use of LaTeR provides significant computational advantages in the treatment of (temporal) queries.

The theoretical approach proposed in the paper can also be a basis for query optimization, which will be the subject of further study.

Notice that, although we focused our proposal on an extension of historical relational databases, some aspects for dealing with incomplete information could be extended beyond the temporal part, and applied also to data stored in tuples (as done, for instance, by [9]).

References

[1] J. Allen. Maintaining knowledge about temporal intervals. *Communications of the ACM*, 26:832–843, 1983.

[2] V. Brusoni, L. Console, B. Pernici, and P. Terenziani. LaTeR: a general purpose manager of temporal information. In *Methodologies for Intelligent Systems 8*, pages 255–264. LNCS 869, Springer Verlag, 1994.

[3] V. Brusoni, L. Console, B. Pernici, and P. Terenziani. A relational model for historical databases dealing with absolute, qualitative and incomplete information. Technical report, Dip. di Informatica, Università di Torino, 1995.

[4] V. Brusoni, L. Console, and P. Terenziani. On the computational complexity of querying bounds on differences constraints. *Artificial Intelligence (to appear)*, 1995.

[5] S. Chaudhuri. Temporal relationships in databases. In *Proc. 14th Conference on Very Large Databases*, Los Angeles, 1988.

[6] J. Chomicki. Temporal databases. In *Tutorial presented at 12th ACM SIGACT-SIGMOD-SIGART Symposium on Principles of Database Systems*, Washington, D.C., 1993.

[7] L. Console, B. Pernici, and P. Terenziani. Towards the development of a general temporal manager for temporal databases: a layered and modular approach. In *Proc. of the Int. Work. on an Infrastructure for Temporal Databases*, Arlington, Texas, 1993.

[8] C. Dyreson and R. Snodgrass. Valid-time interminacy. In *Proc. IEEE Conf. on Data Engineering*, Vienna, 1993.

[9] S.K. Gadia, S.S. Nair, and Y.-C. Peon. Incomplete information in relational temporal databases. In *Proc. 18th Conference on Very Large Databases*, Vancouver, 1992.

[10] M. Koubarakis. Representation and querying in temporal databases: the power of temporal constraints. In *Proc. IEEE Conf. on Data Engineering*, pages 327–334, 1993.

[11] M. Koubarakis. Database models for infinite and indefinite temporal information. *Information Systems*, 19(2):141–173, 1994.

[12] L. McKenzie and R. Snodgrass. Evaluation of relational algebras incorporating the time dimension in databases. *ACM Computing Surveys*, 23(4):501–543, 1991.

[13] S.B. Navathe and R. Ahmed. A temporal relational model and a query language. *Information Sciences*, 48:147–175, 1988.

[14] P. VanBeek. Temporal query processing with indefinite information. *Artificial Intelligence in Medicine*, 3:325–339, 1991.

[15] M. Vilain and H. Kautz. Constraint propagation algorithms for temporal reasoning. In *Proc. AAAI 86*, pages 377–382, 1986.

[16] M. Vilain, H. Kautz, and P. VanBeek. Constraint propagation algorithms for temporal reasoning: a revised report. In D.S. Weld and J. de Kleer, editors, *Readings in Qualitative Reasoning about physical systems*, pages 373–381. Morgan Kaufmann, 1989.

Managing Time in GIS
An Event-Oriented Approach

Christophe Claramunt
Swiss Federal Institute of Technology
Department of Rural Engineering
Spatial Information Systems
Lausanne, CH-1015, Switzerland

Marius Thériault
Laval University
Department of Geography
Planning and Development Research Center
Quebec, G1K 7P4, Canada

Abstract

Time integration within GIS requires a comprehensive analysis of spatio-temporal phenomena. This paper presents a conceptual model of time and space suitable for geographic applications. A topological temporal framework for representing entity-based events and processes is proposed. An event-oriented model, extended from the versioning concept, describes different evolution levels. The temporal operations possible with this architecture are defined in terms of time- and event-based queries. Performance and some implementation issues are also discussed.

1   Introduction

The distribution of land-based phenomena and activities is directly dependent on transformation and diffusion processes that have led to the mutation and evolution of entities occupying geographic space. Conceptually, time is an essential dimension for understanding and modeling space [6], which is illustrated by the increase of publications concerning databases and temporal GIS (TGIS) over the last ten years [4].

Interest in the relationship between space and time greatly preceded the emergence of GIS. Geographic literature [1, 14, 23] is replete with studies that associate time and space in analyzing or explaining processes related to the distribution, evolution and diffusion of geographic phenomena. Modeling both space and time covers a wide spectrum of applications, from bio-physical sciences to epidemiological research, as well as the social, economic and political sciences [11, 21, 32]. If we consider real-time GIS applications for transportation, along with applications for management and planning which require both retrospective and prospective views of processes, we can easily presume that adding a temporal character will substantially increase GIS use for scientific and administrative needs. In this paper, we propose a TGIS architecture based on two complementary stages:

a) identifying the spatio-temporal processes and the related spatio-temporal operators, at the conceptual level;

b) designing the logical architecture for such a conceptual model.

The approach retained associates the Newtonian concept of time (seen as a measurable flow) with Leibnitz's relational theory, which defines time as a succession of events. This condition is mandatory because ordered events are more frequent than precisely dated events [40]. According to Hazelton [24], we use metaphors to work with time in order to avoid the inherent difficulties of temporal concepts. It is thus possible to define four basic metaphors for integrating time into GIS [22]: linear time (past, present, future), cyclical time (seasons, day/night, etc.), branching (inter-entity time dependencies) and multi-dimensional time (world time, survey time, valid time, display time).

We propose a conceptual model of time that integrates its topologic and metric dimensions. Our goal is to demonstrate the feasibility of such a system by using existing spatial data structures. The proposed solution is based on the versioning concept. According to Easterfield [15], versioning is a mechanism for recording the history of the database. We propose to extend this notion to management of spatio-temporal processes in the real world: Extended-versioning is a mechanism for recording the history of the database and for describing successive events in the real world.

This paper is organized as follows. In Section 2, we define events and processes. In Section 3, we propose a framework for spatio-temporal modeling. In Section 4, we present two event-oriented diagrams. In Section 5, we define an event-oriented typology of spatio-temporal operators. In Section 6, we discuss the indexation mechanism, data access issues and quality control. Section 7 summarizes our work and presents conclusions.

2   Events and processes

A TGIS should simultaneously consider the events behind changes and the facts which enable observation of these changes [6]. Beller notes that browsing through the events may lead to an understanding of causal relationships and help with hypothesis generation [6]. There is a clear need for a temporal GIS capable of monitoring and analyzing successive states of the spatial entities.

Events are things that happen; they are conditions, processes, or objects that exist and can be observed [1]. We can thus model events as a set of processes that transform entities. We may also define several temporal scales. A mountain is immobile from our point of view, but its shape and elevation vary on the geological scale (orogenesis and erosion processes). Each TGIS application must define the chronon (the shortest duration of time; [26]) to describe all the processes involved. An appropriate chronon avoids producing useless data, without obscuring significant phenomena.

To respond adequately to scientific needs, a TGIS should explicitly preserve known links between events and their consequences. Observed relationships should be noted (e.g. entities A and B generate entity C) to help scientists develop models that reproduce the dynamics of spatio-temporal processes. Researchers will thus be able to study complex relationships, draw conclusions and verify causal links that associate entities through influence and transformation processes.

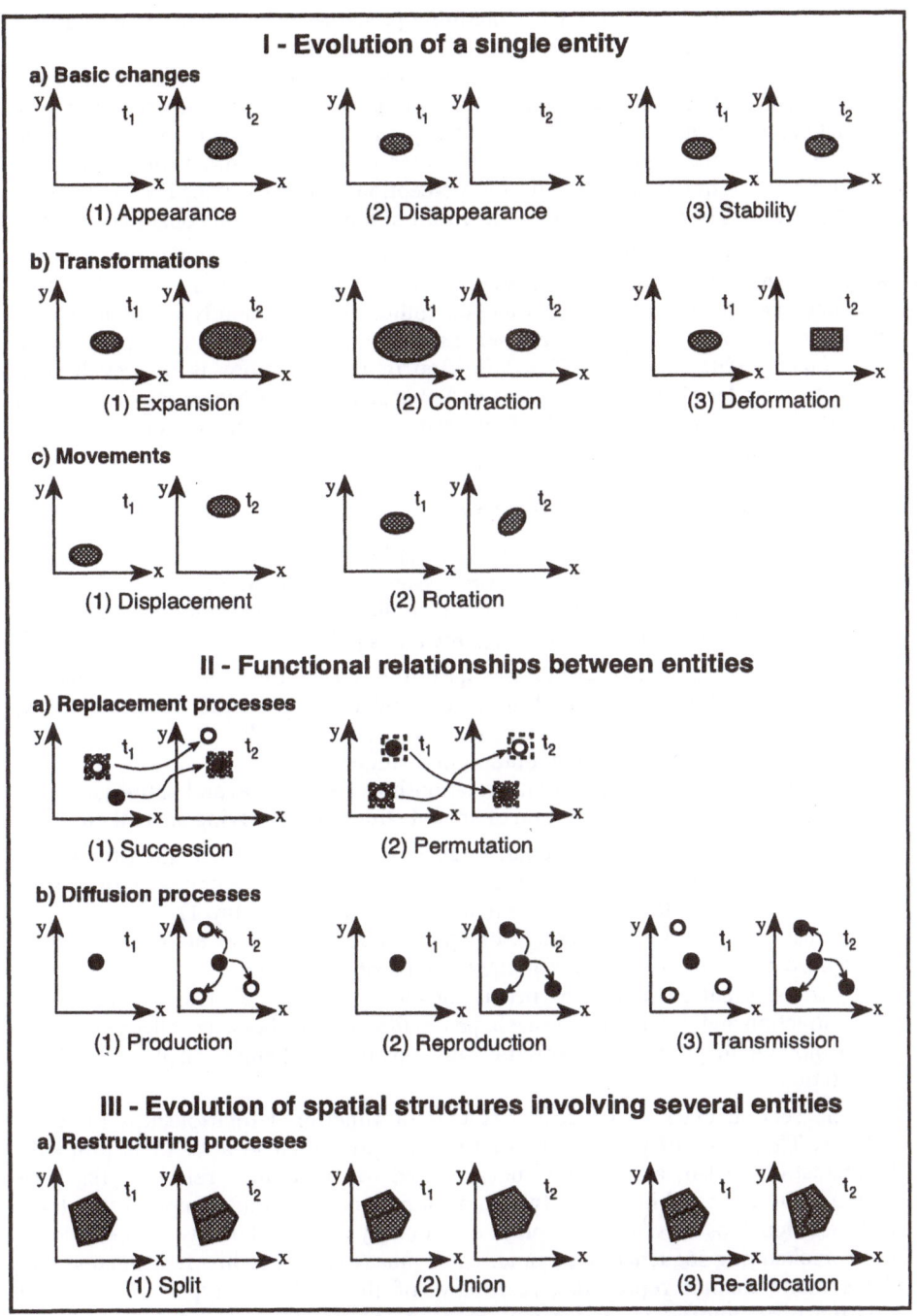

Figure 1. **Typology of spatio-temporal processes**

Langran notes the importance of defining processes conceptually to establish a proper link between time and space in GIS [28]. This involves three components: a definition of the notion of change and particularly that differentiates between evolving and mutating entities, an inventory of spatio-temporal processes and a rule for making a clear demarcation between the spatial, temporal and thematic domains. All geographic phenomena have a spatio-temporal component as time and space constitute the frame of reference for our perceptions. The processes lead to changes in entity states. These changes show the result of the process and constitute events.

In the field of GIS, the term 'entity' is generally used to designate an observed phenomenon. For each application, an entity has an essence that, if changed, causes it to become a different entity altogether; other changes merely result in a new version of the same entity. These essences must be defined prior to implementing the temporal database [28]. The definition of these entities is the result of a conceptual model of land, phenomena and changes. Change occurs when there is a significant evolution of an entity's characteristics over time. Changes and events are a natural way to define processes.

2.1   Spatio-temporal processes

Mutations provide evidence of change and must be used to define events. The events are then used to model geographic processes. Event abstraction should not be limited to a single level. It is thus preferable to devise conceptual models that allow higher-order events using hierarchical aggregations [6].

Figure 1 shows the basic processes used to describe low-order spatio-temporal events and to define a framework to accommodate our scientific research needs. Three main types of spatio-temporal processes may be defined:

I -   those that concern the evolution of a single entity;
II -   those that involve functional relationships between several entities;
III -   those that are the evolution of spatial structures involving several entities.

Evolution of a single entity constitutes an indispensable foundation for TGIS. Therefore, a process is represented as the aggregation of simultaneous or related changes. We propose three categories to describe evolution (figure 1):

a) basic processes: appearance, disappearance and spatial stability to allow representation of attribute variation without spatial effects;

b) transformation processes involving change in shape or size: expansion, contraction and deformation (i.e. shape modification without size change),

c) movement processes involving only positional change: displacement and rotation.

The second class of processes is that of functional relationships between entities. The range of phenomena that can be processed in a TGIS is probably inexhaustible. Also, a rule must be provided to distinguish relationships with predominant temporal incidence (which must be modeled in the temporal structure) from relationships in which time plays a secondary role. Certain events are ordered in an unchanging sequence (e.g. an ancestor must live before his descendants) that dates alone cannot reproduce. A review of the principal types of temporal relationships studied in geography leads us to set forth the following rule: functional processes that involve a dependence link between entities, while they impose a precedence constraint, must be modeled on the temporal structure in order to clarify the topologic relationships they convey. Furthermore, processes with only one time-period overlap constraint may be described in the thematic base without creating confusion. This is the criterion that motivates keeping the production process in the temporal structure because one entity creates another entity of a different nature, thereby explaining the appearance of the new one. By contrast, we can dismiss notions of ownership and inclusion among spatial and thematic relationships as verifying that the two entities are contemporaneous is sufficient to validate the relationship. Functional relationships with a dominant temporal characteristic may be grouped into two categories:

a) Replacement processes involve a sequence of entities of comparable types that accomplish the same function or occupy the same position in space (without necessarily having identical locations). Figure 1 distinguishes between succession and permutation processes, although the latter may be likened to a double succession.

b) Diffusion processes involve a transfer of characteristics between two or more spatial entities. It seems useful to distinguish between production phenomena (creation of new entities by the actions of one or more entities of different natures), reproduction phenomena (creation of new entities of the same type as the parents) and transmission phenomena (modification of the characteristics of a receiver due to the influence of a transmitter). Each process carries a precedence constraint. Contagion is a specific form of diffusion.

The third class concerns the evolution of spatial structures and takes into account constraints linked to the position of the other entities. Many consistency constraints implicit in a GIS must become explicit in a TGIS because elements move. Evolving spatial patterns in a population of individuals describe overall tendencies. As such changes are reproducible by combining individual movements they do not require elementary operators. By contrast, land is partitioned according to a system of mutually exclusive zones for several administrative applications (e.g. counties, municipalities, census tracts). These divisions undergo periodic rezoning, which creates an obvious problem for time series analysis because the delimitation of statistical areas varies between censuses. Geographers call this a 'split tract problem' [25], which corresponds to the notion of restructuring processes in figure 1. We retain three fundamental cases: division of a zone into 'n' parts (split), fusion of 'n' zones into a single entity (union) and reallocation of land covered by 'n' initial zones to form 'p' new zones. However, the case of land exchange between two existing zones (by modification of the common border) is comparable to a change of shape of the concerned zones (transformation processes).

Finally, we retain at least five basic classes that can be aggregated to model more complex processes: evolution of an entity, succession, production, reproduction and transmission.

2.2 Temporal topology

According to the temporal resolution considered, changes are perceived as instantaneous (mutation) or progressive (evolution). If we admit that time is one-dimensional, two types of time-stamps must be defined: the instant (the equivalent of a point in space) and the period (time interval). Furthermore, we could retain a cyclical vision of time as several natural and economic processes evolve according to cyclical rhythms. However, for the purpose of this paper, let us assume time is straight and linear.

Events involving several entities play the same role as communication networks: they form ordered temporal networks. They link series of events and enable deduction of lineages (e.g. precedence or connectivity relationships) even if precise dates are unknown. The topologic properties obtained may be used to verify connectivity between versions of the same entity or between different entities linked by functional or structural processes.

In the context of this paper, we will use the term 'instance' to designate versions that do not necessarily concern the same entity. In the database, object versions correspond to successive states of the represented entity. They are delimited by the events that have modified (thematic or spatial changes) the entities in a significant way.

2.3   Spatio-temporal topology

Cole and King propose entities be divided into three categories according to the pace of their evolution: those that are static (for a given temporal resolution), those that change slowly, and those that are dynamic [14]. Static entities require a single version in a TGIS as they are spatial and thematic constants. Entities that evolve slowly will use a reduced number of versions. Their spatial structure is described efficiently and compactly using current topologic spatial models [36].

Dynamic entities evolve rapidly (in space or by their attributes) and require a large number of versions, which takes up a significant amount of space for data storage. If entity positions vary, classic representation methods pose a major problem because all of the coordinates of the moving object and adjacent object must be redefined in order to express the topology clearly. As well as consuming a large amount of space, the required processes slow the system, creating a touchy problem for real-time GIS applications [16].

Different spatial representations must be developed for moving entities in order to simplify their coding while making the most of the invariable spatial characteristics. Two structures may then model the spatial domain in a TGIS, the first being of topologic type for static and slowly evolving entities, the second being object-oriented for mobile entities. As an application nearly always implies both types of entities, it is therefore essential to model time in a distinct structure to preserve its unicity and maintain data consistency.

3   A framework for spatio-temporal modeling

Since our purpose is to model changes among a set of entities and to provide an operational environment, the vector-based model is the most suitable considering its general properties. Issues of matrix encoding modes and continuous spatial variation phenomena are beyond the scope of this paper. The reader is refered to Peuquet and Duan for a discussion about raster TGIS [39].

3.1   The need for an explicit temporal topology

The spatio-temporal processes described above require an explicit representation. The architecture developed must associate the date and duration of events with the logical sequence of successive versions (e.g. a series of crops on the same plot with fallow periods of varying durations).

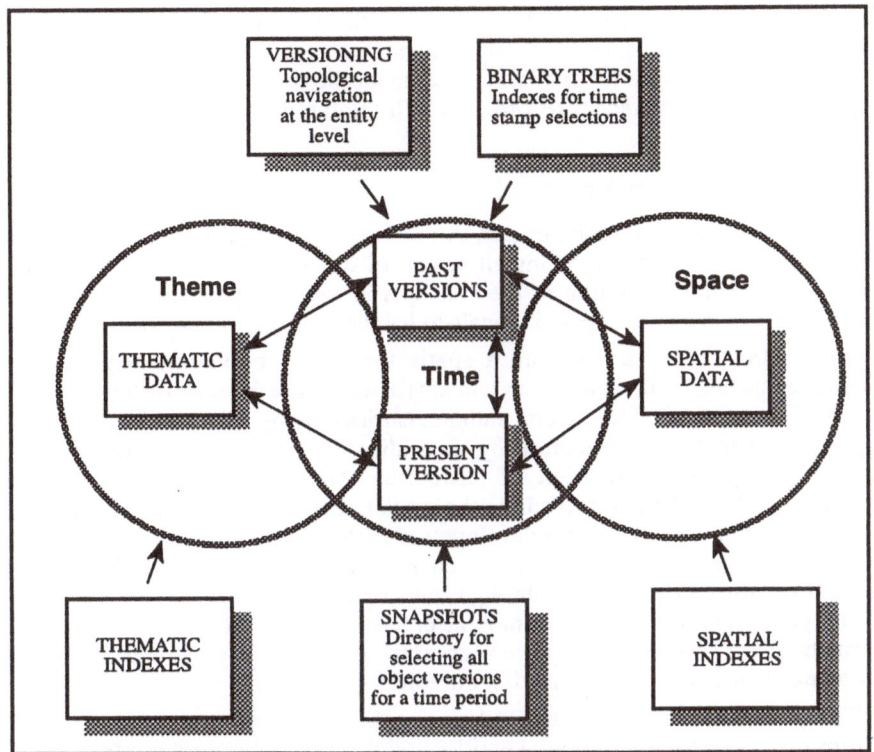

Figure 2.   **Spatio-temporal framework**

It is possible to derive successions from time-stamps, but this procedure requires significant calculation time and runs the risk of confusion similar to what occurs when spatial topology is deduced from a spaghetti-type model. Processing only dates may create false successions and ignore significant links between entities (events). This risk is well known in the spatial domain (creation of false polygons and lost adjacency relationships). Furthermore, spatio-temporal processes corresponding to phenomena involving mutation, succession, production, repro-duction and transmission must be explicit encoded in order to be distinguished.

It is preferable, therefore, to treat time as a complementary and independent facet of spatial and thematic domains (figure 2). The proposed framework separates themes, time and space, which enables the use of existing models [36, 38] and preserves compatibility with the spatial data structures currently used in GIS packages. From the user's point of view, it is the query language and its interface that constitute the integrating element for the three domains. The domains are separated into distinct structures but are united by domain links that form the intersections of the three circles in figure 2. The temporal domain is represented by successive object versions accumulated in temporal structures. The structure's links describe events explicitly. Versions refer to thematic and spatial structures to produce a complete description of entities at different moments of their evolution.

This structure avoids redundancy because several versions can refer to the same spatial object if the mutation is thematic, or to the same thematic description if the process is spatial. Current versions are preserved in a structure (present version) that is distinct from past versions (past generally beeing accessed in read-only mode) to optimize processing time for spatial queries about the present situation. Users want fast access to the most recent records but will tolerate slower access to the older, historical records [30].

3.2 Properties and restrictions

Although this approach distributes data throughout separate structures, it allows the user to formulate a query involving all or part of the domains. It can be reconciled with the foreseeable evolution of the concepts in each domain and, in particular, authorizes the extension of spatial models to handle the time dimension.

Most GIS are developed with a spatio-thematic architecture that includes specialized management of attribute and spatial data. The interest of this approach has already been detailed by several authors, particularly by Aref and Samet [5]. We propose to keep this architecture by extending this principle to the temporal component. The specialization of structures will facilitate the autonomous development of functions for handling the spatial, thematic and temporal aspects of a query. This approach allows for development of the most appropriate structures for storing and accessing information in each domain. Spatial entities and their temporal versions are associated through links that describe the sequence of events and the properties of the spatio-temporal processes involved. Access to temporal information will be guaranteed, according to the objectives, by methods suitable to the context, which will be described in the following sections.

To maintain a certain amount of coherence, the approach described in this article requires certain restrictions. Spatial entities and their versions are discrete or can be represented by a finite partition of space and time. Furthermore, to avoid ambiguity, we assume that time is represented with a granularity that forbids temporal overlapping of two versions of the same spatial entity [34].

By contrast, it is essential to anticipate the following properties to allow for the integration of spatio-temporal processes and simulation in GIS. An event may be instantaneous or have a duration (progressive temporal variation), which is noted as an explicit attribute of the temporal link. Temporal links are bidirectional to access previous and following versions of an object by means of a topologic navigation procedure. Several types of links (succession, production, reproduction, transmission) may be used simultaneously to make dependence relationships between several objects explicit by defining the event that unites their respective versions. The data structure should allow access and selections with temporal, spatial or thematic criteria or any combination of the three domains. The access structure should allow windowing of space, specification of periods of interest and establishment of thematic coverages.

4 Event-oriented diagrams

Using an event-oriented approach means that the model focuses on spatio-temporal events and their significance (as opposed to a snapshot approach, which focuses on time stamps). The diagrams presented in this section illustrate the feasibility of the event-oriented approach. The logical model proposed is rendered explicit by using relational formalism. Besides being frequently used for developing temporal architectures, this formalism has the advantage of being well-known to GIS users.

Our approach is to extend the 'tuple-level versioning' method proposed by Lum *et al.* for structuring temporal databases [31].

4.1   General structure

The general structure distinguishes between thematic, temporal and spatial domains (figure 3). These three sets of characteristics are distributed in distinct tables. These tables describe the appropriate attributes for each spatial or aspatial object version. A new version is added to the temporal table each time an object undergoes a thematic or spatial change. A thematic change also creates a new tuple in the thematic table. A spatial process modifies the reference in the spatial table. The new version continues to point to the old description as long as there is no change in the domain concerned. The three sets of tables are interconnected by domain links. Bidirectional temporal links allow forward and backward movement through time.

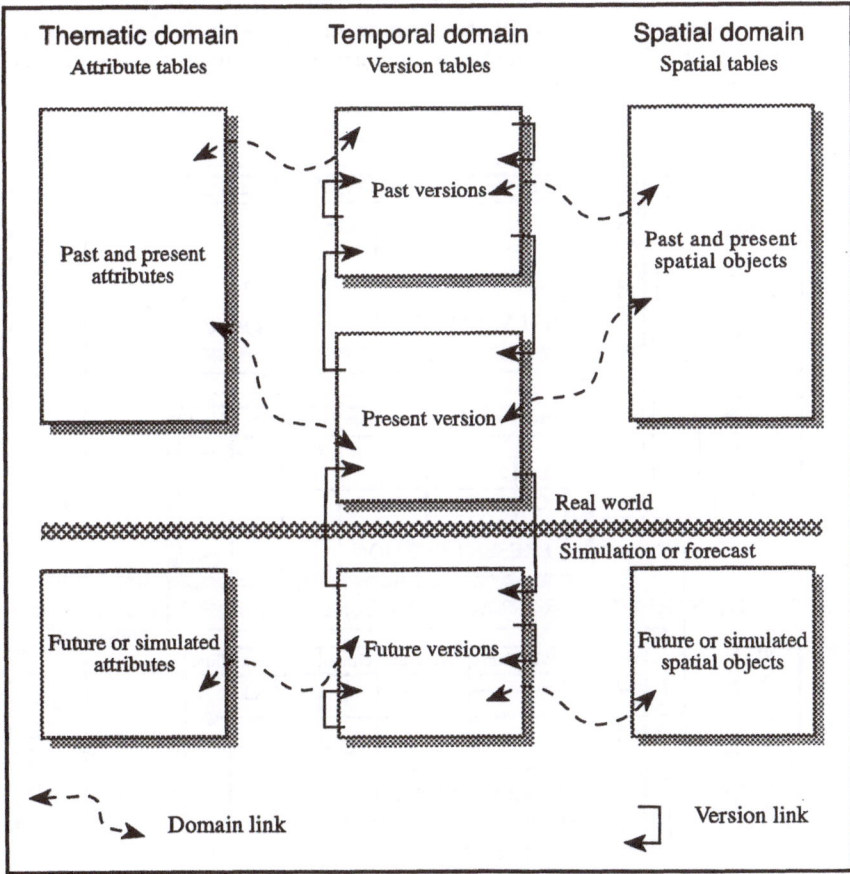

Figure 3.   **General structure**

Version tables provide an explicit representation of the chronological sequence of changes and, in a way, act as temporal indexes to access spatial and attribute descriptions of objects. Versions are distributed in past, present and future temporal tables to identify events with respect to the present and to optimize queries about the current situation. Attribute and spatial tables for past and present versions are joined to allow description sharing. This characteristic enables efficient determination of the date of the last change.

Future tables receive prediction data (simulation and forecast). They are stored separately to facilitate cancellation of simulation data but they maintain the same structure in order to simplify manipulations.

4.2   Basic versioning diagram

Figure 4 is a rough outline of a logical schema based on the tuple-level versioning model of Lum et al. [31]. Version tables order changes by means of bi-directional temporal links (*Prev* and *Next*) completed by real-world (*WD_Time*) and valid time (*VL_Time*). A special field (*Last*) in the past versions table establishes a link with the present versions. Each tuple of the attribute and spatial tables references the last version that used it. Thus we can retrace the history of changes based on a thematic or spatial query.

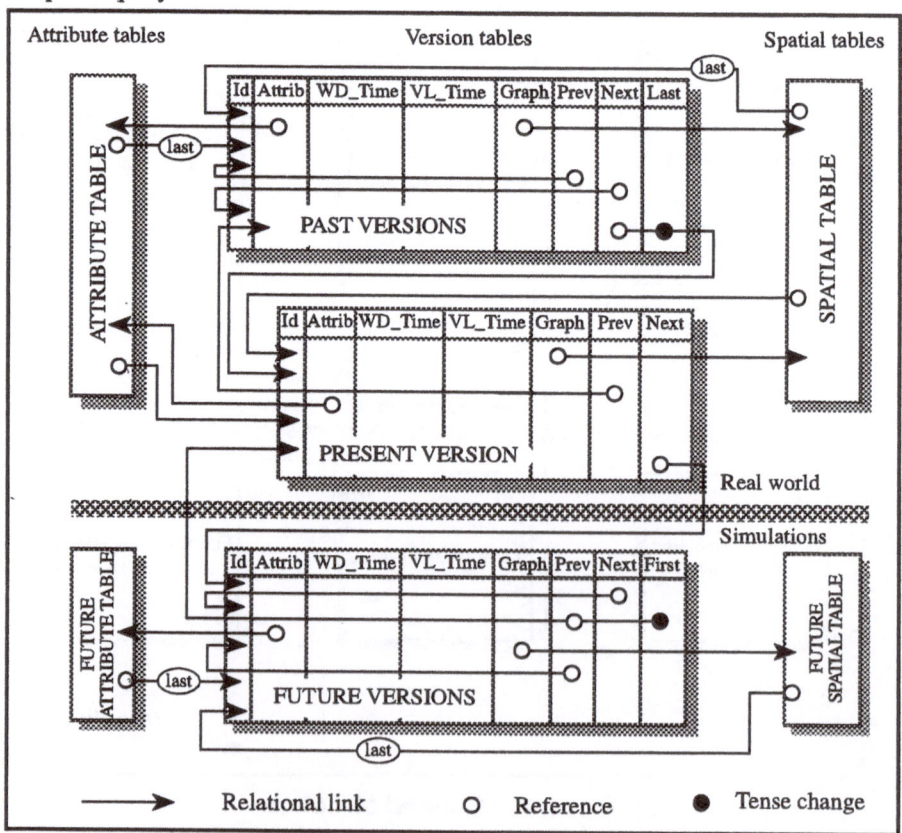

Figure 4.   **Basic versioning diagram**

This architecture enables the temporal mutations (or evolution) of each entity to be represented. Its sequential character does not allow for specification of complex spatio-temporal processes such as succession and diffusion that involve several entities.

4.3   Extended-versioning diagram

Figure 5 is an extension of the previous diagram which can describe events involving several entities. Version tables are accessed through intermediary logical tables (Past events, Present events and Future events) that enable these multiple links to be represented. These intermediary tables can simultaneously reference several different entities and thus permit description of complex succession, production, reproduction and transmission processes. The same tuple in the event table can reference previous or subsequent versions of an entity while describing the processes and the other entities involved in the change.

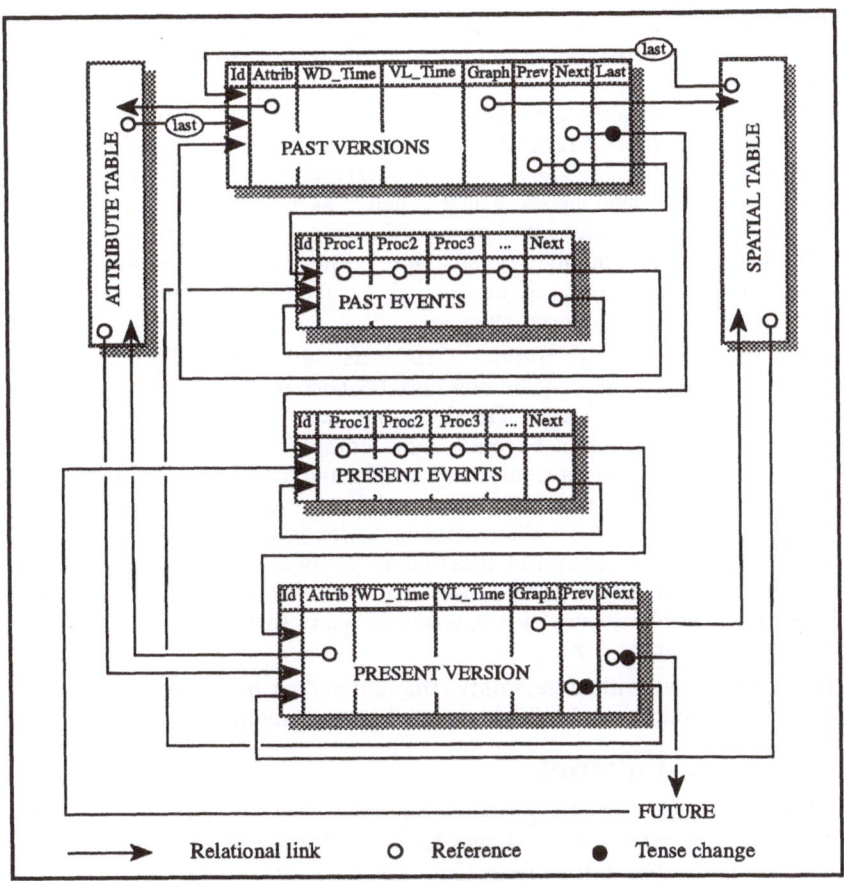

Figure 5.   **Extended-versioning diagram**

Each event marks the passage between two or more instances and is described by a set of complementary processes. Each process is described by a complex attribute that references the version it generates.

Process: [**Version**: Longint; {Ref. to the appropriate version; null if no version}
            Process_Type: Char; {E: evolution; S: succession; P: production;
                                R: reproduction; T: transmission}
            Date: Time; {Event time-stamp}
            Duration: Real; {Process duration}
            Source: Text; {Meta-data about change notification}]

5   Query capabilities

This section defines basic rules of designing query language for a temporal database according to the extended diagram.

5.1   Typology of queries

We can define four main classes of queries required to operate a TGIS:

a) Thematic queries select tuples according to criteria involving simple attributes.

b) Temporal queries are generally subdivided into simple temporal queries and temporal range queries [28]. We propose to further distinguish between time-stamp-based and topologically-based temporal queries.

c) Spatial queries have the same dual structure as temporal queries [37]. The first form is quantitative and involves coordinate or distance measurements. The second is topologic and involves spatial relationships among entities.

d) Spatio-temporal queries are used to link events with locations and share all the characteristics of the previous classes.

Since the purpose is to provide GIS users with full spatio-temporal query capabilities, the language may be complex because it will integrate all thematic, temporal and spatial concepts. On the other hand, the likelihood of a query diminishes significantly as it becomes more complex. The proposed approach is modular. It integrates current research on spatial and temporal query languages and allows the request to be defined at the minimum level of complexity. Since the simple query will only access the necessary tables in the database, it will execute more efficiently. It is common practice in software engineering to measure performance as both the computer processing time needed to perform a task and the delay the user considers acceptable to answer a query (evaluated as a function of its complexity and database size).

In this paper, we will address only temporal and spatio-temporal query classes. Spatial query operators are described in detail by many authors [18, 37, 41].

5.2   Temporal queries

Many languages can be used to process temporal queries [12, 20, 27, 43]. The reader is referred to McKenzie and Snodgrass for an evaluation of relational algebras that incorporate the temporal dimension [33]. TSQL, a superset of SQL developed by Navathe and Ahmed , provides an exhaustive set of temporal operators to retrieve information from a temporal database: comparing time-intervals, computing the intersection between time periods, analyzing time discontinuities, specifying the time domain, aggregating over time periods and choosing the length of a time-interval [34].

Since TSQL is an extension of SQL, it provides an obvious starting point to integrate time-based queries in many existing GIS packages. The original operators defined by Navathe and Ahmed complement the WHEN clause and return a boolean result based on the relative sequence of two time-intervals [34]. They operate with time-stamps stored in flat tables and represent a time-point with a zero duration time-interval (i.e. begin-time = end-time).

BEFORE	[a,b] BEFORE [c,d]	b<c	boolean
AFTER	[a,b] AFTER [c,d]	a>d	boolean
DURING	[a,b] DURING [c,d]	(a≥c) & (b≤d)	boolean
EQUIVALENT	[a,b] EQUIVALENT [c,d]	(a=c) & (b=d)	boolean
ADJACENT	[a,b] ADJACENT [c,d]	(c-b=1) I (a-d=1)	boolean
OVERLAP	[a,b] OVERLAP [c,d]	(a≤d) & (c≤b)	boolean
FOLLOWS	[a,b] FOLLOWS [c,d]	(a-d=1)	boolean
PRECEDES	[a,b] PRECEDES [c,d]	(c-b=1)	boolean
STARTS	[a,b] STARTS [c,d]	a=c	boolean
FINISHES	[a,b] FINISHES [c,d]	b=d	boolean

Notes: [a,b] and [c,d] symbolize the two periods begin- and end-time. The EQUIVALENT, ADJACENT, STARTS, FINISHES and OVERLAP operators are commutative.

Table 1. Time-stamp-based operators
(adapted from Navathe and Ahmed [34]; Allen and Hayes [3])

The previous operators compare time periods but do not provide an explicit way to model and distinguish evolution, succession, production, reproduction and transmission processes. There is a need for a new class of topological operators used in the WHEN clause to access the explicit topological links between instances stored in the tables. Indeed, time-stamp-based operators use time measurements to compute relative positions between potentially independant entities as opposite to the topological operators linking interdependant entities. Here "instance" has the meaning of a generalized data type in the temporal domain. The implementation of this function and the logical links to be considered are kept transparent to the user, and the system must provide mechanisms to avoid constraint violations (e.g. an entity that is generated by its descendant; or an instance that replaces itself).

EVOLUTION	[InstanceA1] CHANGES TO [InstanceA2]	A1=A2	boolean
SUCCESSION	[InstanceA] REPLACED BY [InstanceB]	A≠B	boolean
PRODUCTION	[InstanceA] PRODUCES [InstanceB]	A≠B	boolean
REPRODUCTION	[InstanceA] GENERATES [InstanceB]	A≠B	boolean
TRANSMISSION	[InstanceA] TRANSMITS [InstanceB]	A≠B	boolean

Notes: All these operators involve Instances as operands and are not commutative. The symbol A1=A2 means that the operator is restricted to two versions of the same entity, while A≠B implies two different entities.

Table 2. Events-based operators

The CHANGES TO operator returns 'true' when InstanceA2 is an entity mutation immediately following InstanceA1. The evolution processes are always modeled according to a 'one to one' relationship.

The REPLACED BY operator returns 'true' when InstanceB is an immediate successor of InstanceA. Both instances may survive the replacement, InstanceA being permuted to another position tracked with the appropriate CHANGES TO query. The succession process is encoded as a 'one to many' or a 'many to one' relationship. The re-allocation process described in figure 1 ('many to many' case) is modeled by a 'many to one' followed by a 'one to many' relationship using an intermediate virtual entity.

The PRODUCES operator returns 'true' when InstanceA is the producer of InstanceB. The production process is modelled as a 'one to many' relationship where the production and the product are different entities or different classes (e.g. a plant and the cars produced). Multiple cooperating producers use many independant relationships and each product may refer to many producers.

The GENERATES operator returns 'true' when InstanceA is an immediate ancestor of InstanceB. The reproduction process is modeled as a 'one to many' relationship where the ancestor and its children must be different entities of the same class. Multiple ancestors (i.e., father and mother) use many independent topological links, and many descendants (i.e. children) can share one or many ancestors to define a full 'n to n' relationship. The child entity is born with this instance and the link table shows its relationship to both the parent entity and the first child version.

The TRANSMITS operator returns 'true' when InstanceB has its attributes modified by some contact with instanceA. The main difference with the production and reproduction processes is that InstanceB existed prior to transmission. Its previous history is tracked with a CHANGES TO query. The transmission process is generally (but not restricted to) a 'one to many' relationship.

The CHANGES TO operator is generally sufficient to operate with the adjacent versions of an entity, even if time-stamps are missing or corrupted. The other operators are mandatory for time-dependent applications in genealogy (e.g. two parents and many children), in business (e.g. to track employees playing musical chairs with their positions) in communications and in epidemiology (e.g. one or many sources linked with one or many receptors). A fully topologic spatio-temporal database can track movements of all family members (spatial distribution) simultanously describing their reproduction (child birth), production (sold products), influence networks (ideas or diseases transmission) and succession history (heritage).

The topologic operators suggested here access only immediately adjacent entities or versions. There is still a need to provide an efficient way to find the grandparents and grandchildren or to check if two entities share a common lineage. This is a challenging subject for future research. A preliminary solution may involve a recursive procedure based on transitive closure of the relations or a deductive query [7].

5.3 Spatio-temporal queries

Spatial and temporal data have dimensional properties (geometry, topology, relative position and graphic presentation) that the user needs to use in a single integrated query language [17]. In this context, the query language must provide tools to retrieve and display data in various forms (snapshot maps, time-ordered graphs, animated maps, etc.). The ultimate goal is to replicate, as closely as possible, human thinking about space and time when defining such an integrated query language. An appropriate use of semantically defined, dimension-independent domains (i.e. abstract data types for "version", "instance", "spatial", etc.), graphical presentation language [17] and icon symbols can further add to system user-friendliness.

Spatial and temporal relations are significantly different from standard relations, since they involve specific properties such as topology and direction. These properties make use of one-dimensional objects in the time domain [28] and are based on one-, two- and three-dimensional objects in the spatial domain [17]. These dimensions are used to compute duration, distance, direction and angle, providing relationships between entities. The same applies to topology, which is used to explicitly define adjacency, inclusion, intersection, (etc.) in space [18] or event succession and dependence in time.

Defining a new language to deal simultaneously with space and time is a challenging task. However, spatio-temporal processes are extremely complex in conceptual terms because they simultaneously involve spatial, temporal and thematic mutations. It is crucial that such a query language be able to express all four query classes (thematic, temporal, spatial and spatio-temporal) and avoid unnecessary overhead when the question at hand is simple. Many approaches, which extend SQL by incorporating temporal or spatial capabilities (operators and functions), are efficient and productive [18, 34, 41]. Despite its well-known flaws [13], SQL is a simple, powerful and technologically mature language with a short learning period. SQL's presence in the worldwide activities of standards organizations (ANSI, ISO, etc.) ensures that it will be in use for some time. It will evolve in the near future to integrate time (TSQL2 Language Design Committee). Some related issues include new database developments such as object-oriented [42] or active database concepts [19]).

Research on temporal and spatial queries must now address the need to merge space and time and to relate them to adimensional thematic data to produce a syntactically correct and conceptually flexible language. An efficient query language can reduce the cycle time scientists need to formulate theories, develop models and check their validity. There is a real need to incorporate events in any environmentally-based TGIS so that the database can contain and relate both explicit and implicit causal information about the natural processes embedded in the data.

6   Implementation issues

The proposed model draws a clear distinction between thematic, temporal and spatial characteristics of an entity. We propose to maintain this separate approach for database access considering that aspatial, spatial and temporal access requirements are separate issues. These complementary methods will be integrated with a single query interface, using SQL or object-oriented query languages, with an approach proposed by Ooi [35]. This integration will be linked with a query optimizer based on query decomposition in basic sequences nested with an acyclic dependency graph. Common queries could be determined with a database catalog [35]. This divide and conquer strategy can reduce complex queries to their manageable components, thus reducing the computing time.

6.1   Indexation mechanism

Several indexation methods have been proposed to support temporal structures. Most of them are based on one-dimensional and primary keys index such as B+Trees for time-date value-oriented queries and multi-dimensional approaches such as R-Trees for time-interval queries [44].

For application purposes, real world time is the most appropriate key for the date value reference of a version. We have to allow for version access based on the "begin time" for present versions (considering that the current system time is the same for all versions) and on both "begin-" and "end-time" for past and future versions. This leads us to propose a B+Tree value-oriented index for the present version table and a multi-dimensional R-Tree for past and future tables. A secondary index could be applied for other database times where range queries on these keys are not often used. Temporal and continuous modification of the database updates only the pointer list of the tree structure; on the other hand, the index tree has to be modified for random and retroactive temporal modifications. The efficiency of these index methods will increase in proportion to the non-uniform temporal distribution of the data.

Topologic navigation allows for retrieval of the successive states of the same entity. It is well known and has been used for spatial applications [9]. The event-oriented logical structure stores version links explicitly and then constitutes an efficient access method for entity evolutions through the topologic operators. Considering that temporal topology is linear and leads to a single active version per moment, navigation allows entity evolution to be traced. Topologic navigation is also efficient for navigating from one entity to other linked entities (succession, reproduction, transmission).

Snapshots have been widely studied in the database world [12]. A temporal snapshot permits the design of a static database view for a specific time. Temporal snapshots are created dynamically and stored if necessary for application needs. Materialized snapshots are especially useful for applications that require a view of information at a specific time. Regular refreshes are a guarantee of snapshot consistency after database modifications. Snapshots are mandatory for comprehensive evolution studies. An alternate and more dynamic form of snapshot defines a list of pointers to the appropriate versions.

Database views extend snapshot principles and provide a framework for interactive database queries. A spatial database view extends this concept and may be defined as the necessary integration, for spatial data, of visualization parameters within a classic view model [10]. Both derived or materialized spatial views provide the user with an independent and application-oriented view of the database. Further research is needed on the definition of a spatio-temporal view and on the integration of temporal operators.

Due to the huge amount of data to manipulate, access performance is a vital issue for the operation of a TGIS. Evaluation of the performance of temporal databases has already been completed [2]. Each specific application has its own characteristics and requirements. Together, these indexation methods provide efficient support for time management in GIS if the query mechanism is task- or context-sensitive [35]. The query optimization strategy is also retained by Raper and Bundock to speed up data access for the UGIX system [41].

6.2   Quality control

Quality control and data integrity are important issues for spatio-temporal applications due to the intricate mix of dependencies between time and space [8]. An efficient quality control procedure has to check integrity for both space and time components as well as for their multiple interactions. Temporal quality control must re-examine the procedures used for quality control in a conventional GIS [28, 29]. The event-based structure adds many temporal and spatio-temporal quality control levels to complement the spatial topology:

a)   Entity-level temporal topology entails a strict order for successive entity versions through the database. This ordinal structure may be used to cross-check the time-stamps. Furthermore, bi-directional links (previous and next versions) are a great help in checking for data integrity and completeness because information is redundant at this level.

b)   Between-entities temporal topology linking entities within the structure allows us to validate between-entities time-stamps with logical constraints (e.g. an entity birthdate must precede that of its successors). It is also possible to check if many different polygons linked by a replacement relationship still cover the same space and use chains shared with their common adjacent polygons.

c)   Independent spatio-temporal topologies introduce a time constraint for entities that are topologically connected in the space domain (e.g. two adjacent entities in space must also share an overlapping time interval). It is also feasible to check time consistency using logical rules, for example, "two polygons of the same type (e.g. municipalities) must never overlap in both space and time" (space-time exclusivity constraint).

d)   Spatio-temporal process control leads to semantic (e.g. a road cannot later be transformed to a river) and quantitative constraints (a split process is a one to many relationship).

All these consistency checks have to be integrated into the time-oriented GIS package. This way, application programs can use such a comprehensive quality control framework to elaborate dynamic, efficient and secure data management tools.

7   Conclusion

Time is too complex to be reduced to a simple collection of time-stamps. Events connect entities that are distributed across land to form independent networks that must be expressed explicitly within TGIS to bring out the functional components of the temporal topology. Versions are appropriate for recording the successive states of an entity. The described functional and structural processes (replacement, diffusion, restructuring) connect entities and define the necessary lineages to discover the causal relations that produce the observed events.

A TGIS that integrates the event concept is useful and technically achievable. However, such a project involves further research. There is a need to extend the interrogative part of SQL to incorporate high-level spatial and temporal operators. There is also a need to devise efficient spatial structures to describe entity movements. Current spatial data models preserve the topology between entities on the same thematic layers. However, independent objects can retain or change their geometric parameters while they are moving. This information may be fundamental to understanding spatial dynamic. The model presented involves well delimited objects and could be extended to handle phenomena that are continuous in space or in time (imprecise spatio-temporal relationships) by defining sharing functions based on fuzzy-sets. Finally, a dynamic graphic semiology must be developed to illustrate temporal entity sequences connected by functional processes.

The proposed approach aims for a harmonious integration of TGIS for the study of spatio-temporal processes. Furthermore, it ensures security and improves performance for administrative use by its retrospective view of events. It favors development of real-time applications that preserve successive states of each entity. Finally, the type of TGIS proposed describes functional links between entities and facilitates analysis of sequences of events, an important asset for scientists researching causal links.

Acknowledgments

The authors acknowledge François Golay, Stefano Spaccapietra, Dean Louder as well as several anonymous reviewers for many useful comments on several issues in this paper. We would like also to thank Laura Vidale and Patricia Dyksterhuis for their attentive reading of preliminary versions of this paper. The authors gratefully acknowledge the support of this work by the GERMINAL project, funded by the Rural Engineering Department through the Swiss Federal Institute of Technology in Lausanne, Switzerland.

References

[1] ABLER, R., ADAMS, J. S., and GOULD, P., 1971, *Spatial Organization. The Geographer's View of the World.* (Englewood Cliffs: Prentice Hall).

[2] AHN, I., and SNODGRASS, R. T., 1986, Performance evalutation of a temporal database management system. In *Proceedings of ACM SIGMOD International Conference on Management of Data* (Washington: ACM), pp. 96-107.

[3] ALLEN, J. F., and HAYES P. J., 1989, Moments and points in an interval-based temporal logic. *Computational Intelligence,* **5** (4), 225-238.

[4] AL-TAHA, K. K., SNODGRASS, R. T., and SOO, M. D., 1994, Bibliography on spatiotemporal databases. *International Journal of Geographical Information Systems,* **8** (1), 95-103.

[5] AREF, W. G., and SAMET, H., 1991, Extending a DBMS with spatial operations. In *Advances in Spatial Databases, Proceedings of the Second International Symposium, SSD '91,* edited by O. Günther and H. J. Schek (Berlin: Springer-Verlag), pp. 299-318.

[6] BELLER, A., 1991, Spatial/temporal events in a GIS. In *Proceedings of GIS/LIS '91* (Bethesda, Maryland: ASPRS/ACSM), **2**, pp. 766-775.

[7] BOURSIER, P., and MAINGUENAUD, M., 1992, Spatial query languages: Extended SQL vs. Visual languages vs. hypermaps. In *Proceedings of the Fifth International Symposium on Spatial Data Handling* (Charleston: IGU Commision on GIS), pp. 249-259.

[8] CHRISMAN, N. R., 1984, The role of quality information in the long-term functioning of a geographic information system. *Cartographica,* **21**, 79-87.

[9] CHRISMAN, N. R., 1990, Deficiencies of sheets and tiles: building sheetless databases. *International Journal of Geographical Information Systems,* **4** (2), 157-167.

[10] CLARAMUNT, C., and MAINGUENAUD, M., 1994, Identification of a definition formalism for a spatial view. In *Proceedings of Advanced Geographic Data Modelling* (Molenaar M. and de Hoop S., eds., Delft: Netherlands Geodetic Commission), pp. 191-203.

[11] CLIFF, A. D., HAGGET, P., and ORD, J. K., 1981, *Spatial Diffusion: An Historical Geography of Epidemics in an Island community* (Cambridge University Press).

[12] CLIFFORD, J., and WARREN, S. S., 1983, Formal semantics of time in databases. *ACM Transactions on DB Systems*, **8** (2), 214-254.

[13] CODD, E. F., 1988, Fatal flaws in SQL. *Datamation*, **34** (16), 45-48.

[14] COLE, J. P., and KING, C. A. M., 1968, *Quantitative Geography. Techniques and Theories in Geography*. (London: Wiley).

[15] EASTERFIELD, M., NEWELL, R. G., and THERIAULT, D., 1991, Modelling spatial and temporal information. In *Proceedings of the Second European Conference on Geographical Information Systems* (Brussels: EGIS), pp. 294-304.

[16] EDWARDS, G., GAGNON, P., and BÉDARD, Y., 1993, Spatio-temporal topology and causal mechanisms in time-integrated GIS: from conceptual model to implementation strategies. In *Proceedings of the Canadian Conference on GIS'93*, (Ottawa: The Canadian Institute of Geomatics), pp. 842-851.

[17] EGENHOFER, M. J., 1994, Spatial SQL: A query and presentation language. *IEEE Transactions on knowledge and data engineering*, **6** (1), 86-95.

[18] EGENHOFER, M. J., and SHARMA, J., 1993, Topological relations between regions in IR^2 and Z^2: In *Advances in Spatial Databases, Proceedings of the Third International Symposium, SSD '93*, edited by D. Abel and B. C. Ooi (Berlin: Springer-Verlag), pp. 316-336.

[19] ETZION, O., GAL, A., and SEGEV, A., 1992, Temporal support in active databases. In *Proceedings of the Second International Workshop on an Infrastructure for Temporal Databases* (Arlington: TX).

[20] GADIA, S. K., and CHOPRA, V., 1992, *A relational model for seamless query of temporal data*. Technical Report No. TR-92-05, Computer Science Department, Iowa State University.

[21] GOLUB, A., GOR, W. L., and GOULD, P. R., 1993, Spatial diffusion of the HIV/AIDS epidemic: Modeling implications and case study of AIDS incidence in Ohio. *Geographical Analysis*, **25** (2), 85-100.

[22] GOULD, S. J., 1987, *Time's Arrow Time's Cycle. Myth and Metaphor in the Discovery of Geological Time* (Cambridge, Massachussets: Harvard Univ. Press).

[23] HÄGERSTRAND, T., 1953, *Innovation diffusion as a spatial process*. (Chicago: University of Chicago Press).

[24] HAZELTON, N. W. J., 1992, Developments in spatio-temporal GIS. In *Proceedings of the First Regional Conference on GIS Research in Victoria and Tasmania* (Ballarat Ballarat University College).

[25] HOWENSTEIN, E., 1993, Measuring demographic change: The split tract problem. *The Professional Geographer* **45** (4), 425-430.

[26] JENSEN, C. S., CLIFFORD, J., GADIA, S. K., SEGEV, A., AND SNODGRASS, R. T., 1992, A glossary of temporal database concepts. *Sigmod Record*, 21 (3), 35-43.

[27] JONES, S., and MASON, P. J., 1980, Handling the time dimension in a database. In *Proceedings of the International Conference on Databases* (Aberdeen: British Computer Society), pp. 65-83.

[28] LANGRAN, G., 1992, *Time in geographic information systems* (London: Taylor & Francis).

[29] LESTER, M., 1990, Tracking the temporal polygon: a conceptual model of multi dimensional time for GIS. In *Proceedings of Temporal Workshop* (University of Maine).

[30] LOMET, D., and SALZBERG, B., 1989, Access methods for multiversion data. In *Proceedings of International Conference on the Management of Data* (Portland: ACM SIGMOD records), **18** (2), 315-324.

42

[31] LUM, V., DADUM, P., ERBE, R., GUENAUER, J., PISTOR, P., WALCH, G., WERNER, H., and WOODFILL, J., 1984, Designing DBMS support for the temporal dimension. In *Proceedings of the SIGMOD'84 Conference*, (New York: ACM), pp. 115-126.

[32] MATTINGLY, P. F., 1991, The changing location of physician offices in Bloomington-Normal, Illinois: 1870-1988. *The Professional Geographer*, **43** (4), 465-474.

[33] MCKENZIE, E., and SNODGRASS, R. T., 1991, An evaluation of relational algebras incorporating the time dimension in databases. *ACM Computing Surveys*, **23** (4), pp. 501-543.

[34] NAVATHE, S. B., and AHMED, R., 1988, TSQL: A language interface for history databases. *Information Sciences*, **49**, 109-121.

[35] OOI, B. C., 1990, *Efficient Query Processing in Geographic Information System* (Berlin: Springer-Verlag).

[36] PEUQUET, D. J., 1988a, Representations of geographic space: Toward a conceptual synthesis. *Annals of the Association of American Geographers*, **78** (3), 375-394.

[37] PEUQUET, D. J., 1988b, Toward the definition and use of complex spatial relationships. In *Proceedings of the Third International Sysposium on Spatial Data Handling* (Sydney: International Geographic Union), pp. 211-224.

[38] PEUQUET, D. J., 1994, It's About Time: A Conceptual Framework for the Representation of Temporal Dynamics in Geographic Information Systems. *Annals of the Association of the American Geographers*, **84** (3), 441-461

[39] PEUQUET, D. J., and DUAN N., 1995, An event-based spatiotemporal data model (ESTDM) for temporal analysis of geographical data. *International Journal of Geographical Information Systems*, **9** (1), 7-24.

[40] PISSINOU, N. *et al.*, 1994, Toward an infrastructure for temporal databases. *Report of an Invitational Workshop* (Arlington: ARPA/NSF).

[41] RAPER, J. F., and BUNDOCK, M. S., 1991, UGIX: A layer based model for a GIS user interface. In *Cognitive and Linguistic Aspects of Geographic Space*, edited by D. M. Mark and A. U. Frank (Dordrecht: Kluwer Academic Publishers), pp. 449-475.

[42] ROSE, E., and SEGEV, A., 1992, A temporal object-oriented algebra and query language. *Lawrence Berkeley Laboratory Technical Report LBL-32013*.

[43] SNODGRASS, R. T., 1987, The temporal query language - TQUEL. *ACM Transactions on Database Systems*, **12**, 247-298.

[44] SNODGRASS, R. T., 1992, Temporal databases. In *Proceedings of Theories and Methods Spatio-temporal Reasonning*, edited by. A.U. Franck, I. Campari and U. Formentini, (New York: Spingler-Verlag), pp. 22-64.

Temporal connectives versus explicit timestamps in temporal query languages

(preliminary report)

Serge Abiteboul, Laurent Herr, Jan Van den Bussche*

INRIA Rocquencourt[†]

Paris, France

Abstract

Some temporal query languages work directly on a timestamp representation of the temporal database, while others provide a more implicit access to the flow of time by means of temporal connectives. We study the differences in expressive power between these two approaches. We first consider first-order logic (i.e., the relational calculus). We show that first-order future temporal logic is strictly less powerful than the relational calculus with explicit timestamps. We also consider extensions of the relational calculus with iteration constructs such as least fixpoints or while-loops. We again compare augmentations of these languages with temporal left and right moves on the one hand, and with explicit timestamps on the other hand. For example, we show that a version of fixpoint logic with left and right moves lies between the explicit timestamp versions of first-order and fixpoint logic, respectively.

1 Introduction

A simple, natural and common way of representing a temporal relational database over a finite time period is to augment each relation with a "timestamp" column holding the time instants of validity of each tuple. Such representations can then be queried using standard relational query languages with built-in linear order on the timestamps. An alternative way of providing temporal facilities to query languages is by means of constructs yielding a more implicit access to the flow of time, such as the typical temporal connectives *next*, *previous*, *until*, and *since* of temporal logic [9]. Illustrations of these two approaches can be found in [11]. The question of how temporal connectives versus explicit timestamps in temporal query languages relate to each other with respect to expressive power, arises naturally [7, 8]. In the present paper, we study this question from various angles.

---

*On leave from the University of Antwerp. Research Assistant of the Belgian National Fund for Scientific Research.

[†]INRIA, Domaine de Voluceau, Rocquencourt, B.P. 105, F-78153 Le Chesnay Cedex, France.

First, we compare the relational calculus (i.e., first-order logic) with timestamps (TS-FO) to past-future first-order temporal logic (TL). We start by showing that *future* first-order temporal logic (FTL) is strictly weaker than TL. This should be contrasted with the conventional propositional case, where past connectives are known to be redundant [9]. This result should be related to [1] where it is shown that TL is strictly weaker than TS-FO.

We also look at more powerful languages, in particular, the languages WHILE and FIXPOINT which augment the relational calculus with while-loops and with inflationary fixpoint iteration, respectively [2]. When used on timestamp representations of temporal databases, they give rise to powerful temporal query languages denoted by TS-WHILE and TS-FIXPOINT. Alternatively, they can be extended with a more implicit access to the flow of time. We study their extension with instructions for moving left and right in time, giving rise to temporal query languages denoted by T-WHILE and T-FIXPOINT. In the case of T-FIXPOINT, this involves extra non-inflationary language features which are interesting in their own right.

We compare TS-WHILE, TS-FIXPOINT, T-WHILE, and T-FIXPOINT. We also compare T-FIXPOINT with TS-FO, and with ETL, an "extended" temporal logic which is closely related to fixpoint extensions to temporal logic proposed in the propositional setting [13, 12, 5]. Our results are summarized in Figure 1. Note that the only new languages are T-FIXPOINT and T-WHILE. Note also the central position of T-FIXPOINT. We believe this is an important language: it can be evaluated in polynomial time; it accesses time only implicitly; and it generalizes TL, TS-FO, and ETL.

The paper is organized as follows. In Section 2, we define temporal databases and timestamp representations, recall TL, and compare it to TS-FO. In Section 3, we recall WHILE, introduce T-WHILE, and compare it to TS-WHILE and TS-FO. In Section 4, we recall the inflationary language FIXPOINT, study its augmentation with certain non-inflationary features, and introduce the central language T-FIXPOINT. In Section 5, we compare T-FIXPOINT to all other languages. Finally, in Section 6, we indicate special cases of temporal databases (including some notion of "local time") where the distinction between explicit versus implicit access to time in the context of WHILE and FIXPOINT disappears. In this preliminary report, the proofs of the technical results are only sketched.

2 First-order temporal queries

A *temporal database* is a non-empty finite sequence $\mathbf{I} = I_0, \ldots, I_n$ of instances of a common relational database scheme. Each element of the sequence is called a *state*. We can represent this sequence $\mathbf{I}$ as one single instance $\bar{\mathbf{I}}$ of an extended scheme, where each relation is extended with an additional column holding for each tuple the numbers of the states at which the tuple belongs to the relations. We call $\bar{\mathbf{I}}$ the *timestamp representation of* $\mathbf{I}$. More formally, for each relation

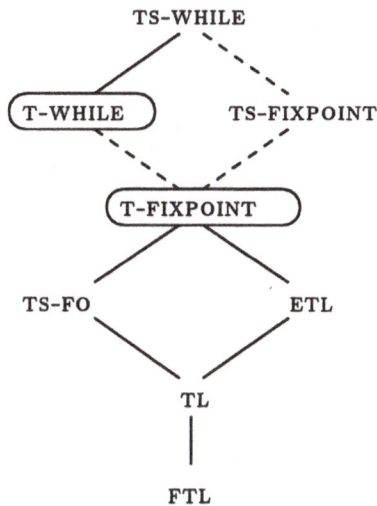

Figure 1: The relative power of temporal languages. Solid upward edges indicate strict containment. Dashed lines indicate that the strictness of the containment depends on unresolved questions in complexity theory.

R, we have an extended relation $\bar{R}$ whose value in $\bar{\mathbf{I}}$ is:

$$\bar{\mathbf{I}}(\bar{R}) := \bigcup_{t=1}^{n} I_t(R) \times \{t\}.$$

Furthermore, the total order on the timestamps is given in $\bar{\mathbf{I}}$ in a binary relation $<$.

Example 1 Consider the scheme consisting of a single unary relation S. Temporal databases over this scheme are basically sequences of sets. An example and its timestamp representation are shown in Figure 2. ■

A very direct way to express temporal queries on $\mathbf{I}$ is to use first-order logic (i.e., relational calculus) on the timestamp representation $\bar{\mathbf{I}}$. We denote this temporal query language by TS-FO.

Example 2 On databases as in Example 1, the query "give the elements that have been deleted but have later been re-inserted" can be expressed in TS-FO as

$$\{x \mid (\exists t)(\exists t')(\exists t'')(t < t' \wedge t' < t'' \wedge S(x,t) \wedge \neg S(x,t') \wedge S(x,t''))\}.$$

On the database of Figure 2, the answer to this query is $\{a, c\}$. ■

$$
\mathbf{I} =
\begin{array}{ccc}
I_0 & I_1 & I_2 \\[2pt]
\boxed{\begin{array}{c} a \\ b \\ c \end{array}} &
\boxed{\begin{array}{c} b \\ d \end{array}} &
\boxed{\begin{array}{c} a \\ c \end{array}}
\end{array}
\qquad
\boxed{\begin{array}{cc}
a & 0 \\
b & 0 \\
c & 0 \\
b & 1 \\
d & 1 \\
a & 2 \\
c & 2
\end{array}}
$$

Figure 2: A temporal database and its timestamp representation.

Note that queries expressed in TS-FO can also return timestamps. For example, the query $\{t \mid (\forall x)(S(x,t) \leftrightarrow S(x,0))\}$ returns the numbers of all states that are equal to the first state. However, in the remainder of this discussion, we focus on queries returning data elements only.

An alternative way of expressing temporal queries is by using first-order temporal logic (abbreviated TL). This language is defined on the original database scheme, and does not involve timestamps. Instead, it extends the relational calculus by adding the binary connectives since and until. Syntactically, they are used to build formulas in the same way as the connective $\wedge$: if φ and ψ are formulas, then so are φ since ψ and φ until ψ.

Semantically, TL formulas, when evaluated on a given temporal database $\mathbf{I} = I_0, \ldots, I_n$, are evaluated with respect to some given time instant $t \in \{0, \ldots, n\}$. Formally, let θ be a TL formula, and let v be a valuation assigning domain values in $\mathbf{I}$ to the variables that are free in θ. The satisfaction of θ on $\mathbf{I}$ at t under v, denoted $\mathbf{I}, t \models \theta[v]$, is defined as follows:

- If θ is a relational atom $R(x_1, \ldots, x_k)$, then $\mathbf{I}, t \models \theta[v]$ if $(v(x_1), \ldots, v(x_k)) \in I_t(R)$.

- If θ is an equality predicate $x = y$, or is of one of the forms $(\exists x)\varphi$, $(\forall x)\varphi$, $\neg\varphi$, or $\varphi \wedge \psi$, satisfaction is defined in the standard way.[1]

- If θ is of the form φ until ψ, then $\mathbf{I}, t \models \theta[v]$ if

$$\exists t'' > t : \mathbf{I}, t'' \models \psi[v] \wedge \forall t' : t < t' < t'' \Rightarrow \mathbf{I}, t' \models \varphi[v].$$

- Finally, if θ is of the form φ since ψ, then $\mathbf{I}, t \models \theta[v]$ if

$$\exists t'' < t : \mathbf{I}, t'' \models \psi[v] \wedge \forall t' : t'' < t' < t \Rightarrow \mathbf{I}, t' \models \varphi[v].$$

In the above, the quantifiers on t' and t'' naturally range over $\{0, \ldots, n\}$.

Conventionally, queries expressed in TL are evaluated in the first state. So, if θ is a TL formula with free variables $x_1, \ldots, x_k$, then the result of the query $\{x_1, \ldots, x_k \mid \theta\}$ on a temporal database $\mathbf{I}$ is the relation $\{v \mid \mathbf{I}, 0 \models \theta[v]\}$.

---

[1] Quantifiers range over the active domain.

Example 3 The query of Example 2 can be expressed in TL as

$$\{x \mid \mathsf{sometimesfuture}(S(x) \wedge \mathsf{sometimesfuture}(\neg S(x) \wedge \mathsf{sometimesfuture}\, S(x)))\},$$

where $\mathsf{sometimesfuture}\, \theta$ is an abbreviation for $\theta \vee (\mathit{true}\ \mathsf{until}\ \theta)$ (i.e., "θ is true now or some time in the future"). The other usual temporal connectives $\mathsf{next}\, \theta$ ("θ holds in the next state"), $\mathsf{alwaysfuture}\, \theta$ ("θ holds now and always in the future"), and the duals for the past (previous, sometimespast and alwayspast) are also easily definable in terms of since and until.

Since TL queries are evaluated in the first state, one may wonder if the past connective since is really necessary. Actually, in *propositional* TL (corresponding to the case where the database scheme consists of nullary relations[2] only), it is well-known that every formula is equivalent, with respect to the first time instant, to a pure future formula (i.e., using only until as temporal connective). We now show that this does not carry over to the setting of temporal databases:

Theorem 4 *The yes/no query Q:* $(\exists t > 0)(\forall x)(S(x,t) \leftrightarrow S(x,0))$ *is expressible in* TL *but not in pure future* TL.

Proof. (Sketch) We can express Q in TL as

$$\mathsf{next}\ \mathsf{sometimesfuture}(\forall x)(S(x) \leftrightarrow \mathsf{sometimespast}(\mathbf{first} \wedge S(x))),$$

where **first** is the formula $\neg(\mathit{true}\ \mathsf{since}\ \mathit{true})$ (this formula is only true in the first state).

To show that Q is not expressible in pure future TL, we use a combinatorial argument. Let θ be an arbitrary closed pure future TL formula. Let D be some arbitrary fixed finite domain of data elements, let d be the cardinality of D, and let n be some arbitrary fixed positive natural number. We consider temporal databases $I_0, \ldots, I_n$, and define the function F on the "tails" of such databases by

$$F(I_1, \ldots, I_n) := \{I_0 \mid (I_0, I_1, \ldots, I_n), 0 \models \theta\}.$$

If θ would express the query Q, then the cardinality of the image of F would be

$$\sum_{k=1}^{n} \binom{2^d}{k}.$$

However, it can be shown that the cardinality of the image of F is at most $2^{d^{\alpha}}$, for some integer α depending only on θ. The theorem then follows by elementary asymptotic calculus. ∎

Note that, by symmetry, pure past TL (evaluated in the last state) is also strictly weaker than TL. Pure past TL is often used to specify dynamic integrity constraints [6].

---

[2] A nullary relation can either contain the empty tuple or be empty, and can thus be used to represent a proposition (i.e., True or False).

We now turn to the question of how full past-future TL relates to TS-FO. Clearly, TS-FO is at least as expressive as TL. This inclusion is strict: it is shown in [1] that the TS-FO-query Q: $(\exists t)(\exists t')(\forall x)(S(x,t) \leftrightarrow S(x,t'))$ is not expressible in TL.

3 Iterative queries

Let us first briefly recall how relational calculus is extended with iteration to obtain the language WHILE. (See [2] for a more detailed presentation of the languages WHILE and FIXPOINT considered in the following sections.)

An *assignment statement* is an expression of the form $X := E$, where X is a *auxiliary relation* and E is a relational calculus query which can involve both relations from the database scheme and auxiliary relations. Each auxiliary relation has a fixed arity; in the above assignment statement, the arity of the result of E must match with the arity of X.

We can now build *programs* from assignment statements using sequencing $P_1; P_2$ and *while-loops*: if P is a program, then so is **while** φ **do** P **od**, where φ is a relational calculus sentence. The query language thus obtained is called WHILE. The execution of a program on a database instance is defined in the natural manner. The result of the query expressed by a program is the value of some designated output relation at completion of the execution[3].

The language WHILE on the timestamp representations of temporal databases provides a very powerful temporal query language which is denoted by TS-WHILE.

Example 5 The query "give the elements that belong to all even-numbered states" is not expressible in the relational calculus with timestamps, but it is expressible in TS-WHILE as follows:

> $Current := \{0\}$;
> $A := \{x \mid S(x,0)\}$;
> **while** $(\exists t)(\exists t')(Current(t) \wedge t' = t + 2)$ **do**
> $Current := \{t' \mid (\exists t)(Current(t) \wedge t' = t + 2)\}$;
> $A := A \cap \{x \mid (\exists t)(Current(t) \wedge S(x,t))\}$
> **od**.

In the above program, A is the answer relation, and $t' = t + 2$ is only an abbreviation which can be directly expressed in terms of the order on the timestamps. ∎

An alternative temporal query language based on WHILE, not involving timestamps, can be obtained by extending WHILE with more implicit temporal features. One way to do this is to execute programs on a machine which can move back and forth over time. Formally, we provide, in addition to assignment

---

[3]If the execution loops indefinitely, the result is defined to be empty by default. Such loops can always be detected [3].

statements, the two statements **left** and **right** which move the machine one step in the required direction[4]. Furthermore, we partition the auxiliary relations into *state relations*, which are stored in the different states, and *shared relations*, which are stored in the memory of the machine itself. So, the values of (and assignments to) state relations depend on the current state the machine is looking at, while this is not the case for shared relations. Finally, we assume two built-in nullary state relations *First* and *Last*, with *First* being true only in the first state, and *Last* being true only in the last state. The machine always starts execution from the first state.

The temporal query language WHILE extended with left and right moves just described is denoted by T-WHILE.

Example 6 The query from Example 5 can be expressed in T-WHILE as follows:

> shared $A(1)$, $Even(0)$;
> $A := \{x \mid S(x)\}$; $Even := \{()\}$;
> **while** $\neg Last$ **do**
>   **right**;
> $Even := \{()\} - Even$;
>   **if** $Even$ **then** $A := A \cap \{x \mid S(x)\}$
>   **od**.

In the above program, A and $Even$ are both shared relations. Note how they are "declared" as variables in the beginning of the program, indicating their status of shared relation and their arity; we will always use such declarations when presenting T-WHILE programs in the sequel. The if-then construct is only an abbreviation and can be expressed in the relational calculus. ∎

We next study the expressive power of T-WHILE. We will see in the next section that it strictly encompasses TS-FO, and hence TL as well. We now show:

Proposition 7 T-WHILE *is strictly contained in* TS-WHILE.

Proof. (Sketch) The simulation of T-WHILE by TS-WHILE is straightforward, using a *Current* relation as in Example 5 holding the current temporal position of the machine.

The argument for strictness is based on complexity. The complexity of TS-WHILE programs in terms of the length n of the temporal database only is precisely PSPACE. However, the space complexity of T-WHILE programs in terms of n is linear: we only have to store the state relations at each state. The proposition then follows from the space hierarchy theorem [10]. ∎

---

[4]In the first state, **left** has no effect; in the last state, **right** has no effect.

4 Fixpoint queries

General WHILE programs can only be guaranteed to run in polynomial space
(PSPACE) and hence their computational complexity is probably intractable
in general. However, there is a well-known restriction of WHILE which runs in
polynomial time (PTIME). This restriction consists of allowing only *inflationary*
assignment statements, of the form $X := X \cup E$ (abbreviated $X \mathrel{+}= E$).
Executing an inflationary WHILE program with all auxiliary relations initialized
to the empty set will either finish or repeat a configuration after an at most
polynomial number of steps.[5] The computation has then "reached a fixpoint"
and the result of the query is determined. The query language thus obtained
is therefore called FIXPOINT.

Actually, on *ordered* databases[6], a query is in PTIME if and only if it is
expressible in FIXPOINT. It is an open question whether FIXPOINT is strictly
weaker than WHILE, but it is shown in [4] that this question is equivalent to the
renowned open problem in computational complexity on the strict containment
of PTIME in PSPACE.

Similarly to TS-WHILE, the language FIXPOINT on timestamp representations of temporal databases provides a powerful yet computationally tractable
temporal query language denoted by TS-FIXPOINT.

Example 8 The query of Example 5 can also be expressed in TS-FIXPOINT as
follows:

$Current \mathrel{+}= \{0\};$
$B \mathrel{+}= \{x \mid \neg S(x,0)\};$
while $(\exists t)(\exists t')(Current(t) \wedge \neg Current(t') \wedge t' = t + 2)$ **do**
$\quad Current \mathrel{+}= \{t' \mid (\exists t)(Current(t) \wedge t' = t + 2)\};$
$\quad B \mathrel{+}= \{x \mid (\exists t)(Current(t) \wedge \neg S(x,t))\}$
$\quad$**od**;
$A \mathrel{+}= \{x \mid \neg B(x)\}.$ ∎

Alternatively, we could depart from the language T-WHILE and restrict it
to inflationary assignments only, to obtain a PTIME temporal query language.
However, this language would be rather inflexible, since a pure inflationary restriction is an obstacle to the inherently non-inflationary back-and-forth movements along time involved in temporal querying. (For simple temporal queries
involving only one single scan, this would suffice.)

This obstacle can also be analyzed using a complexity argument. As we
have seen in Proposition 7 for T-WHILE, the available space is linear in the
length n of the sequence. In FIXPOINT, the restriction to PTIME is achieved
by a careful inflationary use of space. Thus, the restriction of T-WHILE to
inflationary assignments would lead to a computation that would run in time
linear in n.

---

[5] As for WHILE, infinite loops can always be detected.
[6] This means that a linear order on the active domain is available.

This problem can be alleviated by adding two extra, non-inflationary features to standard FIXPOINT that allow to use non-inflationary variables in a controled manner: "local variables" and "non-inflationary variables".

(a) Local variables to blocks: Certain auxiliary relations can be declared as local variables to program blocks. These relations can only be assigned to within the block, and each time the block is exited, they are emptied. (If the local variables are state relations, they are emptied in each state.) Syntactically, if P is a program then [**local** $V_1, \ldots, V_r; P$] is a program block with local auxiliary relations $V_1, \ldots, V_r$.

(b) Non-inflationary variables: Certain auxiliary relations can be declared to be non-inflationary. They can be assigned to without any inflationary restriction. However, they are not taken into account in determining whether the program has reached a fixpoint. (Hence, this remains in PTIME.) Syntactically, these variables will be declared using the keyword **noninf**.

The inflationary restriction of T-WHILE, to which the above two extra non-inflationary features are added, yields a temporal query language that we call T-FIXPOINT. Note that configurations of T-FIXPOINT programs now include the position of the machine in time, which is taken into account to see whether the computation has reached a fixpoint (i.e., repeated a configuration).

It is important to note that the extra features of local and non-inflationary variables only make a difference in the context of T-FIXPOINT: in the standard FIXPOINT language, they can be simulated as shown in the next proposition. This result is interesting in its own right, since it facilitates expressing PTIME computations in FIXPOINT. It also indicates a fundamental distinction between temporal querying and standard querying.

Proposition 9 *Adding program blocks with local variables and noninflationary variables with the restrictions described above to* FIXPOINT *does not increase the expressive power of the language.*

Proof. (Sketch) The key observation is that, due to the inflationary nature of the computation, a program block can be executed only so many times as tuples are inserted in the auxiliary relations that are global (i.e., not local) to this block. Hence, the contents of the local variables can be simulated by versioning their tuples with the tuples inserted in the global variables since the previous invocation of the program block (using Cartesian product). Emptying the local variables then simply amounts to creating a new version. The old versions are accumulated in a separate relation. In this manner the process is entirely inflationary, as desired.

We can also simulate the noninflationary variables using a similar versioning technique. The version consists of the tuples inserted in the ordinary, inflationary variables since the previous non-inflationary assignment. Since the program terminates as soon as the inflationary variables reach a fixpoint, we will not run out of versions. ∎

We now illustrate the use of local variables and non-inflationary variables in T-FIXPOINT by means of the following two examples. We first illustrate local variables.

Example 10 Assume the database scheme contains two unary relations S and T. One way to express the temporal logic query $\{x \mid S(x) \text{ until } T(x)\}$ in T-FIXPOINT is as follows:

```
state Mark(0);
shared N(1), A(1);
Mark += {()};
while ¬Last do
  right;
  A += ¬N ∩ T;
  N += ¬S
od;
while ¬Mark do left.
```

In the above program, $Mark$ is a (nullary) state relation which is used to mark the initial state. Relations A and N are shared: A is the answer relation, and N keeps track of the elements that are not in S in some state encountered so far; if x is in N the first time it is found to be in T, x does *not* satisfy $S(x)$ until $T(x)$. The final while-loop returns to the marked state (the use of this will become clear immediately).

Suppose now that we have an additional third unary database relation R, and we want to express the more complex temporal logic query $\{x \mid R(x) \text{ until } (S(x) \text{ until } T(x))\}$. A simply way to do this would be to use the above program as a subroutine. However, in doing this, care must be taken that the auxiliary relations $Mark$, A and N are cleared after each invocation of the subroutine. This is precisely the facility provided by the local variables in T-FIXPOINT. Written out in full, we can thus express the query in T-FIXPOINT as follows:

```
shared N_0(1), A_0(1);
while ¬Last do
  right;
  [ local state Mark(0);
    local shared N(1), A(1);
    Mark += {()};
    while ¬Last do
      right;
      A += ¬N ∩ T;
      N += ¬S
    od;
    while ¬Mark do left;
    A_0 += ¬N_0 ∩ A
  ];
  N_0 += ¬R
```

od. ∎

We next illustrate the kind of computations that can be performed using noninflationary variables.

Example 11 Assume the database scheme consists of a single binary relation R. Consider the program:

> **noninf** shared $S(2)$;
> $S := R$;
> **while** $\neg Last$ **do**
>   **right**;
> $S := \{x, y \mid (\exists z)(S(x, z) \land R(z, y))\}$
> **od.**

At the end, if the last state of the temporal database is numbered n, S contains the set of pairs (x_0, x_n) such that there exist $x_0, x_1, \ldots, x_n$ with such that (x_i, x_{i+1}) is in R in the i-th state, for each $i \in \{0, \ldots, n-1\}$. ∎

5 Comparisons

In this section, we first show that the expressive power of T-FIXPOINT lies between TS-FO and TS-FIXPOINT. Then we recall the extended temporal logic ETL and show that it can be simulated in T-FIXPOINT. Finally, we compare T-FIXPOINT and T-WHILE.

We first show:

Theorem 12 TS-FO *is strictly contained in* T-FIXPOINT.

Proof. (Sketch) Each timestamp variable is represented by a nullary state relation which is true exactly in the state numbered by the current value of the variable, plus all states to the left of that state. The simulation now proceeds by induction on the structure of the formulas. An atomic formula $S(x, t)$ is simulated by searching for the state where t is true and returning S in that state. A comparison $t < t'$ between timestamp variables is simulated by a left-to-right scan checking whether t is true before t'. Disjunction, negation, and existential quantification of data variables are simulated using union, complementation, and projection as usual. Finally, existential quantification of a timestamp variable is performed by a while-loop which repeatedly sets the variable true from left to right. Nested quantifiers are simulated using a nested program block for each quantifier, with the marking relation as a local variable to that block.

The inclusion is strict because TS-FO cannot compute the transitive closure of a graph stored in one of the states. ∎

Since TL is subsumed by TS-FO, as an immediate corollary we obtain that TL is strictly contained in T-FIXPOINT.

We next show:

54

Theorem 13 T-FIXPOINT *can be simulated in* TS-FIXPOINT.

Proof. (Sketch) The simulation is analogous to that of T-WHILE by TS-WHILE of Proposition 7. The relation *Current* used there is non-inflationary, but by Proposition 9 we know that this does not pose a problem. ∎

It is not clear whether the converse of Theorem 13 holds. This is again because of the linear space complexity in the number of states of T-WHILE (and hence also of T-FIXPOINT) programs already mentioned in the proof of Proposition 7. Indeed, we can reduce the containment of TS-FIXPOINT in T-FIXPOINT to the containment of PTIME in the following class of complexity:

> A problem is in PLINSPACE if it can be solved by a Turing machine in polynomial time using only linear space.

Observe that if PTIME is included in PLINSPACE, then in particular, PTIME is included in LINSPACE which is an open question of complexity theory. We observe:

Theorem 14 *Assuming ordered databases,* TS-FIXPOINT = T-FIXPOINT *if and only if* PTIME = PLINSPACE.

Proof: (Sketch) Suppose that PTIME = PLINSPACE, and consider a TS-FIXPOINT query Q. Then Q is in PTIME, so in PLINSPACE. It is possible (although somewhat intricate) to show that PLINSPACE queries can be computed in T-FIXPOINT. The linear tape of the Turing machine is simulated by splitting it into n pieces (where n is the number of states) and assigning one piece to each state of the database. Non-inflationary variables are used to simulate the non-inflationary nature of the Turing machine computation. Local variables are used to "count" the number of steps (polynomial) that the machine is allowed to perform. Thus Q is in T-FIXPOINT.

Conversely, suppose that TS-FIXPOINT = T-FIXPOINT. Let Q be a PTIME problem. Consider the coding of this problem as a query on a propositional temporal database (each letter in the input word is represented by one state). As mentioned in the beginning of Section 4, any PTIME query on ordered databases is expressible in FIXPOINT. Hence, Q can be computed by a TS-FIXPOINT-program. So Q can be computed by a T-FIXPOINT-program. This program runs in PTIME, and since the database is propositional, it uses only linear space. Thus, Q is in PLINSPACE. ∎

Fixpoint extensions of temporal logic have been studied extensively in the propositional case [9]. One of these extensions is the *extended temporal logic* ETL [13, 12]. This language offers general temporal connectives expressed in terms of regular expressions. Indeed, the standard connective φ until ψ of TL corresponds to searching for the regular expression ab^*c, where the letter a stands for *True*, b stands for φ, and c stands for ψ. It is not difficult to define ETL in the context of first-order predicate logic (i.e., databases) rather than propositional logic (e.g., [5]). We can show:

Theorem 15 ETL *is strictly contained in* T-FIXPOINT.

Proof. (Sketch) The simulation of ETL in T-FIXPOINT is analogous to the simulation of TL in T-FIXPOINT illustrated in Example 10. We now consider the finite automaton corresponding to the regular expression, and for each state of the automaton we use an auxiliary relation playing a role similar to N in Example 10, keeping track of the status of the elements during the simulation of the automaton. The state-changes of the automaton are performed while moving over the states of the temporal database. The state-changing relations must be implemented using non-inflationary variables, since the working of the automaton is not inflationary.

The inclusion is strict because TS-FO cannot compute the transitive closure of a graph stored in one of the states. (Actually, also on propositional databases the inclusion is strict: ETL can only recognize regular properties [9], while it is possible to write a T-FIXPOINT program checking whether the length of the temporal database is a prime number.)

Finally, we compare T-FIXPOINT to T-WHILE. It turns out that their equality is very unlikely:

Proposition 16 *If* T-FIXPOINT = T-WHILE, *then* PTIME = PSPACE.

Proof. (Sketch) Suppose that T-FIXPOINT = T-WHILE. Then, in particular, T-FIXPOINT equals T-WHILE on temporal databases consisting of a single state, and hence, FIXPOINT equals WHILE. As mentioned in the beginning of Section 4, this is known to imply PTIME = PSPACE.

It remains open whether the converse of the above proposition holds. In some sense, the equality of T-FIXPOINT and T-WHILE could even be more unlikely that the equality of PTIME and PSPACE.

6   Local time

A temporal database $I = I_0, \ldots, I_n$ is said to have *local time* if at each state, the number of that state in some relation. Formally, assume the database scheme contains a unary relation *Time*. Then I has local time if for each $t \in \{0, \ldots, n\}$, $I_t(Time) = \{t\}$. We naturally assume that the linear order on timestamps is available to query languages working on temporal databases with local time.

In practice, local time will often be present. It can be shown that on temporal databases with local time, T-WHILE is equivalent to TS-WHILE and T-FIXPOINT is equivalent to TS-FIXPOINT.

We will obtain this result as a corollary of the following much stronger result stating that, in some cases, it is possible to simulate local time using the data elements. Thereto, we need to assume that the temporal databases are ordered, i.e., that a linear order is available on the active domain. (We will remove this restriction later.)

Theorem 17 *Let p be a natural number. On ordered temporal databases of length at most d^p, where d is the size of the active domain,* T-WHILE *is equivalent to* TS-WHILE *and* T-FIXPOINT *is equivalent to* TS-FIXPOINT.

Proof. (Sketch) First assume that local time is present. We already know that TS-WHILE can simulate T-WHILE and that TS-FIXPOINT can simulate T-FIXPOINT. To show the converse simulations, it suffices to show that the timestamp representation of a temporal database with local time can be constructed in T-FIXPOINT, since T-FIXPOINT is a sublanguage of T-WHILE. This is easily done using the following program (for simplicity assuming that the database scheme consists of a single relation S):

$$\textbf{while } \neg Last \textbf{ do } R \mathrel{+}= S \times Time; \textbf{ right od}$$

It now suffices to observe that local time can be simulated using the tuples in D^p. This is done by a straightforward T-FIXPOINT program which generates them one after the other in lexicographical order while moving over the temporal database from left to right.

Note that in order to prove Theorem 18 we do not even need the facilities of local and noninflationary variables in T-FIXPOINT.

In the above, we assumed that the domain of the database is ordered. Using a similar argument, the theorem remains true without the ordering assumption if we replace d^p by i^p, where i the *k-type index* of the database for some k. For the formal definition of type index we refer to [2]; we simply recall that it is a polynomial in d on ordered databases, and that the k-type index[7] can be computed in FIXPOINT. Now for temporal databases, one can show that it can be computed in T-FIXPOINT; and it is easy to demonstrate that for databases with local time, the k-type index is always larger than the number of states. From these observations, it follows:

Corollary 18 *On temporal databases with local time,* T-WHILE *is equivalent to* TS-WHILE *and* T-FIXPOINT *is equivalent to* TS-FIXPOINT.

References

[1] S. Abiteboul, L. Herr, and J. Van den Bussche. Temporal connectives versus explicit timestamps in temporal query languages. Technical report, INRIA, 1995. in preparation.

[2] S. Abiteboul, R. Hull, and V. Vianu. *Foundations of Databases*. Addison-Wesley, 1994.

[3] S. Abiteboul and E. Simon. Fundamental properties of deterministic and nondeterministic extensions of Datalog. *Theoretical Computer Science*, 78:137–158, 1991.

---

[7]Actually, the collection of k-types with an order on them.

[4] S. Abiteboul and V. Vianu. Generic computation and its complexity. In *Proceedings 23rd ACM Symposium on Theory of Computing*, pages 209–219, 1991.

[5] A. Casanova and A. Furtado. On the description of database transition constraints using temporal constraints. In H. Gallaire, J. Minker, and J.-M. Nicolas, editors, *Advances in Data Base Theory*, pages 211–236. Plenum Press, 1984.

[6] J. Chomicki. History-less checking of temporal integrity constraints. In *Proceedings 8th International Conference on Data Engineering*. IEEE, 1992.

[7] J. Chomicki. Temporal query languages: a survey. In D.M. Gabbay and H.J. Ohlbach, editors, *Temporal Logic: ICTL'94*, volume 827 of *Lecture Notes in Computer Science*, pages 506–534. Springer-Verlag, 1994.

[8] J. Clifford, A. Croker, and A. Tuzhilin. On completeness of historical relational query languages. *ACM Transactions on Database Systems*, 19(1):64–116, 1994.

[9] E.A. Emerson. Temporal and modal logic. In J. van Leeuwen, editor, *Handbook of Theoretical Computer Science*, volume B, chapter 16. Elsevier science publishers, 1990.

[10] J.E. Hopcroft and J.D. Ullman. *Introduction to Automata Theory, Languages, and Computation*. Addison-Wesley, 1979.

[11] A. Tansel et al., editors. *Temporal Databases: Theory, Design, and Implementation*. Benjamin/Cummings, 1993.

[12] M.Y. Vardi. A temporal fixpoint calculus. In *Proceedings 5th ACM Symposium on Principles of Programming Languages*, pages 250–259, 1988.

[13] P. Wolper. Temporal logic can be more expressive. *Information and Control*, 56:72–93, 1983.

II. Temporal Constraints

Design of Temporal Relational Databases Based on Dynamic and Temporal Functional Dependencies

Jozef Wijsen

Departement Toegepaste Economische Wetenschappen
Katholieke Universiteit Leuven
Naamsestraat 69, 3000 Leuven, Belgium
Jef.Wijsen@econ.kuleuven.ac.be

Abstract

In earlier work, we introduced dynamic and temporal functional dependencies (DFDs and TFDs), which are used in conjunction with conventional functional dependencies. The purpose of this paper is to study how DFDs and TFDs affect database design in a temporally ungrouped historical data model. The result is a generalization of conventional normalization theory for temporal databases.

1. Introduction

During the last decade temporal databases have become an important field of research [14,21]. A dozen temporal data models and temporal query languages have been developed, among others HRDM [5], TempSQL [10], TRM and TSQL [17], HSQL [18], TQuel [20], TEER [8], TDM [19]. Relatively few studies have addressed temporal database integrity (examples are [1,3,4,15,24,27]). Nevertheless, integrity is an important issue. If a temporal database is to be used for tasks whose successful execution is important in the real world then it is of the utmost importance that the temporal data involved are correct. This paper contributes to a theory of integrity for temporal databases. In particular, we propose temporal extensions to conventional normalization theory.

A temporally ungrouped historical data model is used to study the effect of static and temporal constraints on database design. The static constraints considered are *functional dependencies (FDs)*. The temporal constraints considered are restricted to certain temporal extensions of FD, called *dynamic functional dependencies* and *temporal functional dependencies (DFDs and TFDs)*. DFDs and TFDs are motivated by their tractability and frequent occurrence in real situations. Like FDs, DFDs and TFDs can cause data redundancy, which, in turn, leads to anomalous update behavior. Decomposing relations to avoid data redundancy is at the center of (temporal) relational database design. The purpose of this paper is to characterize "good" database design in the presence of FDs, DFDs and TFDs.

DFDs and TFDs were first introduced in an identity-based framework [25,26]. They were used there to study the identification of objects in time. In this paper, we follow a value-based approach.

The paper is divided in seven sections. The next section is devoted to preliminary concepts. The formal description of the data model and constraints, and a motivating example, are presented in section 3. In section 4 it is shown that DFDs and TFDs can cause data redundancy, which is characterized by temporal normal forms. Section 5 concerns the notion of DFD/TFD-preservation and its connection with (temporal) normal forms. Section 6 contains a comparison with related work. Finally, section 7 contains some conclusions and a discussion of future work.

2. Preliminaries

In this section, we introduce the well-known concepts of tuple, (snapshot) relation and FD. We assume the existence of the following two sets: a set $ATTR$ of attributes and a set $VALS$ of (atomic) values. The term *relation schema* is commonly used for a set of attributes. We write $A_1 A_2 ... A_n$ as a shorthand for the set $\{A_1, A_2, ..., A_n\}$, where $A_1, A_2, ..., A_n \in ATTR$. We write $Z_1 Z_2 ... Z_n$ as a shorthand for the set $Z_1 \cup Z_2 \cup ... \cup Z_n$, where $Z_1, Z_2, ..., Z_n \subseteq ATTR$.

Definition 1.
Let f be a function and let S be a set. We define, $f[S] := \{\langle x, y \rangle \in f : x \in S\}$, the restriction of f to S.

Let Z be a set of attributes (i.e., $Z \subseteq ATTR$).
A *tuple over* Z (or simply *tuple*, if Z is understood) is a total function from Z into $VALS$.

A *snapshot relation over* Z (or simply *snapshot relation*, if Z is understood) is a set of tuples over Z. We sometimes use the term relation for snapshot relation.

A *functional dependency (FD)* is a statement $X \to Y$, where X and Y are sets of attributes.

The FD $X \to Y$ is said to be satisfied by snapshot relation R if and only if whenever $s, t \in R$ such that $s[X] = t[X]$, then $s[Y] = t[Y]$. ◆

3. The Model

We assume that time is discrete and bounded in the past and in the future. Notably, time is represented by the set $TIME = \{0, 1, 2, ..., maxTime\}$. Time is incorporated in snapshot relations by extending each tuple with a set of time points. We assume the existence of a special element VT not in $ATTR$, which is used to denote valid timestamps. Our data model is a temporally ungrouped historical data model in the classification of [6]. A *valid-time relation* over {EMPL, RANK, SAL} is shown in figure 1. We require that no two distinct tuples of a valid-time relation have the same value for all regular attributes. The (valid-)timeslice at time i of a valid-time relation T is denoted by T_i.

EMPL	RANK	SAL	VT
Ed	E	100	{0}
Ed	E	110	{2,3}

Fig. 1. Valid-time relation.

Definition 2. Let Z be a set of attributes.
A *valid-time tuple over* Z (or simply *valid-time tuple*, if Z is understood) is a function t with domain $Z \cup \{VT\}$ such that $t[Z]$ is a tuple over Z and $t(VT) \subseteq \textbf{TIME}$.

Let s and t be valid-time tuples over Z. s and t are said to be *value-equivalent* if and only if $s[Z] = t[Z]$; otherwise s and t are said to be *nonvalue-equivalent*.

A *valid-time relation over* Z (or simply *valid-time relation*, if Z is understood) is a set of pairwise nonvalue-equivalent valid-time tuples over Z.

Let T be a valid-time relation over Z. Let $i \in \textbf{TIME}$. The *timeslice at time* i *of* T, denoted by T_i, is the smallest snapshot relation over Z containing $t[Z]$ whenever $t \in T$ and $i \in t(VT)$.

Let S and T be valid-time relations over Z. S and T are said to be *snapshot equivalent*, denoted by $S == T$, if and only if for every $i \in \textbf{TIME}$, $S_i = T_i$. ◆

Demonstrably, if two valid-time relations S and T are snapshot equivalent, then they are equal. That is, $S == T$ implies $S = T$. As a consequence, a valid-time relation T can be represented, without loss of information, as the sequence $\langle T_0, T_1, ..., T_{maxTime} \rangle$. The constraints that are used in conjunction with the data model are FDs, DFDs and TFDs. They are formalized by definition 3. First, however, we present an example that motivates our dynamic and temporal constraints.

Example 1. Consider the relation schema {EMPL, CITY, BIRTH, RANK, SAL} of an "employee" database. EMPL uniquely identifies each employee. RANK is a letter between A and F, A being the highest rank. BIRTH is the year of birth, and SAL the salary. The FD

$$\{EMPL\} \rightarrow \{CITY, RANK, SAL\}$$

expresses that each employee lives in exactly one city, has one rank, and earns one salary. Every employee has a single year of birth, which, moreover, remains unchanged over all time. The FD

$$\{EMPL\} \rightarrow \{BIRTH\}$$

states that each EMPL-value has associated with it precisely one BIRTH-value *at any one time*. To express that each EMPL-value has associated with it precisely one BIRTH-value *over all time*, we use the "temporal" functional dependency:

$$\{EMPL\} \ G \ \{BIRTH\}.$$

The policy of the company is to increase or decrease the salary of an employee whenever his rank is changed (promotion or demotion). Hence, if EMPL- and SAL-values in a tuple are preserved between times i and $i+1$, then the associated RANK-value must be preserved as well; otherwise, the rank of the employee under consideration changed, while his salary remained unchanged. This is expressed by the "dynamic" functional dependency:

$$\{EMPL, SAL\} \ N \ \{RANK\}.^* \ \blacklozenge$$

Definition 3. Let $i \in TIME$.
The FD $X \rightarrow Y$ is said to be satisfied by valid-time relation T at time i if and only if it is satisfied by T_i.

A *temporal functional dependency (TFD)* is a statement of the form $X \ G \ Y$, where X and Y are sets of attributes.

The TFD $X \ G \ Y$ is said to be satisfied by valid-time relation T at time i if and only if $X \rightarrow Y$ is satisfied by $T_i \cup T_{i+1} \cup ... \cup T_{maxTime}$.

A *dynamic functional dependency (DFD)* is a statement of the form $X \ N \ Y$, where X and Y are sets of attributes.

The DFD $X \ N \ Y$ is said to be satisfied by valid-time relation T at time i if and only if (1) $X \rightarrow Y$ is satisfied by $T_i \cup T_{i+1}$ in case $i < maxTime$, and (2) $X \rightarrow Y$ is satisfied by $T_{maxTime}$ in case $i = maxTime$.

A *dependency* is an FD, a TFD or a DFD.

Dependency U is said to be satisfied by valid-time relation T if and only if it is satisfied by T at every time $j \in TIME$. $\blacklozenge$

---

* The connectors G and N hint at the henceforth- and the nexttime-operators of temporal logic.

XNY and XGY have mathematically simple and elegant semantics in terms of satisfaction of $X \to Y$ by unions of timeslices. Importantly, the semantics is fully expressed in terms of timeslices. As a consequence, the foregoing definition applies to any temporal relational data model with discrete time and a (valid-)timeslice operator that yields snapshot relations. FD, DFD and TFD frequently occur in real situations. They allow us to constrain the set of possible valid-time relations. In this way, more real-world semantics can be captured in the data model. It is interesting to consider reasoning about FD, DFD and TFD together.

Definition 4. Let $F \cup \{U\}$ be a set of dependencies (i.e., FDs, DFDs and TFDs). U is said to be logically implied by F if and only if U is satisfied by every valid-time relation that satisfies all dependencies of F.

The *logical closure of* F, denoted by F^+, is the smallest set containing every dependency that is logically implied by F.

U is said to be *trivial* if $U \in \varnothing^+$; otherwise U is *nontrivial*.

Let Z be a set of attributes. The *projection of* F *on* Z, denoted by $\pi_Z F$, is the smallest set containing dependency $X \theta Y$ whenever $X \theta Y \in F^+$ and $XY \subseteq Z$, where θ (Greek lowercase theta) is a syntactic variable ranging over $\{\to, N, G\}$. In simple words, $\pi_Z F$ is the smallest set containing every dependency that is logically implied by F and that consists of attributes of Z only. ♦

Two important logical implications are as follows: $\{XGY\}$ logically implies XNY and $\{XNY\}$ logically implies $X \to Y$. In simple words, the TFD XGY is stronger than the DFD XNY, which, in turn, is stronger than the FD $X \to Y$. Logical implication of FD, DFD and TFD together can be axiomatized; axioms A1 through A5 below constitute a sound and complete axiomatization, where θ is a syntactic variable ranging over $\{\to, N, G\}$.

> A1. *Reflexivity:* Infer $X \theta \varnothing$.
> A2. *Transitivity:* From $X \theta Y$ *and* $Y \theta Z$ infer $X \theta Z$.
> A3. *Augmentation:* From $X \theta Y$ infer $XZ \theta YZ$.
> A4. From XNY infer $X \to Y$.
> A5. From XGY infer XNY.

A1, A2 and A3 are similar to Armstrong's axioms [23]. The implication problem is the task of effectively computing whether or not a dependency $X \theta' Y$ is logically implied by a given set F of dependencies. This problem can be transformed into the classical implication problem for FD, for which algorithms exist [28]. Let us indicate how this is done. Let F' be the smallest set that contains every dependency of F as well as every dependency that can be inferred from F by applying A4 and A5 only. Demonstrably, $X \theta' Y$ is inferable from F if and only if it is inferable from F' by applying A1, A2 and A3 only with θ' substituted for θ. The latter problem resolves itself into the classical implication problem for FD.

What is the significance of DFD and TFD? First, DFD and TFD characterize a tractable and meaningful class of temporal integrity constraints. Some existing temporal database concepts can be expressed in terms of DFD and TFD, and hence are less general. An example is the concept of *(fully-)synchronous attributes* [16]. A comparison with related work is given in section 6. Second, DFD and TFD can contribute to a design theory for relational databases -- also known as *normalization theory*. They can be used in classical normalization through the principle of preservation of DFD and TFD (section 5). Furthermore, DFD and TFD can cause data redundancy, which gives rise to "temporal normalization" (section 4).

4. Temporal Normalization

DFDs and TFDs, like FDs, can cause data redundancy. Consider the valid-time relation of figure 2(a). The values for *?1* and *?2* are predictable, and hence redundant. To satisfy {EMPL} G {BIRTH}, *?1* must be equal to *1964*. To satisfy {EMPL, SAL} N {RANK}, *?2* must be equal to *E*. The redundancy under consideration leads to update anomalies. In figure 2(a), for example, if we correct the year of birth of an employee, we must update all valid-time tuples about that employee; otherwise, the database will become inconsistent. The redundancy can be eliminated by decomposing the valid-time relation as shown in figure 2(b).

Redundancy caused by FD is dealt with by conventional normalization theory [9,23]. Loosely speaking, normalization refers to the process of decomposing a universal relation, *without loss of information*, into smaller relations such that (1) redundancy caused by FDs decreases or disappears, and (2) FDs are preserved. *Without loss of information* means that the original universal relation can be re-constructed from the smaller component relations. This aspect is formalized by the concept of lossless-join decomposition. Redundancy caused by FDs is characterized by the formalism of 3NF and BCNF. Preservation of FDs means that there is no need to re-construct the original universal relation to test satisfaction of FDs. This aspect is formalized by the concept of (functional) dependency-preserving decomposition. We refer to the literature for a formal description of lossless-join, normal forms, and (functional) dependency-preservation [9,13,23].

Importantly, the decomposition shown in figure 2 is not implied by classical normalization theory. The original relation schema {EMPL, CITY, BIRTH, RANK, SAL} is in BCNF (and even 5NF) w.r.t. the FDs that are logically implied by the dependencies under consideration ({EMPL} $\rightarrow$ {CITY, RANK, SAL}, {EMPL} G {BIRTH}, and {EMPL, SAL} N {RANK}).

(Functional) dependency-preservation can be extended to involve DFDs and TFDs. This extension is carried out in the next section. In this section we focus on temporal normal forms entailed by DFD and TFD. We point out that we do not define temporal extensions of the lossless-join property. We found that, in our theory, preservation of time-related information is adequately described by the conventional lossless-join property.

{EMPL} → {CITY, RANK, SAL}
{EMPL} *G* {BIRTH}
{EMPL, SAL} *N* {RANK}

EMPL	CITY	BIRTH	RANK	SAL	*VT*
Ed	*Paris*	*1964*	*E*	*100*	{0}
Ed	*Paris*	*- ?1 -*	*E*	*110*	{2}
Ed	*London*	*1964*	*- ?2 -*	*110*	{3}

(a)

EMPL	RANK	SAL	*VT*
Ed	*E*	*100*	{0}
Ed	*E*	*110*	{2,3}

EMPL	CITY	*VT*
Ed	*Paris*	{0,2,3}
Ed	*London*	{3}

EMPL	BIRTH	*VT*
Ed	*1964*	{0,2,3}

(b)

Fig. 2. Decomposition into T3NF.

Redundancy caused by DFD and TFD is very similar to redundancy caused by FD. Redundancy emerges whenever some, *but not all*, attributes are dependent on certain other attributes. For example, the redundancy characterized by *?2* emerges because BIRTH and RANK are "dynamically functionally dependent" on {EMPL, SAL}, while CITY is not. Likewise, the redundancy characterized by *?1* emerges because BIRTH is "temporally functionally dependent" on {EMPL}, while CITY, RANK and SAL are not. As a consequence, redundancy caused by DFD and TFD can be characterized in the same way as redundancy caused by FD. This gives rise to temporal variants of classical normal forms. Temporal normal forms are defined shortly (definitions 5 and 6). First, however, we note that in figure 2(b), *E* appears twice in the valid-time relation over {EMPL, RANK, SAL} (one appearance is printed in bold). Nevertheless, neither occurrence of *E* can be predicted from other values using the dependencies under consideration. In other words, we can separately replace each occurrence of *E* by another value, without violating the constraints under consideration. We conclude that neither occurrence of *E* is really redundant.

In conventional normalization theory, the construct of key is defined in terms of FD. Definition 5 introduces analogous key constructs in terms of DFD and TFD. The formalism of →-key corresponds to the conventional construct of key in normalization theory. No two distinct tuples of any one timeslice of a valid-time relation can have the same value for a given →-key. The formalism of G-key serves to uniquely identify valid-time tuples in a valid-time relation, irrespective of time. In other words, no two distinct valid-time tuples of a valid-time relation can have the same value for a given G-key. The formalism of N-key is less intuitive; it distinguishes tuples within pairs of "adjacent" timeslices of a valid-time relation (i.e., timeslices at times i and $i + 1$).

Definition 5. Let F be a set of dependencies. Let $K \subseteq Z \subseteq ATTR$.
K is said to be a θ-*key w.r.t.* $\langle Z, F \rangle$ if and only if (1) $K \theta Z \in F^+$, and (2) *Minimality:* if K' is a proper subset of K, then $K' \theta Z \notin F^+$.

An attribute A of Z is said to be θ-*prime w.r.t.* $\langle Z, F \rangle$ if and only if it is contained in some θ-key w.r.t. $\langle Z, F \rangle$; otherwise A is θ-*nonprime w.r.t.* $\langle Z, F \rangle$.

A subset of Z is said to be a θ-*superkey w.r.t.* $\langle Z, F \rangle$ if it contains a θ-key w.r.t. $\langle Z, F \rangle$. ♦

In the example, {EMPL} is a →-key, {EMPL, CITY, SAL} is a N-key, and {EMPL, CITY, RANK, SAL} is a G-key. Demonstrably, every G-key is a N-superkey, and every N-key is a →-superkey. Definition 6 extends the formalism of 3NF for temporal databases. →-3NF characterizes the redundancy caused by FDs; it corresponds to classical 3NF. N-3NF and G-3NF characterize the redundancy caused by DFDs and TFDs respectively. T3NF is a combination of →-3NF, N-3NF and G-3NF.

Definition 6. Let F be a set of dependencies. Let Z be a set of attributes.
Z is said to be in θ-*3NF w.r.t.* F if and only if whenever $K \theta \{A\}$ is a nontrivial dependency of $\pi_Z F$, then either (1) K is a θ-superkey w.r.t. $\langle Z, F \rangle$, or (2) A is →-prime w.r.t. $\langle Z, F \rangle$.

A *decomposition (of ATTR)* is a set $\{Z_1, Z_2, ..., Z_n\}$ where $Z_1, Z_2, ..., Z_n$ are subsets of $ATTR$ such that $ATTR = Z_1 \cup Z_2 \cup ... \cup Z_n$.

Decomposition ζ is said to be in θ-*3NF w.r.t.* F if and only if for every $Z \in \zeta$, Z is in θ-3NF w.r.t. F.

Decomposition ζ is said to be in *T3NF w.r.t.* F *(Temporal 3NF)* if and only if ζ is in θ-3NF w.r.t. F for every $\theta \in \{\rightarrow, N, G\}$. ♦

Demonstrably, the relation schema of figure 2(a) is not in N-3NF nor in G-3NF w.r.t. the dependencies under consideration. The decomposition of figure 2(b) is in

T3NF. Note that θ-3NF does not imply θ'-3NF if θ and θ' are distinct. For example, {A, B, C} is in G-3NF w.r.t. {A $\rightarrow$ B, B $\rightarrow$ C}, but not in $\rightarrow$-3NF; {A, B, C} is in $\rightarrow$-3NF w.r.t. {A $\rightarrow$ B, A N C}, but not in N-3NF.

5. Preservation of DFD and TFD

Definition 7 extends, in a straightforward manner, the concept of (functional) dependency-preservation to involve DFD and TFD.

Definition 7. Let F be a set of dependencies. Let $\zeta = \{Z_1, Z_2, ..., Z_n\}$ be a decomposition.

ζ is said to *preserve* dependency U of F if and only if U is logically implied by $\pi_{Z_1} F \cup \pi_{Z_2} F \cup ... \cup \pi_{Z_n} F$.

ζ is said to be *FD-preserving w.r.t.* F if it preserves every FD of F.

ζ is said to be *ALL-preserving* w.r.t. F if it preserves every dependency of F. ♦

An algorithm for testing preservation of dependencies (FD, DFD and TFD) is presented in [28]. Demonstrably, the decomposition of figure 2(b) is ALL-preserving w.r.t. the dependencies under consideration. It is reasonable to ask whether we can always find a lossless-join and ALL-preserving decomposition in T3NF. Unfortunately, the answer is "no". In particular, there does not always exist a lossless-join and ALL-preserving decomposition in $\rightarrow$-3NF. (A fortiori, there does not always exists a lossless-join and ALL-preserving decomposition in T3NF.) Constructing a counterexample is easy. Still we have the following significant result: there always exists a lossless-join and FD-preserving decomposition in T3NF (theorem 1). That is, redundancy caused by DFD and TFD can always be eliminated without violating the conventional properties of lossless-join and FD-preservation.

Theorem 1. Let F be a set of dependencies.
There always exists a lossless-join and FD-preserving decomposition that is in T3NF (w.r.t. F). ♦

Preservation of DFDs and TFDs is still useful. Classical normalization theory provides criteria by which to evaluate the "goodness" of a given decomposition, viz. the lossless-join property, FD-preservation and normal forms. A good decomposition might not be unique. Usually, in fact, there will be multiple ways of reducing a universal relation schema to 5NF. Conventional normalization theory provides no objective criteria for choosing among alternative decompositions. Adding preservation of DFDs and TFDs as "quality criteria" for a decomposition, is reasonable. This is motivated by the following example.

Example 2. Consider the relation schema {EMPL, DEPT, MGR}. DEPT uniquely identifies each department; MGR is the manager of a department. The FDs

$$\{DEPT\} \rightarrow \{MGR\} \text{ and } \{MGR\} \rightarrow \{DEPT\}$$

express a one-to-one relationship between departments and managers. The FD

$$\{EMPL\} \rightarrow \{MGR\}$$

expresses that an employee works for exactly one manager. Assume for a while that employees cannot change department, which is expressed by the TFD:

$$\{EMPL\} \ G \ \{DEPT\}$$

Consider the following two decompositions:

$$\zeta_1 = \{\{EMPL, MGR\}, \{DEPT, MGR\}\}, \text{ and}$$
$$\zeta_2 = \{\{EMPL, DEPT\}, \{DEPT, MGR\}\}.$$

Demonstrably, both decompositions are lossless-join, FD-preserving and in 5NF w.r.t. the FDs that are logically implied by the dependencies under consideration. Hence, conventional normalization theory provides no criterion for choosing between ζ_1 and ζ_2. Nevertheless, ζ_2 is ALL-preserving, while ζ_1 is not. Notably, ζ_1 does not preserve {EMPL} G {DEPT} (however it preserves {EMPL} $\rightarrow$ {DEPT}). We therefore prefer ζ_2. This choice is intuitively correct. A relation over {EMPL, DEPT} is stable, whereas the corresponding relation over {EMPL, MGR} has to be modified each time a department changes manager. ♦

A final remark: one could object that, in the foregoing example, no rational designer would ever come up with decomposition ζ_1. Common sense tells a designer that ζ_2 is the right choice. We understand this objection, but point out that it misses the point. The very goal of normalization theory is precisely to provide a formalization of commonsense reasoning. Normalization theory aims to capture the reasoning made by a designer, and to mechanize it in axiomatizations and algorithms. Date makes a similar remark with respect to conventional normalization [7, p. 546].

6. Comparison with Related Work

6.1. Temporal Dependency of Jensen et al.

Jensen et al. [11,12] extend the construct of FD for temporal relations as follows:

Let X and Y be sets of explicit attributes of a temporal relation schema, R. A temporal functional dependency, denoted X -T$\rightarrow$ Y, exists on R if, for all instances r of R , all snapshots of r satisfy the functional dependency $X \to Y$. [12, p. 60]

Assumably, the intention of this definition is to assert that an FD is satisfied by a temporal relation if it is satisfied at each timeslice. However, we point out that the definition is deficient. Notably, if $X \to Y$ is nontrivial, then one can always construct a snapshot relation falsifying $X \to Y$. As a consequence, the requirement *"all snapshots of r satisfy the functional dependency $X \to Y$ "* in the above definition can only be fulfilled for trivial FDs. The inaccuracy here is to view FDs as characteristic properties of relation schemas, instead of defining FDs as constraints that can be satisfied or not by (temporal) relations. Extending the notion of satisfaction of FD -- rather than FD itself -- is more accurate: An FD $X \to Y$ is satisfied by temporal relation r if all snapshots of r satisfy $X \to Y$. The latter definition is contained in our definition 3. The temporal normal forms proposed by Jensen et al. repeat classical normal forms.

6.2. Temporal Normal Form of Navathe and Ahmed

Navathe and Ahmed in [16,17] introduce a temporal dependency to define a temporal normal form (TNF). They demonstrate that data replication occurs in a valid-time relation if attribute values within a valid-time tuple change at different rates. Figure 3(a) shows again the valid-time relation over {EMPL, RANK, SAL} of figure 2(b). If the salary of an employee changes, we add a new valid-time tuple with the new salary. This tuple replicates the "old" rank, unless the rank changes at the same time. In figure 3(a), for example, the value E is duplicated in the second valid-time tuple. To avoid such data replication, TNF requires the relation schema {EMPL, RANK, SAL} to be decomposed into {EMPL, RANK} and {EMPL, SAL} (figure 3(b)).

From our standpoint, the decomposition under consideration is not desirable. First, as was argued before, neither occurrence of E in figure 3(a) is really redundant, in the sense that it can be predicted from other values using the dependencies under consideration. We can separately replace each occurrence of E by another value, without violating the constraints under consideration. Second, the decomposition does not preserve the DFD {EMPL, SAL} N {RANK}. That is, after the decomposition, a join is required to test whether this DFD is satisfied, which is not practical.

TNF first assumes that a key is predetermined (a so-called *time-invariant key*) and then requires that all nonkey attributes are (fully-)synchronous, in the sense that they always change simultaneously. Interestingly, the notion of synchronism can be expressed in terms of DFDs, and hence is less general (example 3).

Example 3. The policy of the company is to change the salary of an employee whenever his rank is changed. This is expressed by the DFD:

$$\{EMPL, SAL\} \; N \; \{RANK\}$$

Assume for a while that a change of salary is always accompanied by a change of rank. This is expressed by the DFD:

$$\{EMPL, RANK\}\ N\ \{SAL\}$$

The two DFDs together express that the SAL- and RANK-values associated with a given EMPL-value always change simultaneously. ♦

$$\{EMPL\} \rightarrow \{RANK, SAL\}$$
$$\{EMPL, SAL\}\ N\ \{RANK\}$$

EMPL	RANK	SAL	VT
Ed	E	100	{0}
Ed	E	110	{2,3}

(a)

EMPL	RANK	VT
Ed	E	{0,2,3}

EMPL	SAL	VT
Ed	100	{0}
Ed	110	{2,3}

(b)

Fig. 3. Decomposition into TNF.

Navathe and Ahmed introduce a temporal dependency to expresses the absence of synchronism. Importantly, they assume that the conventional normalization process is carried out before the detection of temporal dependencies [16, p. 157]. As a consequence, the following inconveniences may arise:

- A designer cannot impose temporal dependencies before carrying out conventional normalization. This may be frustrating. A designer would like to define temporal dependencies at the same time that he defines functional dependencies.
- Conventional normalization cannot benefit from temporal information, since such information is only introduced afterwards. As was illustrated in the previous section, temporal information can be helpful to conventional normalization (example 2).
- Temporal dependencies are only formulated after the initial universal relation schema has been decomposed. At that time, it is not evident how to detect (and to formulate) temporal dependencies that span several relation schemas. It is

quite natural to formalize such dependencies on the universal relation schema before decomposition.

DFDs and TFDs can be defined by a designer at the same time that functional dependencies are defined. They do not suffer from the deficiencies listed above.

6.3. Dynamic Functional Dependency of Vianu

In the work of Vianu [24], a temporal relation is viewed as a sequence of snapshot relations in time. Each new snapshot relation is obtained from the previous one by global updates, which affect several (or all) tuples simultaneously. Tuples preserve their identity through updates. Both static and dynamic constraints are used in conjunction with the data model. The static constraints considered are FDs. The dynamic constraints involve global updates and are restricted to certain analogs of FDs, called dynamic functional dependencies. To avoid any confusion with our formalism of DFD, we use the acronym VDFD for Vianu's dynamic functional dependency.

Example 4. The policy of the company is to have an annual salary increase. Each new salary is determined strictly on the basis of the current salary and the year of birth. Hence, two employees with the same salary and year of birth receive the same new salary as a result of a salary increase. For each attribute A, let $@A$ refer to values after an update. The policy relating to salary increases is expressed by the VDFD:

$$\{SAL, BIRTH\} \rightarrow \{@SAL\}.$$

Two tuples with the same value for SAL and BIRTH must agree on SAL after an update. ♦

Our initial data model, unlike that of Vianu, does not incorporate the notion of tuple-identity. Nevertheless, our DFDs can be applied to Vianu's data model in a straightforward manner. Importantly, we demonstrated that our DFDs cannot be expressed by VDFDs, and vice versa [28]. In particular, we proved (1) a non-trivial DFD $X N Y$ is *not* equivalent to any set containing FDs and VDFDs only, and (2) a non-trivial VDFD $\{X \rightarrow @X\}$ is *not* equivalent to any set containing FDs and DFDs only. As a consequence, combining VDFDs and our DFDs results in a net increase of expressive power.

6.4. Other Formalism

DFDs and TFDs can be represented as sentences of first-order temporal logic (FOTL) [3,4]. Let us demonstrate how this is done for the relation schema $\{A, B, C\}$ and the DFD $A N B$. Consider the predicate symbol R with arity 3. A corresponds to the first argument of predicate symbol R etc. The DFD $A N B$ is expressed by the sentence:

$$\forall x \forall y \forall z \forall y_1 \forall z_1[(R(x,y,z) \wedge (R(x,y_1,z_1) \vee \textbf{next } R(x,y_1,z_1))) \Rightarrow (y = y_1)].$$

The only assumption we made about values for nontemporal attributes is that they can be compared for equality. *TIME,* on the other hand, is an interpreted domain. Constraint-generating dependencies, proposed by Baudinet et al. [2], are a generalization of functional dependencies where equality requirements are replaced by constraints on an interpreted domain. DFDs and TFDs are a special form of constraint-generating 2-dependencies. Consider the valid-time relation r. The DFD $X N Y$ is expressed by the sentence:

$$\forall t_1 \forall t_2[[r(t_1) \wedge r(t_2) \wedge (t_1[X] = t_2[X]) \wedge$$
$$\exists i[(i \in t_1[VT]) \wedge ((i \in t_2[VT]) \vee (i+1 \in t_2[VT]))]] \Rightarrow (t_1[Y] = t_2[Y])].$$

7. Concluding Remarks and Future Research

In this paper, a temporally ungrouped historical data model was used to study data redundancy caused by certain types of static and temporal constraints (FD, DFD and TFD). Conventional normalization theory was extended to cope with this kind of redundancy. T3NF and preservation of DFD/TFD were defined as new goals in temporal database design. We proved that T3NF can always be achieved in combination with classical design goals (i.e., lossless-join and FD-preservation -- theorem 1). Unfortunately, preserving all DFDs and TFDs as well, is not always possible. Further research is required to find out to what extent DFDs and TFDs can be preserved in combination with lossless-join, T3NF and FD-preservation.

Certain redundancy in conventional relational databases can be attributed to the requirement of first normal form, and can be eliminated by switching to the nested relational data model. Analogously, certain redundancy in temporal relational databases can be eliminated by switching to a temporally grouped historical data model. The introduction of *repeating groups* is a fundamental deviation from the conventional relational data model. This option is beyond the scope of this study, but deserves future attention. Note, however, that the meaning of DFD and TFD is defined in terms of timeslices, irrespective of a particular timestamping strategy.

At the center of this paper is the formalism of FD. Studying temporal extensions of other dependencies (e.g., inclusion dependencies) may be interesting.

References

[1]   Arapis C.: Temporal specifications of object behavior. In *MFDBS 91, 3rd Symposium on Mathematical Fundamentals of Database and Knowledge Base Systems*, Rostock, Germany, 1991, LNCS 495, Springer-Verlag, Berlin, 1991, 308-324.

[2] Baudinet M., Chomicki J., Wolper P.: Constraint-generating dependencies. In *Database Theory - ICDT'95, 5th Internat. Conf.*, Prague, Czech Republic, 1995, LNCS 893, Springer-Verlag, Berlin, 1995, 322-337.

[3] Chomicki J.: Efficient checking of temporal integrity constraints using bounded history encoding. To appear in *ACM Trans. on Database Systems*.

[4] Chomicki J.: On the feasibility of checking temporal integrity constraints. To appear in *Journal of Computer and System Sciences*.

[5] Clifford J., Croker A.: The historical relational data model (HRDM) revisited. Chapter 1 of *Temporal Databases: Theory, Design and Implementation*. Benjamin/Cummings, Redwood City, CA, 1993, 6-27.

[6] Clifford J., Croker A., Tuzhilin A.: On completeness of historical relational query languages. *ACM Trans. on Database Systems*, 19(1), 1994, 64-116.

[7] Date C.J.: *An Introduction to Database Systems, Volume I*. Addison-Wesley, Reading, MA, 1990.

[8] Elmasri R. , Wuu G.T J. , Kouramajian V.: A temporal model and query language for EER databases. Chapter 9 of *Temporal Databases, Theory, Design, and Implementation*, Benjamin/Cummings, Redwood City, CA, 1993, 212-229.

[9] Elmasri R., Navathe S.: *Fundamentals of Database Systems, Second Edition*. Benjamin/Cummings, Redwood City, CA, 1994.

[10] Gadia S.K., Nair S.S.: *Temporal databases: a prelude to parametric data. Chapter 2 of Temporal Databases: Theory, Design, and Implementation*, Benjamin/Cummings, Redwood City, CA, 1993, 28-66.

[11] Jensen C.S. , Snodgrass R.T. , Soo M. D.: Extending normal forms to temporal relations. Technical Report 92-17, Computer Science Department, University of Arizona, 1992.

[12] Jensen C.S., Clifford J., Elmasri R., et al. (eds.): A consensus glossary of temporal database concepts. *ACM SIGMOD RECORD*, 23(1), 1994, 52-64.

[13] Kanellakis P.C.: Elements of relational database theory. Chapter 17 of *Handbook of Theoretical Computer Science, Vol. B: Formal Models and Semantics*, Elsevier, Amsterdam, 1990.

[14] Kline N.: An update of the temporal database bibliography. *ACM SIGMOD RECORD*, 22(4), 1993, 66-80.

[15] Lipeck U.W. , Saake G.: Monitoring dynamic integrity constraints based on temporal logic. *Information Systems*, 12(3), 1987, 255-269.

[16] Navathe S.B. , Ahmed R.: A temporal relational model and a query language. *Information Sciences*, 49, 1989, 147-175.

[17] Navathe S.B. , Ahmed R.: Temporal extensions to the relational model and SQL. Chapter 4 of *Temporal Databases: Theory, Design and Implementation*, Benjamin/Cummings, Redwood City, CA, 1993, 92-109.

[18] Sarda N.L.: HSQL: A historical query language. Chapter 5 of *Temporal Databases: Theory, Design and Implementation*. Benjamin/Cummings, Redwood City, CA, 1993, 110-140.

[19] Segev A., Shoshani A.: A temporal data model based on time sequences. Chapter 11 of *Temporal Databases: Theory, Design and Implementation.* Benjamin/Cummings, Redwood City, CA, 1993, 248-270.

[20] Snodgrass R.: An overview of TQuel. Chapter 6 of *Temporal Databases: Theory, Design and Implementation,* Benjamin/Cummings, Redwood City, CA, 1993, 141-182.

[21] Soo M.D.: Bibliography on temporal databases. *ACM SIGMOD RECORD,* 20(1), 1991, 14-23.

[22] Tansel A.U., Clifford J., Gadia S., Jajodia S., Segev A., Snodgrass R. (eds.): *Temporal Databases: Theory, Design and Implementation.* Benjamin/Cummings, Redwood City, CA, 1993.

[23] Ullman J.D.: *Principles of Databases and Knowledge-Base Systems, Volume I.* Computer Science Press, Rockville, MD, 1988.

[24] Vianu V.: Dynamic functional dependencies and database aging. *Journal of the ACM,* 34(1), 1987, 28-59.

[25] Wijsen J.: A theory of keys for temporal databases. In *Actes 9èmes Journées Bases de Données Avancées,* Toulouse, France, 1993, 35-54.

[26] Wijsen J., Vandenbulcke J., Olivié, H.: Functional dependencies generalized for temporal databases that include object-identity. In *Proc. 12th Internat. Conf. on Entity-Relationship Approach,* Arlington, Texas, U.S.A., 1993, LNCS 823, Springer-Verlag, Berlin, 1994, 99-109.

[27] Wijsen J., Vandenbulcke J., Olivié H.: On time-invariance and synchronism in valid-time relational databases. *Journal of Computing and Information,* 1(1), Special Issue: *Proc. 6th Internat. Conf. on Computing and Information,* Peterborough, ON, Canada, 1994, 1192-1206.

[28] Wijsen J.: *Extending Dependency Theory for Temporal Databases,* Ph.D. thesis, K.U.Leuven, Belgium, February 1995.

"Temporal" Integrity Constraints in Temporal Databases

Michael Gertz and Udo W. Lipeck

Institut für Informatik, Universität Hannover
Lange Laube 22, D-30159 Hannover, Germany
{mg|ul}@informatik.uni-hannover.de

Abstract

In this paper we consider a class of integrity constraints which describe admissible lifecycles of database objects, and which can be specified by transition graphs. We present an algorithmic scheme for monitoring such constraints in temporal databases which efficiently support the concept of valid-time. The keys to efficient monitoring lie in storing lifecycle situations with respect to constraints, in utilizing the property of graphs being iteration-invariant, and in using basic operations of temporal databases to determine validity intervals. In particular, we give hints how to extend monitoring to transactions that involve retroactive and proactive modifications.

1 Introduction

Specifying and monitoring integrity constraints is essential for every kind of database application system in order to ensure its correctness and reliability. This applies to temporal databases as it has applied to conventional (non-temporal) databases.

In conventional databases, integrity constraints are partitioned into static constraints which restrict possible properties of database objects (thus they restrict possible database states), transitional constraints which restrict possible object changes (state transitions), and "temporal" constraints which restrict possible lifecycles of objects (state sequences) to admissible ones.

Now temporal databases store information about the history, the presence, and possibly (e.g., for planning purposes) the future of application objects, if we assume that a concept of valid-time [16, 17] is supported. Thus they are able to store complete lifecycles, i.e. conventional state sequences are now represented within one temporal database state (for an overview of temporal databases see [23]). Using corresponding temporal query languages like TSQL [15], TSQL2 [18] or TQuel [21], it has become possible to express an integrity check that refers to some lifecycle as one query. So the question arises whether we still need the above differentiation of integrity constraints.

Depending on the constraint to check, however, queries can become difficult to be formulated and very complex to be processed. As in conventional databases, techniques for constraint simplification are strongly needed in order to obtain efficient monitoring mechanism. Such simplification techniques shall be applied in monitors at database runtime or by designers at database definition time, e.g., when designing integrity-preserving transactions or triggers. Typically simplification aims at filtering out from a constraint those subconditions and those instances which are critical with respect to the result of a given transaction, whereas the remaining parts can be assumed to hold already due to the knowledge about the database before the transaction and about the transaction itself. For example, monitoring static constraints relies heavily on knowing that the constraint must have been true in the state before the transaction. Techniques for monitoring "temporal" constraints in conventional databases like in [13, 20, 2, 22] basically rely on stepwise maintaining lifecycle situations with respect to the constraint.

It would of course be rather expensive to monitor such constraints in temporal databases just by queries on the full temporal information. But lifecycle information and associated constraints have become particularly interesting for applications in the context of temporal databases. Therefore we want to investigate how to utilize "temporal" constraints and corresponding monitoring techniques, as they have been proposed for conventional databases, together with the special features of temporal databases. Thus we want to present an important class of integrity constraints for temporal databases that allows for systematic simplification.

In [8, 13] we have proposed integrity constraints which can be expressed in temporal logic and which control sequences of (conventional) database states. In order to reduce conditions on full sequences to conditions on state transitions we have utilized so-called transition graphs which can be constructed from temporal formulae. Such a transition graph equivalently describes all the admissible lifecycles of objects with respect to the underlying constraint. Nodes in a graph correspond to the situations an object can reach in such a lifecycle and edges give the conditions under which a change into another situation is admissible. Thus one might also relate a transition graph to a finite deterministic automaton. Monitoring the constraint can then be realized by storing and updating the situations of all database objects, and by checking situation-dependent transitional conditions. The graph nodes (situations) represent the minimal historic information needed for monitoring lifecycles with respect to the given constraint. In [13, 20] we have introduced the basic monitoring scheme, [13, 9, 11] contain algorithms to construct transition graphs from temporal formulae, [10, 11, 12] give rules how to transform the monitoring behavior into pre/postconditions of transaction specifications, and [6] presents rules how to derive triggers as integrity-maintaining mechanisms from transition graphs.

As an alternative to temporal logic formulae, transition graphs may be used directly to specify such constraints if a graphical, but flow-oriented view is preferred to a declarative style. In this paper we still call these constraints "temporal", although we of course do not claim to treat arbitrary constraints on temporal databases. They may be considered to be "transitional", but in a generalized sense since full transition graphs can be handled, or from an application point of view they may be considered as "lifecycle" constraints.

We do not want to emphasize temporal logic as a specification language since temporal quantifiers can be seen as or simulated by appropriate aggregating operators of temporal query languages like TSQL2 [18] or others proposed in the literature [23]. But we want to study a class of integrity constraints dealing with object lifecycles over the course of time so that we will work here directly with transition graphs as descriptions of temporal integrity constraints.

We want to incorporate the monitoring framework for such constraints into temporal databases which store objects and attribute values together with their times of validity.

In the following section we provide the basic definitions and notations for this paper; they deal with temporal databases as far as needed here, and with monitoring temporal integrity constraints in non-temporal databases. Section 3 presents the monitoring scheme for temporal databases and discusses impacts on retroactive and proactive transactions, i.e. transactions updating past or future values, respectively.

2 Basic Definitions and Notations

2.1 Temporal Data Model

For our approach we assume a temporal data model which supports storing information about the past, present and future. In this data model time is represented by a discrete domain of time instants called *valid-time*, which is isomorphic to the natural numbers. Valid-time is assumed to be equally spaced and ordered such that for two time points t and t', either t is before t' or t' is before t. A *time interval*, denoted by $[s, e]$, is any consecutive set of time points designated by its boundary time instants s and e where s is the first time instant and e is the last time instant in the interval. A single discrete time instant is simply denoted by t. In the temporal data model t_0 denotes the starting time of the modelled application. Since we require to store also future information and the future typically is not limited to a certain time point, we introduce an artificial time instant for the end of time, denoted by $t_\dashv$ (for a discussion on concepts for handling infinite future see, e.g., [1]).

In our approach we utilize valid-time to denote when a modelled fact becomes effective, i.e. true, in reality. A *database state*, denoted by σ_t, is a snapshot at a certain instant t consisting of all object/value combinations valid at that instant. A *state sequence* consists of snapshots at adjacent time instants. A temporal database thus may contain the past, present and future information best known at the present point of time, denoted by t_{now}.

In order to be general for modelling temporal data we utilize an ER model which offers a temporal extension to capture temporal information on objects and relationships. Thus we do not have to restrict ourselves to a concrete representation of a data model which supports storing temporal information, e.g., by using tuple timestamping or attribute timestamping, which is not essential for this presentation. For an overview of different data models and implementations of temporal data models supporting valid-time see, e.g., [23, 7]. The used model is similar to the extended ER model introduced in [4], for which an extension for handling temporal dimensions and a corresponding temporal query language have been proposed in [3, 5].

In the temporal ER Model, an *object type* is a set O of objects of the same type having the same attributes. Each object type O_i has a set of attributes $\{a_{i1}, \ldots, a_{in}\}$ where each attribute a_{ij} is associated with a domain of values $dom(a_{ij})$. Since we assume that future information can be modelled, each object o of type O is associated with one time interval $t(o) \subseteq [t_0, t_{\dashv}]$, which gives the *lifespan* of the object. For each object of type O it is assumed that a system defined surrogate attribute exists whose value is unique for every object in the database and which is determined when an object is created and does not change throughout the lifespan of the object. The temporal value of each attribute a_j of an object o, which is referred to as $a_j(o)$, is a partial function $a_j(o) : t(o) \rightarrow dom(a_j)$. The subset of $t(o)$ in which $a_j(o)$ is defined is denoted by $t(a_j(o))$.

Temporal modifications on objects of the data model are defined as follows (relationships referencing objects by their key attributes are handled in an analogous way) :

- **insert into** <*object type*>(<*attribute_values*>[, s, e])
  A new object of the given object type is inserted with the specified attribute values valid in interval $[s, e]$ which also builds the (initial) object lifespan. If no interval is specified it is assumed to be $[t_{now}, t_{\dashv}]$.

- **modify** <*object*>({<*attribute*> := <*value*>}[, s, e])
  New values are assigned to attributes of a given object. For each old attribute value the last valid-time instant is set to $s - 1$. If no valid-time interval is given, $[s, e]$ is assumed to be $[t_{now}, t_{\dashv}]$. A modification also allows to extend the lifespan of an object, e.g., when the specified interval is adjacent to the lifespan.

- **delete** <*object*>[(s, e)]
  The given object is updated such that all attribute values are set to null in the specified valid-time interval. If for the object o with its lifespan $[s', e']$ either $s < s' < e$, or $s < e' < e$ holds then the lifespan of the object is shortened to $[e + 1, e']$, respectively to $[s', s - 1]$. If no time interval is specified it is assumed to be $[t_{now}, t_{\dashv}]$, i.e. the lifespan of the object ends before the time instant t_{now}.

A *transaction* on a temporal database is a finite sequence Δ of temporal modifications $\{\omega_1, \ldots, \omega_l\}$. The parameters of the modifications $\omega_i \in \Delta$ (or the implicit assumptions about them) determine a finite union of *update intervals* containing all time instants when attribute values are modified by Δ.

2.2 Temporal Integrity Constraints and Transition Graphs

In this subsection we concentrate on monitoring temporal integrity constraints in non-temporal databases, based on transition graphs. The presented framework will then serve as the basis for our approach to maintaining temporal constraints in temporal databases discussed in Section 3.

In contrast to static integrity constraints which are used to describe the desired properties of objects that must hold at each time instant, temporal integrity constraints are used to restrict the possible lifecycles of objects to admissible ones. Temporal constraints are built from non-temporal formulae of the underlying calculus by iteratively applying logical connectives and temporal quantifiers **always** and **sometime**, and temporal bounds like **from ... holds**, **before**, etc. (for more details on the specification of temporal integrity constraints see, e.g., [13, 12] using future-oriented temporal logic or [2, 22] using past temporal logic).

Most of the *temporal* constraints for temporal databases considered in the literature are inherent to the data model, e.g., temporal extensions to referential integrity. There objects referenced in a relationship by their key attributes are required to exist during the specified valid-time for the relationship. For data models supporting the concept of supertypes/subtypes a similar class of temporal constraints requires that the lifespan of each object of a subtype has to be a subset of the the lifespan of the object in the respective supertype [24]. More general temporal integrity constraints describing restrictions imposed on the modelled application domain, however, are not considered, but can be formulated as ad-hoc queries.

In order to concentrate on the approach and not on examples our illustration database schema only consists of one object type *EMPLOYEE* having the attributes *emp_name, dname, job, salary* where *dname* denotes the name of the department where the employee works.

Example 2.1:
Assume the temporal constraint *DYC* stating that "before an employee can become a member in the headquarters (s)he must have been working (sometime) in the administrative department, and once (s)he joins the headquarters (s)he always belongs to that department (until (s)he leaves the company)."

This constraint can be stated as a temporal formula using an extension of an object calculus by the temporal quantifiers mentioned above as follows:

> **during-existence**(e: *EMPLOYEE*):
>   **from** e.dname <> "undefined" **holds**
>   ((**sometime** e.dname = "administration"
>   **before** e.dname = "headquarters")
>   **or** (**always** e.dname <> "headquarters"))
>   **and from** e.dname = "headquarters" **holds**
>   (**always** e.dname = "headquarters")

Since in a temporal database past as well as future information of objects is available, temporal constraints can be checked by issuing queries for constraint violations. The above constraint is future oriented, thus it is not obvious which queries have to be performed. For example, it is necessary to check the condition for all employees who are currently working in the headquarters. Additionally the condition has also to be checked for those employees who will be working in the headquarters in the future (as far as already stored in the database).

In order to monitor temporal constraints on state sequences in non-temporal databases in [13, 10, 14, 19] a method was proposed to utilize *transition graphs* which describe the admissible lifecycle(s) of objects and which can be constructed from temporal constraints at schema definition time. The main advantage of using transition graphs for monitoring is that checks of complete state sequences can be reduced to checks on "state transitions", i.e. adjacent time instants.

Formally, a transition graph for a temporal constraint referring to an object of type O by a respective variable *ooi* (object of interest) is defined as follows:

Definition 2.2 (Transition Graph):
A *transition graph* $T = \langle V, E, F, \nu, \eta, v_0 \rangle$ with a free object variable *ooi* consists of

- a directed graph $\langle V, E \rangle$ having a finite set V of nodes and a set $E \subseteq V \times V$ of edges,
- a set of *final nodes* $F \subseteq V$,
- a *node labelling* $\nu : V \to \mathbb{N}$,
- an *edge labelling* η on E with non-temporal formulae of the underlying calculus with *ooi* as the only free variable and which can be interpreted in a single snapshot,
- and an *initial node* $v_0 \in V$.

Furthermore a transition graph is here required to be *deterministic*, i.e. at each node $v \in V$ the labels of different outgoing edges exclude each other. $\square$

Note that this definition can be generalized to combinations of objects and data variables (compare references above), but this presentation is simplified in that respect.

A transition graph T can now be used to analyze a state sequence by searching for a corresponding path whose edge labels successively hold in the states of the sequence. For that, the node (situation) which has been reached by an object θ that can be assigned to the variable *ooi* must be "marked": A node v' is marked after passing a state σ iff there exists an edge $e = (v, v')$ such that the edge label $\eta(e)$ is valid in σ. If no edge satisfies this condition, no node gets marked. That graph processing, of course, starts in the initial node v_0. A deletion of θ (end of lifespan) is only allowed if a final node has been reached.

From this explanation, it is clear that a marking must be maintained for each object θ of the object type O relevant to the graph throughout the lifecycle of θ. This is done by adding a new attribute *situation$_T$* to the object type O where the marked node of θ (the "situation" reached by θ) is stored for the graph T.

Normally each node $v \in V$ is a final node, except there are liveness constraints imposed on the objects of interest, e.g., that a condition must hold sometime in the future. In our example such non-final nodes do not appear but we consider them in our algorithms.

Instead of constructing transition graphs from a temporal formula, what requires a respective underlying calculus supporting temporal logic, it can be more intuitive in many applications to start directly with the graphical representation of admissible lifecycles of objects. However, what is automatically ensured by the graph construction algorithms [13, 9, 11] must be preserved when specifying transition graphs directly:

Transition graphs must be *iteration-invariant*, i.e. at each node v in a graph there exists a loop labelled with δ such that for each ingoing edge e into v the condition $\eta(e) \Rightarrow \delta$ holds. This property ensures that the situation of an object will not change on simple state repetitions or modifications which leave the loop label δ valid. This is guaranteed whenever the underlying temporal formula can be expressed without referring to a "next" or "previous" state.

Example 2.3:
The following transition graph is deterministic and iteration-invariant and corresponds to the description of admissible lifecycles of employees working in the headquarters as stated in the temporal constraint DYC (cf. Example 2.1):

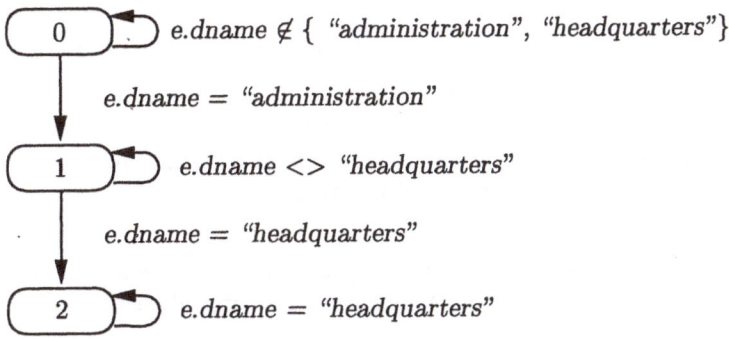

Figure 1: Transition graph for DYC

The variable e referring to objects of the type EMPLOYEE is the free object variable in the graph. The initial node v_0 is 0. All nodes in the graph are final nodes. □

We will explain the semantics and usage of a transition graph by our example above. Therefore we assume only modifications of present information like in conventional non-temporal databases, i.e. on the snapshot corresponding to t_{now}.

A lifecycle of an object θ begins by entering the graph via an edge which leaves the initial node v_0. Thus these edges have to be checked when the object has been inserted during the current transaction. In our example, inserting an employee who is working at the administration department leads to entering the situation 1. Hence the insertion is valid with regard to the transition graph. This node then gets marked for the object θ in the poststate of the transaction. Note that an insertion of an employee who works in a department different from the administration or headquarters is valid; the employee then remains in situation 0. Note that an insertion of an employee with $dname =$ "headquarters" is not allowed since then no valid outgoing edge from the initial node 0 exists.

Now assume a state where an object θ has reached the situation v. This node must have been entered via one ingoing edge valid at the previous state when that situation was computed. Since we consider iteration-invariant graphs only, the loop label δ at node v must be a logical implication of each ingoing edge label. So this label δ has been valid in the previous state and can be assumed to hold before the present state. The subsequent state transition is acceptable iff there exists one outgoing edge from node v which is valid in the new state; e.g., an employee in situation 1 can be moved to the headquarters. If the loop label at node v is invariant under the transaction, i.e. remains valid, the situation of the object θ remains invariant, too. E.g., all modifications not touching the department attribute of an employee leave the loop labels invariant.

A deletion of θ is only admissible if the object has reached a final node before the deletion. In the graph above deletions of employees are allowed in any situation.

The admissibility of lifespans of objects is summarized as follows:

Definition 2.4 (Admissible Lifespan):
The lifecycle of an object θ that can be assigned to the variable ooi of a transition graph T is admissible w.r.t. T up to the state σ iff there is a node marked for θ in σ. It is completely admissible iff a final node has been reached at its end. □

We now give a basic (non-optimized) algorithmic scheme for monitoring that will serve as a skeleton for the later monitoring algorithm for temporal databases.

Algorithm 2.5:
We assume a set of deterministic transition graphs, each graph T with a final node set F_T. The following procedure **MONITOR** has to be called after each transition from an old database state σ_{old} into a state σ_{now}, including the initialization into σ_0 as well as the exit after the last state (σ_{now} undefined).

  procedure MONITOR :
      /* global variables: $\sigma_{old}, \sigma_{now}$, new_situation */
      for each transition graph T and

```
    for each object θ of object type O from σ_old ∪ σ_now only
        do case of
        θ inserted: new_situation := CHECK(T, θ, v_0, σ_now);
                    /* v_0 is the initial node of T */
                    modify θ(situation_T := new_situation);
        θ updated:  new_situation := CHECK(T, θ, θ.situation_T, σ_now);
                    modify θ(situation_T := new_situation);
        θ deleted:  CHECK_COMPLETE(T, θ.situation_T)
endproc

function CHECK(T, θ, v, σ) : situation :
    /* get new situation for object θ in T by checking which
       edge outgoing from its current situation node v is valid */
    for each outgoing edge e = (v, v') in T
        do if edge label η(e) is valid in state σ then return v'
    if no edge label has been valid
        then ERROR("transition rejected: no edge applicable")
endfunc

procedure CHECK_COMPLETE(T, v) :
    if v ∉ F_T then ERROR("no final node reached")
endproc                                                          □
```

The property that a transition graph is iteration-invariant allows an important simplification of monitoring: if the state σ_{now} or the part relevant for the constraint (edge formulae) has not changed from σ_{old}, the situation of the object θ remains unchanged, i.e. no outgoing edge from the situation node of θ has to be checked in the new state. For our example assume a transaction which only performs modifications on the salary of employees. None of the loop labels in the transition graph for DYC is affected by these modifications; thus the situation nodes of employees remain unchanged. Such additional simplifications are possible due to the knowledge about the modifications by the transaction which has induced a state transition. Remember that only static constraints (edge labels) need to be checked based on the known situation each object has reached in its lifecycle.

3   Checking Temporal Constraints

We will now incorporate the above monitoring approach into temporal databases.

An often neglected problem of temporal constraints in conventional databases is that actually only the lifecycles of database objects with respect to transaction-time can be checked. Typical specifications, however, shall describe lifecycles of corresponding real-world objects, i.e. lifecycles of database objects with respect to valid-time. Thus a database application system shall be used as an instrument to control developments in the application world. This goal, however, can be achieved in temporal databases which offer a valid-time concept.

Here we assume that a state in a conventional database corresponds in a temporal database to a snapshot at a certain instant of valid-time. Theoretically, the monitoring algorithm above has to be applied to check a temporal constraint in a given temporal database by iteratively calling CHECK for every snapshot transition in the database: Depending on the current object situations the monitor again checks the validity of outgoing edges or deletions (end of lifespans) and computes the reached situations as far as no error occurs.

As a first improvement these checks can be limited to the snapshots between the minimal lower and maximal upper time instants t_{min} and t_{max} of the update intervals which were specified in the modifications of the given transaction as depicted in the following figure:

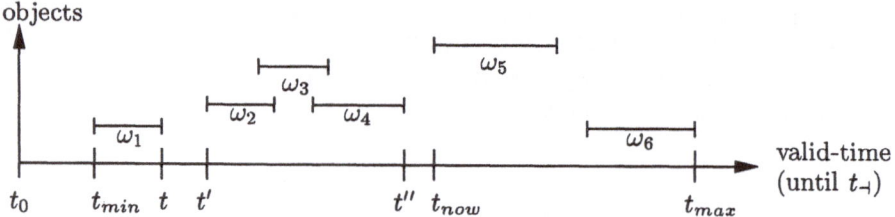

Figure 2: Example of valid-time modifications

The monitor algorithm then has to be applied to the snapshot at time instant $t_{min} - 1$, and for each two consecutive snapshots, until at some instant after t_{max} the new object situations coincide with the situations before the transaction. This of course requires that object situations with respect to transition graphs are stored as additional (now temporal) attributes. By utilizing the iteration-invariance of the graph and by using basic operations of temporal databases to determine validity intervals, this monitoring can be done rather efficiently.

Algorithm 3.1:

Let a transaction Δ updating the temporal database be given. In order to check the integrity constraint represented by a transition graph T the information about situations has to be maintained for the objects of interest at least at all time instants when attributes mentioned in T have been changed. But additionally, the transitions into the spaces between/after update intervals have to be checked as well. Thus we assume that the transaction determines an ordered set of maximal update intervals $U_i = [s_i, e_i] \subseteq [t_0, t_\dashv]$, $i = 1, ..., k$, and that these intervals can be extracted from the transaction by the monitor. In Figure 2, this sequence would start with $U_1 = [t_{min}, t], U_2 = [t', t'']$, etc. For technical reasons we set $e_0 := t_0$ and $s_{k+1} := t_\dashv + 1$ (an artificial value greater than $t_\dashv$).

Let the situation v of an object θ at time t with regard to the graph T be stored as $\theta.situation_T(t)$. In the algorithm the invariant $\Phi(i, t)$ of the while-loop will be that situations of objects have already been checked within all update intervals $[s_j, e_j], j \leq i$, completely and at all instants $< t$. This is illustrated in the figure below (Fig. 3).

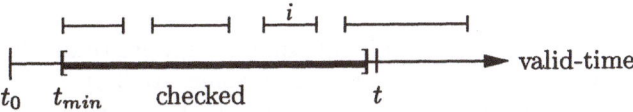

Figure 3: Invariant of the while-loop

for each transition graph T **do**
for each object θ of type O **do**
begin
    $t := \max\{s_1, \textit{lifespan}(\theta).\textit{start}\};$ /* $t \hat{=}$ current instant */
    $i := 0;$ /* $i \hat{=}$ number of last checked interval */

    /* get situation before current instant */
    if $t = \textit{lifespan}(\theta).\textit{start}$ **then** $v := v_0$ /* assume initial node */
    else $v := \theta.\textit{situation}_T(t-1);$ /* get situation before current instant */

    while $i \le k$ **and** $t \le \min\{t_\lnot, \textit{lifespan}(\theta).\textit{end}\}$ **do**
    /* consider the object lifespan in the update intervals */
    begin
       /* get former object situation at t */
       $v_{old} := \theta.\textit{situation}_T(t);$

       /* calculate (and store) new situation v in snapshot σ_t at
            instant t as in the conventional monitoring algorithm
            (see Remark (1) below) */
       $v := \text{CHECK}(T, \theta, v, \sigma_t);$

       if $t > e_i$ **then** $i := i + 1;$

       /* check if the situation has remained unchanged outside an update
            interval; then subsequent situations remain unchanged, too   */
       if $v_{old} = v$ **and** $i = k$
          then $i := k + 1$ /* after last update interval */
       else if $v_{old} = v$ **and** $t < s_{i+1}$
             then $t := s_{i+1}$ /* go to next update interval */

       else begin
          $t_{end} := \max\{t' \mid t' \ge t \land \forall t'' \le t' : \delta \text{ valid in } \sigma_{t''}\}$
          /* end of validity interval (starting from t) of the loop
             condition δ at node v in T (see Remark (2) below) */
          modify $\theta(\textit{situation}_T := v, t, t_{end});$
          $t := t_{end} + 1; \; i := \max\{j \mid t > e_j, j \ge i\}$
       end

       $v := \theta.\textit{situation}_T(t - 1)$ /* get situation before current instant */
    end

    if $t = \textit{lifespan}(\theta).\textit{end} + 1$ **then** CHECK_COMPLETE(T, v)
end

Remark (1): Since the new situation node for θ in T has to be checked at time instant t, the evaluation of the valid outgoing edge from v has to be done in the snapshot σ_t.

Remark (2): Due to iteration-invariance of graphs recalculation of situations is only needed at interval limits where some attribute, which is needed for evaluating the current loop, is changing. The calculation of a validity interval thus is an important operation to optimize monitoring. It can be assumed to be supported by basic features of temporal databases. The algorithm is robust against taking a non-maximal long validity interval; thus one might simply take the intersection of valid-time intervals of the current values of attributes explicitly mentioned in the loop label δ. Of course, unnecessary recomputations of unchanged situations can be avoided if the database language offers a powerful built-in mechanism for querying validity intervals of arbitrary conditions.

Remark (3): Note that invariance of subconditions under the given transaction cannot be utilized directly, since here snapshot transitions (e.g., from an updated snapshot to a non-updated snapshot) are relevant to the above algorithm, but not the original temporal transaction commands. Instead we have utilized update intervals, i.e. knowledge, where attributes were changed.   □

One problem that arises in modifications of past and future information is that it is often useful or even required to have *gaps* of information, e.g., for planning purposes. Consider for example a modification ω that inserts future information (e.g., *e.dname*="*headquarters*") about an already existing employee with its lifespan $[s', e']$ into the database (Fig. 4). Here the lifespan of the object is extended to the time instant e, but in the gap $[e' + 1, s - 1]$ (indicated by the dotted line) its attribute values are undefined.

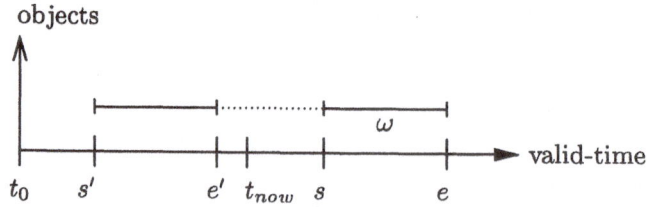

Figure 4: Example of a proactive modification

From a formal point of view this modification is not admissible with regard to our example transition graph since the situation of the object is not known at time instant $s - 1$. Thus the situation of the object at time instant s cannot be determined using the function CHECK. A similar problem arises when we delete a valid-time part $[s, e]$ of the information of an object's lifespan $[s', e']$ such that $s > s'$ and $e < e'$, what is indicated by the dotted line in Figure 5.

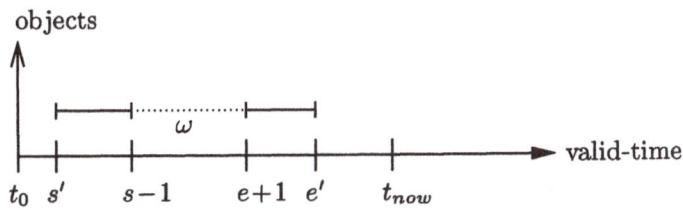

Figure 5: Example of a retroactive modification

Here we also get an information gap on the lifespan of an object. A recomputation of the situation of the object at time instant e is not possible since we do not know the situation at time instant e and thus cannot compute the situation for the object in $e + 1$.

A transition graph, however, allows to check whether there exists a path in the transition graph from the situation node the object had in $s - 1$ to a node v such that the loop label δ at v is valid for the object in $e + 1$ (since the loop labels are characteristic, though not necessarily unique conditions for nodes). If there exists such a path, its length (i.e. the number of the edges) must then be less or equal to the number of time instants between s and e (inclusive) such that it is possible to "fill" the gap by further modifications completing the lifecycle. Such a path checking procedure can be incorporated into the monitoring algorithm 3.1.

Another approach to handle such information gaps, which can also be combined with a path checking procedure as above, requires a re-specification of the corresponding transition graph. Therefore extra nodes have to be introduced which correspond to *undefined situations* an object is allowed to reach in its lifespan. Different nodes for undefined situations are necessary, e.g., to distinguish different modifications of an object depending on its given attribute values. Re-entries into the "desired" lifecycle then can be specified by edges going from undefined situations to defined ones and which have certain re-entry conditions.

Such an approach, however, can lead to the fact that the transition graph and the monitoring process is not deterministic anymore since re-entry conditions from an undefined situation do not necessarily have to be disjoint. If the underlying temporal database system supports triggers one solution for such cases would be to utilize these triggers which are automatically invoked by respective checking procedures in our monitoring algorithm 3.1. Therefore, however, the underlying monitoring algorithm has to be extended. This extended functionality is subject to future research.

4 Conclusions

It is undoubted that in particular temporal integrity constraints, either speci-fied as formulae of a calculus for temporal logic or directly as transition graphs describing admissible lifecycles of objects, play an important role in temporal databases for modelling real-world applications. Based on our former work on monitoring temporal integrity constraints in non-temporal databases, we have extended the monitoring algorithm by incorporating the valid-time dimension. Thus retroactive as well as proactive modifications on objects can be checked efficiently for admissibility. The advantage of using transition graphs is that (1) by storing the situations of an object with respect to a given transition graph, (2) by utilizing the iteration-invariance of the graph and (3) by using basic op-erations of temporal databases to determine validity intervals, this monitoring can be done much more efficiently and goal-directed than performing complex temporal queries checking for constraint violations.

Based on our work for monitoring temporal integrity constraints in active databases [6] we want to extend the approach presented here to temporal active databases. The integrity checking triggers are then used to imitate the monitor within the temporal database system itself, and thus avoid an external monitor. Additionally triggers can be utilized for active corrections of constraint viola-tions, in particular for handling gaps on information as discussed at the end of Section 3. Since the proposed monitoring algorithm is very general and mainly independent of the underlying data model (if at least valid-time is supported) we also want to study our approach in different proposed temporal data models like, e.g., TSQL2 or the temporal extension of GORDAS [5].

References

[1] J. Clifford, C. Dyreson, R. T. Snodgrass, T. Isakowitz, C. S. Jensen: Now in TSQL2. Technical Report, The TSQL2 Language Design Committee, 1994.

[2] J. Chomicki: History-less Checking of Dynamic Integrity Constraints. In F. Golshani (ed.), *Eighth International Conference on Data Engineering 1992*, IEEE Computer Society Press, 1992, 557–564.

[3] R. Elmasri, I. El-Assal, V. Kouramajian: Semantics of Temporal Data in an Extented ER Model. In F. H. Lochovsky (ed.), *Entity-Relationship Approach to Database Design and Querying*, North-Holland, Amsterdam, 1990, 239–254.

[4] R. Elmasri, S. B. Navathe: *Fundamentals of Database Systems.* Ben-jamin/Cummings, Redwood City, CA, 1989.

[5] R. Elmasri, G. T. Wuu, V. Kouramajian: A Temporal Model and Query Language for EER Databases. In [23], 212–229.

[6] M. Gertz, U. W. Lipeck: Deriving Integrity Maintaining Triggers from Transition Graphs. In *Proceedings Ninth International Conference on Data Engineering*, IEEE Computer Society Press, 1993, 22–29.

[7] C. S. Jensen, R. T. Snodgrass, M. D. Soo: The TSQL2 Data Model. Technical Report, The TSQL2 Design Committee, 1994.

[8] U. W. Lipeck, H.-D. Ehrich, M. Gogolla: Specifying Admissibility of Dynamic Database Behaviour Using Temporal Logic. In A. Sernadas, J. Bubenko, A. Olive (eds.), *Theoretical and Formal Aspects of Information Systems (Proc. IFIP Work. Conf. TFAIS'85)*, North-Holland, Amsterdam, 1985, 145–157.

[9] U. W. Lipeck, D. Feng: Construction of Deterministic Transition Graphs from Dynamic Integrity Constraints. In J. v. Leeuwen (ed.), *Graph-Theoretic Concepts in Computer Science — International Workshop WG '88*, Lecture Notes in Computer Science 344, Springer-Verlag, Berlin, 1989, 166–179.

[10] U. W. Lipeck: Transformation of Dynamic Integrity Constraints into Transaction Specifications. In M. Gyssens, J. Paredaens, D. Van Gucht (eds.), *ICDT '88 — 2nd International Conference on Database Theory, Proceedings*, Lecture Notes in Computer Science 326, Springer-Verlag, Berlin, 1988, 322–337.

[11] U. W. Lipeck: *Dynamische Integrität von Datenbanken: Grundlagen der Spezifikation und Überwachung* (Dynamic Integrity of Databases: Foundations of Specification and Monitoring, in German). Informatik-Fachberichte 209, Springer-Verlag, Berlin, 1989.

[12] U. W. Lipeck: Transformation of Dynamic Integrity Constraints into Transaction Specifications. *Theoretical Computer Science 76 (1990)*, 115 – 142.

[13] U. W. Lipeck, G. Saake: Monitoring Dynamic Integrity Constraints Based on Temporal Logic. *Information Systems 12:3 (1987)*, 255–269.

[14] U. W. Lipeck, H. Zhou: Monitoring Dynamic Integrity Constraints on Finite State Sequences and Existence Intervals. In J. Göers, A. Heuer, G. Saake (eds.), *Third Workshop on Foundations of Models and Languages for Data and Objects*, Informatik-Bericht 91/3, TU Clausthal, Clausthal, 1991, 115–130.

[15] S. B. Navathe, R. Ahmed: Temporal Extensions to the Relational Model and SQL. In [23], 92–109.

[16] R. Snodgrass, I. Ahn: A Taxonomy of Time in Databases. In S. Navathe (ed.), *Proc. ACM SIGMOD Int. Conf. on Management of Data 1985, Austin*, ACM Press, New York, 1985, 236–246.

[17] R. Snodgrass, I. Ahn: Temporal Databases. *IEEE Computer 19:9 (1986)*, 35–42.

[18] R. Snodgrass, I. Ahn, G. Ariav, et al: A TSQL2 Tutorial. *SIGMOD Record 23:3 (1994)*, 27–34.

[19] G. Saake: Descriptive Specification of Database Object Behaviour. *Data & Knowledge Engineering 6:1 (1991)*, 47–73.

[20] G. Saake, U. W. Lipeck: Foundations of Temporal Integrity Monitoring. In C. e. a. Rolland (ed.), *Temporal Aspects in Information Systems (Proc. IFIP Work. Conf. TAIS'87)*, North-Holland, Amsterdam, 1988, 235–249.

[21] R. Snodgrass: An Overview of TQuel. In [23], 141–182.

[22] S. Schwiderski, G. Saake: Monitoring Temporal Permissions Using Partially Evaluated Transition Graphs. In U. W. Lipeck, B. Thalheim (eds.), *Modelling Database Dynamics , Volkse, Oct.1992*, 196–217, Workshops in Computing, Springer-Verlag, London, 1993.

[23] A. Tansel, J. Clifford, S. Gadia, S. Jajodia, A. Segev, R. Snodgrass (eds.): *Temporal Databases: Theory, Design, and Implementation.* Database Systems and Applications Series, Benjamin/Cummings, Redwood City, CA, 1993.

[24] G. Wuu, U. Dayal: A Uniform Model for Temporal Object-Oriented Databases In *Proceedings Eigth International Conference on Data Engineering*, IEEE Computer Society Press, 1992, 584-593.

Databases and Temporal Constraints: Semantics and Complexity

Manolis Koubarakis

Dept. of Computation, UMIST

P.O. Box 88

Manchester M60 1 QD

U.K.

manolis@sna.co.umist.ac.uk

Abstract

We continue the development of a theory of constraint databases with indefinite information which we originated in our previous research. Initially we review the schemes of $\mathcal{L}$-constraint databases and indefinite $\mathcal{L}$-constraint databases where $\mathcal{L}$, the parameter, is a first-order constraint language. Then we consider several instances of these schemes where $\mathcal{L}$ is a language for expressing information about atomic data values and time. We collectively refer to these models as temporal constraint databases and indefinite temporal constraint databases. We give a detailed characterization of the computational complexity of query answering for various classes of temporal constraint databases and queries. Our results results are theoretical but can be summarized as follows for a wider database audience: The worst-case complexity of query evaluation does not change when we move from queries in relational calculus over relational databases, to queries in relational calculus with temporal constraints over temporal constraint databases. This fact remains true even if we consider indefinite relational databases vs. indefinite temporal constraint databases.

1 Introduction

In this paper we continue the development of the theory of *indefinite constraint databases* which we originated in our previous research [21, 25, 24, 23, 22]. The starting point of our study is the model of constraint databases proposed in [19]. This model is useful for the representation of *unrestricted* (i.e., finite or infinite) *definite* information. However, indefinite information is also important in many applications e.g., planning and scheduling, medical expert systems, geographical information systems and natural language processing systems. Motivated by these practical considerations, we have developed the model of *indefinite constraint databases* which allows the representation of *definite, indefinite, finite* and *infinite* information in a single unifying framework [21, 25]. More precisely, we have developed the scheme of *indefinite $\mathcal{L}$-constraint databases* where $\mathcal{L}$, the parameter, is a first-order *constraint language*. This parameterized model extends the scheme of [19] to include indefinite information in the style of [13, 11]. We have also defined declarative and procedural query languages for indefinite $\mathcal{L}$-constraint databases: the *modal relational calculus with*

Complexity type	Query Type	
	RC+TC	$\exists_k$ RC+TC
Data	LOGSPACE	—
Combined	PSPACE	Σ_k^p

Complexity type	Query Type		
	$\Diamond$+RC+TC	$\Box$+RC+TC	$\exists_k$ $\Box$+RC+TC
Data complexity	NP	co-NP	—
Combined complexity	PSPACE	PSPACE	Π_{k+1}^p

Figure 1: Complexity of query evalution

$\mathcal{L}$-constraints and the *modal $\mathcal{L}$-constraint algebra*. Our analysis has been carried out in an abstract setting and subsumes previous work on specific classes of constraints [19, 17, 22, 24, 20, 29].

Initially we review the schemes of $\mathcal{L}$-constraint databases and indefinite $\mathcal{L}$-constraint databases as defined in [21, 25]. Then we consider several instances of these schemes where $\mathcal{L}$ is a language for expressing information about *atomic data values and time*. We collectively refer to these models as temporal constraint databases and indefinite temporal constraint databases. We give a detailed characterization of the computational complexity of query answering for various classes of temporal constraint databases and queries. Our results are summarized in Figure 1. The first table refers to definite temporal constraint databases while the second refers to indefinite ones.

The notation RC+TC stands for relational calculus with temporal constraints while $\exists_k$ QL stands for queries in language QL which are in prenex normal form with k alternations of quantifiers beginning with an existential one. $\Diamond$+RC+TC (resp. $\Box$+RC+TC) stands for "possibility" (resp. "certainty") queries in modal relational calculus with temporal constraints. Finally, an entry $\mathcal{C}$, where $\mathcal{C}$ is a complexity class, means that the corresponding query answering problem is complete for class $\mathcal{C}$.

Although our results are theoretical, they demonstrate the following important fact which must be of interest to database theoreticians and practitioners alike. *The worst-case complexity of query evaluation does not change when we move from queries in relational calculus over relational databases, to queries in relational calculus with temporal constraints over temporal constraint databases. This fact remains true even if we consider indefinite relational databases vs. indefinite temporal constraint databases.* This analysis complements the results of [32, 6] and extends the results of [19, 35]. It also answers the questions posed in [5] with respect to the model of [22].

The paper is organized as follows. The next section defines the abstract notions of constraints, constraint languages and constraint databases, and their concrete manifestations as temporal constraints, temporal constraint languages and temporal constraint databases. In Section 3 we review the constraint query languages proposed in [21, 25]. In Section 4 we analyze the computational complexity of query evaluation in temporal constraint databases (with or without indefinite information). Finally, in Section 5 we present our conclusions and discuss future research. The proofs of all results are omitted and can be found in [21].

2 Constraints and Databases

In this section we review the basic concepts of [21, 24, 25]. In Subsection 2.1, we explain what we mean by constraint languages in general, and then define the temporal constraint languages that we will deal with in the rest of this paper. In Subsection 2.2 we show how to integrate temporal constraints in the relational model of data.

2.1 Constraint Languages

In this paper we consider many-sorted first-order languages, structures and theories as defined in [9]. Every many-sorted first-order language $\mathcal{L}$ will be interpreted over a *fixed* structure, called the *intended structure*, which will usually be denoted by $\mathbf{M}_{\mathcal{L}}$. If $\mathbf{M}$ is a structure then $Th(\mathbf{M})$ will denote the theory of $\mathbf{M}$ i.e., the set of sentences which are true in $\mathbf{M}$. For every language $\mathcal{L}$, we will distinguish a class of quantifier free formulas called $\mathcal{L}$-*constraints*. The atomic formulas of $\mathcal{L}$ will be included in the class of $\mathcal{L}$-constraints. There will also be two distinguished $\mathcal{L}$-constraints *true* and *false* with obvious semantics. Similar assumptions have been made in [28] in the contex of the CLP scheme. A set of $\mathcal{L}$-constraints will be the algebraic counterpart of the logical conjunction of its members. Thus we will freely mix the terms "set of $\mathcal{L}$-constraints" and "conjunction of $\mathcal{L}$-constraints". We will assume that the reader is familiar with the notions of *solution, consistency* and *equivalence* of sets of constraints [28].

The following are some examples of a constraint language which will be our focus in this paper:

1. *ECL* (*Equality Constraint Language*): this language allows us to make statements about *atomic data values* [19]. ECL has predicate symbols $=$, $\neq$ and an infinite number of constants (the atomic data values). The intended structure for this language interprets $=$ as equality, $\neq$ as non-equality and constants as "themselves". An *ECL-constraint* is an ECL formula of the form $x_1 = x_2$ or $x_1 \neq x_2$ where x_1, x_2 are variables or constants. ECL has been used by [19] for the development of an extended relational model based on ECL-constraints.

2. *dePCL* (*dense Point Constraint Language*): this language allows us to make stamements about points in dense time. dePCL is a first-order language with equality and the following set of non-logical symbols: the set of rational numerals, function symbol $-$ of arity 2 and predicate symbol $<$ of arity 2. The *terms* and *atomic formulas* of dePCL are defined as follows. Constants and variables are terms. If t_1 and t_2 are variables or constants then $t_1 - t_2$ is a term. An *atomic formula* of dePCL is a formula of the form $t \sim c$ or $c \sim t$ where $\sim$ is $<$ or $=$ and t is a term.

   The intended structure for dePCL is $\mathbf{Q}$. $\mathbf{Q}$ interprets each rational numeral by its corresponding rational number, function symbol $-$ by the subtraction operation over the rationals and $<$ by the relation "less than". The theory $Th(\mathbf{Q})$ is a subtheory of real addition with order [30].

A *dePCL-constraint* is a dePCL formula of the form $t \sim c$ where t is a term, c is a constant and $\sim$ is $=$, $<$, $>$, $\leq$ or $\geq$. For example, the formulas $p_1 < p_2$, $p_3 - p_4 \geq 15$, $p_3 = 5/4$ are dePCL-constraints.

3. *diPCL* (*discrete Point Constraint Language*): this language allows us to make stamements about points in discrete time. It is defined exactly as dePCL except that the constants of diPCL are the *integer* numerals. The intended structure for diPCL is $\mathbf{Z}$. $\mathbf{Z}$ interprets each integer numeral by its corresponding integer number, and symbols $-$ and $<$ in the obvious way. The theory $Th(\mathbf{Z})$ is a subtheory of integer addition with order (Presburger arithmetic) [30]. *diPCL-constraints* are defined similarly to *dePCL-constraints*.

4. *diTCL* (*discrete Temporal Constraint Language*): this language is a 2-sorted extension of diPCL which allows us to make stamements about *points* and *intervals* (i.e., pairs of points) in discrete time. The sorts of diTCL are $\mathcal{Z}$ (for points or integers) and $\mathcal{I}_{\mathcal{Z}}$ (for integer intervals). The non-logical symbols of diTCL include a countably infinite set of constant symbols of sort $\mathcal{Z}$ (the point or integer constants), function symbols L and R of sort $(\mathcal{I}_{\mathcal{Z}}, \mathcal{Z})$, function symbol $-$ of sort $(\mathcal{Z}, \mathcal{Z}, \mathcal{Z})$ and predicate symbol $<$ of sort $(\mathcal{Z}, \mathcal{Z})$. The intended structure for diTCL is $\mathbf{ZI}_{\mathbf{Z}}$ and is defined in the obvious way. It is important to note that relations like *before, after, during* etc. [2] have not been introduced as primitives since they can be defined in this language.

A *diTCL-constraint* is a diTCL formula of the form $t \sim c$ or $t_1 - t_2 \sim c$ where (i) c is a constant, (ii) $\sim$ is $=$, $<$, $>$, $\leq$ or $\geq$ and (iii) t, t_1, t_2 are point variables or terms of the form i_L or i_R where i is an interval variable. For example, the formulas $p < 12$, $i_L < p$, $i_R - i_L \geq 15$ are diTCL-constraints.

5. *deTCL* (*dense Temporal Constraint Language*): this language is a 2-sorted extension of dePCL. The definitions are similar with the ones for diTCL.

6. ECL$+\mathcal{L}$ (the union of ECL and $\mathcal{L}$) where $\mathcal{L}$ is diPCL, dePCL, diTCL or deTCL. These languages are the most important ones because they enable us to express information about atomic data values (via ECL) and time (via $\mathcal{L}$). This will be demonstrated in the examples of the next section.

For every $\mathcal{L}$, the language ECL$+\mathcal{L}$ is formally defined in the obvious way. For example, the sorts of ECL$+$dePCL are $\mathcal{D}$ (for the infinite set of constants of ECL) and $\mathcal{Q}$ (for the rational numerals of dePCL). The symbols of ECL$+$dePCL are interpreted by the many-sorted structure which is the union of the intended structures for ECL and dePCL.

Let us now define the concept of *variable elimination*.[1]

---

[1]Notation: The vector of symbols $(o_1, \ldots, o_n)$ will be denoted by $\bar{o}$. The natural number n will be called the *size* of $\bar{o}$ and will be denoted by $|\bar{o}|$. This notation will be used for vectors

Definition 2.1 Let $\mathcal{L}$ be a many-sorted first-order language. The class of $\mathcal{L}$-constraints *admits variable elimination* iff for every boolean combination ϕ of $\mathcal{L}$-constraints in variables $\overline{x}$, and every vector of variables $\overline{z} \subseteq \overline{x}$, there exists a disjunction ϕ' of conjunctions of $\mathcal{L}$-constraints in variables $\overline{x} \setminus \overline{z}$ such that

1. If $\overline{x}^0$ is a solution of ϕ then $\overline{x}^0 \setminus \overline{z}^0$ is a solution of ϕ'.

2. If $\overline{x}^0 \setminus \overline{z}^0$ is a solution of ϕ' then this solution can be extended to a solution $\overline{x}^0$ of ϕ.

The following definition will be useful in the forthcoming sections.

Definition 2.2 Let $\mathcal{L}$ be a many-sorted first-order language. The class of $\mathcal{L}$-constraints is *weakly closed under negation* if the negation of every $\mathcal{L}$-constraint is equivalent to a disjunction of $\mathcal{L}$-constraints.

In the rest of this paper we will only be interested in constraints which admit variable elimination and are weakly closed under negation. Many interesting classes of constraints fall under this category. The following proposition shows that this is also the case for the constraint classes defined in this section [21].

Proposition 2.1 *For any language $\mathcal{L}$ presented in this section, the class of $\mathcal{L}$-constraints admits variable elimination and is weakly closed under negation.*

2.2 Relational Databases with Constraints

In this section we present a family of models which integrate temporal constraints and relational databases and achieve the representation of *definite, indefinite, finite* and *infinite* temporal information in a single unified framework. Initially, we define $\mathcal{L}$-constraint databases and indefinite $\mathcal{L}$-constraint databases in the abstract (i.e., for any given constraint language $\mathcal{L}$ which satisfies some conditions) [25]. Then we define temporal constraint databases and indefinite temporal constraint databases as instances of these abstract schemes.

Let $\mathcal{L}$ be a many-sorted language and $\mathbf{M}_{\mathcal{L}}$ be the *intended $\mathcal{L}$-structure*. Let us assume that the class of $\mathcal{L}$-constraints admits variable elimination and is weakly closed under negation. For each sort $s \in sorts(\mathcal{L})$, let U_s be a countably infinite set of *attributes* of sort s. The set of all attributes, denoted by $\mathcal{U}$, is $\bigcup_{s \in sorts(\mathcal{L})} U_s$. The sort of attribute A will be denoted by $sort(A)$. With each $A \in \mathcal{U}$ we associate a set of values $dom(A) = dom(s, \mathbf{M}_{\mathcal{L}})$ called the *domain* of A.[2] A *relation scheme* R is a finite subset of $\mathcal{U}$.

We will first define $\mathbf{M}_{\mathcal{L}}$-relations which are unrestricted (i.e., finite or infinite) standard relations. $\mathbf{M}_{\mathcal{L}}$-relations are a theoretical device for giving semantics to indefinite $\mathcal{L}$-constraint relations.

---

of variables but also for vectors of domain elements. Variables will be denoted by x, y, z, t etc. and vectors of variables by $\overline{x}, \overline{y}, \overline{z}, \overline{t}$ etc. If $\overline{x}$ and $\overline{y}$ are vectors of variables then $\overline{x} \setminus \overline{y}$ will denote the vector obtained from $\overline{x}$ by deleting the variables in $\overline{y}$. If $\overline{x}$ is a vector of variables then $\overline{x}^0$ will be a vector of constants of the same size.

[2]If s is a sort and $\mathbf{M}$ is a structure then $dom(s, \mathbf{M})$ denotes the domain of s in structure $\mathbf{M}$.

Definition 2.3 Let R be a relation scheme. An $\mathbf{M}_{\mathcal{L}}$-*relational tuple* t over scheme R is a mapping from R to $\bigcup_{s \in sorts(\mathcal{L})} dom(s, \mathbf{M}_{\mathcal{L}})$ such that $t(A) \in dom(sort(A), \mathbf{M}_{\mathcal{L}})$. An $\mathbf{M}_{\mathcal{L}}$-*relation* r over scheme R is an *unrestricted* set of $\mathbf{M}_{\mathcal{L}}$-relational tuples over R.

For every $s \in sorts(\mathcal{L})$, we now assume the existence of two disjoint countably infinite sets of *variables*: the set of *u-variables* $UVAR_{\mathcal{L}}^s$ and the set of *e-variables* $EVAR_{\mathcal{L}}^s$. Let $UVAR_{\mathcal{L}}$ and $EVAR_{\mathcal{L}}$ denote $\bigcup_{s \in sorts(\mathcal{L})} UVAR_{\mathcal{L}}^s$ and $\bigcup_{s \in sorts(\mathcal{L})} EVAR_{\mathcal{L}}^s$ respectively. The intersection of the sets $UVAR_{\mathcal{L}}$ and $EVAR_{\mathcal{L}}$ with the domains of attributes is empty.

Notation 2.1 U-variables will be denoted by letters of the English alphabet, usually x, y, z, t, possibly subscripted. E-variables will be denoted by letters of the Greek alphabet, usually $\omega, \lambda, \zeta, \nu$, possibly subscripted.

Definition 2.4 Let R be a relation scheme. An *indefinite $\mathcal{L}$-constraint tuple* t over scheme R is a mapping from $R \cup \{CON\}$ to $UVAR_{\mathcal{L}} \cup WFF(\mathcal{L})$ such that (i) $t(A) \in UVAR_{\mathcal{L}}^{sort(A)}$ for each $A \in R$, (ii) $t(A_i)$ is different than $t(A_j)$ for all distinct A_i, $A_j \in R$, (iii) $t(CON)$ is a conjunction of $\mathcal{L}$-constraints and (iv) the free variables of $t(CON)$ are included in $\{t(A) : A \in R\} \cup EVAR_{\mathcal{L}}$. $t(CON)$ is called the *local condition* of the tuple t while $t(R)$ is called the *proper part* of t.

Definition 2.5 Let R be a relation scheme. An *indefinite $\mathcal{L}$-constraint relation* over scheme R is a *finite* set of indefinite $\mathcal{L}$-constraint tuples over R. Each indefinite $\mathcal{L}$-constraint relation r is associated with a boolean combination of $\mathcal{L}$-constraints $G(r)$, called the *global condition* of r.

Similarly we can define database schemes, $\mathbf{M}_{\mathcal{L}}$-relational databases and indefinite $\mathcal{L}$-constraint databases [21]. Database schemes and databases will usually be denoted by $\widetilde{R}$ and $\widetilde{r}$ respectively.

The above definitions extend the model of [19] by introducing *e-variables* which have the semantics of marked nulls of [13]. As in [11], the possible values of the e-variables can be constrained by a *global condition*.

In the remainder of this paper we will be mostly interested in $\mathcal{L}$-constraint databases and indefinite $\mathcal{L}$-constraint databases when $\mathcal{L}$ is any of the constraint languages defined in Section 2.1. Collectively, we will refer to these models as *temporal constraint databases* and *indefinite temporal constraint databases*.

Example 2.1 The indefinite temporal constraint relation BOOKED in Figure 2 gives the times that rooms are booked.[3] The first tuple says that room WP212 is booked from 1:00 to 7:00. For room WP219 the information is indefinite: it is booked from 1:00 until some time between 5:00 and 8:00. This indefinite information is captured by the *e-variable* ω and its global condition $5 \leq \omega \leq 8$. *E-variables* can be understood as being existentially quantified and their scope is the entire database. They represent values that exist but are not known precisely [13, 11]. All we know about these values is captured by the global condition. *U-variables* (e.g., x_1, x_2, t_1, t_2) can be understood as being universally quantified and their scope is the tuple in which they appear [19].

---

[3]More precisely, BOOKED is an indefinite ECL+dePCL-constraint relation.

BOOKED

Room	Time	CON
x_1	t_1	$x_1 = WP212,\ 1 \leq t_1 < 7$
x_2	t_2	$x_2 = WP219,\ 1 \leq t_2 < \omega$

$$G(BOOKED) :\ 5 \leq \omega \leq 8$$

Figure 2: An indefinite temporal constraint relation

2.3 Semantics

Let us first define two special kinds of valuations. An *e-valuation* in $\mathbf{M}_{\mathcal{L}}$ is a valuation whose domain is restricted to the set $EVAR_{\mathcal{L}}$. Similarly, a *u-valuation* in $\mathbf{M}_{\mathcal{L}}$ is a valuation whose domain is restricted to the set $UVAR_{\mathcal{L}}$. The symbols $Val^e_{\mathbf{M}_{\mathcal{L}}}$ and $Val^u_{\mathbf{M}_{\mathcal{L}}}$ will denote the set of e-valuations and u-valuations in $\mathbf{M}_{\mathcal{L}}$ respectively. The result of applying an e-valuation v to an indefinite $\mathcal{L}$-constraint relation r over R will be denoted by $v(r)$. $v(r)$ is an $\mathcal{L}$-constraint relation over R obtained from r by substituting each e-variable ω of r by the constant symbol whose denotation in structure $\mathbf{M}_{\mathcal{L}}$ is $v(\omega)$. The result of applying a u-valuation of $\mathbf{M}_{\mathcal{L}}$ to the proper part of a tuple can be defined as follows. If t is an $\mathcal{L}$-constraint tuple on scheme R and u is a u-valuation in $\mathbf{M}_{\mathcal{L}}$ then $u(t)$ is an $\mathbf{M}_{\mathcal{L}}$-tuple over R such that for each $A \in R$, $u(t)(A) = u(t(A))$.

The semantics of an $\mathcal{L}$-constraint relation is given by the function *points* [19]. *points* takes as argument an $\mathcal{L}$-constraint relation r over R and returns the $\mathbf{M}_{\mathcal{L}}$-relation over R which is finitely represented by r:

$$points(r) = \{u(t) :\ t \in r,\ u \in Val^u_{\mathbf{M}_{\mathcal{L}}}\ \text{and}\ \mathbf{M}_{\mathcal{L}} \models t(CON)[u]\}.$$

The *semantics* of an indefinite $\mathcal{L}$-constraint relation r over scheme R is defined to be the following set of $\mathbf{M}_{\mathcal{L}}$-relations:

$$sem(r) = \{points(v(r)) :\ \text{there exists}\ v \in Val^e_{\mathbf{M}_{\mathcal{L}}}\ \text{s.t.}\ \mathbf{M}_{\mathcal{L}} \models G(r)[v]\}.$$

The function *rep* will also be useful in the rest of this paper. If r is an indefinite $\mathcal{L}$-constraint relation over scheme R then *rep* gives the set of $\mathcal{L}$-constraint relations represented by r:

$$rep(r) = \{v(r) :\ \text{there exists}\ v \in Val^e_{\mathbf{M}_{\mathcal{L}}}\ \text{s.t.}\ \mathbf{M}_{\mathcal{L}} \models G(r)[v]\}$$

The functions *points*, *sem* and *rep* can be extended to databases in the obvious way. The above definitions imply that indefinite $\mathcal{L}$-constraint relations are interpreted in a *closed-world* fashion. They are assumed to represent all facts relevant to an application domain. However the exact value of any attribute of these facts may not be known precisely.

3 Query Languages for Relational Databases with Constraints

[19] proposed *relational calculus with $\mathcal{L}$-constraints* as a declarative query language for $\mathcal{L}$-constraint databases. [21, 25] proposed *modal relational calculus with $\mathcal{L}$-constraints* as a declarative query language for indefinite $\mathcal{L}$-constraint databases. Similar modal query languages have been investigated in [27, 26, 31]. Let us review some definitions from [25].

Definition 3.1 Let $\widetilde{R}$ be a database scheme and $R(C_1, \ldots, C_m)$ be a relation scheme. An expression over $\widetilde{R}$ in *modal relational calculus with $\mathcal{L}$-constraints* is $\{R(C_1, \ldots, C_m), x_1/s_1, \ldots, x_m/s_m \;:\; OP\ \phi(x_1, \ldots, x_m)\}$ where $s_i \in sorts(\mathcal{L})$ is the sort of C_i, OP is an *optional* modal operator $\Diamond$ or $\Box$, ϕ is a well-formed formula of relational calculus with $\mathcal{L}$-constraints and $x_1, \ldots, x_m$ are the only free variables of ϕ. If an expression does not contain a modal operator then it will be called *pure*, otherwise it will be called *modal*.

We will now define the *value* of expressions in modal relational calculus.

Definition 3.2 Let f be the pure expression

$$\{R(C_1, \ldots, C_m), x_1/s_1, \ldots, x_m/s_m \;:\; \phi(x_1, \ldots, x_m)\}$$

over $\widetilde{R}$ in modal relational calculus with $\mathcal{L}$-constraints. If $\widetilde{r}$ is an indefinite $\mathcal{L}$-constraint database over $\widetilde{R}$ then the *value* of f on the set of $\mathbf{M}_{\mathcal{L}}$-relational databases $sem(\widetilde{r})$, whose finite representation is $\widetilde{r}$, is the following set of $\mathbf{M}_{\mathcal{L}}$-relations:

$$f(sem(\widetilde{r})) = \{\ \{(a_1, \ldots, a_m) \in dom(s_1) \times \cdots \times dom(s_m) : (\mathbf{M}_{\mathcal{L}}, Dom, \widetilde{r}') \models \phi(a_1, \ldots, a_m)\} \;:\; \widetilde{r}' \in sem(\widetilde{r})\}$$

The question left open by the above definition is whether we can guarantee *closure* as required by the constraint query language principles laid out in [19]. In other words, given a pure expression f of modal relational calculus with $\mathcal{L}$-constraints, and an indefinite $\mathcal{L}$-constraint database $\widetilde{r}$, is it possible to find an indefinite $\mathcal{L}$-constraint relation which finitely represents $f(sem(\widetilde{r}))$? As we explain in Section 4 (and in more detail in [21, 25]), the answer to this question is in the affirmative.

Example 3.1 The query "Find all rooms that are booked at 6:00" over the database of Example 2.1 can be expressed as

$$\{BOOKED\_AT\_6(Room), x/\mathcal{D} : BOOKED(x, 6)\}.$$

The answer to this query is given by the following relation:

BOOKED_AT_6

Room	CON
x_1	$x_1 = WP212$
x_2	$x_2 = WP219,\ \omega > 6$

This answer is *conditional*. Room WP212 is booked on time 6. However, room WP219 is booked on time 6 *only under the condition* that ω is greater than 6. In Section 4 we will explain how to evaluate calculus queries and compute a finite representation of the answer.

Definition 3.3 Let f be the modal expression

$$\{R(C_1, \ldots, C_m), x_1/s_1, \ldots, x_m/s_m \; : \; \Box \, \phi(x_1, \ldots, x_m)\}$$

over $\widetilde{R}$ in modal relational calculus with $\mathcal{L}$-constraints. If $\widetilde{r}$ is an indefinite $\mathcal{L}$-constraint database over $\widetilde{R}$ then the *value* of f on the set of $\mathbf{M}_\mathcal{L}$-relational databases $sem(\widetilde{r})$, whose finite representation is $\widetilde{r}$, is the following *singleton* set of $\mathbf{M}_\mathcal{L}$-relations:

$$f(sem(\widetilde{r})) = \{ \; \{(a_1, \ldots, a_m) \in dom(s_1) \times \cdots \times dom(s_m) : \text{for every}$$
$$\mathbf{M}_\mathcal{L}\text{-relational database } \widetilde{r}' \in sem(\widetilde{r})$$
$$(\mathbf{M}_\mathcal{L}, Dom, \widetilde{r}') \models \phi(a_1, \ldots, a_m)\} \; \}$$

The value of a $\Diamond$-expression is defined in the same way but now the quantification over $\mathbf{M}_\mathcal{L}$-relational databases in $sem(\widetilde{r})$ is existential. Section 4 demonstrates that expressions of modal relational calculus with $\mathcal{L}$-constraints can also be evaluated in closed form. In summary, for every expression f (pure or modal) in modal relational calculus with $\mathcal{L}$-constraints and indefinite $\mathcal{L}$-constraint database $\widetilde{r}$, it is possible to find an indefinite $\mathcal{L}$-constraint relation which finitely represents $f(\widetilde{r})$.

Example 3.2 The query "Find all rooms that are possibly booked at 6:00" over the database of Example 2.1 can be expressed as

$$\{POSS\_BOOKED\_AT\_6(Room), x/\mathcal{D} : \Diamond BOOKED(x, 6)\}.$$

If this query is evaluated as explained in Section 4, the answer will be the following relation:

POSS_BOOKED_AT_6

Room	CON
x_1	$x_1 = WP212$
x_2	$x_2 = WP219$

The above answer is *unconditional*. It is possible that both rooms WP212 and WP219 are booked on time 6.

The next lemma demonstrates an intuitive property of modal relational calculus with $\mathcal{L}$-constraints. If $\mathcal{S}$ is a set of sets then $\bigcap \mathcal{S}$ (resp. $\bigcup \mathcal{S}$) denotes the set $\{\cap_{s \in \mathcal{S}} s\}$ (resp. $\{\cup_{s \in \mathcal{S}} s\}$).

Lemma 3.1 Let f be a $\Box$-expression (resp. $\Diamond$-expression) over $\widetilde{R}$ in modal relational calculus with $\mathcal{L}$-constraints. Let f' be the pure expression which corresponds to f. Then for all indefinite $\mathcal{L}$-constraint databases $\widetilde{r}$ over $\widetilde{R}$, $f(sem(\widetilde{r})) = \bigcap f'(sem(\widetilde{r}))$ (resp. $f(sem(\widetilde{r})) = \bigcup f'(sem(\widetilde{r}))$).

Let us now sketch very briefly three procedural query languages, one for each of the models discussed in Section 2.2: the $\mathbf{M}_{\mathcal{L}}$-*relational algebra*, the $\mathcal{L}$-*constraint algebra* and the *modal $\mathcal{L}$-constraint algebra*. The $\mathbf{M}_{\mathcal{L}}$-relational algebra is a procedural query language for $\mathbf{M}_{\mathcal{L}}$-relational databases. It is interesting only from a theoretical point of view because $\mathbf{M}_{\mathcal{L}}$-relations are unrestricted. The operations of $\mathbf{M}_{\mathcal{L}}$-relational algebra can be defined verbatim as in the case of finite relations [18].

The operations of the $\mathcal{L}$-constraint algebra are extensions of similar operations of standard relational algebra [18]. The $\mathcal{L}$-constraint algebra has not been presented in [19] where the model of $\mathcal{L}$-constraint databases was originally defined. However its definition is straightforward and can be found in [21].

The operations of the *modal $\mathcal{L}$-constraint algebra* take as input one (or two) indefinite $\mathcal{L}$-constraint relations associated with a common global condition and return an indefinite $\mathcal{L}$-constraint relation associated with the *same* global condition. The modal $\mathcal{L}$-constraint algebra contains an operation for every $\mathcal{L}$-constraint algebra operation. The definitions of these operations were originally given in [22] for the special case of indefinite dePCL-constraint relations.[4] These operations treat e-variables as uninterpreted parameters thus they are defined exactly as the $\mathcal{L}$-constraint algebra operations. Similar operations were defined in [13, 11] for the special case of conditional tables.

The modal algebra also includes two additional operations $POSS$ and $CERT$, which take a more active stand towards e-variables. Given an indefinite $\mathcal{L}$-constraint relation r, the expression $POSS(r)$ evaluates to an $\mathcal{L}$-constraint relation which finitely represents the set of all tuples contained in *any* relation of $sem(r)$. The expression $CERT(r)$ evaluates to an $\mathcal{L}$-constraint relation which finitely represents the set of all tuples contained in *every* relation of $sem(r)$.

Possibility. Let r be an indefinite $\mathcal{L}$-constraint relation on scheme R. Then $POSS(r)$ is an *$\mathcal{L}$-constraint relation* defined as follows:

1. $sch(POSS(r)) = sch(r)$

2. $POSS(r) = \{poss(t) : t \in r\}$.

For each tuple t on scheme R, $poss(t)$ is a tuple on scheme R such that $poss(t)(R) = t(R)$ and $poss(t)(CON) = \psi$ where ψ is obtained by eliminating all e-variables from the boolean combination of $\mathcal{L}$-constraints $G(r) \wedge t(CON)$. The expression $poss(t)(CON)$ is well-defined since the class of $\mathcal{L}$-constraints admits variable elimination.

Certainty. Let r be an indefinite $\mathcal{L}$-constraint relation on scheme R. Then $CERT(r)$ is an $\mathcal{L}$-constraint relation defined as follows:

1. $sch(CERT(r)) = sch(r)$

2. $CERT(r) = \{cert(t) : t \in r^{\downarrow}\}^{\uparrow}$.

For each tuple t on scheme R, $cert(t)$ is a tuple on scheme R such that $cert(t)(R) = t(R)$ and $cert(t)(CON) = \neg\psi$ where ψ is obtained by eliminating all e-variables from the boolean combination of $\mathcal{L}$-constraints $G(r) \wedge \neg t(CON)$. The expression $cert(t)(CON)$ is well-defined since the class of $\mathcal{L}$-constraints admits variable elimination.

---

[4] [22] uses the term *temporal tables* for indefinite dePCL-constraint relations.

The operation $r^{\downarrow}$ has the effect of *denormalizing* $\mathcal{L}$-constraint relation r. This is achieved by collecting all tuples $\{t_1, \ldots, t_{|r|}\}$ of r into a single tuple t' on scheme R such that $t'(R) = (x_1, \ldots, x_{|R|})$ and $t'(CON) = t'_1(CON) \vee \cdots \vee t'_{|r|}(CON)$. In the new tuple t' u-variables have been standardized apart: $x_1, \ldots, x_{|R|}$ are brand new u-variables, and for $1 \leq i \leq |r|$, $t'_i(CON)$ is the same as $t_i(CON)$ except that $t(X)$ has been substituted by $t'(X)$ for each $X \in R$.

The operation $r^{\uparrow}$ has the effect of *normalizing* the local conditions of a relation r in order to obtain a true $\mathcal{L}$-constraint relation. This is done by the following three steps:

- Application of De Morgan's laws to transform the negated parts of each local condition of r into a disjunction whose disjuncts are $\mathcal{L}$-constraints. This operation is well-defined since the class of $\mathcal{L}$-constraints is weakly closed under negation.

- Application of the law of associativity of conjunction with respect to disjunction to transform each local condition of r into a disjunction of conjunctions of $\mathcal{L}$-constraints.

- Splitting of disjuncts into different tuples.

Let us now define modal $\mathcal{L}$-constraint algebra expressions.

Definition 3.4 A *pure expression* over scheme $\widetilde{R}$ in modal $\mathcal{L}$-constraint algebra is any well-formed expression built from constant $\mathcal{L}$-constraint relations, relation schemes from $\widetilde{R}$ and the above operators excluding $POSS$ and $CERT$. A *modal $\mathcal{L}$-constraint algebra expression* is a pure expression, or an expression of the form $CERT(g)$ or $POSS(g)$ where g is a pure expression. Expressions of the form $CERT(g)$ or $POSS(g)$ are called *CERT-expressions* or *POSS-expressions* respectively.

Modal $\mathcal{L}$-constraint algebra expressions define functions from indefinite $\mathcal{L}$-constraint databases to indefinite $\mathcal{L}$-constraint relations. The result of applying an expression e to an indefinite $\mathcal{L}$-constraint database $\widetilde{r}$ is defined as for the $\mathcal{L}$-constraint algebra. Let us simply stress that $G(e(\widetilde{r})) = G(\widetilde{r})$ for all indefinite $\mathcal{L}$-constraint databases $\widetilde{r}$ and expressions e over $\widetilde{R}$.

The following lemma gives an intuitive property of $POSS$ and $CERT$.

Lemma 3.2 *Let e be a pure expression over scheme $\widetilde{R}$ in modal $\mathcal{L}$-constraint algebra. Then for all indefinite $\mathcal{L}$-constraint databases $\widetilde{r}$ over $\widetilde{R}$*

$$sem(CERT(e(\widetilde{r}))) = \bigcap sem(e(\widetilde{r})) \text{ and } sem(POSS(e(\widetilde{r}))) = \bigcup sem(e(\widetilde{r})).$$

4 Query Evaluation in Databases with Temporal Constraints

In [25] we have shown that expressions of modal relational calculus with $\mathcal{L}$-constraints have equivalent expressions in modal $\mathcal{L}$-constraint algebra. Thus we can evaluate a calculus expression by evaluating an equivalent algebraic expression. As we have seen in Section 3, algebraic query evaluation can be done bottom-up and the answer is obtained in closed form. Therefore calculus expressions can also be evaluated bottom-up in closed form on indefinite $\mathcal{L}$-constraint databases. Our results (as well as the analogous theorems of [20, 24, 29]) provide a translation of calculus expressions into algebraic expressions. This translation can be the first step in optimizing the evaluation of expressions in relational calculus with $\mathcal{L}$-constraints.

Query evaluation over indefinite $\mathcal{L}$-constraint databases can also be viewed as quantifier elimination in the theory $Th(\mathbf{M}_\mathcal{L})$. This idea was originally presented in [19] in the less general scheme of $\mathcal{L}$-constraint databases. Quantifier elimination is always possible in our framework since $Th(\mathbf{M}_\mathcal{L})$ admits quantifier elimination. The following theorem is from [19].[5]

Theorem 4.1 Let $\widetilde{r}$ be an $\mathcal{L}$-constraint database over $\widetilde{R}$ and f be the expression $\{R(\overline{X}), \overline{x}/\overline{s} : \phi(\overline{x})\}$ over $\widetilde{R}$ in relational calculus with $\mathcal{L}$-constraints. Then $f(points(\widetilde{r})) = \{ \overline{a} : \mathbf{M}_\mathcal{L} \models \psi[\overline{x} \leftarrow \overline{a}] \}$ where ψ is the formula of $\mathcal{L}$ corresponding to ϕ and $\widetilde{r}$.

The formula of $\mathcal{L}$ corresponding to ϕ and $\widetilde{r}$ can be obtained from ϕ by substituting each occurence of a database predicate $R(\overline{x})$ by the disjunction of conjunctions of $\mathcal{L}$-constraints which is equivalent to the relation over scheme R.

Let us now consider indefinite $\mathcal{L}$-constraint databases.

Theorem 4.2 Let $\widetilde{r}$ be an indefinite $\mathcal{L}$-constraint database over $\widetilde{R}$. Let $G(\overline{\omega})$ be the global condition of $\widetilde{r}$ where $\overline{\omega}$ is a vector of e-variables of sort $\overline{s}'$. Let f be the expression $\{R(\overline{X}), \overline{x}/\overline{s} : OP \; \phi(\overline{x})\}$ over $\widetilde{R}$ in modal relational calculus with $\mathcal{L}$-constraints. If OP is $\Diamond$ then

$$f(sem(\widetilde{r})) = \{ \; \{ \; \overline{a} : \mathbf{M}_\mathcal{L} \models (\exists \overline{z}/\overline{s}')(G[\overline{z}/\overline{\omega}] \wedge \psi'(\overline{x}, \overline{z}))[\overline{x} \leftarrow \overline{a}] \; \} \; \}.$$

If OP is $\Box$ then $f(sem(\widetilde{r})) = \{ \; \{ \; \overline{a} : \mathbf{M}_\mathcal{L} \models (\forall \overline{z}/\overline{s}')(G[\overline{z}/\overline{\omega}] \supset \psi'(\overline{x}, \overline{z}))[\overline{x} \leftarrow \overline{a}] \; \} \; \}$. In the previous expressions $G[\overline{z}/\overline{\omega}]$ is the formula of $\mathcal{L}$ obtained from $G(\omega)$ by substituting $\overline{z}$ by $\overline{\omega}$, and $\psi'(\overline{x}, \overline{z})$ is the formula of $\mathcal{L}$ which is obtained from the formula corresponding to ϕ and $\widetilde{r}$ by substituting $\overline{z}$ for $\overline{\omega}$.

The theorem implies that queries in modal relational calculus with $\mathcal{L}$-constraints over $\mathcal{L}$-constraint databases can be evaluated in closed form by eliminating quantifiers from a formula of $\mathcal{L}$. The resulting formula in DNF can be turned into an indefinite $\mathcal{L}$-constraint relation which is the answer to the query f.

Example 4.1 The query "Find all rooms that are possibly booked between 4:00 and 6:00" over the database of Example 2.1 can be expressed as follows:

$$\{BOOKED\_4TO5(RN), x/\mathcal{D} : \Diamond(\exists t/\mathcal{Q})(BOOKED(x,t) \wedge 4 \leq t \leq 5)\}$$

This query can be evaluated by eliminating quantifiers from the following EQL+dePCL formula:

---

[5]Notation: We will use $\overline{x}, \overline{y}, \overline{z}, \ldots$ to represent vectors of variables of $\mathcal{L}$, $\overline{a}, \overline{b}, \overline{c}, \ldots$ to represent vectors of domain elements, $\overline{X}, \overline{Y}, \overline{Z}, \ldots$ to represent vectors of attributes of relations, $\overline{s}, \overline{s}', \ldots$ to represent vectors of sorts and $\overline{\omega}$ to represent vectors of e-variables.

$$(\exists \omega / \mathcal{Q})(5 \leq \omega \leq 8 \wedge (\exists t / \mathcal{Q})((x = WP212 \wedge 1 \leq t \wedge t \leq 7) \vee (x = WP219 \wedge 1 \leq t \wedge t \leq \omega)) \wedge 4 \leq t \wedge t \leq 6).$$

The result is $x = WP212 \vee x = WP219$.

The importance of the above results will be demonstrated immediately. Given the complexity analysis of [23], Theorems 4.1 and 4.2 enable us to analyze the computational complexity of query answering for the concrete case of temporal constraint databases (with or without indefinite information).

Let us first recall some results from [23, 21].

Theorem 4.3 *Let $\mathcal{L}$ be any of the constraint languages of Section 2.1. If ϕ is a sentence of $\mathcal{L}$ then the problem of deciding whether $\mathbf{M}_{\mathcal{L}} \models \phi$ is PSPACE-complete.[6] If ϕ is a $\exists_k$ sentence of $\mathcal{L}$ then the problem is Σ_k^p-complete. If ϕ is a formula of $\mathcal{L}$ then a quantifier-free formula equivalent to ϕ in DNF can be computed in PSPACE.*

We can now use the transformations of Theorems 4.1 and 4.2 to obtain the following results. The upper bounds in these theorems are original while the lower bounds follow easily from previous work [4, 36, 37, 1]. We assume the reader is familiar with the notions of *data* and *combined* complexity [36].

Theorem 4.4 *Let $\mathcal{L}$ be any of the constraint languages of Section 2.1. Let $\widetilde{r}$ be an $\mathcal{L}$-constraint database and f be a yes/no query in relational calculus with $\mathcal{L}$-constraints. The problem of deciding whether $f(\widetilde{r}) = $ yes has LOGSPACE data complexity and PSPACE-complete combined complexity. If f is a $\exists_k$ yes/no query then this problem has Σ_k^p-complete combined complexity.*

Proof: (sketch) For the combined complexity case the upper bounds follow from Theorems 4.1 and 4.3. For the data complexity case the LOGSPACE bounds follow from [10] or modifications of the algorithms of [23]. The lower bounds follows from [4]. ∎

The above theorem complements the results of [32, 6] and extends the results of [19]. [32, 6] have studied Datalog with integer gap-order constraints i.e., a subset of diPCL-constraints. They have shown that evaluating queries in Datalog with integer gap-order constraints can be done with PTIME data complexity [32] and EXPTIME combined complexity [6]. [19] have studied $\mathcal{L}$-constraint databases where $\mathcal{L}$ is the language of rational order with constants i.e., a sublanguage of dePCL. They have shown that relational calculus queries with rational order constraints can be evaluated with LOGSPACE data complexity. Grumbach, Su and Tollu have recently improved the LOGSPACE data complexity bound of the above theorem when $\mathcal{L} = diPCL$ [12]. In this case, it follows from the main theorem of [12] that query evaluation can be done in AC^0 (the class of functions computable in constant time with a polynomial amount of hardware [16]).

Theorem 4.5 *Let $\mathcal{L}$ be any of the constraint languages of Section 2.1. Let $\widetilde{r}$ be an indefinite $\mathcal{L}$-constraint database and f be a yes/no $\Diamond$-query in modal relational calculus with $\mathcal{L}$-constraints. The problem of deciding whether $f(\widetilde{r}) = $ yes is NP-complete for data complexity and PSPACE-complete for combined*

---

[6]More precise DSPACE upper-bounds are also given [23].

complexity. If f is a yes/no □-query then this problem has co-NP-complete data complexity and and PSPACE-complete for combined complexity. If f is a $\exists_k$ yes/no □-query then the combined complexity becomes Π^p_{k+1}-complete.

Proof: (sketch) The upper bounds follow from Theorems 4.2 and 4.3. The lower bounds follow from [4, 37, 35]. ■

The above theorem extends the upper bounds of [35] who has only considered positive existential queries over indefinite $\mathcal{L}$-constraint databases where $\mathcal{L}$ is the language of rational order (i.e., a sublanguage of dePCL) or discrete order (i.e., a sublanguage of diPCL).

5 Conclusions and Future Research

The contribution of this paper was to demonstrate that the worst-case complexity of query evaluation does not change when we move from queries in relational calculus over relational databases, to queries in relational calculus with temporal constraints over temporal constraint databases. This fact remains true even if we consider indefinite relational databases vs. indefinite temporal constraint databases.

In future research we would like to use this work as a basis to study the complexity of query evaluation in other temporal database models particularly the ones allowing indefinite information [8, 3]. Indefinite temporal information is important in many applications and has been included in TSQL2. Yet, in most cases, the presence of indefinite information makes query evaluation intractable. Therefore it is important to know what are the interesting cases where indefinite information can be handled efficiently. This knowledge can be very useful to designers of temporal query languages such as TSQL2.

We are also investigating constraint database models and query languages more expressive than the ones based on diPCL and dePCL. We are particularly interested in languages for *spatial constraint databases.* An interesting question here is whether the techniques and results of [21] carry over to these languages.

Finally we would like to have an implementation of the temporal constraint database model as soon as possible. Our complexity results suggest that an efficient implementation is indeed possible when *only definite* information is present (considering discrete or dense time). In this effort we can be guided by implementations of similar temporal reasoning systems [7], implementations of constraint logic programming languages and preliminary results on constraint query languages [15, 34, 33, 14]. Handling indefinite information will be more challenging. From the existing systems only TMM has addressed this case in some depth by considering polynomial time algorithms that are sound but incomplete.

Acknowledgements

The work presented in this paper was performed while the author was at the National Technical University of Athens and at Imperial College, London. At Imperial College this work was supported by project CHRONOS funded by DTI/EPSRC. I would like to thank Timos Sellis and Barry Richards for their support and encouragement. I am also grateful to Jan Chomicki for interesting comments and questions concerning this work.

References

[1] S. Abiteboul, P. Kanellakis, and G. Grahne. On the Representation and Querying of Sets of Possible Worlds. *Theoretical Computer Science*, 78(1):159–187, 1991.

[2] J.F. Allen. Towards a General Model of Action and Time. *Artificial Intelligence*, 23(2):123–154, July 1984.

[3] V. Brusoni, L. Console, B. Pernici, and P. Terenziani. Extending temporal relational databases to deal with imprecise and qualitative temporal information. In *Proceedings of the International Workshop On Temporal Databases*, 1995.

[4] A. Chandra and D. Harel. Structure and Complexity of Relational Queries. *Journal of Computer and System Sciences*, 25:99–128, 1982.

[5] Jan Chomicki. Temporal Databases. Unpublished notes from a tutorial presented at the 12th ACM SIGACT-SIGMOD-SIGART Symposium on Principles of Database Systems, May 1993.

[6] J. Cox and K. McAloon. Decision Procedures for Constraint Based Extensions of Datalog. In F. Benhamou and A. Colmerauer, editors, *Constraint Logic Programming: Selected Research*. MIT Press, 1993. Originally appeared as Technical Report No. 90-09, Dept. of Computer and Information Sciences, Brooklyn College of C.U.N.Y.

[7] T. Dean. Using Temporal Hierarchies to Efficiently Maintain Large Temporal Databases. *Journal of ACM*, 36(4):687–718, 1989.

[8] C. Dyreson and R. Snodgrass. Valid-time Indeterminacy. In *Proceedings of the 9th International Conference on Data Engineering*, pages 335–343, 1993.

[9] H.B. Enderton. *A Mathematical Introduction to Logic*. Academic Press, 1972.

[10] J. Ferrante and C. Rackoff. A Decision Procedure for the First Order Theory of Real Addition with Order. *SIAM Journal on Computing*, 4(1):69–76, 1975.

[11] Gosta Grahne. The Problem of Incomplete Information in Relational Databases. Technical Report Report A-1989-1, Department of Computer Science, University of Helsinki, Finland, 1989. Also published as Lecture Notes in Computer Science 554, Springer Verlag, 1991.

[12] S. Grumbach, J. Su, and C. Tollu. Linear constraint databases. In D. Leivant, editor, *Proceedings of the Logic and Computational Complexity Workshop*, Indianapolis, 1994. Springer Verlag. To appear in LNCS.

[13] T. Imielinski and W. Lipski. Incomplete Information in Relational Databases. *Journal of ACM*, 31(4):761–791, 1984.

[14] Jaffar J., A. Brodsky, and M. Maher. Towards Practical Constraint Databases. In *Proceedings of 19th International Conference on Very Large Databases (VLDB-93)*, pages 567–580, 1993.

[15] J. Jaffar, S. Michaylov, P. Stuckey, and R. Yap. The CLP($\mathcal{R}$) language and system. *ACM Transaction on Programming Languages and Systems*, 14(3):339–395, July 1992.

[16] D.S. Johnson. A Catalog of Complexity Classes. In J. van Leeuwen, editor, *Handbook of Theoretical Computer Science*, volume A, chapter 2. North-Holland, 1990.

[17] F. Kabanza, J.-M. Stevenne, and P. Wolper. Handling Infinite Temporal Data. In *Proceedings of ACM SIGACT-SIGMOD-SIGART Symposium on Principles of Database Systems*, pages 392–403, 1990.

[18] Paris Kanellakis. Elements of Relational Database Theory. In J. van Leeuwen, editor, *Handbook of Theoretical Computer Science*, volume B, chapter 17. North-Holland, 1990.

[19] Paris C. Kanellakis, Gabriel M. Kuper, and Peter Z. Revesz. Constraint Query Languages. In *Proceedings of the 9th ACM SIGACT-SIGMOD-SIGART Symposium on Principles of Database Systems*, pages 299–313, 1990. Long version to appear in Journal of Computer and System Sciences.

[20] P.C. Kanellakis and D. Goldin. Constraint Programming and Database Query Languages. In *Proceedings of Theoretical Aspects of Computer Software (TACS)*, volume 789 of *Lecture Notes in Computer Science*, pages 96–120. Springer-Verlag, April 1994.

[21] M. Koubarakis. *Foundations of Temporal Constraint Databases*. PhD thesis, Computer Science Division, Dept. of Electrical and Computer Engineering, National Technical University of Athens, February 1994. Available by anonymous ftp from host passion.doc.ic.ac.uk, file IC-Parc/Papers/M.Koubarakis/phd-thesis.ps.Z.

[22] Manolis Koubarakis. Representation and Querying in Temporal Databases: the Power of Temporal Constraints. In *Proceedings of the 9th International Conference on Data Engineering*, pages 327–334, April 1993.

[23] Manolis Koubarakis. Complexity Results for First-Order Theories of Temporal Constraints. In *Principles of Knowledge Representation and Reasoning: Proceedings of the Fourth International Conference (KR'94)*, pages 379–390. Morgan Kaufmann, San Francisco, CA, May 1994.

[24] Manolis Koubarakis. Database Models for Infinite and Indefinite Temporal Information. *Information Systems*, 19(2):141–173, March 1994.

[25] Manolis Koubarakis. Foundations of Indefinite Constraint Databases. In A. Borning, editor, *Proceedings of the 2nd International Workshop on the Principles and Practice of Constraint Programming (PPCP'94)*, volume 874 of *Lecture Notes in Computer Science*, pages 266–280. Springer Verlag, 1994.

[26] H.J. Levesque. Foundations of a Functional Approach to Knowledge Representation. *Artificial Intelligence*, 23:155–212, 1984.

[27] Witold Jr. Lipski. On Semantic Issues Connected with Incomplete Information Databases. *ACM Transcactions on Database Systems*, 4(3):262–296, September 1979.

[28] M. Maher. A Logic Programming View of CLP. In *Proceedings of the 10th International Conference on Logic Programming*, pages 737–753, 1993.

[29] J. Paredaens, J. Van den Bussche, and D. Van Gucht. Towards a theory of spatial database queries. In *Proceedings of the 13th ACM SIGACT-SIGMOD-SIGART Symposium on Principles of Database Systems*, pages 279–288, 1994.

[30] M.O. Rabin. Decidable theories. In *Handbook of Mathematical Logic*, volume 90 of *Studies in Logic and the Foundations of Mathematics*, pages 595–629. North-Holland, 1977.

[31] Ray Reiter. On Integrity Constraints. In *Proceedings of the 2nd Conference on Theoretical Aspects of Reasoning About Knowledge*, pages 97–111, Asilomar, CA, 1988.

[32] Peter Z. Revesz. A Closed Form for Datalog Queries with Integer Order. In *Proceedings of the 3rd International Conference on Database Theory*, pages 187–201, 1990. Long version to appear in Theoretical Computer Science.

[33] Divesh Srivastava. Subsumption and Indexing in Constraint Query Languages with Linear Arithmetic Constraints. In *Proceedings of the 2nd International Symposium on Artificial Intelligence and Mathematics*, Fort Lauderdale, Florida, January 1992.

[34] Divesh Srivastava and Raghu Ramakrishnan. Pushing Constraint Selections. In *Proceedings of the 11th ACM SIGACT-SIGMOD-SIGART Symposium on Principles of Database Systems*, pages 301–315, 1992.

[35] Ron van der Meyden. The Complexity of Querying Indefinite Data About Linearly Ordered Domains (Preliminary Version). In *Proceedings of the 11th ACM SIGACT-SIGMOD-SIGART Symposium on Principles of Database Systems*, pages 331–345, 1992.

[36] Moshe Vardi. The Complexity of Relational Query Languages. In *Proceedings of ACM SIGACT/SIGMOD Symposium on Principles of Database Systems*, pages 137–146, 1982.

[37] Moshe Vardi. Querying Logical Databases. *Journal of Computer and System Sciences*, 33:142–160, 1986.

III. Critical Evaluations of TSQL2

Experience Using TSQL2 in a Natural Language Interface

I. Androutsopoulos,   G.D. Ritchie

Department of Artificial Intelligence, University of Edinburgh
Scotland, U.K.

P. Thanisch

Department of Computer Science, University of Edinburgh
Scotland, U.K.

Abstract

Attempting to use TSQL2 in a natural language interface for temporal databases has focused our attention on certain points in the semantics of TSQL2 where we believe that clarifications or modifications are needed. It has also led us to some extensions to TSQL2 that seem generally useful, regardless of natural language issues.

1   Introduction

For many years, there have been interfaces to databases which allowed the user to frame queries in natural language, such as English (see [2], [4], [10] for reviews). Until recently, the databases involved have mainly been conventional "snapshot" database systems, that do not facilitate the handling of temporal information. We are attempting to build an experimental natural language interface for temporal databases, using methods similar to those already in use for natural language interfaces to non-temporal databases (see [3] for a description of our project). In particular, our architecture has an English query parsed into a syntactic structure and converted into a formal expression (in a logic-like language) encoding the relevant aspects of its meaning. This expression is then translated into TSQL2 [13], a temporal extension of SQL-92 [9]. The evaluation of the TSQL2 query against the temporal database supplies the answer to the original English query. Unfortunately, we are not aware of any available system that can evaluate TSQL2 queries. Hence, our natural language interface simply translates English questions to TSQL2 queries, without evaluating the resulting TSQL2 queries.

We have studied the evolving definitions of TSQL2 very closely. The aim of constructing a natural language interface has concentrated our scrutiny in two ways: in order to prove that the translation from our logic-like language to TSQL2 was correct, we had to think very rigorously about the semantics of TSQL2; also, because our TSQL2 statements are created dynamically by a program (instead of statically by a human user), we had to be very sure of what was and was not possible within TSQL2. It has become apparent as a result of these deliberations that the current definitions of TSQL2, particularly the informal outlines of its semantics, are still in need of some development. There are several inclarities and inconsistencies in the available TSQL2 documents, and a few points which we believe could be defined in a more appropriate way. We also devised some extensions to the current TSQL2 definition, that seem generally useful, regardless of natural language issues.

Some parts of this paper may be based on misunderstandings of the available TSQL2 definition. We note that although [13] defines the syntax of TSQL2 rigorously, the semantics of the language is often left to the intuition of the reader, or to the TSQL2 commentaries; these do not always agree with [13]. Our confusion may serve as pointers to sections in the TSQL2 documentation whose clarity could be improved.

Although we propose clarifying or modifying the TSQL2 definition, we do not question the value of TSQL2 as an extension of SQL-92. On the contrary, the built-in temporal support of TSQL2 (especially built-in temporal functions like CONTAINS, BEGIN, INTERSECT, and the PERIOD data-type, none of which is supported by SQL-92) has proven valuable in our project, and it has greatly simplified the task of formulating the translation from the logic-like language to a database query language.

This paper assumes that the reader is familiar with SQL-92. Section 2 provides an introduction to the aspects of TSQL2 on which our criticisms will be focused. Section 3 discusses the points in the definition of TSQL2 where the semantics of TSQL2 is unclear or where we think that the semantics of TSQL2 should be modified. Section 4 describes our extensions to TSQL2, and section 5 summarises.

2   TSQL2 basics

Temporal ontology

TSQL2 assumes that time in the real world is linear, and that it consists of *instants* (time-points). TSQL2 remains agnostic on whether time in the real world is continuous, dense or discrete (see [7]).

In TSQL2 an instant can only be specified with respect to a particular *granularity*. For example, at the granularity of years, one can specify that an instant falls within the granule (year) 1995. At the granularity of days, one can specify that the instant falls within the granule (day) March 2nd 1995. TSQL2 supports a variety of granularities (e.g. years, months, days, seconds), and application-specific granularities can also be defined (e.g. academic semesters; see [6]).

The TSQL2 granularities form a lattice that shows how the granularities relate to each other (e.g. that the granularity of months is finer than the granularity of years, that a year-granule contains twelve month-granules, etc.). The finest available granularity is that of *chronons*. Depending on the database application, a chronon could correspond to a day, a second, a nano-second, etc. A granule (even at the level of chronons) is much bigger than an instant, and there is at least one instant within each granule. Hence, an instant can never be specified precisely in TSQL2. One can only specify the containing granule.

A *period* is a convex set of instants. ("Convex set" of instants means that if the set contains two instants i_1 and i_2, then it also contains all the instants between i_1 and i_2.) To specify a period, it is enough to specify the period's earliest and latest instants. In TSQL2 a period can only be specified with respect to a particular granularity. One determines the granules where the earliest and the latest instants of the period are located. For example, at the granularity of years, one can specify a period by determining that the earliest instant of the period falls within the year-granule 1991, and that the latest instant of the period falls within the year-granule 1995. (According to section 2.4 of [7], both the earliest and the latest instant of a period must be specified with respect to the same granularity.) A period can be represented as a convex set of granules of some granularity. ("Convex set of granules" means that if the set contains two granules g_1 and g_2 of some granularity G, then it also contains all the granules of G between g_1 and g_2.) For example, at the granularity of years a period that starts at some instant in 1991 and ends at some instant in 1995 can be represented as the set that contains the year-granules 1991, 1992, 1993, 1994, and 1995.

In TSQL2 the term *interval* is used to denote a duration. TSQL2 intervals are expressed as numbers of granules. For example, one can specify an interval (duration) of 5 year-granules, or an interval of 2 minute-granules, etc.

Relations

Apart from the ordinary relations of the traditional relational model, which are called *snapshot relations* in TSQL2, TSQL2 provides *valid-time relations*, *transaction-time relations*, and *bitemporal relations*. Transaction-time relations and bitemporal relations are ignored in this paper, as they have not been used in our project.

Valid-time relations are further divided into *state valid-time relations* and *event valid-time relations*. (This and the following paragraphs are based on our interpretation of [12]. The distinction between state and event relations also applies to bitemporal relations.) In all valid-time relations, there is a special unnamed attribute, the *implicit attribute*, the values of which are called *time-stamps*. (The other attributes are called *explicit attributes*.) Each tuple of a valid-time relation represents a situation in the world. The tuple's time-stamp shows when the situation was/is/will be true in the world. Each time-stamp is a set of granules of some granularity. The same granularity has to be used in all the time-stamps of a valid-time relation. (Section 5.2 of [8] assumes that time-stamps are always sets of *chronons*. We do not see how this is compatible with TSQL2's multiple granularities. Instead, we follow section 3.2 of [5], and assume that each time-stamp is a set of granules, not necessarily a set of chronons.)

The exact semantics of the time-stamps of a valid-time relation depend on whether the relation is a state or an event one. Let us assume that manager_of is a state valid-time relation of the following form, and that the time-stamps of manager_of are specified at the granularity of years.

manager_of		
name	department	
K.Prince	sales	{1987, 1988, 1989, 1992, 1993, 1994}
J.Pappas	personnel	{1987, 1988, 1989, 1990}
...	...	...

The semantics in manager_of above is that K.Prince was the manager of the sales department all the time from some instant in 1987 to some instant in 1989, and all the time from some instant in 1992 to some instant in 1994. To interpret the time-stamp of a state valid-time relation, one first forms the maximal subsets of the time-stamp, such that each subset is convex. In the case of the tuple for K.Prince and sales, the maximal subsets are {1987, 1988, 1989} and {1992, 1993, 1994}. The periods represented by the maximal subsets are called *maximal periods* of the time-stamp. (The reader is reminded that periods can be represented as convex sets of granules). The semantics of a time-stamp in a state valid-time relation is that the situation represented by the corresponding tuple is true at all the instants of the maximal periods of the time-stamp.

In the case of event valid-time relations, the semantics of each time-stamp is that the corresponding situation is true at some instant within each granule of the time-stamp. Let us assume that `become_employed` is an event valid-time relation of the following form, and that the time-stamps of `become_employed` are specified at the granularity of years:

become_employed	
name	
K.Prince	{1987, 1992}
J.Pappas	{1987}
T.Smith	{1991,1992}
...	...

The semantics of `become_employed` above is that, for example, K.Prince became employed at some instant in 1987, and then again at some instant in 1992. Unlike tuples of state valid-time relations, the tuple for T.Smith above does not mean that T.Smith was becoming employed all the time from an instant in 1991 to an instant in 1992. It simply means that T.Smith became employed at some instant in 1991, and again at some instant in 1992.

The distinction between state valid-time relations and event valid-time relations shows up when some TSQL2 functions are used. For example, when the TSQL2 function FIRST is applied to the time-stamp of a state valid-time relation, it returns the set of granules that represents the earliest maximal period of the time-stamp. In contrast, when FIRST is applied to the time-stamp of an event valid-time relation, it returns the earliest granule of the time-stamp.

The time-stamps of state valid-time relations are called *temporal elements*, while the time-stamps of event valid-time relations are called *instant sets*. (According to this definition, the term "instant set" is unfortunate, since if an instant set is a time-stamp, then it is a set of granules, not a set of instants.) Actually, the TSQL2 documents often try to distinguish between the terms "temporal element" and "instant set" by saying that temporal elements are unions of periods, while instant sets are simply sets of instants (see for example section 2.1 of [12]). In our view, this definition is problematic. A union of periods in the real world is a union of convex sets of instants, i.e. simply a set of instants. (The union of two convex sets of instants is not necessarily a convex set of instants.) Hence, one cannot distinguish between unions of periods and simple sets of instants. Perhaps when the TSQL2 documents refer to "unions of periods" they mean unions of convex sets of granules (a period can be represented as a convex set of granules), and when they refer to sets of instants they mean sets of granules (an instant can be represented as a granule). Even in this case, however, a union of convex sets of granules is simply a set of granules. (The union of two convex sets of granules is not necessarily a convex set of granules.) Hence, again one cannot distinguish between unions of convex sets of granules and simple sets of granules. In our view, both temporal elements and instant sets are sets of granules. The term "temporal element" simply means that the set of granules is used as a a time-stamp in a state valid-time relation, while the term "instant set" means that the set of granules is used as time-stamp in an event valid-time relation (and as discussed above, the semantics of the time-stamps depend on whether the time-stamps are used in state valid-time relations or in event valid-time relations).

In BCDM, the conceptual data model of TSQL2, a relation can never contain *value equivalent* tuples, i.e. tuples that contain the same values in their explicit attributes (see section 5.2 of [8]). TSQL2, however, provides *partitioning units*, special keywords that can be used in TSQL2 queries, and that cause a relation to be viewed within a query as if it contained value-equivalent tuples. For example, the (PERIOD) partitioning unit would cause manager_of to be viewed as if each tuple were time-stamped by a set of granules representing a single maximal period of the corresponding time-stamp in the unpartitioned manager_of:

manager_of partitioned with (PERIOD)		
name	department	
K.Prince	sales	{1987, 1988, 1989}
K.Prince	sales	{1992, 1993, 1994}
J.Pappas	personnel	{1987, 1988, 1989, 1990}
...	...	...

TSQL2 also supports a partitioning unit called (INSTANT); this will be discussed in section 4.3.

Literals

TSQL2 provides three kinds of *temporal literals*: literals that specify *instants*, literals that specify *periods*, and literals that specify *intervals* (see [14] and [15]). For example, the literal TIMESTAMP 'March 3, 1995' DAY specifies an instant at the granularity of days that falls within March 3rd 1995. Instants can also be specified by DATE and TIME literals. The status of DATE and TIME literals in TSQL2 is unclear. The assumption seems to be that DATE literals are syntactic sugar for TIMESTAMP literals at the granularity of days. For example, DATE 'March 3, 1995' is the same as TIMESTAMP 'March 3, 1995' DAY. TIME literals seem to be intended to specify an instant within a day, but without determining that day (e.g. TIME '08:54:32'). DATE and TIME literals will be discussed further in section 3.1.

TSQL2 supports closed-closed, closed-open, open-closed, and open-open period literals (see [13], section 10.2, additional syntax rule 11, and additional general rule 5). For example, PERIOD '[March 3, 1995 – March 20, 1995]' DAY is a closed-closed period literal that specifies a period at the granularity of days, that starts at some instant on March 3rd 1995, and ends at some instant on March 20th 1995. PERIOD '(March 3, 1995 – March 20, 1995]' DAY is an open-closed period literal that specifies a period at the granularity of days. In this case, the period starts at some instant on March 4th 1995 (the day after March 3rd 1995), and ends at some instant on March 20th 1995. Closed-open and open-open period literals have similar meanings. Finally, to give an example of an interval literal, INTERVAL '5' DAY specifies an interval 5 days long.

In the rest of this paper, we adopt a notation similar to TSQL2 period literals to refer informally to periods specified at some granularity. For example, we write [June 1993 – May 1994] to refer to the period specified by the TSQL2 literal PERIOD '[June 1993 - May 1994]' MONTH.

Calendars

TSQL2 supports multiple *calendars*. Roughly speaking, a TSQL2 calendar describes a system that people use to measure time (e.g. Gregorian calendar, Lunar calendar, etc.). TSQL2 calendars also specify the strings that are allowed to appear within the quotes of temporal literals (e.g. DATE 'December 31, 1991', DATE 'Ramadam 1, 1872'), the meanings assigned to these strings, and the available granularities (e.g. days, weeks, academic semesters, etc.). According to section 3 of [11], TSQL2 calendars are defined by the database administrator, the DBMS vendor, or third parties. Users can then select the calendar they wish to use, or even use combinations of calendars.

SCALE *and* CAST

TSQL2 provides two functions, SCALE and CAST, that can be used to change the granularity of TSQL2 temporal expressions; see sections 4.5 – 4.11 of [6]. (Section 11.16 of [13] does not allow SCALE to be used with expressions that specify instant sets. We see no reason for this restriction, and propose adding an extra syntax rule in section 11.16 of [13] to remove this restriction. The extra rule would be very similar to the rule for SCALE in section 11.14 of [13].) CAST can also be used to convert non-temporal expressions from one data-type to another; see section 6.3 of [9]. CAST was already supported in SQL-92, but TSQL2 has enhanced its functionality. SCALE is a new function introduced in TSQL2.

The following examples illustrate the behaviour of SCALE in the case of instant-specifying expressions. The examples are a modified version of the examples in section 4.5 of [6]. We use "=" as a shorthand for "is equivalent to".

```
SCALE(TIMESTAMP 'May 6, 1994' DAY AS YEAR) =
    TIMESTAMP '1994' YEAR
SCALE(TIMESTAMP 'May 6, 1994' DAY AS MONTH) =
    TIMESTAMP 'May 1994' MONTH
SCALE(TIMESTAMP 'May 6, 1994' DAY AS DAY) =
    TIMESTAMP 'May 6, 1994' DAY
SCALE(TIMESTAMP 'May 6, 1994' DAY AS MINUTE) =
    TIMESTAMP 'May 6, 1994 00:00 ~ May 6, 1994 23:59' MINUTE
```

In the last example above, TIMESTAMP 'May 6, 1994 00:00 ~ May 6, 1994 23:59 MINUTE is an *indeterminate* instant-specifying literal, that reflects the fact that we do not know the exact minute of May 6th 1994 where the instant should be placed (the instant could be placed at any minute of that day).

The behaviour of SCALE and CAST can be explained in terms of the granules or sets of granules that correspond to the temporal expressions to which SCALE or CAST are applied.

In the case of instant-specifying expressions, when converting from a finer to a coarser granularity (e.g. DAY to YEAR), SCALE maps the granule g that represents the instant at the old granularity to the granule g' of the new granularity that contains g. For example, in the first case above the day-granule May 6th 1994 is mapped to the year-granule 1994. When converting from a coarser to a finer granularity (e.g. from DAY to MINUTE) using SCALE, the granule g that represents the instant at the old granularity is mapped to an indeterminate granule g' ranging over all the granules of the new granularity that are contained within g. For example, in the last case above the day-granule May 6th 1994 is mapped to an indeterminate minute-granule that ranges over all the minute-granules of May 6th 1994. In contrast, when converting from a coarser to a finer granularity using CAST, the granule g that represents the instant at the old granularity is mapped to the *earliest* granule of the new granularity that is contained within g. For example, below the day-granule May 6th 1994 is mapped to the minute-granule May 6th 1994 00:00.

```
CAST(TIMESTAMP 'May 6, 1994' DAY AS MINUTE) =
    TIMESTAMP 'May 6, 1994 00:00' MINUTE
```

When converting from a finer to a coarser (or to the same) granularity (e.g. DAY to MONTH), CAST behaves in the same way as SCALE.

The behaviour of SCALE and CAST in the case of period-specifying expressions is similar. The granules that specify the earliest and latest instants of the period are mapped to granules of the new granularity as in the case of instant-specifying expressions. The following examples illustrate the behaviour of SCALE and CAST with periods.

```
CAST(PERIOD '[1991 - 1995]' YEAR AS DAY) =
    PERIOD '[Jan 1, 1991 - Jan 1, 1995]' DAY
SCALE(PERIOD '[1991 - 1995]' YEAR AS DAY) =
    PERIOD '[Jan 1, 1991 ~ Dec 31, 1991 -
            Jan 1, 1995 ~ Dec 31, 1995]' DAY
```

The behaviour of CAST in the case of period-specifying expressions will be discussed further in section 3.2.

[6] does not provide much information on the behaviour of SCALE and CAST with expressions that refer to time-stamps of valid-time relations (instant sets or temporal elements). We assume that in the case of instant sets, each granule of the instant set is mapped to a granule of the new granularity, as in the case of instant-specifying expressions. For example, assuming that the set of day-granules {May 5 1994, August 13 1994, March 20 1995} is used as an instant-set, when converting from DAY to YEAR, both SCALE and CAST would generate the set of year-granules {1994, 1995}. Notice that the first two day-granules are merged into one single year-granule.

In the case of temporal elements, we assume that first each maximal period of the temporal element is converted individually to the new granularity, as when SCALE and CAST are used with period-specifying expressions. Then, the sets of granules that represent the maximal periods at the new granularity are formed, and the resulting temporal element is the union of these sets. The resulting temporal element may have fewer maximal periods than the original one. Let us consider the temporal element whose maximal periods are [May 1991 – July 1991]. [Nov 1992 – March 1993], and [March 1995 – May 1995]. When converting to the granularity of years, both SCALE and CAST would map the first maximal period to [1991 – 1991] (the period starts at some instant in 1991 and ends at some instant in the same year), the second maximal period to [1992 – 1993], and the third one to [1995 – 1995]. These periods are represented by the sets of year-granules {1991}, {1992, 1993}, and {1995} respectively. The resulting temporal element is the union of these sets of year-granules, i.e.

{1991,1992,1993,1995}, and it has only two maximal periods: [1991 – 1993] and [1995 – 1995].

3 Clarifications and modifications in the semantics of TSQL2

3.1 Granularities of temporal literals

As mentioned in section 2, TSQL2 provides DATE literals, TIME literals, TIMESTAMP literals, PERIOD literals, and INTERVAL literals. These literals specify instants, periods, or intervals at some granularity. In the case of INTERVAL literals, the granularity is always specified explicitly within the literal. For example, in INTERVAL '5' DAY the granularity is DAY. In TIME, TIMESTAMP, and PERIOD literals the granularity may or may not be specified explicitly within the literal. For example, both TIMESTAMP '10:00am Jan 1, 1994' MINUTE and TIMESTAMP '10:00am Jan 1, 1994' are valid TSQL2 literals. Using the terminology of section 10.2 of [13], TIME, TIMESTAMP, and PERIOD literals may or may not contain "precision" specifications. These precision specifications in effect determine the granularities of the literals. (Actually, the rule for TIME literals in section 10.2 of [13] does not allow precision specifications in TIME literals. We assume that this is an unintended omission, since additional general rule 1 of the same section refers to the precision specifications of TIME literals.) In DATE literals, the granularity can never be specified explicitly (see the syntax rules in section 10.2 of [13]). For example, DATE 'Jan 1, 1994' DAY is *not* a valid TSQL2 literal.

The various TSQL2 documents do not agree on how the granularities of TIME, TIMESTAMP, PERIOD, and DATE literals are determined when the granularities are not specified explicitly within the literals:

Section 4.2 of [6] assumes that in these cases the granularity is decided by the TSQL2 calendar that interprets the literals. This seems to agree with the discussion in section 3.3 of [14], where an example is given showing how a TIMESTAMP literal with no explicitly defined granularity is passed to all the available TSQL2 calendars, with each calendar that manages to interpret it returning a granularity for the literal.

In contrast, additional general rules 1 and 2 in section 10.2 of [13] specify that if the granularity is not defined explicitly within a TIME or a TIMESTAMP literal, then the granularity is SECOND. Section 10.2 of [13] does not specify what happens in the case of DATE and PERIOD literals when the granularity is not defined explicitly by the literals.

Finally, although this is not stated in [14], section 3.2 of [14] (which contains some discussion on declaring attributes of type DATE) seems to suggest that a DATE literal is simply syntactic sugar for a TIMESTAMP literal that specifies explicitly the granularity DAY.

Our proposal is that in the case of DATE literals, the underlying granularity should always be DAY. In the case of TIME, TIMESTAMP, and PERIOD literals, we propose adopting the view of [6]. That is, if the literals do not specify explicitly granularities, the granularities of the literals should be determined by the calendar that interprets each literal. This seems to allow greater flexibility than the approach whereby for each one of these types of literals a default calendar-independent granularity is specified. (As mentioned above, the latter approach is partially adopted in section 10.2 of [13], where a calendar-independent default granularity, SECOND, is assumed for TIME and TIMESTAMP literals.) The approach of [6], that we propose for adoption in the case of TIME, TIMESTAMP, and PERIOD literals, allows each calendar to choose the most natural granularity for each temporal literal. For example, the calendar interpreting TIMESTAMP '10:00am Jan 1, 1994' is free to assign to the literal the granularity MINUTE, which is the most reasonable choice. In contrast, if the approach of section 10.2 of [13] is adopted, TIMESTAMP '10:00am Jan 1, 1994' will be assigned the default calendar-independent granularity SECOND. A conversion mechanism, similar to CAST or SCALE would have to be invoked, that would cause TIMESTAMP '10:00am Jan 1, 1994' to be treated as equivalent to TIMESTAMP '10:00:00am Jan 1, 1994' SECOND (in the case of CAST), or as equivalent to TIMESTAMP '10:00:00am Jan 1, 1994 ∼ 10:00:59am Jan 1, 1994' SECOND (in the case of SCALE).

There are some outstanding questions concerning what happens in the case of literals like TIMESTAMP '10:00am Jan 1, 1994' SECOND, or TIMESTAMP '10:00am Jan 1, 1994' DAY, where the explicitly defined granularity (SECOND or DAY) differs from the granularity that would be returned by the interpreting TSQL2 calendar if there were no explicit granularity (assuming that the interpreting calendar would return the most reasonable granularity, as discussed above, i.e. MINUTE). Do such literals cause errors? Or are the literals converted to the explicitly specified granularity (e.g. TIMESTAMP '10:00am Jan 1, 1994' DAY is treated as equivalent to TIMESTAMP 'Jan 1, 1994' DAY, ignoring the "10:00am")? If the literals are converted to the explicitly specified granularity, how is the conversion carried out? Is it carried out invoking the mechanism of CAST, or is it carried out invoking the mechanism of SCALE? If the conversion is carried out using the CAST mechanism, then TIMESTAMP '10:00am Jan 1, 1994' SECOND would be treated as equivalent to TIMESTAMP '10:00:00am Jan 1, 1994' SECOND. If it is carried out using the SCALE mechanism, then TIMESTAMP '10:00am Jan 1, 1994' SECOND would be treated as equivalent to TIMESTAMP '10:00:00am Jan 1, 1994 ∼ 10:00:59am Jan 1, 1994' SECOND.

We propose that when literals specify explicitly a granularity other than the granularity that would be returned by the interpreting calendar if no granularity were specified, the literals should be converted to the specified granularity (i.e. no errors should arise), provided that the calendar that interprets the quoted part of the literal (e.g. '10:00am Jan 1, 1994') also supports the specified granularity (e.g. DAY). Otherwise, an error should occur. The exact conversion mechanism (CAST or SCALE) to be used when converting a literal should be determined by the calendar that interprets the literal.

3.2 Casting periods from coarser to finer granularities

As discussed in section 2, the following:

CAST(PERIOD '[1993 - 1994]' YEAR AS DAY)

generates a period specified at the granularity of days, which is the same as the period specified by:

PERIOD '[Jan 1, 1993 - Jan 1, 1994]' DAY

The Tsql2 view is that in the case of periods like the one specified by PERIOD '[1993 - 1994]' YEAR, the exact day on which the period starts or ends is not known (see sections 3.2 and 3.3 of [6]). The period could start on any day in 1993, and it could end on any day in 1994. When converting from YEAR to DAY using SCALE, this ignorance of the exact starting and ending days is expressed by generating an indeterminate period. For example,

SCALE(PERIOD '[1993 - 1994]' YEAR AS DAY)

produces the same indeterminate period as the one specified by:

PERIOD '[Jan 1, 1993 ~ Dec 31, 1993 - Jan 1, 1994 ~ Dec 31, 1994]' DAY

CAST, however, is not allowed to generate indeterminate results. Hence, it has to choose a particular starting day from 1993, and a particular ending day from 1994. According to the current Tsql2 definition, CAST chooses the first day of 1993 and the first day of 1994, i.e. it chooses the earliest possible granules of the new granularity for both the left and the right boundaries of the original period.

This way, however, casting a period from a coarser to a finer granularity causes the boundaries of the original period to be treated asymmetrically. In the example above where PERIOD '[1993 - 1994]' YEAR is cast to DAY, CAST has chosen to include in the result the whole left boundary of the original period (the whole 1993). In contrast, the right boundary of the original period is excluded almost completely (only the first day of 1994 has been included). This asymmetrical behaviour seems unreasonable to us. It would be more consistent to (a) include both the whole of 1993 and the whole of 1994 in the result, or (b) include only the last day of 1993 and the first day of 1994. We propose adopting (a). That is, when casting a period from a coarser to a finer granularity, the resulting period should start at the earliest granule of the new granularity that falls within the original left boundary, and it should end at the latest granule of the new granularity that falls within the original right boundary. For example,

CAST(PERIOD '[1993 - 1994]' YEAR AS DAY)

would produce a period that is the same as the period specified by:

PERIOD '[Jan 1, 1993 - Dec 31, 1994]' DAY

Apart from treating both boundaries of the original period in a symmetrical manner, our proposal is also more intuitive. We believe that when a user specifies a period by using, say, PERIOD '[1993 - 1994]' YEAR, in most cases he/she means that the period contains the *whole* of 1993 and the *whole* of 1994. Hence, when converting from YEAR to DAY, the most reasonable result is [Jan 1, 1993 – Dec 31, 1994], i.e. the result that CAST would produce according to our proposal.

3.3 State and event relations

As explained in section 2, Tsql2 distinguishes between state valid-time relations and event valid-time relations. It is unclear how one can check whether a valid-time relation is a state or an event one. For valid-time relations stored directly in the database (tables of the database), the VALID_TIME attribute of the system table TABLES can be consulted. (This attribute shows whether a table in the database is event or state; see [1], and section 18.1 of [13].) In the case, however, of valid-time relations computed by SELECT statements (relations not stored in the database), there does not seem to be any TSQL2 mechanism to find out whether the relations are state or event. In fact, in many cases it unclear whether the computed relations are supposed to be state or event. Consider the statement:

```
SELECT *
VALID PERIOD '[1990 - 1995]' YEAR
FROM table1, table2
```

where table1 is a state valid-time relation, and table2 is an event valid-time relation. (The VALID clause specifies that all the tuples in the computed relation are time-stamped by the set of granules that represents the period [1990 - 1995].) The TSQL2 documents do not state clearly whether the result is supposed to be a state or an event valid-time relation.

4 Extensions to TSQL2

4.1 Coarser/finer granularity semantics by default

When the arguments of a temporal operator are specified at different granularities, TSQL2 by default enforces *left argument granularity semantics* (see section 4.9 of [6], and additional syntax rule 7 in section 16.1 of [13]). This means that in effect CAST or SCALE operators are inserted to convert the granularities of all the arguments to the granularity of the first argument. The user can specify whether this default conversion should be carried out by inserting CASTs or SCALEs, using the statements SET CAST AS DEFAULT or SET SCALE AS DEFAULT respectively (see section 4.9 of [6], and section 16.1 of [13]). For example, if a SET CAST AS DEFAULT statement is in force, then:

```
INTERSECT(PERIOD '[May 1994 - July 1994]' MONTH,
          PERIOD '[April 20, 1994 - June 5, 1994]' DAY)
```

is treated as equivalent to:

```
INTERSECT(PERIOD '[May 1994 - July 1994]' MONTH,
          CAST(PERIOD '[April 20, 1994 - June 5, 1994]' DAY AS MONTH))
```

i.e. the result is a period at the granularity of months, that is the same as the period specified by the literal PERIOD '[May 1994 - June 1994]' MONTH. (Here, the TSQL2 function INTERSECT returns the period that corresponds to the overlap of the periods specified by the two arguments; see section 3.3 of [15].) The SET CAST and SET SCALE statements can also be used to cast or scale all temporal expressions to a particular granularity. For example, SET CAST MINUTE causes all temporal expressions to be cast to the granularity of minutes (see section 4.10 of [6], and section 16.1 of [13]).

Section 4.9 of [6] comments that although left argument granularity semantics is enforced by default, other granularity semantics (e.g. finest/coarsest

granularity semantics, i.e. converting all the arguments to the granularity of
the argument that is specified at the finest/coarsest granularity) can be effected
by explicitly inserting cast or scale operators. For example, in the INTERSECT
example above, finest granularity semantics can be effected by using:

```
INTERSECT(CAST(PERIOD '[May 1994 - June 1994]' MONTH AS DAY),
          PERIOD '[April 20, 1994 - May 5, 1994]' DAY)
```

This comment of [6] is certainly true in cases where the granularities of the
various expressions are known. However, in programs that generate TSQL2
code dynamically (and our natural language interface is an example of such
a program), it is often difficult to determine the granularities of the various
expressions. For example, a program may utilise a generic SELECT pattern, that
when given two expressions arg_1 and arg_2 that specify two valid-time relations
r_1 and r_2, computes a new valid-time relation r. Each tuple t in r derives
from a tuple t_1 in r_1 and a tuple t_2 in r_2, such that t_1 and t_2 agree on an
attribute called key, and t contains all the explicit attribute values of t_1 and t_2.
The time-stamp of t is the intersection of the sets of granules that time-stamp
t_1 and t_2, with the intersection computed with *coarsest granularity semantics*.
That is, if the time-stamp of t_1 is a set of day-granules, and the time-stamp
of t_2 is a set of year-granules, then t_1 should be converted to the granularity
of years before computing the intersection. (Since any time-stamp conversion
will be from a finer to the coarsest granularity, it does not matter whether the
conversions will be carried out using SCALE or CAST.) The problem is that the
granularities of the time-stamps of t_1 and t_2 are not known in advance.

One could try to formulate the SELECT pattern as follows. (The VALID clause
specifies the time-stamp of each tuple in the resulting relation. VALID(t1) and
VALID(t2) return the time-stamps of t_1 and t_2 respectively.)

```
SELECT t1.*, t2.*
VALID INTERSECT(VALID(t1), VALID(t2))
FROM arg1 AS t1, arg2 AS t2
WHERE t1.key = t2.key
```

The expressions arg_1 and arg_2 would be computed at run-time. For example,
they could be table names chosen at run-time, or embedded SELECT statements
generated by other parts of the program. Similar patterns are used in our natural language interface. (We note that section 3.3 of [15] allows the INTERSECT
function to be used only with expressions specifying periods, not with expressions referring to time-stamps, i.e. not with temporal elements or instant sets.
Sections 11.12, 11.14, and 11.16 of [13], however, indicate that INTERSECT can
be used with both of its arguments specifying periods, or with both of its arguments referring to temporal elements, or with both of its arguments referring
to instant sets. We follow [13].)

Unfortunately, assuming TSQL2 defaults, the pattern above would not always produce the correct results, because TSQL2 by default enforces left argument granularity semantics. This means that the intersection would always be
computed at the granularity of the time-stamps of r_1, which is not guaranteed
to be the coarsest one. It is also not possible to solve the problem by inserting
CAST or SCALE operators in the INTERSECT of the VALID clause, because we do not
know the granularities of VALID(t1) and VALID(t2), and we do not know which

one of these granularities is the coarsest one. Neither is it possible to solve the problem by using a statement like SET CAST MINUTE, because this would cause the intersection to be computed at the granularity of minutes, which is not guaranteed to be the coarsest of the granularities of VALID(t1) and VALID(t2).

To solve problems of this kind, we propose enhancing the repertoire of SET CAST and SET SCALE, so that finest or coarsest granularity semantics can be enforced by default using statements of the form: SET CAST AS COARSEST, SET CAST AS FINEST, SET SCALE AS COARSEST, and SET SCALE AS FINEST. Using the statement SET CAST AS COARSEST at the beginning of the TSQL2 session would cause the SELECT pattern above to produce the correct results.

4.2 Period constructors

Although TSQL2 allows closed-closed, closed-open, open-closed, and open-open period literals (see section 2), there is only one period constructor, PERIOD($expr_1$, $expr_2$), that can only be used to construct periods by specifying them in their closed-closed form (see section 11.12 of [13], and sections 3.1.3 and 3.3 of [15]). The arguments of the PERIOD constructor, $expr_1$ and $expr_2$, are always instant-specifying expressions. PERIOD($expr_1$,$expr_2$) constructs the period whose earliest instant is the one specified by $expr_1$, and whose latest instant is the one specified by $expr_2$. Intuitively, PERIOD($expr_1$,$expr_2$) constructs the period $[expr_1, expr_2]$. There are cases, however, where the period that has to be constructed is $(expr_1, expr_2]$, or $[expr_1, expr_2)$, or $(expr_1, expr_2)$.

Let us imagine a job centre that uses a state valid-time relation, called employment, to store information showing when in the past the persons registered at the centre were employed. Assuming that the granularity of the time-stamps of employment is DAY, employment could have the following form. (For simplicity, in the remainder of this paper when showing a state valid-time relation, we often show the sets of maximal periods of the time-stamps of the relation, instead of the time-stamps themselves. For example, below we write {[May 1994 – July 1994], [Nov 1994 – Jan 1995]} instead of the set of granules {May 1994, June 1994, July 1994, Nov 1994, Dec 1994, Jan 1995}.)

employment		
id	name	
10345	T.Smith	{ [May 1994 - July 1994], [Nov 1994 - Jan 1995] }
10478	J.Adams	{ [July 1992 - May 1994] }
...	...	...

Let us assume that we want to compute a new state valid-time relation, that associates with each person in employment a time-stamp of only one maximal period, with the maximal period being ($month_1$, $month_2$], where $month_1$ is the last month during which the person was employed, and $month_2$ is the present month. For example, if the current month is March 1995, the time-stamp for T.Smith in the new relation should have only one maximal period, the period (Jan 1995 – March 1995], i.e. the time-stamp should be the set of granules {Feb 1995, March 1995}. For simplicity, let us also assume that no person in employment was employed during the current month. The new relation would show the last periods of unemployment of the persons registered at the centre.

Using the following TSQL2 query would not compute the correct relation.

```
(1)   SELECT t.*
      VALID PERIOD(END(LAST(VALID(t))), TIMESTAMP 'now')
      FROM employment AS t
```

In (1), for each tuple of `employment`, `LAST(VALID(t))` returns the set of granules that represents the latest maximal period of the time-stamp of the tuple, and `END(LAST(VALID(t)))` returns the latest granule of that set. Assuming again that the current month is March 1995, in the resulting relation the time-stamp of T.Smith will be {Jan 1995, Feb 1995, March 1995}, while we want it to be {Feb 1995, March 1995}. In other words, the (single) maximal period of the new time-stamp of T.Smith will be [Jan 1995 – March 1995], while we want it to be (Jan 1995 – March 1995], i.e. [Feb 1995 – March 1995].

Of course, in cases like the example above, where the granularities of the expressions that are used as arguments of `PERIOD` are known, one can still produce the required result using interval arithmetic. In our example, the granularity of the first argument of `PERIOD` is known to be `MONTH` (the same as the granularity of the time-stamps of `employment`). Instead of (1) one could use (2), that would yield the correct result:

```
(2)   SELECT t.*
      VALID PERIOD(END(LAST(VALID(t))) + INTERVAL '1' MONTH,
                   TIMESTAMP 'now')
      FROM employment AS t
```

If, however, we did not know the granularity of the expression that is used as the first argument of `PERIOD`, then we would not be able to deduce whether we should add to the first argument of `PERIOD` an interval one `MONTH` long, or one `DAY` long, or one `MINUTE` long, etc. As mentioned in section 4.1, in programs that generate TSQL2 code dynamically, like for example our natural language interface, it is not always possible to predict the granularities of the various expressions.

In our natural language interface project we have added an extra argument to the `PERIOD` function, with possible values '(]', '[)', '()', and '[]'. If $expr_1$ and $expr_2$ specify instants at the granularity G, and $expr_1$ specifies an instant located within a granule g_1, and $expr_2$ specifies an instant located within a granule g_2, `PERIOD(`$expr_1$, $expr_2$, '(]')` constructs the period whose earliest instant is located within the granule immediately after $g_1$ in $G$, and whose latest instant is located within $g_2$ (intuitively the result is the period $(g_1, g_2]$). Similarly, `PERIOD(`$expr_1$, $expr_2$, '()')` constructs the period whose earliest instant is located within the granule immediately after g_1 in G, and whose latest instant is located within the granule immediately before g_2 in G (intuitively the result is the period (g_1, g_2)). The semantics of `PERIOD(`$expr_1$, $expr_2$, '[)')` and `PERIOD(`$expr_1$, $expr_2$, '[]')` are similar. To preserve compatibility with the current TSQL2 definition, `PERIOD(`$exrp_1, expr_2$)` is the same as `PERIOD(`$exrp_1, expr_2$,'[]')`.

Instead of adding an extra argument to the `PERIOD` function, an alternative solution (suggested to us by Hugh Darwen and Mike Sykes) would be to introduce two new functions, `PREVIOUS` and `NEXT`. `PREVIOUS(`$expr$)` would return the granule immediately before $expr$, and `NEXT(`$expr$)` the granule immediately after $expr$. For example, instead of using `PERIOD(`$expr_1$, $expr_2$, '(]')`, one could use `PERIOD(NEXT(`$expr_1$), $expr_2$)`.

4.3 Calendric tables

Let us imagine a chemical company with many sites. Various technical problems arise occasionally at the sites of the company, and specialised company technicians (called "visiting technicians") are sent from the headquarters to the sites to help solve the problems. The company uses a state valid-time relation, called technician_visits, to keep track of the time each visiting technician has spent at each site. The time-stamps of technician_visits are specified at the granularity of minutes. technician_visits may have the following form. (We show the sets of maximal periods of the time-stamps rather than the time-stamps.)

technician_visits		
technician	site	
T.Smith	Glasgow Central	{ [9:00am Jan 1, 1995 - 10:20am Jan 1,1995], [4:30pm Jan 2, 1995 - 6:10pm Jan 2, 1995], [11:30pm Feb 6, 1995 - 1:40am Feb 7, 1995] }
T.Smith	Edinburgh Leith	{ [2:15pm Dec 28, 1994 - 2:55pm Dec 28, 1994] }
J.Adams	Glasgow Central	{ [4:00am Jan 7, 1995 - 9:45am Jan 7, 1995], [4:40pm Feb 10, 1995 - 6:35pm Feb 10, 1995] }
J.Adams	North Sea	{ [10:00am May 25, 1994 - 5:30pm June 4, 1994] }
...	...	...

Given a table like technician_visits, there does not seem to be any easy way to express questions like the following in TsQL2:

(3) Report any visiting technician who was at some site on a Sunday in 1994.

(4) Report any visiting technician who was at Glasgow Central (for some time) on every Monday in 1994.

Similar problems arise in questions involving "every February", "some summer", etc. The only way, for example, to express (3) seems to be to use a TsQL2 query that mentions explicitly all the 1994 Sundays, as in (5). (The reader is reminded that (PERIOD) is a partitioning unit; see section 2. It is unclear whether or not an expression referring to a temporal element may be used as an argument of OVERLAPS. Section 3.6.2 of [15] does not allow it. Table 2 in section 13.4 of [13] allows it, but additional syntax rule 3 of the same section seems to forbid it.. If an expression referring to a temporal element *can* be used as an argument of OVERLAPS, then the (PERIOD) partitioning unit in (5) and in other similar SELECT statements of this section can be omitted.)

```
(5)    SELECT DISTINCT SNAPSHOT t.technician
       FROM technician_visits(PERIOD) AS t
       WHERE VALID(t) OVERLAPS
           PERIOD '[00:00 Jan 2, 1994 - 23:59 Jan 2, 1994]'
       OR VALID(t) OVERLAPS
           PERIOD '[00:00 Jan 9, 1994 - 23:59 Jan 9, 1994]'
       OR VALID(t) OVERLAPS
           PERIOD '[00:00 Jan 16, 1994 - 23:59 Jan 16, 1994]'
       OR ...
```

(5) reports the technician value of any tuple t in technician_visits, such that a maximal period of the time-stamp of t overlaps a 1994 Sunday-period.

Alternatively, one could try to express (3) using the TSQL2 EXTRACT function. In SQL-92, EXTRACT can be used to extract a field from a datetime (instant-specifying) expression or from an interval expression (see section 5.9.1 of [9]). For example, in SQL-92 the expression EXTRACT(YEAR FROM DATE '1992-06-01') returns the numeric value 1992. TSQL2 generalises EXTRACT, so that a granularity can be extracted from a datetime or interval expression (see section 3.5 of [14]). It is unclear exactly what can be extracted from an instant-specifying or interval-specifying expression in TSQL2, and exactly what the result of the extraction is supposed to be. Let us assume, however, that EXTRACT can be used to find out the name of the day that corresponds to an instant-specifying expression, and that the result of EXTRACT is an integer showing the name of the day (1 for Monday, 2 for Tuesday, etc.; according to section 5.9.1 of [9], the result of EXTRACT is a number). Then one could try to express (3) using a SELECT statement of the form:

```
(6)   SELECT DISTINCT SNAPSHOT t.technician
      FROM technician_visits(INSTANT) AS t
      WHERE EXTRACT(DAYNAME FROM VALID(t)) = 7
```

The (INSTANT) partitioning unit causes a valid-time relation to be viewed as if it were allowed to contain value-equivalent tuples, with each tuple time-stamped by a single granule. For each tuple t' in the unpartitioned form of the relation, if t' is time-stamped by the set of granules $\{g_1, g_2, g_3, \ldots, g_n\}$, there are n tuples in the partitioned form of the relation, one time-stamped by the granule g_1, one time-stamped by g_2, etc. These n tuples in the partitioned form of the relation are all value-equivalent to the original tuple t'. The granules in the partitioned form of the relation are interpreted as specifying instants. For example, (INSTANT) causes technician_visits to be viewed as if it had the following form.

technician_visits		
technician	site	
T.Smith	Glasgow Central	9:00am Jan 1, 1995
T.Smith	Glasgow Central	9:01am Jan 1, 1995
T.Smith	Glasgow Central	9:02am Jan 1, 1995
...	...	...
T.Smith	Glasgow Central	1:40am Feb 7, 1995
T.Smith	Edinburgh Leith	2:15pm Dec 28, 1994
...	...	...

Unfortunately, the (INSTANT) partitioning unit can only be used with event tables (see [13], section 11.3, additional syntax rule 7, and [12]), not with state tables like technician_visits. Even if partitioning state tables with (INSTANT) were allowed, it seems there would still be no easy way to express questions like (4) (universal quantification over Mondays).

TSQL2 already supports multiple calendars. As mentioned in section 2, a TSQL2 calendar describes a system that people use to measure time. TSQL2 calendars also specify the strings that can appear within the quotes of temporal literals, the meanings of these strings, and the available granularities. We propose that a TSQL2 calendar should also be allowed to define *calendric tables*. Calendric tables behave like ordinary tables stored in the database, except that they are defined by the creator of the TSQL2 calendar, and they cannot be updated. (We have not examined which mechanisms TSQL2 would have to provide to allow calendar creators to define calendric tables. It is also unclear exactly how TSQL2 calendars are created. For example there does not seem to be any CREATE CALENDAR TSQL2 command.)

The exact purpose and contents of each calendric table are left to the calendar creator. We assume, however, that a calendric table provides information about the time-measuring system described by the TSQL2 calendar that defines the calendric table. For example, in the case of the Gregorian calendar, the calendar creator may have defined a calendric table listing the Monday-periods, the Tuesday-periods, etc. Other calendric tables may list the periods that correspond to the various seasons (spring-periods, summer-periods, etc.), the periods that correspond to the various months (January-periods, February-periods, etc.), special days (e.g. Easter days), etc.

Let us assume that a state valid-time calendric table &year_month_day is available. (To distinguish calendric tables from ordinary tables, the names of calendric tables start with an ampersand.) We assume that the time-stamps of our calendric table are specified at the granularity of chronons. &year_month_day has the form shown below. (We show the sets of maximal periods of the time-stamps, instead of the time-stamps.)

&year_month_day				
year	month	day_num	day_name	
...	...	...	...	...
1994	September	2	Friday	$\{[c_{n_1} - c_{n_2}]\}$
1994	September	3	Saturday	$\{[c_{n_3} - c_{n_4}]\}$
...	...	...	...	...
1995	February	9	Thursday	$\{[c_{n_5} - c_{n_6}]\}$
1995	February	10	Friday	$\{[c_{n_7} - c_{n_8}]\}$
...	...	...	...	...

The calendric table above means that the period that starts at the chronon c_{n_1} and ends at the chronon c_{n_2} is a Friday, the second day of September 1994; that the period that starts at the chronon c_{n_3} and ends at the chronon c_{n_4} is a Saturday, the third day of September 1994, etc. Of course, the cardinality of &year_month_day will be very large, though it will not be infinite (since time in TSQL2 is bounded; see [7]). It is important, however, to realise that although &year_month_day behaves like a table stored in the database, it does not need to be physically present in the database. Its tuples could be computed dynamically, whenever they are needed, using some algorithm specified by the TSQL2 calendar.

Assuming that the calendric table &year_month_day is available, (3) can be expressed in TSQL2 as follows:

```
(7)   SELECT DISTINCT SNAPSHOT t.technician
      FROM technician_visits(PERIOD) AS t, &year_month_day(PERIOD) AS d
      WHERE d.day_name = 'Sunday'
          AND d.year = 1994
          AND VALID(t) OVERLAPS VALID(d)
```

(7) reports the technician value of any tuple t in technician_visits, such that a maximal period of the time-stamp of t overlaps a 1994 Sunday-period. Similarly, the answer to (4) can be found using the following TSQL2 query:

```
(8)   SELECT DISTINCT SNAPSHOT t1.technician
      FROM technician_visits AS t1
      WHERE NOT EXISTS
         ( SELECT *
           FROM &year_month_day(PERIOD) AS d
           WHERE d.day_name = 'Monday'
             AND d.year = 1994
             AND NOT EXISTS
               ( SELECT *
                 FROM technician_visits(PERIOD) AS t2
                 WHERE t2.technician = t1.technician
                   AND t2.site = 'Glasgow Central'
                   AND VALID(t2) OVERLAPS VALID(d)  ))
```

Intuitively, the TsQL2 query above means: *"Report any visiting technician, for which there is no 1994 Monday on which the technician did not visit Glasgow Central."*.

Questions involving counts like (9) can also be formulated easily, provided that the appropriate calendric tables are available. For example, the question:

(9) On how many Sundays was J.Adams at Glasgow Central in 1994?

can be expressed as:

```
(10)   SELECT SNAPSHOT COUNT(DISTINCT d.*)
       FROM &year_month_day(PERIOD) AS d, technician_visits(PERIOD) AS t
       WHERE d.year = 1994
         AND d.day_name = 'Sunday'
         AND VALID(t) OVERLAPS VALID(d)
         AND t.technician = 'J.Adams'
         AND t.site = 'Glasgow Central'
```

The TsQL2 query above counts the 1994 Sunday-periods during which J.Adams was at Glasgow Central. We cannot see how questions like (9) could be expressed without using calendric tables.

5   Conclusions

Although the built-in temporal support of TsQL2 has proven valuable in our experimental natural language interface, there are some points in the definition of TsQL2 where we think that the semantics of the language should be clarified or modified. These points have to do with the granularities of temporal literals, the behaviour of CAST when converting period-specifying expressions from coarser to finer granularities, and the distinction between state and event relations. Some extra features were added to TsQL2 during our project, namely a statement to enforce coarser or finer granularity semantics by default, an enhanced period constructor, and calendric tables. These extra features seem generally useful, regardless of natural language issues.

Acknowledgements

The authors wish to thank Hugh Darwen and Mike Sykes for comments on an earlier version of this paper. This paper was written while the first author was a postgraduate student at the University of Edinburgh under the supervision of the other two authors. The first author wishes to thank the Greek State Scholarships Foundation for funding his studies in Edinburgh.

Contact addresses

Correspondence concerning this paper may be addressed to: I. Androutsopoulos, Department of Artificial Intelligence, University of Edinburgh, 80 South Bridge, Edinburgh EH1 1HN, Scotland, U.K.; G.D. Ritchie, Department of Artificial Intelligence, University of Edinburgh, 80 South Bridge, Edinburgh EH1 1HN, Scotland, U.K.; P. Thanisch, Department of Computer Science, University of Edinburgh, King's Buildings, Mayfield Road, Edinburgh EH9 3JZ, Scotland, U.K.

References

[1] I. Ahn. System Tables for TSQL2. TSQL2 commentary, available by anonymous ftp from cs.arizona.edu, September 1994.

[2] I. Androutsopoulos, G.D. Ritchie, and P. Thanisch. Natural Language Interfaces to Databases – An Introduction. Research paper 709, Department of Artificial Intelligence, University of Edinburgh, 1994. To appear in the *Journal of Natural Language Engineering*, Cambridge University Press.

[3] I. Androutsopoulos, G.D. Ritchie, and P. Thanisch. A Framework for Natural Language Interfaces to Temporal Databases. Research Paper 734, Department of Artificial Intelligence, University of Edinburgh, 1995.

[4] A. Copestake and K. Sparck Jones. Natural Language Interfaces to Databases. *The Knowledge Engineering Review*, 5(4):225–249, 1990.

[5] C.E. Dyreson and R.T. Snodgrass. A Timestamp Representation for TSQL2. TSQL2 commentary, available by anonymous ftp from cs.arizona.edu, September 1994.

[6] C.E. Dyreson and R.T. Snodgrass. Temporal Granularity in TSQL2. TSQL2 commentary, available by anonymous ftp from cs.arizona.edu, September 1994.

[7] C.E. Dyreson, M.D. Soo, and R.T. Snodgrass. The TSQL2 Data Model for Time. TSQL2 commentary, available by anonymous ftp from cs.arizona.edu, September 1994.

[8] C.S. Jensen, R.T. Snodgrass, and M.D. Soo. The TSQL2 Data Model. TSQL2 commentary, available by anonymous ftp from cs.arizona.edu, September 1994.

[9] J. Melton and A.R. Simon. *Understanding the New SQL: A Complete Guide*. Morgan Kaufmann Publishers, San Mateo, California, 1993.

[10] C.R. Perrault and B.J. Grosz. Natural Language Interfaces. In H.E. Shrobe, editor, *Exploring Artificial Intelligence*, pages 133–172. Morgan Kaufmann Publishers Inc., San Mateo, California, 1988.

[11] R.T. Snodgrass. A TSQL2 Tutorial. Available by anonymous `ftp` from `cs.arizona.edu`, September 1994.

[12] R.T. Snodgrass. Event Tables in TSQL2. TSQL2 commentary, available by anonymous `ftp` from `cs.arizona.edu`, September 1994.

[13] R.T. Snodgrass, I. Ahn, G. Ariav, D. Batory, J. Clifford, C.E. Dyreson, R. Elmasri, F. Grandi, Jensen C.S., W. Kaefer, N. Kline, K. Kulkarni, T.Y.C. Leung, N. Lorentzos, J.F. Roddick, A. Segev, M.D. Soo, and S.M. Sripada. TSQL2 Language Specification. Available by anonymous `ftp` from `cs.arizona.edu`, September 1994. An earlier version of this document has appeared in *SIGMOD Record*, 23(1):65–86, March 1994.

[14] R.T. Snodgrass and M. Soo. Supporting Multiple Calendars in TSQL2: An Overview. TSQL2 commentary, available by anonymous `ftp` from `cs.arizona.edu`, September 1994.

[15] M. Soo and R. Snodgrass. User-defined Time in TSQL2. TSQL2 commentary, available by anonymous `ftp` from `cs.arizona.edu`, September 1994.

Using Temporal Constructs in Temporal Databases

Wayne Harris[1], W.A. Gray[2]
[1]University of the West of England,
Bristol BS16 1QY United Kingdom
email: wj-harri@csm.uwe.ac.uk
[2]University of Wales, College of Cardiff,
Cardiff United Kingdom
email: wag@cm.cf.ac.uk

Abstract

Temporal Databases have developed to the point where there is a proposed query language, TSQL2, [1] and a database implementation, Multical, [2] based on this language. It is now appropriate to review the power and relevance of this approach. It is accepted that TSQL2 is appropriate for a number of types of temporal query. This paper examines TSQL2 with respect to the requirements of an application area to see how well it can be applied to solving the problems with temporal querying in this area. The weaknesses of TSQL2 in this application area are identified and an alternative graphical query language, called GEST is presented to overcome these weaknesses. GEST has the same power as TSQL2, but improves on it, in three ways: it is based on a WIMP interface; it can cope with incomplete temporal information; and it can also support a variety of temporal constructs that are difficult to implement in TSQL2.

1   Introduction

There has been a great deal of interest in Temporal Databases over the last 10 years with the number of papers published in the area rising steadily. There are numerous models for temporal databases which have been designed using both object oriented [3], [4] and relational databases [5], [6], [7], [8], [9], [10], [11], [12], [13], [14], [15] as the underlying database models. The basic understanding of temporal databases has progressed to the point where a standard temporal language and infrastructure, have been proposed [1], [16], [17] and a database utilising these standards, Multical, has been built [2]. Most of the work done to date has identified the basic properties of temporal information and various data models and associated algebras have been produced in order to manipulate data with a temporal component. Multical has demonstrated that a temporal query language can be implemented allowing for different calendars and a variety of temporal operators.

It is apparent from the difficulties of implementing a temporal query language that time is one of the most complex phenomena that can be modelled on a computer, and yet we all use this complexity in our daily life. This is reflected in the complexity of temporal languages such as TSQL2.

One type of task where time is an essential feature is planning. This area is difficult to represent in the TSQL2 approach because it often has incomplete temporal information. For instance, we often know the sequence of planning events needed to run an international conference and their temporal relationships to each other but, because the dates of the conference have not been finalised, it is difficult to store and manipulate this information.

Knowledge Based Systems (KBSs) which attempt to solve simple problems involving plans demonstrate both the complexity and the difficulty of the task [18], as well as the time taken [19]. Even apparently simple characteristics of time, such as periodically repeating events can be difficult to model and use. For example, Chomicki [20] has produced a temporal logic which can model regular, recurring intervals starting from some fixed point in time using the expression a + bx, where a is the start time, b is some period between recurrences of the event and x is a positive integer varying from 0 to infinity.

The conclusion to draw from these observations is that while the subject of temporal databases has made some excellent progress, it is now time to extend the language further to meet the needs of the user in complex application areas. To provide fuller temporal facilities for the naive user we must have a definition of a temporal structure and its manipulation where the temporal component is incomplete but can be related to other events to provide partial information.

In a temporal database system there must be a temporal data model with an associated temporal algebra for manipulating these data structures which map into the query language constructs of the database system. A temporal data model has the notion of a time axis with an origin, with time going from minus infinity to plus infinity at a given granularity. Against this time axis, a basic temporal model has three data constructs: A time point, a time interval and a time duration as discussed in [21] and [22]. A duration is a passage of time which has not been anchored to any specific point on the time axis, while an interval starts from a specific point in time and continues for some duration.

All temporal models for relational databases, including TSQL2, are based on this standard temporal representation. All events are stored with respect to some fixed, absolute underlying time base. This data model is awkward when handling missing temporal values.

This paper investigates an application which requires the user to manipulate events occurring at unknown times to identify what information is available. It will then demonstrate that TSQL2 is either difficult to use, unable to implement such temporal requirements or the data structures and the related queries become so complex that they are too difficult to understand.

An alternative language is proposed using a different conceptual model and based on a Graphical User Interface (GUI) with the capabilities of TSQL2 but easier to use because of the graphic user interface. It also represents temporal information more easily and can implement some temporal constructs not easily represented in TSQL2, such as causal relationships between events, synchronisations, subevents and periodic time. So, it is more natural to use and better at handling incomplete temporal information. It is called GEST for Graphic Events Synchronised in Time. It is theoretically possible to implement GEST in TSQL2 since it is based on a language for manipulating data but it would not be an effective implementation as shown in Section 3.

GEST has the same underlying temporal model as TSQL2 of a time point, a time interval and a time duration. It also has an extensive set of constructs for representing the synchronisation of events, subevents, showing the sequence relationship between temporal events and handling time values not bound to the temporal axis.

Section 2 presents an application area, Financial Trading Systems, and its temporal requirements. We identify five types of temporal query common to this and other application areas which the TSQL2 temporal model either can't handle or handles inadequately. These limitations are illustrated in Section 3 and some TSQL2 queries are presented to demonstrate the nature of the requirements. In Section 4, the GEST data model and query language are introduced. It is being prototyped on an Object Oriented Database (OODB) but could be based on any database. Demonstrations are presented showing how it implements the temporal operators in TSQL2. Section 5 presents further advantages of GEST which enable it to extend the basic capabilities of TSQL2. In Section 6, conclusions are drawn.

2   Description of the Application Area

The following short description of a Financial Trading System is based on the authors' experience of users and characterises the main area of investigation. There is not sufficient space in this paper to demonstrate a detailed analysis of all the appropriate application areas, such as Medical Treatment Plans [23] and Ecological Monitoring. Studies have shown that there are a set of similar queries in each area. The selection of queries fot this paper is chosen to demonstrate the requirements which are difficult to represent and query in TSQL2.

A common feature of these difficult queries is the storage and referencing of future events with a common relationship to another set of events where the absolute time of their occurrence is not known. Often relationships between such events is known, such as durations and causal relationships, so some partial information is available, but not enough for a time to be linked to an absolute time axis and then stored in a database. In many cases, such currently unknown temporal information, must be manipulated to create possible solutions.

The users will want to store and manipulate a generic sequences of events which have durations but are not yet tied to precise points in time, and so cannot be treated as intervals. A query may also be represented as a generic sequence of event durations with fixed start times not specified. Once the query is executed the generic sequences may be bound to actual events on an absolute time axis or to generic sequences, not yet bound to the time axis.

2.1 Financial Trading and Analysis Systems

Financial Trading and Analysis Systems [24] support the Dealers and Analysts who are buying and selling shares, stocks and bonds, all of which have the basic capabilities of making a series of payments, called coupons, and a lifetime, at the end of which they are redeemed by the issuer. There is a bewildering array of these instruments and no single person can keep track of all the combinations for trading. A support system must be able to examine these instruments according to various requirements which often involve the essential use of time. Many trading opportunities only occur at certain times of the month or year, according to many environmental factors.

The major area of investigation involves seeking ideal times for trading and identifying previously unnoticed causal relationships between a variety of events. Often the dealer will be working with many objects with fixed temporal relationships to other objects but with the exact times varying. A typical set of queries that a user might ask are shown in fig 1.

1) Find coupon values for stocks which are calculated one day after the announcement of the Retail Price Index figure?

2) Which alternative stocks and bonds produce a series of coupons with a given (possibly irregular) cycle?

3) List the instruments that can only be traded in the lifetime of a given stock.

4) Which instruments only trade on UK working days?

5) What can delay the redemption of a given bond? The answer to this case is the existence of a trade with a value of less than £100.00.

Figure 1. Typical queries in a Financial Application.

2.2 A Summary of the Queries

The queries in fig 1 have been chosen as they are similar across many applications. For the purposes of this paper the word event will be used to describe any happening that has some associated data, and takes some period of time to occur, so it has a start time, an end time and a duration. It is possible for an event to be instantaneous so this definition allows the start and end to be the same time. This allows events to be instantaneous in the representation's granularity.

Query 1 from fig 1 represents a *consequent event*, where one event is directly triggered by another, possibly, but not necessarily, after a fixed period of time. If the time of the triggering event and the time between events is known the triggered event can be instantiated to a fixed time.

Query 2 represents *periodic events*, where some sequence of events is recurring, possibly at regular intervals. Once the start of such a cycle is known, the remaining events can be instantiated as and when the time between the events is known.

The third query requires the user to be able to represent an event that can only occur within the lifetime of another, which we refer to as a *sub-event*. There are

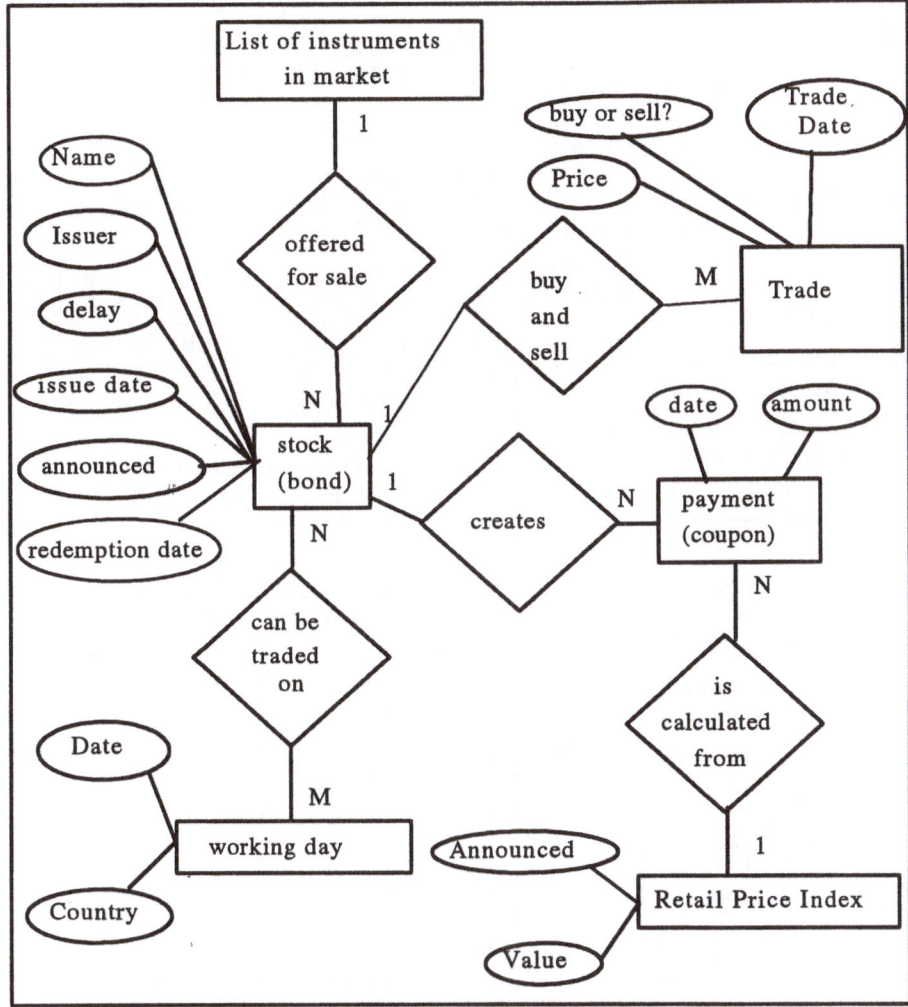

Figure 2. An ER Diagram of the Financial Application with
Time based values shaded

countless examples of such sub-events, e.g. specific tasks within a period of employment or events within a conference timetable.

The fourth query is searching for events that can only occur when two or more events are also occurring. These are a specialised form of the sub-event and are effectively *synchronised* to create a new event.

Sometimes the time between two events depends on the existence of some other event. Public holidays delay the time taken for some work to be done or a visit by an inspector could delay the next stage in the construction of the building. Effectively, while the time between two events is normally fixed, we must allow for these delays which increase the time, hence *delayed events* are a special case of

a) CREATE TABLE
    stock(Name   Character (30),
        Issuer   Character (30),
        announced DateTime) AS
VALID STATE INDETERMINATE

Name	Issuer	Valid Time
Regular Stock	UK	'1995-12-25 2000-12-25 ~ 2002-12-25'
Irregular Stock	UK	'1995-09-25 2015-09-25'

b) CREATE TABLE
    trade (StockName Character(30),
        Price   Integer,
        BuyorSell Logical) AS
VALID EVENT DAY;

StockName	BuyorSell	Price	Valid Time
Regular Stock	Buy	102	'1996-01-02'
Regular Stock	Sell	98	'1996-01-03'
Regular Stock	Buy	96	'1996-01-04'
Regular Stock	Sell	103	'1996-01-05'

c) CREATE TABLE
    RPI (Value Integer) AS
VALID EVENT DAY;

Value	Valid Date
1	'1996-09-25'
5	'1996-12-25'
4	'1997-03-25'

d) CREATE TABLE
    WorkingDay (
        Country character(30),
        Date   DateTime);

Country	Date
UK	'1995-12-29'
UK	'1996-01-02'
UK	'1996-01-03'
UK	'1996-01-04'

e) CREATE TABLE
    payment(
        StockName character (30),
        Value   Integer) AS
VALID EVENT DAY;

StockName	Value	Valid Time
Regular Stock	5	'1996-06-25'
Regular Stock	5	'1996-12-25'
Regular Stock	5	'1997-06-25'
Regular Stock	5	'1997-12-25'
Regular Stock	5	'1998-06-25'
...	...	...
Regular Stock	5	'2000-12-25'
Irregular Stock	1	'1996-09-25'
Irregular Stock	5	'1996-12-25'
Irregular Stock	4	'1997-03-25'
...	...	...
Irregular Stock	1	'2005-09-25'

Figure 3. TSQL2 DDL and Tables for the application data.

unknown times between events but some information is available about expected timings. The fifth query in fig 1 shows a delayed event.

The queries in fig 1 will need to be translated into data structures and operations for the target implementation. Obviously, a major problem in designing a system is this translation. Ideally, a good design, should reflect the real world problems in the final system, hence the introduction of Temporal Databases to facilitate this translation without the need for complex application code.

In order to write TSQL2 queries we need to identify the implied entities in each of the queries, so a simplified ER model for a financial application is shown in fig 2. The interpretations of the queries in fig 1 under the constraints of a temporal query language are translated to TSQL2. Note that all temporal information has been represented as date attributes against entities shaded in the diagram.

3   Implementation in TSQL2

The fig 2 ER model is realised in TSQL2 by the DDL statements shown in fig 3, each of which creates a table corresponding to an entity in the ER diagram. Examples of the tables created are shown with each DDL statement. We will assume that other useful data has been stored in these tables and is available for querying. Notice also that some of the date information, such as issue date, redemption date and delay date do not need to be explicitly stored as attributes since they now become implicit temporal attributes of the tables.

Two stock items are shown: one issues a regular set of payments every 6 months; the other issues an irregular set of payments. They represent some of the many possible combinations of data that it is possible to get in the dealing markets.

Also note, that foreign keys have now been introduced as attributes and that two of the entities, the Dealer and the list of instruments have been dropped as they don't relate directly to the queries being used in our examples.

Finally, only the actual dates and times of events that have occurred are stored in the database. While SQL data structures could be introduced to represent event sequencing and interdependency, they would not use the temporal features of TSQL2, and so would not provide a good comparison of the two approaches.

In many respects, the task of TSQL2 is not to represent complex temporal structures but the detailed existential, temporal data in the application.

The queries in fig 1 can now be cast into TSQL2 DML statements as follows:

Find coupon values for stocks which are calculated one day after the announcement of the Retail Price Index figure?

```
SELECT StockName, Value
VALID  VALID(P)
FROM   payment AS P, RPI AS R
WHERE VALID(R) + DATE '1 DAY' OVERLAPS VALID(P);
```

Note, since TSQL2 only stores existential data, this query cannot differentiate coincidental relationships from causal relationships. Hence, the above query will give all payments that occur one day after the RPI is announced. Whether they occur coincidentally or otherwise is difficult to represent.

Which alternative stocks and bonds produce a series of coupons with a given (possibly irregular) cycle?

Since TSQL2 does not allow direct representation of a periodic cycle, we must assume that we have created a set of dates to indicate the sequence of payments and the query language must be used to determine the sequence.

```
SELECT StockName
VALID VALID(C)
FROM    payment AS C
WHERE (SELECT
            VALID VALID(IS)
            FROM stock AS IS
            WHERE IS.name='Irregular Stock')  CONTAINS VALID(C);
```

List the instruments that can only be traded in the lifetime of a given stock.
TSQL2 is able to handle this query well.

```
SELECT Name
VALID VALID(S)
FROM stock AS S
WHERE (SELECT VALID VALID(IS)
            FROM stock AS IS
            WHERE IS.name='Regular Stock')
            CONTAINS VALID(S);
```

Which instruments only trade on UK working days?
For this query the users want to see all stocks that can be traded on UK working days, whether they are created in the UK or not. It is conceivable (but unlikely in this case) that there is some stock in a foreign market that can only be traded on UK working days due to other circumstances. The query written below only identifies those instruments issued in the UK assuming that they are all the stocks that can be traded only on UK working days. To do the query the users want, we would need to enter all the possible trading times for all stocks and then compare these possible times to the dates in the UK working days table. This would require much data to be stored yet the underlying sequence should be modelled. Ideally, we want to represent the possible trading dates as a logical, repeating sequence.
Hence, although the query below is not complex and uses only the minimum of data, this is purely due to the substitution of a different, simpler query.

```
SELECT name
FROM stock AS S, WorkingDay AS WD
WHERE S.Issuer=WD.Country;
```

What can delay the redemption of a given bond?
The information on why an event has an unknown duration cannot be directly stored in TSQL2, so it is quite difficult to write this query. We either need to store extra information in another table and relate the two in the query language or guess from the juxtaposition of the times. Another table would require extra complexity that would not use the temporal constructs of TSQL2 and so would not be useful in this comparison. On the other hand, using the juxtaposition of times does not

enable us to differentiate with certainty causal links from coincidences. Thus we will not attempt to write this query with our current TSQL2 temporal data model.

4   The GEST System

GEST uses a graphical approach to represent its data model along the principles presented in [21] and [22]. It has constructs for the basic temporal notions of time point, time interval and time duration. These are augmented with additional graphical constructs for showing causal temporal relationships, synchronisations of events, subevents and delayed events. Durations are shown as arcs with times (possibly unknown) attached. Events are drawn as boxes with start and stop times linked by arcs. There is a special event, called the start of time, which is bound to the temporal axis by starting at time zero. Start times for other events can be bound to the temporal axis by an arc from the start of time or by directly entering an absolute time in the start time slot.

These constructs can be used through the GEST query language interface. This supports the standard temporal operations found in TSQL2. Essentially GEST is based on durations and intervals in much the same manner as TSQL2, and hence could actually be implemented using any temporal database.

GEST has been implemented as a set of object classes using C++ on the ONTOS database system [25] using the Tcl/Tk User interface package [26]. These are described in more detail in [24].

4.1   Representing Temporal Structures

Figures 4 to 9 show the constructs of GEST. Events are happenings which start and stop, possible many times. They are named for ease of reference and a few examples are shown in fig 4 as boxes containing their names, with start and stop boxes embedded in them. Delay times, which are durations and not intervals, are shown as arcs between the events, with labels indicating the delay time in the form yy:mm:dd:hh:mm:ss. If the time of the delay is unknown it is represented with the number -1 in all the time fields on its label. Note that any of the fields can be any positive number, months are not limited to 12 or less, and so on. Figure 4 also shows arcs connecting the events using the preparation of a lecture as the example. There are some unusual aspects of this sequence to demonstrate features of GEST. For example, only fifteen minutes are ever allowed at any one time for preparing or reviewing the notes. Similarly, exactly one day must be left between the end of

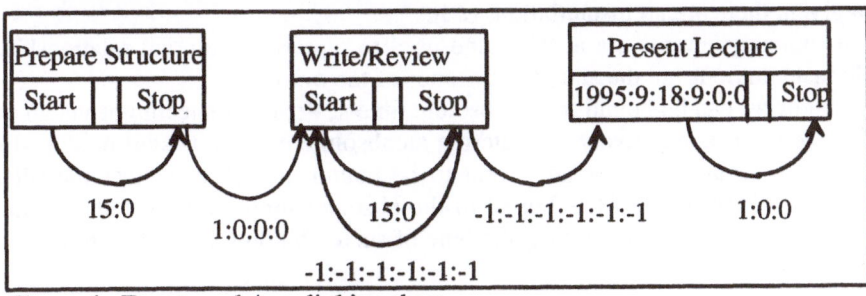

Figure 4. Events and Arcs linking them

142

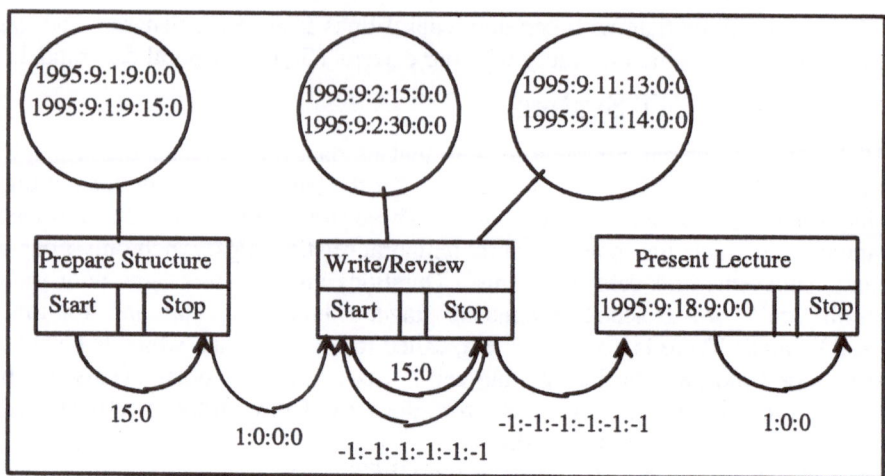

Figure 5. Instantiations against the events.

the preparation of the structure and the first write of the notes. There is a cycle in the arcs on the Write/Review event, indicating that it can occur several times. The arcs indicate that the lecture can occur at any time after the revision of the notes, although the absolute start

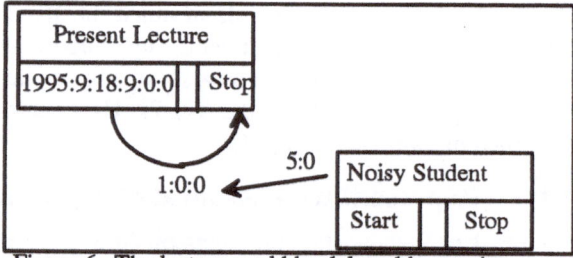

Figure 6. The lecture could be delayed by a noisy student

time on the presentation shows that the time of the lecture is fixed.

Note that at this stage, we are only representing abstract events and how they are connected for manipulation. Figure 5 shows the same events and arcs, but with an associated set of instantiations. Instantiations and their associated stored values are shown in circles connected by lines to their associated events. The instantiations are used to store the actual occurrence of the event and are linked to the associated data and so they contain start and stop times. They could be directly implemented in TSQL2 and are the most basic component of the GEST model. In this case, there were only two attempts at writing the notes and, since the lecture has not yet been given, there are no instantiations of it.

So, in summary, events are abstract and used to represent temporal relationships, while instantiations are the actual occurrence of the event.

Thus, an event can be bound to the absolute time scale, by connecting it via an arc to time zero, or, alternatively, by entering an absolute time in its start or stop slot. There is no requirement for any event to be bound in such a manner until it is necessary. Once the event is bound to the absolute time scale (and if it is in a cycle it can be bound many times) the time of such a binding is used to indicate an instantiation.

The times between events can be varied by the existence of other events. Effectively the time on the arc between the events is affected by the other event. Delay times that depend on other events, are shown with arrows from the other event to the time on the arc, as shown in fig 6 where the presentation time of the lecture has been delayed for 5 minutes by the presence of an unruly student.

If an event can only occur when two or more other events are also occurring, the event is only instantiated by the instantiation of the other events. To indicate such a synchronisation, the flag between the start and stop boxes is set to 'S'. For example, fig 7 shows that the lecture can only proceed if the lecturer is present and an overhead projector is working.

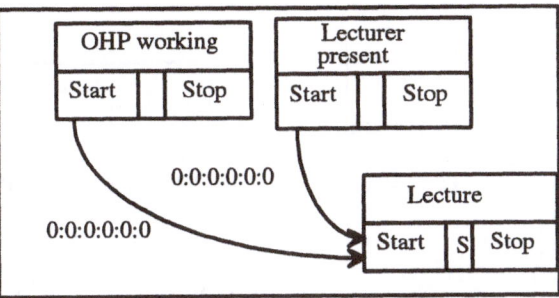

Figure 7. The lecture can only proceed if an OHP is working and the lecturer is present

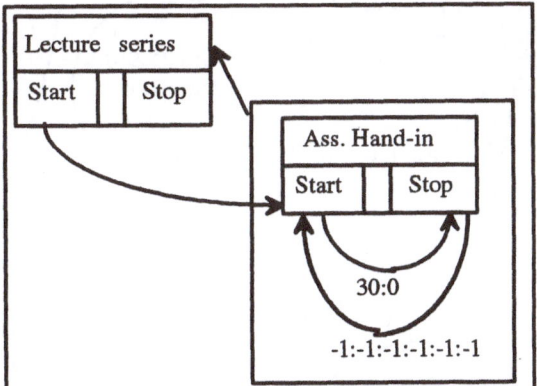

Figure 8. A series of assignments that can only be handed in during the lecture series.

Subevents can only occur in the lifetime of another event, the major event. There are numerous examples of subevents in all our lives and they can be crucial in preventing recurring events from being infinitely instantiated. They are shown in a box with an arrow from the outside of the box to the major event. Effectively, they can only be instantiated at those times when there is an instantiation of the major event, even if they are in a cycle. Figure 8 shows a subevent consisting of a series of assignments, each leading to the next, which can only be handed in during the lecture series. The subevent is drawn in a box with an arrow to the major event. Note that in this case, the subevent is started by the major event, which, while it occurs often is not required.

Finally, after some experimentation it has been shown that some standard events are better created using calendars stored within the database directly and not implemented using the temporal constructs shown here. These calendar events can be specified to occur daily, weekly, monthly or yearly with start and stop times. Examples are months of the year, the days of the week and so on. They are represented in much the same way as an event with a start and a length in a central box. Figure 9 includes such a calendar event in the top left corner, the RPI published event, which occurs on the 25th day of every month.

144

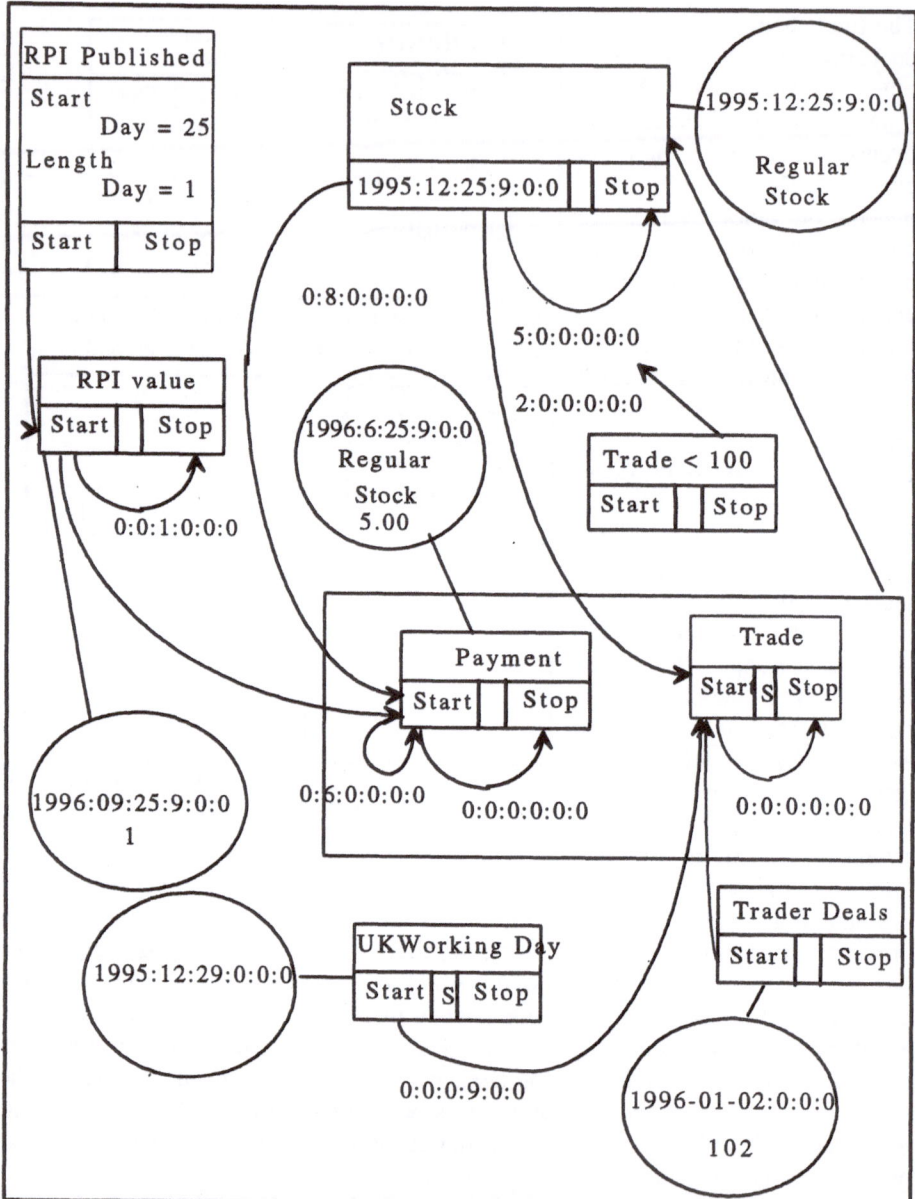

Figure 9 The Regular Stock shown as a Graph

4.2 Constructing a Model of the Financial Application

Figure 9 shows the full complexity of the imaginary stock and its associated payments and trades. The events that can affect all the trades and payments are also shown with a few instantiations of each. Many of these instantiations would not normally be needed by the user when the system is being designed and only the relevant instantiations need to be considered when entering data. A query will only access the required instantiations, hence the diagram in fig 9 is more complex than would appear when a query is being executed.

Examining the diagram we can see that the start time of the Stock is fixed, so a value for its start time is inserted. It could instead have been linked from a start of time event. It stops 5 years later, unless there is a trade with a value of less than £100.00 whereupon the arc time is extended by 2 years.

The payment of coupons is probably the most important part of this diagram. It demonstrates a subevent as coupons are only paid within the lifetime of the Gilt. They recur in a cycle since coupons cause themselves to be re-issued every six months. This is shown by the arc which links back from the start time to the same start time with a 6 month delay. These payments are instantaneous events which stop zero seconds after starting.

The RPI is a Calendar event, which is published on the 25th of every month. since it occurs regularly according to whether the current date meets its conditions. For example, the RPI publication occurs whenever the day of the month is 25 and lasts for one day.

The trade is shown as a synchronised event, occurring when the dealer is ready to make a trade and it is a UK working day. The instantiated value indicates the actual value of the trade. A better example of a synchronised event would be a payment that occurs after the publication of the RPI figure.

4.3   GEST Queries

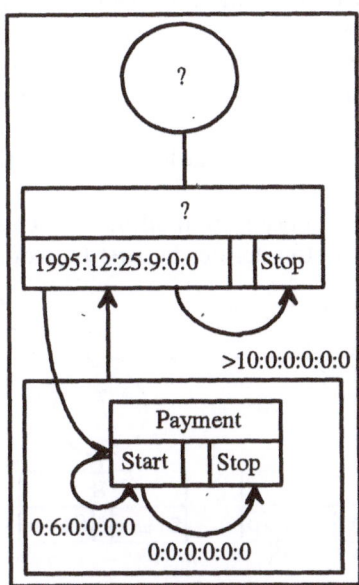

Figure 10, a GEST query selecting all stocks starting at 9am on 25/12/95 and making payments every 6 months

Queries in GEST are created in a similar way to the temporal constructs of the data model. By drawing the structure of the temporal relationships, the database can then query by searching for instantiations of the data which match those drawn in the query. Question marks are used to indicate values to be instantiated in the query, possibly in tabular form. Note that if an event has more arcs attached to it than appear in the query diagram it will still be selected by the matching process, since the query specifies minimum requirements for matching.

For querying we need to be able to represent some more generic information to be matched, so GEST provides two extra features. The first is the ability to match a sequence of events and arcs. This is represented by including a row of dots within the arc from one event to another. Such an arc can be matched to any sequence of events and arcs.

The second ability enables the user to differentiate coincidental temporal data from causal temporal data. If a firm line is drawn for the arc, the query attempts to match events using their structure, hence such a query would select those events where the user deliberately wanted to find causal relationships. Alternatively, the arc could be represented as a dashed line, which indicates that only the instantiations should be searched for a match, hence coincidental temporal relationships will be shown, as well as causal relationships.

We can now demonstrate a simple query for the Financial Application area to find all stock items which are issued at 9am on 25/12/1995 and make payments every six months. This query would be drawn as shown in fig 10. Note, once again, that if we do not care about some feature when we are writing the query, it can be omitted from the diagram, and matching events will still be found. For example, there is no link from the stock to a trade, so we expect to get all stocks, irrespective of whether they have traded. Similarly, the arc from the stock's start to stop slots has an expression, indicating that only those stock items with a lifetime of more than 10 years are to be selected.

Further queries in section 5 give a demonstration of the capabilities of GEST.

4.4   Comparing GEST Operators to TSQL2 Operators

In order to demonstrate that GEST is at least as powerful as TSQL2, we will now examine how two TSQL2 operators LEFT OVERLAPS and CONTAINS can be represented. These have been chosen as representative operators since they are used extensively in the TSQL2 tutorial [16]. Figure 11 shows representations for both operators, using dashed arcs so that it uses the same approach as TSQL2. Note that question marks in the circles indicate that we are searching for instantiations of the data which match the structures.

LEFT OVERLAPS requires that event A starts before B and this is shown by the arc from the start of A to the start of B, with the predicate >0 on it to indicate that only those arcs which are greater than zero are to be matched. Similarly, the arc from the start of B to the stop of A indicates that B must start at least one second before A stops.

We could also have written the LEFT OVERLAPS query to find all those events **designed** to start after the first event but that don't stop before the first by using firm lines for the arcs.

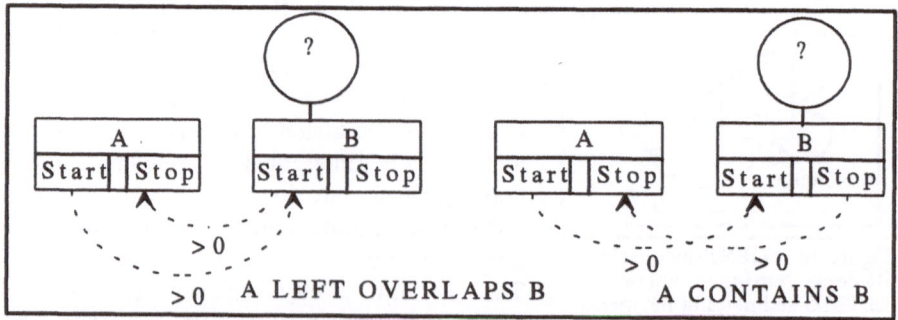

Figure 11. The operators OVERLAPS and CONTAINS represented as GEST queries.

The operator CONTAINS requires that event A starts before B and ends after, hence there is an arc with greater than zero time from the start of A to the start of B, only matching those events that start after A starts. The arc from the stop of B to the stop of A shows that at least one second must elapse after B stops and before A starts. Once again it is dotted in order to be equivalent to the corresponding TSQL2 query which only works on instantiated data.

CONTAINS could actually have been done more easily by using a subevent, but that would not be the operator as implemented in TSQL2.

There is not enough space to examine all of the temporal operators defined in TSQL[16] but it should be apparent that GEST can represent them all, since the start and stop times of intervals are available, and so the normal operators of <, <=, >, >= and <> can be represented by direct reference to these start and stop times.

4.5   A Comparison to TSQL2

The importance of Graphic User Interfaces (GUIs) has been demonstrated in numerous papers, including entire conferences. There is a great deal of evidence that a Graphical Language for querying a database, while not necessarily providing all the power of a textual query language is easier to use [25].

As a result a GUI is felt to be an essential feature of the alternative model and query language demonstrated here. By providing these temporal constructs the user is able to present the complex temporal structure of the information, including indefinite events in time.

If a system is easily usable with minimal training, it must appear in a form that the users are familiar with. Despite the use of English words such as SELECT, FROM, WHERE and ORDER BY, SQL is difficult to learn since these words are not used in an everyday manner. From teaching experience, at least 2 full days of tuition are needed for the average user to learn the basics of SQL. The following points, in the authors' opinion indicate whether a system is easily usable:

- Does it use constructs most people are familiar with?
- Does it provide operators that are intuitively obvious?
- Does it give confidence that the result is correct?

In many respects the points on this list are subjective, but they are also important. While many of the operators such as OVERLAPS seem to be readily apparent, their use is so technically precise that the users may well not realise their effect. The authors claim that the diagrams of GEST are more familiar to users who have already adopted PERT charts. Similarly, the operators are more obvious and the confidence in the result should be improved. So, in addition to having the same power as TSQL2, we feel GEST is easier to use.

5   Working with Incomplete Temporal Data

An examination of the application area chosen for this paper has shown that there is a need to work with incomplete temporal data. This section examines the requirements for such work and demonstrates that GEST can represent durations which are not yet bound to the absolute time axis as well as representing various temporal structures that are required to meet the needs of the applications described in Section 2.

5.1   Power

The power of a language indicates its ability to model the appropriate underlying constructs in some way and, in this case, can be measured by whether the Temporal Database System has the following features:

Temporal Model Features
- store time intervals and time durations of events, when available
- store temporal relationships that occur between objects

Query Language Features
- cope with incomplete temporal information
- represent different calendars and granularities of time
- differentiate coincidences from causality

A temporal database capable of handling the applications we are addressing should be able to provide all of the above features.   TSQL2 does not directly address the issues of incomplete   temporal information and so they must be   implemented   using   the underlying SQL language and application code.   Also, it is difficult   'to   differentiate coincidences   from   causality

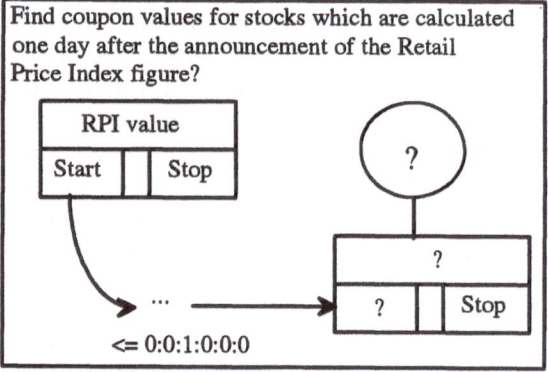

Figure 12. The first query

without extra information added to the underlying data structures. When temporal is stored in the database, the times of the information being stored must be known or complex data structures are needed to represent any temporal relationships.

5.2   GEST Queries with Temporal Structures

A representation for the first query is shown in fig 12. As with all these queries, there is a tool to draw templates to be matched against the event structures. Note the use of a sequence of events and arcs indicated by the dots between the arcs.

Figure 13 demonstrates the query which attempts to match payment sequences. In this case we are seeking any stock which starts on 25th September, 1995, and pays a coupon at any time after with 6 months between payments. The unlabelled arcs can be instantiated with any value, hence the stock can have any lifetime. If we wanted the coupons to be paid irregularly we would need to draw the sequence of payments as a sequence of events or with dots in the arc.

Which alternative stocks and bonds produce a series of coupons with a given (possibly irregular) cycle?

?	
1995:9:25:0:0:0	Stop

Payment	
Start	Stop

0:6:0:0:0:0

Figure 13. The second query.

List the instruments that can only be traded in the lifetime of a given stock.

Regular Stock	
1995:12:25:9:0:0	Stop

?	
?	Stop

Figure 14 The third query

Figure 14 shows a query using a subevent. The expected return from such a query would be a future or an option.

Figure 15 shows the power of being able to represent the synchronisation of two events. The query searches for events that can occur more than 8 hours after the start of trading, providing they occur at the same time as a working day. This is implemented by the expression on the delay time which indicates delays of more than 8 hours and the S between the start and stop slots indicating that the event is synchronised.

Figure 16 shows a query to list the events that can affect the delay time attached to an arc. Because the arc from the query leads to the time of the arc from the start of the stock to its end, it matches those events that affect this time. The question mark on this arc shows that we want to know how long the delay will be if the delaying event exists.

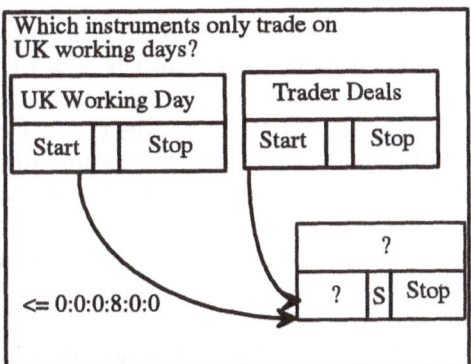

Which instruments only trade on UK working days?

UK Working Day	
Start	Stop

Trader Deals	
Start	Stop

?		
?	S	Stop

<= 0:0:0:8:0:0

Figure 15. The fourth query

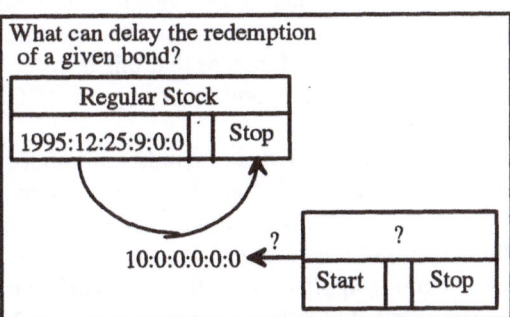

What can delay the redemption of a given bond?

Regular Stock	
1995:12:25:9:0:0	Stop

10:0:0:0:0:0

?	
Start	Stop

Figure 16. The fifth query

5.3   Summary

A review of the two approaches demonstrates first that representing temporal structures with unknown times and querying on them is inherently complex. The TSQL2 queries are based on a different approach, assuming that the data will be

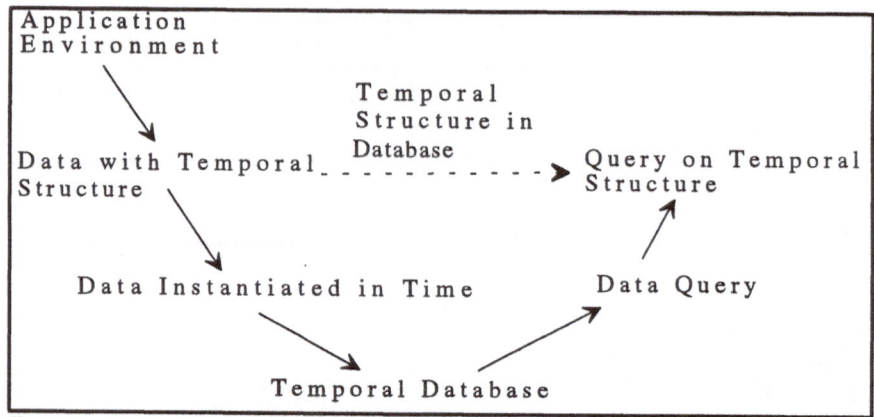

Figure 17   The sequence of temporal data storage and access

readily available, so to represent the incomplete temporal data will require other columns of data, which must be constructed by the user and cannot necessarily take full advantage of the temporal constructs.

The requirement for these higher level constructs is clear from the application. Most planning software is too specific for use in general databases. Unfortunately, until the performance of Temporal Knowledge Based Systems can be improved significantly, the user will be required to model the temporal constructs and to populate the database with the temporal constructs, whatever the temporal language. This seems to be an inherent limitation of representing such temporal information.

By only storing the actual occurrence times of events against data, TSQL2 is not preserving some of the essential information. In effect, we either have to store new information that cannot make use of the temporal database features, or we have to attempt to reconstruct the structure from the stored data, with all the possible incorrect inferences that this brings. Figure 17 shows how the sequence of events, data storage and querying in TSQL2 lose this information, which is preserved in GEST.

For usability, GEST does include a number of extra constructs and operators but, despite this, it is felt that the users will be more confident that the queries are correct. Most of this confidence is based on a subjective view of the confidence of the result, but the graphical approach does seem to provide more power to the user in a planning application without a significant increase in complexity of the model.

In summary, TSQL2 is good for storing and using basic temporal facts, but weak for incomplete temporal information which may require higher level constructs for representation and querying.

This structure has been designed and a prototype written using ONTOS, [26] and a screen drawing tool, Tcl/Tk [27]. The underlying model has been implemented and is functional, although the best ways of entering the instantiations of object values is still being investigated. The query language is now being developed, to investigate whether it will have a sufficiently high performance.

6   Conclusions

As we all use higher order temporal constructs in our everyday life, and in many applications, so they should be available in a temporal database management system. Our use of time is inherently complex and we should be able to introduce such usage, without introducing further complexity. Any representation of a temporal construct should be as obvious as is possible.

We have demonstrated some of the requirements for a temporal model that allows the user to work with events that have a time duration and some sort of relationship to other events but are not tied to a temporal axis. By incorporating this power into a graphical user interface, we believe that GEST has increased the power of a Temporal Database while improving the ease of access by the user. We believe that GEST demonstrates the next steps to be considered in developing temporal database systems, namely operators for working with incomplete temporal data.

The complexity of TSQL2 and GEST shows that more work needs to be done to ensure that any Temporal Database actually provides some advantages over a snapshot database, since they must be, of necessity, more complex. If the resulting Temporal Database Management Systems always introduce greater complexity in an attempt to model as much as possible, they may become too difficult to use in general. It may be better to let the application programmer concentrate only on the temporal features that are necessary for his or her application.

The major conclusion from this work is that more needs to be done on temporal databases and their interfaces to the users, particularly in dealing with incomplete data. The current queries are still based on SQL interfaces, which are now being superseded by GUIs.

7   References

[1]   Pissinou, N., Snodgrass,R.T., Elmasri,R., Mumick,I.S., Ozsu,M.T., Pernici, B. Segev,A., Theodoulidis, B., Dayal,U., "Towards an Infrastructure for Temporal Databases: Report of an Invitational ARPA/NSF Workshop" in SIGMOD Record, Vol 23, No. 1.

[2]   Soo,M., Snodgrass,R. Technical papers on Multical, TempIS Technical Reports, Computer Science Department, University of Arizona, Tucson, Arizona.

[3]   Kafer, W., Ritter, N., and Schoning, H., "Support for Temporal Data by Complex Objects", in Proceedings of the 16th VLDB Conference, Brisbane, Australia, 1990.

[4]   Kafer, W. and Schoning, H., "Realizing a Temporal Complex Object Data Model", in ACM SIGMOD Conference, 1992.

[5]   Chaudhuri, S., "Temporal Relationships in Databases", in Proceedings of the 14th VLDB, Los Angeles, California, 1988.

[6]   Clifford, J., and Tansel, A.U., "On An Algebra for Historical Relational Databases: Two Views", in Proceedings of the ACM SIGMOD International Conference on the Management of Data, 1985.

[7]   Gadia, S.K., Yeung, C-S., "Inadequacy of Interval Timestamps in Temporal Databases", in Information Sciences Vol 54, pages 1 to 22, 1991.

[8]   Jensen, C.S., Clifford, J., Gadia, S.K., Segev, A., Snodgrass, R.T., "A Glossary of Temporal Database Concepts", in SIGMOD Record, Vol. 21,No. 3, September, 1992.

[9]   Lorentzos, N.A., "A Formal Extension of the Relational Model for the Representation and Manipulation of Generic Intervals", in Ph.D. thesis, Birckbeck College, London, 1988.

[10]   McKenzie, L.E., and Snodgrass R.T., "Evaluation of Relational Algebras Incorporating the Time Dimension in Databases", in ACM Computing Surveys, Vol. 23, No. 4, December, 1991.

[11]   Sarda, N.L., "Algebra and Query Language for a Historical Data Model", in The Computer Journal, Vol. 33, No. 1, 1990.

[12]   Tansel, A.U., "Adding Time Dimension to Relational Model and Extending Relational Algebra", in Information Systems, Vol. 11, No. 4, 1986.

[13]   Tansel, A.U., "Modelling Temporal Data", in Journal of Information and Software Technology, Vol. 32, No. 8, October, 1990.

[14]   Tansel, A.U. et al, Temporal Databases, Addison Wesley, 1993.

[15]   Tuzhilin, A., Clifford, J., "A Temporal Relational Algebra as a Basis for Temporal Relational Completeness", in Proceedings of the 16th VLDB Conference, Brisbane, Australia, 1990.

[16]   Snodgrass, R.T., et al, "A TSQL2 Tutorial", in SIGMOD Record, Vol 23, No. 3, September, 1994.

[17]   TSQL2 papers available by anonymous FTP from FTP.cs.arizona.edu.

[18]   Boddy,M., "Temporal Reasoning for Planning and Scheduling", SIGART Bulletin, Vol 4., No. 3, 1993.

[19]   Yampratoom, E., Allen, J.F., "Performance of Temporal Reasoning Systems", in SIGART Bulletin, Vol 4., No. 3, 1993.

[20]   Chomicki, J., Imielinski, T., "Temporal Deductive Databases and Infinite Objects", in Proceedings of the 7th ACM SIGACT-SIGMOD-SIGART Symposium on Principles of Database Systems Austin, Texas, 1988.

[21]   Lingat, J.Y., Nobecourt, P., Rolland, C., "Behaviour Management in Database Applications", in Proceedings of the 13th VLDB Conference, Brighton, 1987.

[22]   Nobecourt, P., Rolland, C., Lingat, J.Y., "Temporal Management in an Extended Relational DBMS", in Proceedings of the Sixth British National Conference on Databases, 1988.

[23]   Kahn, M. G., Ferguson, J. C., Shortliffe, E.H., Fagan, L. M., "Representation and use of temporal information in ONCOCIN", in Proceedings of the Ninth Annual Symposium on Computer Applications in Medical Care, 1985.

[24]   Harris, W.J. and Gray, W.A., "Temporal Constructs Required to Represent Financial Instruments", in Financial Information Systems Conference, Sheffield, UK, 1994.

[25]   Batini,C., Catarci,T., Costabile,M.F., Levialdi,S., "Visual Query Systems: A Taxonomy" in Visual Database Systems II, ed. Knuth,E., Wegner,L.M. Pub: Elsevier,1992.

[26]   ONTOS version 2.1 user manuals, Ontologic Incorporated, 1993.

[27]   Ousterhout, J.K., Tcl and Tk software and documentation distribution on anonymous email from allspice.berkeley.edu.

Evaluating the Completeness of TSQL2

Michael H. Böhlen

Department of Computer Science, University of Arizona
Tucson, AZ 85721, USA

Christian S. Jensen

Department of Mathematics and Computer Science, Aalborg University
Fredrik Bajers Vej 7E, DK–9220 Aalborg Ø, DENMARK

Richard T. Snodgrass

Department of Computer Science, University of Arizona
Tucson, AZ 85721, USA

Abstract

The question of what is a well-designed temporal data model and query language is a difficult, but also an important one. The consensus temporal query language TSQL2 attempts to take advantage of the accumulated knowledge gained from designing and studying many of the earlier models and languages. In this sense, TSQL2 represents a constructive answer to this question. Others have provided analytical answers by developing criteria, formulated as completeness properties, for what is a good model and language.

This paper applies important existing completeness notions to TSQL2 in order to evaluate the design of TSQL2. It is shown that TSQL2 satisfies only a subset of these completeness notions.

1 Introduction

The temporal database community has been prolific in its production of temporal data models and query languages. Over the past fifteen years, more than two dozen temporal relational data models have been proposed, each with one or more associated query languages [24]. This has left the community with a wide, confusing—but also challenging—variety of alternatives.

As one response to this state of affairs, a committee of eighteen temporal database researchers has recently released the TSQL2 Language Specification [25], which defines a temporal extension to the SQL–92 standard [22]. TSQL2 was created partly in an attempt to consolidate, in a single consensual model and language, the insights and experiences gained from the development of the previous data models and languages.

As a quite different approach, other efforts (e.g., [5, 6, 7, 21]) have put focus on the properties of temporal data models and query languages, as well as on the design alternatives available when developing these. This has led to precise definitions of model and language properties that can be used to characterize and evaluate the many models and languages. In the spirit of Codd's original definition of relational completeness [11], some of these properties have been stated as different kinds of completeness.

It then seems appropriate to use the body of work on model and language properties to study the design of TSQL2—this paper does exactly that. It is a fundamental assumption of the paper that when evaluating a data model and query language, both the functionality and the syntax for expressing a certain functionality are important. The completeness notions that we adopt in the investigation thus include both functionality-related and syntactic criteria.

Specifically, we formalize the notion of a data model being *upwards compatible* with another data model and show that TSQL2 is upwards compatible with SQL–92. Briefly, this means that a smooth transition from SQL–92 to TSQL2 is possible.

One of the most widely cited distinctions among temporal data models is that between first normal form and non-first normal form models. This distinction has been formally captured by the concepts of *temporally ungrouped* and *grouped* data models [7]. We show that TSQL2 is temporally ungrouped and not temporally grouped. As this property is inherent in the model, we do not propose to change it. Rather, we put focus on the implications of a model being ungrouped or grouped.

The last two completeness notions considered in this paper are *temporal semi-completeness* and *temporal completeness* [5]. The former notion essentially states that a temporal relational data model must contain temporal generalizations of *all* snapshot relations and queries. Further, temporally generalized queries must be *syntactically similar* to the snapshot queries they generalize. Temporal completeness adds further functional and syntactic requirements, addressing query language aspects not covered by temporal semi-completeness. It is shown that TSQL2 does not fully satisfy these completeness notions.

Related work on completeness has been primarily in the context of non-temporal databases. It is possible to distinguish two basic approaches. The first one takes a particular calculus (usually first order relational calculus) as a metric. Any language having at least the expressive power of the calculus is said to be complete. Original work along these lines was done by Codd for relational databases [11]. There have been generalizations for entity-relationship databases [1] and for temporal databases [30]. One inherent problem with these approaches is the degree of appropriateness of the calculus that is used as a metric. There is no guarantee that the calculus captures *all* reasonable queries. For example, it has been shown [3] that first order relational calculus cannot express the transitive closure of binary relations.

The second approach is to define an appropriately large set of queries and require query languages to express all queries in this set. This kind of completeness was investigated by Bancilhon [4] and Chandra and Harel [8]. The definitions of temporal semi-completeness and temporal completeness are in this spirit. They (in particular temporal semi-completeness) take the set of queries that are expressible by a non-temporal language as a reference and ensure that temporal generalizations of the non-temporal language can express all these queries. Additionally, they establish syntactic restrictions a temporal language must obey, which we believe is also important.

The contributions of the paper are twofold. First, the paper further formalizes some existing definitions of completeness of relevance for temporal data models and query languages, namely the notions of upwards compatibility, temporal semi-completeness and temporal completeness. Second, the paper explores the design of TSQL2 by applying these completeness notions and the notion of temporal (un)groupedness to TSQL2. It is shown that TSQL2 satisfies some of these notions, but does not satisfy all of them.

The paper is structured as follows. Each of Sections 2–5 first defines a particular type of completeness. They then evaluate the completeness of TSQL2 in the context of each completeness notion. During this investigation, some deficiencies of TSQL2 are uncovered.[1] Section 6 summarizes the paper and points to directions for future research.

2   Upwards Compatibility

Completeness is generally a relative property of a data model or a query language. Thus, a model or language satisfies some notion of "completeness" if it is related to another model or query language in a certain way. In this section, we introduce the first of the three types of completeness. Specifically, we formalize the notion that a data model is upwards compatible with respect to another data model. We subsequently consider the upwards compatibility of TSQL2 with respect to SQL–92.

2.1   Definitions

When a new database management system, with an associated data model, is introduced into an organization, often that system replaces an existing system, also with an associated data model. For software engineering reasons, to be discussed in more detail below, it is an important property that the existing data model be upwards (or, forwards) compatible with the new data model. Put differently, the new data model should be a strict superset of the existing data model.

We will adopt the convention that a data model consists of two components, namely a set of data structures and a language for querying the data structures. For example, the central data structure of the relational model is the relation, and the central, user-level query language is SQL. Notationally, $M = (DS, QL)$ then denotes a data model, M, consisting of a data structure component, DS, and a query language component, QL. Thus, DS is the set of all databases expressible by M, and QL is the set of all queries in M that may be formulated on some database in M. We will use db to denote a database and q to denote a query.

Definition 2.1 (upwards compatibility) Let $M_2 = (DS_2, QL_2)$ and $M_1 = (DS_1, QL_1)$ be two data models. Model M_2 is *upwards compatible with* model M_1 if and only if

- $DS_2 \supseteq DS_1$, and

- for each instance db in DS_2 and for each query expression q in QL_1, q is also a legal query expression in QL_2, and the results of evaluating q on db is the same in M_1 and M_2. ∎

---

[1]To answer these deficiencies, the design of Applied TSQL2 (ATSQL2) was initiated. ATSQL2 is a minimal extension of TSQL2 that is temporally complete. An extended version of this paper (ftp://ftp.cs.arizona.edu/reports/1995/TR95-5.ps.gz) sketches syntax and semantics of ATSQL2. A more comprehensive discussion as well as an implementation for public consumption are under way and should be completed by Fall 1995.

This concept captures the conditions that need to be satisfied in order to allow a smooth transition from a current system, with data model M_1, to a new system, with data model M_2. The first condition implies that all existing databases in the old system are also legal databases in the new system and thus need not be modified when the new system is adopted. The second condition guarantees that existing queries will remain legal and will compute the same results in the new system as in the old system. Thus, the bulk of legacy application code is not affected by the transition to a new system.

The definition of upwards compatibility is related to the traditional notion of Codd completeness (Codd originally used the term relational completeness) [11], as formulated in the context of the standard relational model. To see the similarity and differences, we review that completeness notion.

Essentially, a relational or extended relational data model is Codd complete if all queries that can be formulated on arbitrary conventional relations expressible in the model are a superset of all relational algebra queries that can be formulated.

Definition 2.2 (Codd completeness) Let $M = (DS, QL)$ be some data model, and let (SR, RA) be the relational model with the relational algebra as its query language. Model M is *Codd complete* if and only if DS contains SR and each query in RA has an equivalent counterpart in QL when all db in SR are considered. ∎

Two query expressions are equivalent if they always yield mutually identical results when supplied identical arguments. The relational algebra comes in numerous versions[2], and while the definition is dependent on the particular version chosen, the choice is not important in the remainder of this paper.

The similarity between upwards compatibility and Codd completeness is apparent, but there are also important differences. First, Codd completeness is restricted to use the relational algebra as a yardstick for measuring the expressive power of other query languages. Thus, the relevance of Codd completeness is dependent on how "natural" or well-chosen the relational algebra is. On the other hand, upwards compatibility is not tied to any particular data model.

Second, Codd completeness strictly concerns functionality while upwards compatibility concerns both functionality and the syntax for expressing the functionality. Specifically, Codd completeness is defined in terms of the existence of *equivalent*, but possibly different, query expressions. Upwards compatibility requires query expressions that yield identical results to also be syntactically *identical*. Thus, a model being upwards compatible with the relational model/algebra is a stronger criterion than the model being Codd complete.

2.2 Upwards Compatibility among SQL–92 and TSQL2

Clearly, it is an important property for a new data model, such as TSQL2, to be a strict superset of the data model it is intended to supersede, i.e., SQL–92. We now consider this issue.

---

[2]The relational algebra used in conjunction with the original definition of Codd completeness [11] included "cartesian [sic] product," "union," "intersection," "difference," "projection," "θ-join," "division," and "restriction" (a special case of selection).

In TSQL2, there are six kinds of relations[3]: snapshot relation, valid-time event relation, valid-time state relation, transaction-time relation, bitemporal event relation, and bitemporal state relation. The first is the kind of relation found in the conventional relational model; the remaining five are temporal relations. As all the schema specification statements of SQL–92 are included in TSQL2, it follows that the data structures of TSQL2 include those in SQL–92.

TSQL2 is also a strict superset of SQL–92 in its query facilities. In particular, if an SQL–92 select statement does not incorporate any of the constructs added in TSQL2 (e.g., the valid clause, the VALID() and TRANSACTION() expressions, and extensions to the from and group by clauses), and mentions only snapshot relations in its from clause(s), then the language specification states explicitly that the semantics of this statement is identical to its SQL–92 semantics.

It should be noted that the preliminary TSQL2 language specification released in March, 1994 [25] did not have that property. In particular, SQL–92 INTERVALs were termed SPANs in the preliminary TSQL2 specification, and TSQL2 INTERVALs were not present at all in SQL–92. The final TSQL2 language specification [25] retained SQL–92 INTERVALs and added the PERIOD data type, which was previously called INTERVAL in preliminary TSQL2 (confusing, isn't it?). Additional changes to the datetime literals were also made to ensure that TSQL2 was a strict superset of SQL–92.

Hence, both conditions are satisfied, demonstrating that TSQL2 is upwards compatible with SQL–92.

As discussed previously, this directly implies that TSQL2 is Codd complete.

Finally note that, while upwards compatibility is a highly desirable property, it says absolutely nothing about constructs added to a data model or query language to support time. This notion of completeness is thus quite limited in scope, as seen from a temporal data-model perspective.

3 Temporal Groupedness

In this section, we first review the previously proposed notions of temporally ungrouped and grouped data models. We then investigate the temporal groupedness of TSQL2. In contrast to upwards compatibility, temporal groupedness speaks directly to the support of time-varying information in the temporal data model.

3.1 Definition

In temporal data modeling, an informal division among temporal relational data models into first normal form (1NF) and non-first normal form (NFNF) models has developed over the years, and each type of model has attracted its followers[4].

---

[3] In this paper, we use the terminology Codd introduced [10]: relation, tuple, and attribute, rather than the more prosaic terminology used in SQL–92 and subsequently in TSQL2: table, row, and column.

[4] In this particular context, the NFNFness is due to *how time is added* to the relational model, so most NFNF temporal data models do not support general NFNF relations, and the distinction is different from the distinction between the 1NF and the various general NFNF relational data models (e.g., [17]).

With one objective being to clarify this distinction, Clifford et al. [7] have recently given a formal definition of two types of relation structures, termed temporally ungrouped and temporally grouped. While it is debatable whether the data model of TSQL2 is strictly a 1NF model in the generic sense[5], we will show that the model is temporally ungrouped. To set the stage, we review the definition of a temporally ungrouped data model.

A data model is temporally ungrouped if its data structure component is isomorphic to a particular canonical temporally ungrouped data structure, i.e., an onto and 1–1 mapping must exist between the canonical structure and the structure of the model to be proved temporally ungrouped. The canonical structure is defined next.

Definition 3.1 (canonical temporally ungrouped relation structure) [7, pp. 69–70] Let $U_D = \{D_1, D_2, \ldots, D_{n_d}\}$ be a set of non-empty value domains, and let $\mathbf{D} = \cup_{i=1}^{n_d} D_i$ be the set of all values. Let $\mathbf{T} = \{t_0, t_1, \ldots, t_i, \ldots\}$ be a non-empty, finite or countably infinite set of times with "$<$" as the total order relation. Finally, let $U_A = \{A_1, A_2, \ldots, A_n\}$ be a set of attributes, and let *TIME* be a distinguished time attribute.

A canonical temporally ungrouped (TU) relation schema is defined as a triple $< \mathbf{A}, \mathbf{K}, \mathbf{DOM} >$ where

(1) $\mathbf{A} \cup \{TIME\}$ ($\mathbf{A} \subseteq U_A$) is the set of attributes of the schema.

(2) $\mathbf{K} \cup \{TIME\}$ ($\mathbf{K} \subseteq \mathbf{A}$) is the key of the schema, i.e., $\mathbf{K} \cup \{TIME\} \rightarrow \mathbf{A}$.

(3) $\mathbf{DOM}$ is a function from $\mathbf{A} \cup \{TIME\}$ to $U_D \cup \{\mathbf{T}\}$ that assigns domains in U_D to attributes in $\mathbf{A}$ and *TIME* to $\mathbf{T}$.

A TU database schema is a finite set of TU relation schemas. A TU tuple $\mathbf{t}$ on schema $< \mathbf{A}, \mathbf{K}, \mathbf{DOM} >$ is a function from $\mathbf{A} \cup \{TIME\}$ to $\mathbf{D} \cup \mathbf{T}$ that assigns a value in $\mathbf{DOM}(A_i)$ to each attribute A_i in $\mathbf{A}$ and a value in *TIME* to $\mathbf{T}$. A TU relation is then a finite set of TU tuples that satisfy the key constraint in (2) above. A TU database is a finite set of TU relations. ∎

Example 3.2 The following is a sample TU database with one relation.

A	B	TIME
a_1	b_1	1
a_3	b_2	1
a_2	b_1	2
a_3	b_3	2

The relation schema is the structure $< \{A, B\}, \{A, B\}, f >$, where f assigns domains $\{a_1, a_2, a_3\}$ and $\{b_1, b_2, b_3\}$ to A and B, respectively, and the natural numbers to *TIME*. ∎

---

[5]First normal form (1NF) states that each attribute value is *atomic* [10]. This certainly holds for TSQL2's explicit attributes, which can have as types any of the SQL–92 data types or the new type PERIOD. Hence, considering only values of explicit attributes, TSQL2 is a 1NF model. However, the timestamp associated with each tuple in TSQL2 is a *temporal element*, a finite union of periods [15]. While the timestamp is not an explicit attribute, it can be referenced within a query. We thus feel that timestamps should also satisfy the property. Since the partitioning construct in the from clause of TSQL2 (designated "(PERIOD)") effectively iterates over the maximal periods of a temporal element, timestamps are not treated as atomic. TSQL2 is *not* a 1NF model in this strict sense.

A data model cannot be both temporally ungrouped and temporally grouped (see below), and as we will prove that the TSQL2 data model is isomorphic to TU, we need not give a formal definition of the canonical temporally grouped relation structure, TG. Rather, we give an example and point to what makes TG grouped.

Example 3.3 The schema of a temporally grouped relation consists of the same three components as that of an ungrouped relation, with the exception that the component **DOM** assigns a domain of *functions* to each attribute in **A**. These functions map times to some value domain. A tuple, then, consists of some specific function for each attribute in **A**. In addition, a tuple has an associated lifespan, a set of times. The functions of a tuple map each time in the tuple's lifespan to some value.

For example, a TG relation schema may have attributes A and B. The key may be the combination of these attributes, and **DOM** may assign functions to A and B that map from the natural numbers to $\{a_1, a_2, a_3\}$ and $\{b_1, b_2, b_3\}$, respectively. A sample tuple may have lifespan $\{1, 2\}$ and may have the mappings $[1 \rightarrow a_1, 2 \rightarrow a_2]$ as its A-value and $[1 \rightarrow b_1, 2 \rightarrow b_1]$ as its B-value. A relation instance with this and one more tuple is given next.

A	B	lifespan
$1 \rightarrow a_1$	$1 \rightarrow b_1$	
$2 \rightarrow a_2$	$2 \rightarrow b_1$	$\{1, 2\}$
$1 \rightarrow a_3$	$1 \rightarrow b_2$	
$2 \rightarrow a_3$	$2 \rightarrow b_3$	$\{1, 2\}$

In comparison with the TU instance given before, this instance adds a grouping of the temporal information. As before, there are four rows. However, these rows may now be combined in several ways to form tuples. Other legal TG instances with the same rows as that TU instance are the following.

A	B	lifespan
$1 \rightarrow a_1$	$1 \rightarrow b_1$	$\{1\}$
$2 \rightarrow a_2$	$2 \rightarrow b_1$	$\{2\}$
$1 \rightarrow a_3$	$1 \rightarrow b_2$	$\{1\}$
$2 \rightarrow a_3$	$2 \rightarrow b_3$	$\{2\}$

A	B	lifespan
$1 \rightarrow a_1$	$1 \rightarrow b_1$	$\{1\}$
$2 \rightarrow a_2$	$2 \rightarrow b_1$	$\{2\}$
$1 \rightarrow a_3$	$1 \rightarrow b_2$	
$2 \rightarrow a_3$	$2 \rightarrow b_3$	$\{1, 2\}$

Put informally, a TG structure contains more elements than a TU structure. This indicates why it is not possible for a relation structure to be both temporally ungrouped and grouped. ∎

3.2 TSQL2 and Temporal Groupedness/Ungroupedness

The canonical ungrouped relation structure TU is a quite simple one. The relation structure of TSQL2 is more elaborate. TSQL2 relations come in several variations. First, relations may support valid time, transaction time, or both. Second, valid-time support may be for either state or event relations. While each of the resulting six types of relations are important in practice, it is advantageous in this context to consider only valid-time state relations. This permits a focus on the important concepts and is consistent with existing work [7][6]. With this restriction, the relation structures of TSQL2 and TU are quite similar.

The central difference is that in TU, tuples are stamped with a single *TIME* value from domain $\mathbf{T}$ while in TSQL2, tuples are stamped with sets of times, valid-time elements, from domain $\mathbf{T}$. As we shall now demonstrate, this difference is not essential when groupedness is considered.

To show that TSQL2 is temporally ungrouped, we devise an isomorphic mapping between TSQL2 and TU. This mapping takes as argument an arbitrary TSQL2 relation with schema $(A_1, A_2, \ldots, A_n \| T)$ where the A_i are explicit value attributes and T is the implicit, set-valued time attribute (the vertical double-bar is used to emphasize that the A_i's are explicit attributes and that T is a distinguished, implicit attribute). It maps each TSQL2 tuple in turn. A TSQL2 tuple

$$(a_1, a_2, \ldots, a_n \| \{t_{i_1}, t_{i_2}, \ldots, t_{i_k}\})$$

is mapped to the set

$$\{(a_1, a_2, \ldots, a_n \| t_{i_1}), (a_1, a_2, \ldots, a_n \| t_{i_2}), \ldots, (a_1, a_2, \ldots, a_n \| t_{i_k})\}$$

of TU tuples. Note that one TU tuple is generated for each time in the timestamp of the argument TSQL2 tuple. No duplicates are introduced as TSQL2 timestamps are sets of times. Note also that no duplicate tuples are introduced between the sets of tuples generated from individual TSQL2 tuples. This is so because TSQL2 relations do not contain value-equivalent tuples [20] (tuples are *value-equivalent* if they agree on all explicit attribute values [15]).

It should be clear that this mapping is defined for all TSQL2 relations. Next, for any TU relation instance, there exists an TSQL2 instance that maps to it, i.e., the mapping is *onto* the set of all TU relations. To see this, pick an arbitrary TU relation. For each set of value-equivalent tuples, form a single TSQL2 tuple with the same explicit values and with a timestamp that is the union of the timestamps of the value-equivalent tuples. The result is a legal TSQL2 relation, and that relation maps to the initial TU relation. Finally, there is exactly one TSQL2 relation that maps to any TU relation, i.e., the mapping is 1–1. To see this, observe that two different TSQL2 relations map to different TU relations. In conclusion, the mapping is an isomorphism.

It is worth noting that TU and TSQL2 agree regarding duplicates. A TU relation is defined as a *set* of tuples and thus excludes duplicates. TSQL2 relations do not contain value-equivalent tuples, and a timestamp is a *set* of times. A version of TSQL2 changed to allow value-equivalent tuples with overlapping timestamps would contain more instances than the original TSQL2 and would thus not be temporally ungrouped.

It may also be shown that if $\{A_{j_1}, A_{j_2}, \ldots, A_{j_l}\}$ is a temporal key [18] of a TSQL2 relation then $\{A_{j_1}, A_{j_2}, \ldots, A_{j_l}, TIME\}$ is a key of the corresponding TU relation.

We have now seen that TSQL2 is temporally ungrouped and thus not temporally grouped.

---

[6]For simplicity, we also assume that the attribute domains of TU and TSQL2 are the same and that all the domains, including the totally ordered time domain, are finite.

4 Temporal Semi-Completeness

This section first gives refined definitions of *temporal semi-completeness* and *temporal completeness* [5]. The definitions presented here add additional syntactic requirements that were intended in the original definitions, but were not stated explicitly.

These notions reflect a belief that both functionality and syntactic requirements are important when evaluating a data model. Both types of requirements are relative to some chosen non-temporal data model. While the definitions are applicable to any pair of a temporal and a non-temporal data model, they are intended to be applied to pairs of a temporal relational data model and the particular version of the snapshot relational model that the temporal model extends.

The section ends with an evaluation of TSQL2 according to each definition, yielding new insights into this language.

4.1 Definition

To define temporal semi-completeness, we first introduce the auxiliary notion of a snapshot reducible query. We will use r and r^v for denoting a snapshot and a valid-time relation instance, respectively. Similarly, db and db^v are sets of snapshot and valid-time relation instances, respectively.

The definition uses a valid-timeslice operator $\tau_c^{M^v,M}$ (e.g., [15, 19, 27]) which takes as arguments a valid-time relation r^v (in the data model M^v) and a valid-time instant c and returns a snapshot relation r (in the data model M) containing all tuples valid at time c. In other words, r consists of all tuples of r^v whose valid time includes the time instant c, but without the valid time. We assume that the valid timeslice preserves duplicates, i.e., if r^v contains value-equivalent tuples that are valid at time c then $\tau_c^{M^v,M}(r^v)$ will contain duplicates. This becomes important later, when we consider SQL–92 relations with duplicates.

Definition 4.1 (snapshot reducibility) [28] Let $M = (DS, QL)$ be a snapshot relational data model, and let $M^v = (DS^v, QL^v)$ be a valid-time data model. Also, let db^v be a database instance in DS^v. A valid-time query q^v in QL^v is *snapshot reducible with respect to* a snapshot query q in QL if and only if

$$\forall db^v \; \forall c \; (\tau_c^{M^v,M}(q^v(db^v)) = q(\tau_c^{M^v,M}(db^v))). \qquad \blacksquare$$

Graphically, snapshot reducibility implies that for all db^v and for all c, the commutativity diagram shown in Figure 1 must hold.

Temporal semi-completeness of a temporal data model with respect to a snapshot data model requires first that all relation instances in the snapshot data model can be produced by taking timeslices of some relation instance in the temporal data model. Further, it is required that each query q in the snapshot model has a counterpart q^v in the temporal model that is snapshot reducible with respect to it. Observe that q^v being snapshot reducible with respect to q poses no syntactic restrictions on q^v. It is thus possible for q^v to be quite different from q, and q^v might be very involved. This is undesirable,

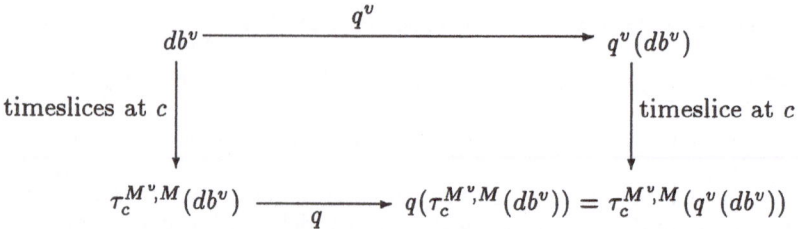

Figure 1: Snapshot Reducibility of Query q^v With Respect To Query q

as we would like the temporal model to be a straight-forward extension of the snapshot model. Consequently, we add to the definition of temporal semi-completeness the restriction that q^v and q be syntactically similar.

Definition 4.2 (temporal semi-completeness) [5] Let $M = (DS, QL)$ be a snapshot data model, and let $M^v = (DS^v, QL^v)$ be a valid-time data model. Data model M^v is *temporally semi-complete with respect to* model M if and only if all three of the following conditions hold.

1. For every relation r in DS, there exists a valid-time relation r^v in DS^v and a time instant c such that $r = \tau_c^{M^v, M}(r^v)$.

2. For every query q in QL, there exists a query q^v in QL^v that is snapshot reducible with respect to q.

3. There exist two (possibly empty) text strings S_1 and S_2 such that for all pairs (q, q^v) of queries, where q^v is snapshot reducible with respect to q, query q^v is syntactically identical to $S_1 q S_2$.   ∎

Note that the same two strings S_1 and S_2 must apply to all (q, q^v) pairs. The strings represent particular syntactic constructs in the language QL^v.

If the valid-time data model treats valid-time relations as a new type of relation, as does TSQL2, it may be possible to use the same syntactic constructs (i.e., q^v and q are identical) for querying snapshot and valid-time relations. In this case, the type of a relation determines the meaning of the syntactic construct.

Temporal semi-completeness of a valid-time data model with respect to a snapshot data model guarantees that the temporal model is a straightforward extension of the snapshot model. Temporal semi-completeness is limited in the sense that it covers only those queries in the temporal data model that are snapshot reducible to a query in the snapshot data model. Most often, a temporal data model allows for the formulation of other queries as well.

4.2 TSQL2 and Temporal Semi-Completeness with Respect to SQL–92

This section identifies where TSQL2 falls short in fulfilling the requirements of temporal semi-completeness. The two related concepts of value-equivalent tuples and duplicates will prove important in this section. The former concept applies only to temporal relations; the latter applies to both valid-time relations and timeslices of valid-time relations.

Example 4.3 Consider the four valid-time relations depicted in Figure 2. Relation r_1 contains no duplicates and no value-equivalent tuples. Thus, no timeslices of r_1 will contain duplicates. Relation r_2 contains no duplicates, but does contain value-equivalent tuples. However, as the timestamps of the value-equivalent tuples are disjoint, no timeslices will contain duplicates. Relation r_3, like r_2, contains no duplicates (i.e., tuples in which the values for A and T are identical), but does contain value-equivalent tuples. Unlike in r_2, the timestamps of the value-equivalent tuples are not disjoint and thus there are timeslices of r_3 (e.g., at time 17) that contain duplicates. Finally, relation r_4 contains duplicates and thus non-disjoint value-equivalent tuples, leading again to timeslices with duplicates. ∎

r_1

A	T
a_1	$[10-20)$
a_2	$[15-50)$

r_2

A	T
a_1	$[10-17)$
a_1	$[17-20)$
a_2	$[15-50)$

r_3

A	T
a_1	$[10-20)$
a_1	$[15-18)$
a_2	$[15-50)$

r_4

A	T
a_1	$[10-20)$
a_1	$[10-20)$
a_2	$[15-50)$

Figure 2: Illustration of Value-equivalent Tuples and Duplicates

Allowing value-equivalent tuples does not necessarily yield duplicates in timeslices. However, if we want to have duplicates in timeslices, we must allow (non-disjoint) value-equivalent tuples.

4.2.1 Lack of Duplicates in TSQL2

One reason why TSQL2 is not temporally semi-complete with respect to SQL–92 is that SQL–92 relations containing duplicates have no counterparts in TSQL2, where relations with value-equivalent tuples (and thus duplicates, either in a timeslice, or in the temporal relation itself) are not allowed. Definition 4.2 requires that for every SQL–92 relation r, there must exist a TSQL2 relation r^v and a time instant c such that $\tau_c^{TSQL2,SQL-92}(r^v) = r$. However, it is not possible to find an r^v in TSQL2 for r's in SQL–92 that contain duplicates. An example illustrates this.

Example 4.4 Let salary relation, *salary_entry*, be given that records (current) monthly incomes of persons. Assume that the person Tom has three incomes because he has three jobs. In two jobs, he makes 1200, and in one he makes 800. This can be represented in SQL–92 as follows.

salary_entry

Name	Amount
Tom	1200
Tom	1200
Tom	800

No timeslice of a TSQL2 relation can yield this relation. The following is a reasonable attempt at adding valid time to the SQL–92 relation to obtain a TSQL2 relation.

salary_entry

Name	Amount	T
Tom	1200	[1994/5 − 1995/3)
Tom	1200	[1994/8 − 1994/12)
Tom	800	[1994/11 − 1995/6)

This relation records that from May 1994 to March 1995, Tom was on one payroll and made a monthly salary of 1200; from August 1994 to December 1994 he was on another payroll where he also made 1200 per month; and from November 1994 to June 1995 he made 800 in a third job. This is not a legal TSQL2 relation because it contains value-equivalent tuples. ∎

The merit of duplicates has already been discussed heatedly (see, e.g., [12, p. 109]). Doubtlessly, SQL–92 would be cleaner in a mathematical sense without duplicates. However, we cannot change SQL–92, so whether we like it or not, it is necessary to deal with duplicates when designing a semi-complete successor to SQL–92. Specifically, for TSQL2 to satisfy the first two criteria of temporal semi-completeness with respect to SQL–92, it must support relations containing value-equivalent tuples with non-disjoint timestamps, permitting duplicates in timeslices.

As a reminder, we note that duplicates may significantly impact the results of queries.

Example 4.5 The following statement computes a relation that associates with every person that person's total salary.

```
SELECT Name, SUM(Amount)
FROM salary_entry
GROUP BY Name
```

Evaluated over the initial nontemporal *salary_entry* relation, the query computes Tom's salary to be $3200. Without duplicates, the result would have been $2000, which is unintended. ∎

4.2.2 Problems with Subqueries

Temporal semi-completeness requires that for every snapshot query, it is possible to formulate a valid-time query that is snapshot reducible and syntactically similar to it. TSQL2 tries to achieve this goal with a carefully designed default valid clause. This works fine for many simple queries, but it does not work for subqueries.

Ignoring duplicates, the following two SQL–92-statements are equivalent [23, p.117].

```
SELECT r5.a              SELECT r5.a
FROM r5,r6               FROM r5
WHERE r5.a=r6.a          WHERE EXISTS (SELECT *
                                       FROM r6
                                       WHERE r5.a=r6.a)
```

If TSQL2 is to be semi-complete with respect to SQL–92, there must be valid-time queries in TSQL2 that are snapshot reducible with respect to the two queries above and are similar to them. Indeed, the default valid clause of TSQL2 was designed to make those two valid-time queries be identical to the two queries above. The valid-time queries are given below, with the implicit default valid clauses shown.

```
SELECT r5.a                            SELECT r5.a
VALID INTERSECT(VALID(r5),VALID(r6))   VALID VALID(r5)
FROM r5,r6                             FROM r5
WHERE r5.a=r6.a                        WHERE EXISTS (SELECT *
                                                     VALID VALID(r6)
                                                     FROM r6
                                                     WHERE r5.a=r6.a)
```

The query to the left behaves as expected. The result ($result_1$) of the query for two sample instances of r_5 and r_6 is shown in Figure 3. The valid clause states that the valid time of a result tuple is the intersection of the valid times of the argument tuples from r_5 and r_6. This means that the left-hand-side valid-time query is snapshot reducible with respect to the left-hand-side snapshot query. The situation gets more complicated when we consider the query to

r_5		r_6		$result_1$		$result_2$	
A	T	A	T	A	T	A	T
a_1	[5−9)	a_1	[7−10)	a_1	[7−9)	a_1	[5−9)

Figure 3: Computing a Valid-time Join Without or With a Subquery

the right. The outermost valid clause implies that the valid time of a result tuples is equivalent to the valid time of the argument tuple from r_5 (see $result_2$ in Figure 3 for an example). This means that the right-hand-side valid-time query is not snapshot reducible with respect to the right-hand-side snapshot query. TSQL2 thus lacks a valid-time query that is snapshot reducible with respect to and is a simple syntactic extension of the right-hand-side snapshot query. Consequently, TSQL2 is not temporally semi-complete with respect to SQL–92.

4.2.3 Summary

We have identified two reasons why TSQL2 is not temporally semi-complete with respect to SQL–92. The first is that, while duplicates are allowed in SQL–92, value-equivalent tuples are not allowed in TSQL2. The second reason is that the valid clause in TSQL2 is not sufficiently powerful to ensure that all SQL–92 queries have similar, snapshot reducible counterparts in TSQL2. We showed this for nested queries. We conjecture that there are also problems with aggregation, grouping, and ordering.

5 Temporal Completeness

Temporal semi-completeness poses useful restrictions on temporal data models. However, temporal semi-completeness poses restrictions on only a subset of the queries that are generally expressible in temporal data models. For example, it does not cover queries that retrieve information concerning relationships between perceived states of the world at *different* points in time. Furthermore, temporal semi-completeness does not say anything about the format of valid time. Both aspects are accounted for by the notion of a temporally complete data model.

5.1 Definition

Definition 5.1 (temporal completeness) [5] A valid-time data model $M^v = (DS^v, QL^v)$ is *temporally complete with respect to* a snapshot data model $M = (DS, QL)$ if and only if all five of the following conditions hold.

1. M^v is temporally semi-complete with respect to M.

2. For every snapshot reducible query q^v in QL^v, it is possible to override snapshot reducibility, either by dropping the syntactic extensions that enforce snapshot reducibility (c.f., Definition 4.2) or by modifying q^v syntactically to $S_1 q S_2$, where S_1 and S_2 are (possibly empty) text strings that depend on QL^v but not on q^v. Overriding snapshot reducibility means to evaluate a query without interpreting valid times.

3. The name of a valid-time relation within a statement can be syntactically substituted (perhaps with other syntactic modifications and additions, such as parentheses) with a query q^v in QL^v that defines the respective valid-time relation without changing the semantics of the statement. The syntactic modifications must depend on QL^v only, not on q^v.

4. Allen's temporal relationships [2] can be used between (a) temporal attributes of stored valid-time relations (i.e., valid time attributes and explicit temporal attributes), (b) implicitly computed valid times associated with temporally semi-complete (sub)queries, and (c) temporal constants.

5. It is possible to retrieve and constrain (a) maximal continuous valid-time periods and (b) valid times as specified by the user. ∎

First, we require that temporally complete languages are temporally semi-complete. This accounts for queries that can be answered by examining (sequences of) snapshots. Overriding snapshot reducibility accounts for a fundamental principle in databases, namely that a query should treat the elements of a database as uninterpreted objects [8, p.158]. Section 5.2.1 provides an example that illustrates this. The third condition ensures that the syntactic construct that is used to enforce snapshot reducibility can be applied not only to whole queries, but also to subqueries. In other words, a temporally complete query may consist of several temporally semi-complete queries. Allen's operators are necessary to state arbitrary temporal relationships. (They were proven to exhaustively describe the relationships between periods [2]. However, other, equally expressive operators are possible as well.) Note that there are various sources of timestamps that are of interest in a temporal database: temporal attributes of base relations, implicitly computed valid times, and temporal constants. We require that all of them can be used together as operands to Allen's operators. Finally the database system has to support maximal continuous periods and valid times as specified by the user. Both kinds of timestamps have been shown necessary in answering temporal queries [29]. It must be possible to retrieve and constrain (i.e., use as operands of functions and predicates) either kind of timestamp.

We emphasize that the notions of temporal semi-completeness and temporal completeness go beyond approaches that define the completeness in terms of an algebra (i.e., by requiring a temporal language to have the same expressive power as an algebra). For example, temporal semi-completeness (and thus temporal completeness) may, depending on the language it is with respect to, cover aggregates, grouping, null values, ordering, and duplicates.

5.2 TSQL2 and Temporal Completeness with Respect to SQL–92

In order to qualify for temporal completeness, a temporal query language must fulfill the five requirements listed in Definition 5.1. We first must modify TSQL2 to make it temporally semi-complete. To ensure temporal completeness, it must in addition be possible to override snapshot reducibility. The valid clause in TSQL2 is intended for this purpose, but as its scope does not extend to set operations such as EXCEPT and UNION, the clause cannot override snapshot reducibility for them, either.

The third condition is that a temporal language must allow a valid-time query to appear in a larger query everywhere a valid-time relation name may appear, so that if the valid-time query computes the named relation, the two forms of the larger queries compute the same result. This feature is provided by table expressions, which were introduced in SQL–92 [22, p.178] and carried over to TSQL2.

The fourth requirement is satisfied by the where clause which is enhanced with temporal predicates that have the same expressive power as Allen's predicates. Temporal attributes of base relations, implicitly computed valid times (e.g., valid times computed by table expressions), and temporal constants can be used as operands to these predicates.

Finally, a temporal language must support maximal continuous valid-time periods and valid times as specified by the user. In the second subsection we will see that TSQL2 ignores the user-specified valid time format.

5.2.1 Overriding Snapshot Reducibility

In TSQL2, the valid clause can be used to override snapshot reducibility—if no valid clause is specified, the semantics defaults to valid-time intersection. However, the scope of the valid clause does not include set operations and, therefore, it is not possible to override valid-time semantics associated with these operations.

Example 5.2 Suppose the valid-time relations r_5 and r_6 of Figure 3. In TSQL2, it is not possible to use **EXCEPT** to retrieve all tuples in r_5 that are not in r_6. Snapshot reducibility is hard-wired into **EXCEPT**, which means that TSQL2 always yields $result_3$ rather than $result_4$, shown below.

$result_3$

A	T
a_1	$[5-7)$

$result_4$

A	T
a_1	$[5-9)$

∎

5.2.2 Beyond Coalescing

The last point of Definition 5.1 requires that a temporal query language be able to retrieve and constrain (a) maximal continuous valid-time periods and (b) valid times as specified by the user. First, TSQL2 falls short in doing this at the outermost level of queries. The results of queries are always coalesced relations, i.e., relations where value-equivalent tuples are eliminated by combining their valid timestamps. This also holds for an individual select statement which may be part of a larger query. Hence, retaining valid times as specified by the user is not possible in TSQL2.

Second, TSQL2 relations are constrained to contain coalesced tuples, which also causes problems.

Example 5.3 Consider relations r_1 and r_2 of Figure 2. We may envision that it is significant to a user whether the explicit attribute value a is associated with one single timestamp, $[10-20)$, or is associated with two separate timestamps, $[10-17)$ and $[17-20)$. These two relations may mean different things to a user. However, r_2 is not a legal TSQL2 relation, and if the user inserts tuples $\langle a_1, [10-17)\rangle$ and $\langle a_1, [17-20)\rangle$ into a TSQL2 relation, the tuples will be coalesced, and relation r_1 will be the result. Put differently, TSQL2 does not consider the difference between r_1 and r_2 (and r_3 and r_4) important and thus only admits coalesced relations. ∎

Temporal completeness requires that TSQL2 respects the valid times as provided by the user. If the user provides two intervals for attribute value a, TSQL2 must maintain those two periods and cannot simply coalesce them. Clearly, this matters for queries. For example, the query "Does there exist an entry with a valid time identical to $[10-17)$" should return "yes" if applied to r_2 (because the user has inserted a tuple with this valid time into r_2) and "no" if applied to r_1 (because the user has not inserted a tuple with this valid time into r_1).

Currently, TSQL2 is a point-based [9], or a snapshot-equivalence preserving [19], temporal query language that uses time periods at the representational level to achieve a reasonable performance. Changing TSQL2 to respect the valid times as specified by the users represents a substantial conceptual change to TSQL2. It may be argued that admitting uncoalesced relations represents a complication, but it also adds to its expressiveness. With implicit coalescing, users do not have to be concerned with the valid times, but they also cannot associate special semantics with valid times (c.f., Section 4.2.1).

5.2.3 Summary

Apart from not being temporally semi-complete, two aspects prevent TSQL2 from being temporally complete. First, it is not possible to override the temporal semantics of set operations. Second, implicit coalescing prevents TSQL2 from respecting valid times as provided by the users.

6 Summary and Future Research

This paper has evaluated the consensus temporal query language TSQL2 using existing notions of completeness, some of which were further formalized in the paper.

In consistency with its design goals, TSQL2 was shown to be upwards compatible with SQL–92 and thus to be relationally complete. TSQL2 was also characterized as temporally ungrouped. This implies that TSQL2 is not temporally grouped. The evaluation of the temporal semi-completeness of TSQL2 with respect to SQL–92 pointed to two important deficiencies: not all SQL–92 relations can be produced taking timeslices of TSQL2 temporal relations, and not all SQL–92 queries have a similar temporal counterpart in TSQL2. Without these deficiencies, TSQL2 would be a "cleaner" extension of SQL–92. The evaluation of temporal completeness of TSQL2 with respect to SQL–92 pointed to two additional problems: with set operations in TSQL2 queries, it is not possible to freely control the valid timestamps of result tuples, and TSQL2 does not respect the valid timestamps of tuples as entered by the users (because value-equivalent tuples are coalesced).

As future research, it would be interesting to use additional completeness notions (e.g., temporally ungrouped complete in [7]) in the evaluation of TSQL2. In particular, it is a possible next step to compare the expressiveness of TSQL2 to those of existing practical or theoretical temporal query languages. Also, a comparative study of completeness notions for temporal databases that sheds light on their interrelations and practical implications, and perhaps leads to new completeness notions, would be worthwhile.

7 Acknowledgments

This work was conducted while the first author visited the University of Arizona. He was supported in part by the Swiss NSF. The second author was supported in part by the Danish Natural Science Research Council through grants 11–1089–1, 11–0061–1, and 9400911. The third author was supported in part by NSF grant IRI-9302244.

We thank John Baer, Jan Chomicki, and Charles Kline for interesting discussions and for their insights.

References

[1] P. Atzeni and P. P. Chen. Completeness of Query Languages for the Entity-Relationship Model. In *Proceedings of the Second International Conference on Entity-Relationship Approach*, P. P. Chen, editor, pages 111–123, October 1981.

[2] J. F. Allen. Maintaining Knowledge about Temporal Intervals. *Communications of the ACM*, 16(11):832–843, 1983.

[3] A. V. Aho and J. D. Ullman. Universality of data retrieval languages. In *Proceedings of the 6th ACM Symposium on Principles of Programming Languages*, pages 110–117, January 1979.

[4] F. Bancilhon. On the Completeness of Query Languages for Relational Databases. In *Proceedings of the 7th Symposium on Mathematical Foundations of Computer Science*. Lecture Notes in Computer Science, Springer Verlag, September 1978.

[5] M. Böhlen and R. Marti. On the Completeness of Temporal Database Query Languages. *Proceedings of the First International Conference on Temporal Logic*, pages 283–300, July 1994.

[6] M. Böhlen. *The Temporal Deductive Database System ChronoLog*. Ph.D. thesis, Departement Informatik, ETH Zürich, 1994.

[7] J. Clifford, A. Croker, and A. Tuzhilin. On Completeness of Historical Relational Query Languages. *ACM Transactions on Database Systems*, 19(1):64–116, March 1994.

[8] A. K. Chandra and D. Harel. Computable Queries for Relational Data Bases. *Journal of Computer and System Sciences*, 21(2):156–178, October 1980.

[9] J. Chomicki. Temporal Query Languages: a Survey. *Proceedings of the First International Conference on Temporal Logic*, pages 506–534, July 1994.

[10] E. F. Codd. A Relational Model of Data for Large Shared Data Banks. *Communications of the ACM*, 13(6):377–387, June 1970.

[11] E. F. Codd. Relational Completeness of Data Base Sublanguages. *Courant Computer Symposia Series*, 6:65–98, 1972.

[12] C. J. Date. *Relational Database Writings 1991–1994*. Addison-Wesley Publishing Company, 1995.

[13] S. K. Gadia. A Homogeneous Relational Model and Query Languages for Temporal Databases. *ACM Transactions on Database Systems*, 13(4):418–448, December 1988.

[14] S. K. Gadia and G. Bhargava. SQL-like Seamless Query of Temporal Data. In R. T. Snodgrass, editor, *Proceedings of the International Workshop on an Infrastructure for Temporal Databases*, Arlington, Texas, June 1993.

[15] C. S. Jensen, J. Clifford, R. Elmasri, S. K. Gadia, P. Hayes, and S. Jajodia (eds.). A Glossary of Temporal Database Concepts. *SIGMOD RECORD*, 23(1):52–64, March 1994.

[16] C. S. Jensen (ed.). A Consensus Test Suite of Temporal Database Queries. Technical Report R 93-2034, Department of Mathematics and Computer, Institute for Electronic Systems, Fredrik Bajers Vej 7, DK 9220 Aalborg, Denmark, November 1993.

[17] G. Jaeschke and H.-J. Schek. Remarks on the Algebra of Non First Normal Form Relations. In *Proceedings of the ACM Symposium on Principles of Database Systems*, pages 124–138, March 1982.

[18] C. S. Jensen, M. D. Soo, and R. T. Snodgrass. Extending Normal Forms to Temporal Relations. Technical Report TR 92-17, University of Arizona, July 1992.

[19] C. S. Jensen, M. D. Soo, and R. T. Snodgrass. Unifying Temporal Models via a Conceptual Model. *Information Systems*, 19(7):513–547, 1994.

[20] C. S. Jensen, R. T. Snodgrass, and M. D. Soo. The TSQL2 Data Model. Chapter 10, *The TSQL2 Temporal Query Language*, R. T. Snodgrass (ed.), Kluwer Academic Pub., 1995, pp. 157–240.

[21] L. E. McKenzie and R. T. Snodgrass. Evaluation of Relational Algebras Incorporating the Time Dimension in Databases. *ACM Computing Surveys*, 23(4):501–543, 1991.

[22] J. Melton and A. R. Simon. *Understanding the New SQL: A Complete Guide*. Morgan Kaufmann Publishers, 1993.

[23] P. O'Neil. *Database: Principles, Programming, and Performance*. Morgan Kaufmann, San Francisco, 1994.

[24] G. Özsoyoğlu and R. T. Snodgrass. Temporal and Real-Time Databases: A Survey. *IEEE Transactions on Knowledge and Data Engineering*, 7(4), August 1995.

[25] R. T. Snodgrass (ed.), I. Ahn, G. Ariav, D. Batory, J. Clifford, C. E. Dyreson, R. Elmasri, F. Grandi, C. S. Jensen, W. Käfer, N. Kline, K. Kulkarni, T. Y. C. Leung, N. Lorentzos, J. F. Roddick, A. Segev, M. D. Soo, and S. M. Sripada. *The TSQL2 Temporal Query Language*. Kluwer Academic Pub., 1995, 674+xxiv pages.

[26] R. T. Snodgrass, I. Ahn, G. Ariav, P. Bayer, J. Clifford, C. Dyreson, F. Grandi, L. Hermosilla, C. S. Jensen, W. Käfer, N. Kline, T. Y. C. Leung, N. Lorentzos, Y. Mitsopoulos, J. F. Roddick, M. D. Soo, and S. M. Sripada. An Evaluation of TSQL2. *TSQL2 Commentary*, September 1994.

[27] B. Schueler. Update reconsidered. In G. M. Nijssen (ed.), *Architecture and Models in Data Base Management Systems*. North Holland Publishing Co., 1977.

[28] R. T. Snodgrass. The Temporal Query Language TQuel. *ACM Transactions on Database Systems*, 12(2):247–298, 1987.

[29] S. M. Sripada. *Temporal Reasoning in Deductive Databases*. Ph.D. thesis, Imperial College of Science and Technology, University of London, 1991.

[30] A. Tuzhilin and J. Clifford. A Temporal Relational Algebra as a Basis for Temporal Relational Completeness. In *Proceedings of the International Conference on Very Large Databases*, D. McLeod, R. Sacks-Davis, and H.-J. Schek, editors, pages 13–23, August 1990.

IV. Alternative Views on Temporal Data Models

Time is just another attribute – or at least, just another dimension.

Christina Davies

Anglia Polytechnic University, East Road,
Cambridge CB1 1PT, UK

Brian Lazell

Medicines Control Agency, London, UK

Martin Hughes and Leslie Cooper

Anglia Polytechnic University, Cambridge, UK

Abstract

Writers on temporal databases frequently claim that most databases hold only a snapshot of the data to be stored in that database and that commonly-used database design tools such as the relational model are unsatisfactory for the development of database systems in which attribute values change over time. Such writers urge that valid time - the interval over which a data item is valid - be treated differently from time which is an ordinary attribute of a relation. This paper argues that, when considering possible extensions to the relational model for such purposes, a distinction must be made between the data model used to represent temporal data and algebras used to specify processing on that model. It is argued that both valid time and user-defined time (as defined in TSQL2 and by many writers in this area) can and should be modelled as simple attributes of a relation within the unextended relational model. This is contrasted with the need for extra facilities in relational query languages for processing of temporal and other interval data. The extra querying facilities identified in these case studies are those for manipulating overlapping intervals and support for recursive querying of version trees. TSQL2 is criticised in terms of its limitations, complexity and reliance on a specific temporal data model.

1 Introduction

The following quotations illustrate a claim that has become commonplace in the literature of temporal databases: "Although conventional databases serve some applications well, they are insufficient for those in which past and/or future data are also required", [23]. "The current contents of a database can be viewed as a snapshot of the real world at a single instant of time", [18]. "In most databases, when an object's attributes assume new values, their previous values are discarded from the database", [22]. "Conventional databases can be viewed as snapshot databases in that they represent the state of an enterprise at one particular time, generally now", [17].

This view that time is inadequately modelled in 'conventional' databases has been largely unchallenged. At the same time, researchers in this field accept that very many applications must store and manipulate values that change with time and that such systems are built, usually using the relational model. No evidence is offered that such systems are built any less satisfactorily than others. With these descriptions of conventional databases as handling time inadequately goes the assumption, again largely unchallenged, that the relational model must be extended for satisfactory modelling of temporal problems. As an example, it is conceded in [23] that temporal applications can be modelled and implemented using the relational model but "perhaps at the expense of higher data redundancy, awkward modelling and unfriendly query languages."

This paper re-examines these assumptions by referring to real case studies in which spatio-temporal problems have been satisfactorily solved using currently available relational software. The conclusions drawn from these studies are that the flexibility and simplicity of the relational model are too valuable to be jettisoned without good reason and that a much stronger case must be made against the unextended relational model before it is rejected or modified for temporal applications. Additionally, considerable intellectual investment has been made by a generation or more of systems developers in acquiring facility with the relational model and analysis and design methods such as SSADM which rely on relational data analysis.

This paper aims

1. to use real case studies to reinforce the accepted point that complex systems requiring manipulation of time are routinely, successfully built,

2. to re-examine the extent to which the unextended relational model can be satisfactorily used to model systems in which data change with time and in which time is an essential component of the enterprise's business,

3. to evaluate the potential usefulness of TSQL2, which is discussed as a representative of the alternative solutions offered by the temporal database research community, in solving our case study problems and hence

4. to offer a more general critique of TSQL2.

These aims are achieved by discussion of three case studies. The first is essentially a family of case studies taken from the field of pharmaceutical licensing, with legal requirements to track the decision-making process for product and manufacturers' licence applications. The second is a case study involving a mixture of temporal and spatial data in which we demonstrate that spatial data can offer the same practical problems as temporal; the theoretical equivalence of spatial and temporal attributes has already been acknowledged (eg [15]). The third study is especially interesting since it requires three dimensions of valid time, two of which are considered in detail, and gives an example of time attributes themselves varying with time. As such it could be considered to give a satisfactory test of the use of the relational model for temporal problems. In all three studies old values of data must be preserved and cannot be over-written or deleted.

The first of these studies has been implemented in a relational DBMS and the second is currently being developed as a relational system The third case which we discuss was implemented in an ad hoc system written in COBOL, almost certainly for reasons of hardware limitation at the time of its commissioning; we offer a relational solution.

In the case studies discussed below, time is stored as an ordinary attribute within the unextended relational model; these time attributes are fully accessible for conventional querying and have no special status as they would if recorded as valid time-stamps in TSQL2. It is argued that, regardless of whether time data stored are classified as user-defined or valid time, the operations likely to be required on them are essentially the same. It is emphasised that extensions to the relational algebra do not have to be accompanied by extensions to the underlying structure of the relational model. In this our thinking parallels that of Codd [4] who distinguishes between structure, manipulative languages and definition of integrity constraints in the relational model. Case studies are used to illustrate desirable extensions to relational query languages and it is further argued that if a set of extensions to relational query languages is to be widely accepted, it should be as simple as possible.

The well-accepted necessity of distinguishing between the conceptual database model and its physical implementation [1], [4] is also emphasised. One criticism of modelling time-stamps as ordinary attributes centres on problems of performance and optimisation [16]. It is argued, for example, that current records will need more frequent access than past ones and that access paths and storage clustering should take account of this. Although optimisation for particular ranges of attribute values may be desirable it is not the proper concern of those working at the logical level, just as objections of poor performance when the relational model was first introduced were rightly not accepted as a fundamental reason for rejecting the model [9].

Like most proposed temporal algebras and temporal extensions to query languages, TSQL2 is based on one specific temporal data model. Its limitations are discussed and it is suggested that attempts to prescribe the data model which should be used are misguided. It is urged that the relational model be retained unless its inadequacies for modelling temporal problems can be convincingly demonstrated.

In summary, it will be argued that the following aspects of TSQL2 are unsatisfactory: First, the fact that it is based on a specific temporal data model, rather than leaving developers to use the relational model to define their own view of time in their particular application area.

Second, even if the need for a specific temporal model were unequivocally demonstrated, that of TSQL2 has the following specific problems:
a) different treatments of valid time and user-defined time, with the limiting of the 'coalesce' function to valid time; if a case were to be made for separate valid time-stamps, then one such time-stamp per row would not be adequate.
b) encouraging the use of hiding of data in data structures (for example' the 'calendar' type)
c) confining any extensions to time intervals only.
d) the creation of an interval data type which is essentially derived from a pair of underlying time attributes.

As alternatives, the following are proposed:

a) retention of the unextended relational model for design of temporal databases.

b) provision of a minimum set of extensions to SQL, to facilitate manipulation of overlapping intervals, whether temporal or spatial. Such extensions can be implemented with no change to the underlying relational model. To minimise redundancy and maintain flexibility, it is suggested that such functions should take as arguments pairs of temporal or spatial data items taken from the same domain.

c) support for recursive querying, the need for which is demonstrated by two of our case studies

d) routine support for user-defined operators, as already provided in some commercial DBMS.

The rest of this document is arranged as follows:

Section 2. Presentation and discussion of a family of case studies from the UK Medicines Control Agency, an Agency of the UK Department of Health.

Section 3. Presentation and discussion of a case study based on a municipal sewer management system.

Section 4. Discussion of a case study originating from [19] based on one of the functions of the UK Department of Social Security (DSS).

Section 5 General Discussion and Summary

2 Case study 1: the Medicines Control Agency

2.1 Introduction

The function of the UK Medicines Control Agency (MCA) is to license manufacturers and wholesalers of pharmaceutical products as well as to grant licenses to the products themselves. It also monitors data on adverse reactions to licensed products. The Agency's information processing is currently handled by several independent systems, all implemented as relational databases, varying in size from about 20 tables to more than 150. One characteristic which they all have in common is the absolute necessity of recording the time of events and of not discarding what could be considered to be old versions of the database. Thus all databases developed for the MCA are concerned with recording historical data. However not only must the systems keep a full history of licence applications (and there are more than 10 different types of licence), they must also support new versions of licences, since companies may apply to vary the terms of their licence at any time. "Any time" means not only any time from the arrival of the application to the death of the licence: dead licences may be resurrected, so that variations may actually be to a re-incarnation of a licence. Every event in the history of a licence (its arrival, referral to a committee, decisions by committees, requests for further information) must be date-stamped and no data item ever discarded. Even should some policy decision be taken to archive data over some particular age, the archiving must remain more or less transparent to the user, since the ultimate users of the data are Government ministers needing to answer questions in Parliament, often at short notice.

These systems, therefore, pose two separate but inter-dependent problems of time recording: the need to record the history of a licence application, and the need to support versions of licences. Although version management has been considered in the literature it is most frequently discussed in the context of design databases. However, in design databases old versions will usually be discarded [8], while the historical nature of the MCA's data requires that all versions be preserved. It has been recognised [26] that databases referred to in the literature as 'historical' databases are also examples of the need for version recording.

2.2   The data model

An example is given from one of the MCA's Information Systems. BLIS (Business-D Licensing Information System) is the MCA's system for tracking the processing of applications for a manufacturer's or wholesale dealer's licence. All companies wanting to supply any licensed product must first obtain a manufacturer's and/or wholesale dealer's licence in which the sites to be used, processes at those sites and personnel responsible are detailed. Like all of the Agency's systems, BLIS supports time even more strongly than most time-oriented systems in that it supports life after death. A licence dies if the company ceases to trade without passing it on to another company, or if it fails to renew at the end of five years. Since a dead licence may be revived at any time, an extra attribute records the incarnation number of a given licence. In BLIS, licence incarnations and their variations are modelled with the following relations:

PHARMACEUTICAL_BUSINESS(Company id, name, address, etc)
LICENCE(Company id, licence type etc)
LICENCE_INCARNATION(Company id, licence type,
incarnation number, birth date, grant date, death date, incarnation status)
LICENCE_INCARNATION_VERSION(Company id, licence type,
incarnation number, version number, parent version number, birth date, grant date,
death date, version status)

The 'status' attributes can have one of three values (PENDING, LIVE or DEAD), reflecting the state of the application at the corresponding date. Should a greater variety of states be needed, a table of states would of course be needed. The status attributes and dates enable the complete history of an application, through any number of versions or incarnations, to be recorded and queries on the history of the application can be routinely satisfied.

2.3   The need for recursive querying

In the present version of the system, only one pending variation is permitted. If new variation applications are received, these are applied to an existing variation 'manually'. An assessor decides if the new application is a reasonable one in the light of existing, outstanding applications. If it is, then there is no reason why it cannot be included as part of the pending variation currently being assessed. If it is not, then the assessors may either deal with it outside the computer system by writing to the applicant suggesting modifications that would enable it to be considered, or they may defer it until the current pending application is decided. In the latter case, however, it might be thought logically acceptable and administratively desirable to record the variation as one parallel to that currently pending, perhaps with a lower priority. Also, there might in future be arguments for recording each variation application that arrives as a separate event. Although the data model is adequate for this, processing would present difficulties. All versions of a given licence can be found since the licence identifier is part of all version identifiers. However to list all 'ancestors' in a direct line back to the original version, a query would be needed that could recursively retrieve the version record which has the version number equal to that of the Parent version number of the version record being currently inspected. Inability to permit recursive querying is a well-known deficiency of relational query languages (see for example [10]). Thus it is not lack of support for time which makes version representation and complete historical querying difficult but lack of support for recursion within relational query languages. Some commercial implementations of SQL already support recursion to varied degrees. However this work has been independent of work on temporal database problems and there is no proposal that TSQL2 should include support for recursion.

2.4 Calculating elapsed time

A second type of time problem, that of work tracking, occurs throughout the work of the Agency and is common in many other application areas. A specific example is the MCA's Biological Licence Application tracking system. Biological Licence Applications are those for products whose active substances are produced by a biological process (for example plant extract, bacterial culture etc). There is the need to track an application from the date of its arrival and, once a licence has been granted (if one is granted) through the lifetime of the company. Apart from the general need to record dates of arrival, completion etc, there are two system requirements which mean that the total amount of time spent working on a licence must be recorded. First, the MCA is required by law to cost its work on a licence and to charge applicants only sufficient to cover the costs of the work involved. Secondly, both a European Union directive and internal performance targets insist that all applications be dealt with within a limited time. It is thus essential to be able to calculate the amount of time that the agency has spent working on the application, subtracting any time for which the MCA cannot be held responsible. Since more than one assessor will be working on a given licence application at any one time, the problem involves manipulation of overlapping time intervals. As part of the calculation, a list of intervals for which at least one assessor was unable to proceed with a given application is also likely to be required.

Although this involves some complex processing, the problem is logically simple. All events in the life of the licence application for which the Agency is not responsible are recorded in appropriate tables. When such an event occurs (for example, a letter of inquiry is sent to the company) the date of the event is recorded. The Agency's 'clock' is conceptually stopped as long as any such event is outstanding. When the delay is resolved, (for example, the company replies to the inquiry), the 'clock' is restarted. The date of restart is known from the date of the resolution of the query. Additionally (although not necessary for the calculation of 'on' and 'off' time) the clock status is recorded in the Licence table. The clock is shown as 'off' as long as any unresolved event for which the Agency does not have responsibility remains outstanding. On resolution of the licence application, a record of all clock-stopping events remains in the form of start-stop date entries in the event tables. A query is then needed to return a table of intervals during which the 'clock' was off and also to compute the total 'off' time. This means that calculations must coalesce overlapping time slots and then aggregate them to report total elapsed time for which the Agency is not responsible.

The authors have given the SQL to solve this problem elsewhere [7]. Briefly, it involves the following steps:

1. Identify all of the time intervals involved.

2. Set up a single-column table holding all of the dates that occur in this set of intervals.

3. For each date in the table set up in (2) we now need to find its successor, and then see if that date lies within a 'clock-off' period or coincides with the upper boundary of a clock-off period. If it does, we include the difference between the two in our 'clock-off' time. The total 'clock-off' time can then be calculated for each licence application.

Note that the table of all intervals during which the clock was stopped can easily be derived from step 3.

2.5   Discussion

If this problem were implemented in TSQL2, the send and receive dates should presumably be defined as 'user-defined time'. In that case the SUM aggregate operator could be used to return the total time for which the clock was off. What seems unclear, however, is how TSQL2 would return the table of all distinct intervals for which the clock was off. It was seen that the SQL solution was capable of giving this as an intermediate result. The appropriate operator in TSQL2 would seem to be 'coalesce', but this is provided only to restructure valid-time interval or instant tables and to merge overlapping valid-time-stamps only. It is hard to see how this could have been used for our data. Defining the send-receive date interval as the valid time stamp would be one, extremely artificial, way of solving the problem, but then the individual dates, which most certainly must be made available, would either have to be stored separately, with resulting redundancy, or obtained by manipulation of the valid time-stamps in ways analogous to retrieving individual parts of text string fields, which is against all principles of relational database design.

Had our users insisted on the facility to store and query complete version histories, some solution in procedural code would have had to have been devised. The case study illustrates that time-related extensions to SQL need to include support for recursive querying.

3 Case study 2: Ipswich Sewer System

3.1 Introduction

Ipswich Borough Council acts as agents for Anglian Water in monitoring and maintaining the town's sewer system. Ipswich has a population of around 160,000 and approximately 450 km of sewers. Currently the council holds data on computer about the layout and structure of the system, but resources have so far been insufficient to develop the system to make the data easily accessible to the engineers who have to monitor them. We are studying ways in which the database could be redesigned and data displayed graphically to make information quickly available about areas of the network where work might be needed.

Our basic data model is as follows: to hold the map of the sewer system there are essentially only three tables. One holds data about nodes on the system. A node could be a manhole, any point where the network branches, a lamphole (small inspection holes) or a pumping station. The Nodes table will hold: some node id, the node type and three numbers to give absolute position of the pipe at that node (eastings, northings, depth). There are of course sub-types of nodes and appropriate details would be held in corresponding tables, but for simplicity they are not considered here. The second table stores data about pipes. A pipe as defined by the engineers is usually a length between only two manholes, although variations occur. A pipe is thus identified by its furthest 'upstream' node and its lowest 'downstream' node. Data held about pipes include construction material, period of construction (to within 20 years), diameter or width, importance to the sewer system as a whole and current state of repair. The third table (all-key) holds information about inter-connectivity by storing the node id and the id of any other node to which it is immediately connected. Note that in large towns the sewer network can be very complex; for example, lengths of sewer pipe can cross each other without being directly connected.

A record of work done on any given length of pipe (a section between two nodes), occurrences such as collapse, blockages etc will all need to be held but again are outside the scope of this discussion. Discussion is limited here to the problem of querying the sewer map. Thus for current purposes the following tables suffice:

Nodes(node_id, eastings, northings, depth, type)
Pipes(upstream, downstream, diameter, construction, min age, max age, importance, state)
Connections(node_id, connected_id)

3.2 Querying the database

The most important requirement is to be able to return a set of node coordinates in order to draw a map of the area in question on the screen. A typical simple query would be to return all nodes in a given geographical area: here we consider the area bounded by MIN-EAST, MAX-EAST, MIN-NORTH, MAX-NORTH.

```
SELECT *
FROM nodes
WHERE
nodes.eastings >= MIN_EAST AND nodes.eastings <= MAX_EAST
AND nodes.northings >= MIN_NORTH AND nodes.northings <= MAX_NORTH;
```

For the sake of simplicity we discuss here only rectangular areas; refinements to return nodes within the boundaries of irregularly-shaped areas are discussed in [25]. See also [14].

Thus this spatial query is straightforward, needing only the equivalent of algebraic SELECT, in the same way that the SQL equivalent of a TSQL WHEN can be performed by querying on the appropriate interval boundary attributes. Neither the temporal nor the spatial case poses any special difficulty. Querying becomes more difficult, however, if there is a requirement to display all nodes connected to a given node within some sector (so nodes belonging to one network within that area are identified; pipes may cross so that any area may contain pipes from more than one network). The same selection criteria are needed, but for the node in question we must perform a natural join with the Connections table:

```
SELECT *
FROM nodes, connections
WHERE
connections.connected_id = NODE_ID
AND nodes.eastings >= MIN_EAST AND nodes.eastings <= MAX_EAST
AND nodes.northings >= MIN_NORTH AND nodes.northings <= MAX_NORTH
AND nodes.node_id = connections.connected_id;
```

This returns all nodes immediately connected to the node with node id NODE-ID; however it would be necessary to run the query repeatedly (recursively) to return the complete network within this area. As with the MCA case study, recursive querying would be needed, and without appropriate extensions to SQL would have to be implemented in procedural code.

Another class of queries involves operations analogous to those needed in the MCA example, where a query was needed to return the aggregate time for which some class of events was true. Suppose that a record is kept of times during which a length of pipe is out of action (for routine maintenance, repair after collapse etc). Such records would be stored in a table of the kind Downtime(upstream, downstream, start_date, end_date, reason), where 'upstream' and 'downstream' are node identifiers of the nodes identifying the ends of the lengths considered. Suppose for a length of pipe with nodes in geographical sequence A, B, C and D the table contains the following:

Upstream	Downstream	start_date	end_date	Reason
A	C	1/1/94	10/2/94	Maintenance
B	D	3/2/94	20/2/94	Emergency repair

Now to answer the query "What total length of pipe was out of action during the first three months of 1994?" it will be necessary not only to identify the rows whose 'downtime' interval is within our time interval of interest, which is relatively straightforward, but also calculate the total lengths of pipe involved without counting overlapping sections twice. This problem is directly analogous to our CLOCK-OFF time problem in the case study described in (2) above, and requires a spatial interval SUM just as the 'clock-off' computation needed a time interval SUM. If there was also the requirement to return the table of lengths of pipe out of use for any reason, the equivalent of the TSQL2 'coalesce' operator function would also be needed.

There are of course many more complex queries which could be formulated, for example involving overlapping areas of sewer networks, but these relatively straightforward examples are offered to underline the essential equivalence of temporal and spatial querying.

3.3   Discussion

The theoretical equivalence of spatial and temporal data has been acknowledged [15]. This case study gives a practical example of the need for manipulations which are equivalent to those needed for overlapping time intervals. If facilities for such queries are to be supplied as extensions to SQL they could be usefully be made available for interval data generally and not restricted to time intervals. This case study illustrates that consideration could be given to a set of interval extensions rather than to a set of purely temporal extensions.

Additionally, as for the version-tree query in section 2, this case study illustrates the need for recursive querying, providing a second illustration of the practical (as distinct from the theoretical) need for the same type of extensions for spatial as for temporal interval data.

4   Case study 3: DSS Income Support Claims

4.1   Introduction

In [19] a solution is described to a problem of retrospective updates. Under UK Social Security legislation, a state benefit (known as Income Support) is payable to those out of work or on low incomes, subject to checks on such matters as number of dependants, savings and financial commitments such as mortgage. As a result of assessing information on these items, applicants will be given an 'adjudication' (a formal decision). This adjudication will be taken on the basis of the financial status of the applicant during periods relevant to his/her claim. Should the data later be held to be incorrect (because the applicant misunderstood the questions, or perhaps deliberately lied when completing the form) then the data have to be revised. There is no limit to the number of times that this could happen. It will be necessary to record:

1. The original data, with the dates for which they were claimed to be true,
2. the date on which they were first believed by the DSS to be true and the date on which the DSS ceased to believe that they were true and
3. the dates on which adjudications were made based upon DSS beliefs then current.

It is never acceptable to 'overwrite' an old value: the applicant's statements about his status are legal documents which may be required as evidence either for or against him, as are DSS adjudications. Note that the dates needed here are the dates on which some event took place in the real world; it may well be necessary also to record the dates on which such changes were recorded in the computer system but we are deliberately leaving that problem aside to keep the case study as simple as possible. This does mean, however, that it would not be acceptable to use the 'transaction time' of TSQL2 to represent the time over which something was thought to be valid. In our ordinary relational model, if we needed to record actual transaction time then we should do so with two extra attributes, whereas if we were to try to model the system so as to use TSQL2 we should use the transaction time- stamps for this purpose.

In what follows we offer a relational solution for the representation of the first and second interval types above. This could be implemented in any relational database; it does not require any extensions to SQL.

4.2   Proposed data model for the DSS system

Our model requires the following relations:
Person(personid,...)
In practice personid would be the person's Social Security number.
Claim(Personid, claimdate, claimplace) One person may make many claims at more than one office.
Change report(personid, claimdate, claimplace, report date, report#, rep. by)
If the applicant reports changes of circumstance or, for example, a fraud enquiry implies that data previously accepted are now held to be false, a change report is filed. This can refer to more than one relevant circumstance. "Rep. by" records who made the report.
Circumstance(personid, claimdate, claimplace, circ#, known, falsified, effective, endeff)
Claims are decided on the basis of many pieces of evidence, such as number of dependants, savings etc. In a full version of the data model, each of these

types of evidence would be regarded as a sub-type of the entity 'circumstance'. In the circumstance relation, meanings of data attributes are as follows:

circ#: an identifying number for circumstances within this claim.

known (date): date from which the circumstance was acknowledged as known to the DSS.

falsified (date): date from which the circumstance was held to be false by the DSS.

effective (date): date from which the acknowledged circumstance applied to the claim under consideration. As an example, the date of birth of a child would be some time before the date at which that fact was known to the DSS but (unless the applicant was extraordinarily late in reporting it) a claim for enhanced benefit dependent on the existence of the child would be back-dated to the child's birth.

endeff (date): date until which this circumstance is relevant to a claim ("end effective date"). Again, if the birth of a child is being reported, it will go on being relevant until its eighteenth birthday. On the other hand, if the circumstance is one of income (or more often, lack of it) no end effective date can be assumed and it will be assumed to be ongoing until change is notified (in TSQL2, the default value would be FOREVER).

Claim state(person id, claimdate, claimplace, known, effective , falsified, endeff)

A claim state is the set of circumstances accepted as relevant to a claim for a given period of time. It will be ended by new evidence being offered in the form of a change of circumstance report. Only if the change report includes evidence that this set of circumstances was false for all or part of its period of currency will the 'falsification date' be set.

The reader will have noticed that this relation is not in third normal form; the structure was chosen to illustrate more clearly the similarity between these temporal attributes and valid time-stamps. Adjudication(personid, claimdate, claimplace, known, effective, superseded date, decision details...)

Many decisions may be made on one set of circumstances, with no change of evidence. This could happen if

i) an adjudication officer made a decision which was then

ii) overturned by his/her immediate superior, which in turn was

iii) overturned on appeal by the applicant.

Since this is a moderately complex problem, an illustrative example is included in the Appendix.

4.3 Querying the relations

Now we can ask queries such as: give me all the circumstances pertinent to a given claim for each of its claim states:

```
SELECT circumstances.*
FROM claimstate, circumstances
WHERE claimstate.claimdate = circumstances.claimdate
AND claimstate.effective >= circumstances.effective
AND (claimstate.effective < circumstances.endeff OR
circumstances.endeff IS NULL)
AND claimstate.known >= circumstances.known
AND (claimstate.known < circumstances.falsified OR
circumstances.falsified IS NULL);
```

This can easily be modified to return, for example, only those circumstances relevant at a given time. Types of queries which are more difficult but which can still be satisfied are of the following type: "Over what total period was any of the information on which adjudications were based subsequently found to be false as the result of false claims by the applicant?" (ie return the total period of any fraudulent claim). This requires the use of both a 'believed valid' time and a 'validity valid' time. What we are actually asking, of course, is the total time over which a set of circumstances was definitely **invalid**. It also requires us to make calculations on overlapping time periods for both types of time interval; since the individual, distinct time intervals over which circumstances were true or believed true may be required, rather than merely the aggregate, TSQL2 'coalesce' operator would be needed for both of these time intervals.

4.4 Discussion

This case study illustrates circumstances in which one valid-time stamp, as proposed in TSQL2, would not be adequate. It could be argued that transaction time could be used to log time over which a set of circumstances were believed to be valid [12]. However this option would not be possible in this case: the distinction between when a change was recorded externally and when it was applied to the system must be maintained. Again, even if this somewhat ad hoc solution were possible, the DSS system could still not be modelled using one valid time stamp and one transaction time stamp since there are other time intervals relative to each row which may be required. The problem would still have to be modelled using 'user-defined' time.

5 General Discussion and Conclusions

5.1 Conclusions from the case studies

1) The distinction between valid time and user-defined time is not always useful. Additionally, however a pair of time interval attributes is classified, their manipulation can need not only the aggregate operators provided in TSQL2 for user-defined time attributes but also the equivalent of TSQL2 'coalesce', which is provided only for valid time-stamps. On the other hand, queries about occurrence of events ("When did we last send an enquiry letter on application

XYZ?") are easy to express in standard SQL and pose no special difficulties. The principle of Occam's razor suggests that no extensions should be provided for such straightforward queries: "entia non multiplicanda sunt praeter necessitatem".

2) The need for support for recursive querying for both historical and some kinds of spatial data was demonstrated. If no specific support for recursion is provided, complete querying of version trees can only be accomplished with procedural code, and then often with much difficulty.

3) Spatial data are not only theoretically equivalent to temporal data (as has been recognised) but, not surprisingly, they pose the same practical problems. In the second case study the need for aggregation of overlapping spatial intervals was illustrated. The essential equivalence between temporal and ordered spatial data suggests that TSQL should not be defined for time-interval data only; rather, an Interval SQL should be considered. Problems such as that discussed by [25], in which they describe ad hoc solutions to the querying of graphical objects stored in a relational database, would benefit from some operators designed to operate on interval data at least as much as those discussed in the context of temporal databases. It would be regrettable if a special-purpose set of operators were to be bolted on to SQL as it now is and the chance lost to extend the usefulness of SQL generally to a much larger, important class of problem.

4) A need for more than one dimension of 'valid time' was illustrated. Our example is not unique; see for example [11]. TSQL2 supports only one time-stamp per row as a valid time-stamp [20], although the consensus glossary of temporal database terms [12] does not limit the interpretation of valid time in this way. The extra operators which would be useful for temporal querying would be equally welcome for both types of time interval.

5) We suggest that user-defined operators might be one solution to the problem of just which operators are needed by which domain of interest. Those aspects of time discussed by the temporal database research community are merely one special domain of interest, and can be generalised as discussed above. The problem of identifying overlapping polygons is discussed as a test for the ability of the relational model to support complex objects [21], [5]. Date [6] argues for the use of database procedures as part of a solution. We suggest that temporal database problems are a subset of those problems discussed by proponents of the Object- Oriented approach. Those extensions to implementations of the relational model proposed by Date and others to allow better support for the manipulation of complex objects would also solve problems associated with manipulation of temporal intervals.

6) A conventional relational solution was offered to all three case studies. While accepting the need for extra functions for the **manipulation** of time and other intervals, there seems nothing in these studies, one of them relatively complex, to suggest that the relational model per se is too limited to provide a **description** of temporal data.

5.2   Problems with TSQL2

1) For all of the querying facilities of TSQL2 to be available to them, systems developers must use an extension to the relational model. TSQL2 itself supports six different table types and three temporal data types. The simplicity of the relational model must be relinquished and be replaced with one specific vision of how time behaves in the user's world. If the user/developer rejects this view then s/he is left to model the system using only 'user-defined time', with not all of the facilities for time manipulation available to him/her. If the proffered temporal model is accepted and used, the meaning of any TSQL2 program can only be known if the data types of all of its variables are known, both tables and attributes. This makes TSQL2 programs extremely difficult to interpret and will make errors very likely. For a given set of processing commands, for N data types there will have to be N definitions of each command. In TSQL2, for example, the aggregate SUM will have different effects on time interval data from that on point data. This has been well-expressed by Codd [4], objecting that "any additional types of compound data add complexity without adding power".

2) There is a specific objection to the use of an interval data type. An interval is defined by a set of start co- ordinates (spatio-temporal) and a set of stop co-ordinates from the same domain. The interval itself is thus a derived or calculated field. If a set of values is to be encapsulated in this manner into one attribute it must be done with care; the designer must be sure that the separate attributes will not be needed in their own right and there should be good reason for considering them as one value. Since this will very often not be the case, extensions to query facilities which need a specific interval data type as argument will force the designer to specify that the interval be held twice, once as separate attributes and once as an interval. Such redundancy seems at best unnecessary.

3) The system developer is encouraged to hide data under the guise of a data structure: what should contain only meta-data will actually contain data (a calendar) . The calendar itself will not be amenable to query. In the relational model the data dictionary itself is intended to be as amenable to query as the user data: "All information in a relational database is represented explicitly at the logical level and in exactly one way - by values in tables" [3]. We agree with Codd's assertion [4] that this principle should not be abandoned without a cast- iron case being made.

4) Facilities for dealing with uncertainty are offered in TSQL2. While these are interesting and may prove to be valuable, the need for them is not central to problems of manipulating interval data, nor would any usefulness be limited to such data. It is puzzling to see such facilities included in a temporal query language.

5) There is no mention of support for recursion in published discussions of TSQL2. An algebra is discussed in [24] which includes a recursive operator but the problem of recursive querying is relatively neglected in the temporal database literature. Although some commercial implementations of SQL have

various levels of support for recursion there is no proposal for such support in TSQL2. It may be argued that this is being discussed and dealt with in another context, since there is an extensive literature on the subject (eg [13]) and support for recursive querying is under discussion for possible inclusion in SQL3 [1]. However the problem is so central to complete querying of historic data sets that one would expect to see the problem at least discussed in the TSQL literature.

In summary, it is suggested that temporal problems can be adequately described using the relational model and that attempts to define one specific temporal model will be unsatisfactory for a significant number of applications. Query language operators which require compound data types as arguments are considered by the authors to be unwise; rather, any operators offered to help interval querying should take two time or space points as arguments. It is accepted that extensions are needed for querying temporal and other interval data but these need not and should not be tied to a new data model.

Ackowledgments

The authors are extremely grateful to Neville Dean and Graham Hughes for assistance in the preparation and formatting of the LaTeX and postscript files.

References

[1] Central Computing and Telecommunications Agency. Database Language SQL Explained. Her Majesty's Stationery Office, Norwich, UK 1993.

[2] Codd E.F. A Relational Model of Data for Large Shared Data Banks. Communications of ACM **13** (6), 377-387 1970.

[3] Codd E.F. Is your DBMS really relational? Computerworld Oct. 14 1985.

[4] Codd E.F. The relational model for database management: Version 2. Addison-Wesley, 1990.

[5] Date C.J. An optimisation problem. In: Date C.J. and Darwen H., Relational Writings, Addison-Wesley, 1992.

[6] Date C.J. An Introduction to Database Systems. Sixth edition, Addison-Wesley, 1995.

[7] Davies C. and Lazell B. How helpful is current theory for the representation of time in real databases? Proceedings of the Third European Conference on Information Systems (ECIS'95), 1207-1219, Athens 1995.

[8] Dittrich K.R .and Lorie R.A. Version support for engineering database systems. IEEE Transactions on Software Engineering **14** (4) 429-437, 1988.

[9] Gallagher L.J. and Draper J.M. Guide on Data Models in the Selection and Use of Database Management Systems. NBS Special Publication 500-108, US Department of Commerce, 1984.

[10] Elmasri R. and Navathe S.B. Fundamentals of Database Systems, Benjamin Cummings, 1994.

[11] Ioannidis E.V., Kokkotos S. and Spyropoulos C.D. A temporal framework for managing retroactive and delayed updates: an application to the payroll

information system of the Greek public sector. European Journal of Information Systems **2** (2) 149-154, 1993.

[12] Jensen C.S. et al. A consensus glossary of temporal database concepts. ACM SIGMOD Record, **23** (1) 52-64, 1994.

[13] Koymen K. and Cai Q. SQL*: a recursive SQL. Information Systems **18** (2) 121-128, 1993.

[14] Laurini R. and Thompson D. Fundamentals of Spatial Information Systems. Academic Press 1992.

[15] Lorentzos N.A. The Interval-extended relational model and its application to valid-time databases. In: Tansel A.U., Clifford J., Gadia S., Jajodia S., Segev A. and Snodgrass R. (Eds), Temporal Databases, Benjamin Cummings, 67-91, 1993.

[16] Leung T.Y.C. and Muntz R.R. Stream Processing: Temporal Query Processing and Optimization. In: Tansel A.U., Clifford J., Gadia S., Jajodia S., Segev A. and Snodgrass R. (Eds): Temporal Databases, Benjamin Cummings, 329-355, 1993.

[17] McKenzie L.E. and Snodgrass R.T. Evaluation of relational algebras incorporating the time dimension in databases. ACM Computing Surveys **23** (4) 501-543, 1991.

[18] Navathe S.B. and Ahmed R. Temporal extensions to the relational model and SQL. In: Tansel A.U., Clifford J., Gadia S., Jajodia S., Segev A. and Snodgrass R. (Eds), Temporal Databases, Benjamin Cummings, 92-109, 1993.

[19] Shearer I. Retrospective Update: Data as it was believed to be. The Computer Journal, **35** (2) 184-186, 1992.

[20] Snodgrass R. et al. A TSQL2 tutorial. ACM SIGMOD Record, **23**, (3), 27-33, 1994.

[21] Stonebraker M. Inclusion of new types in relational database systems. Proceedings of 2nd International Conference on Database Engineering, Los Angeles, 1986.

[22] Tansel A.U. Non first normal form temporal relational model. IEEE Database Engineering Bulletin **11** (4) 224- 230, 1988.

[23] Tansel A.U., Clifford J., Gadia S., Jajodia S., Segev A. and Snodgrass R. (Eds), Temporal Databases, Benjamin Cummings, 1993.

[24] Tuzhilin A. and Clifford J. A temporal relational algebra as a basis for temporal relational completeness. In: Proceedings of the Conference on Very Large Databases, Brisbane 1990.

[25] Waugh T.C. and Healey R.G. The GEOVIEW design: a relational database approach to geographical data handling. International Journal of Geographical Information Systems **1** (2) 101-118, 1987.

[26] Wuu G.T.J. and Dayal U. A uniform model for temporal and versioned object-oriented databases. In: Tansel A.U., Clifford J., Gadia S., Jajodia S., Segev A. and Snodgrass R. (Eds): Temporal Databases, Benjamin Cummings, 230-247, 1993.

Appendix: DSS Case Study, Sample Data

Phase 1: Person number 1000 makes a claim at Norwich on 1/1/94
This gives a row in Claim:

Personid	claimdate	claimplace
1000	1/1/94	Norwich

The claim is on the basis of the following Circumstances:

Personid	claimdate	claimplace	known	falsified	effective	endeff	circ#	reason
1000	1/1/94	Norwich	1/1/94	NULL	1/1/94	NULL	1	unemployed
1000	1/1/94	Norwich	1/1/94	NULL	1/1/94	NULL	2	wife
1000	1/1/94	Norwich	1/1/94	NULL	1/1/94	NULL	3	child1
1000	1/1/94	Norwich	1/1/94	NULL	1/1/94	NULL	4	address
1000	1/1/94	Norwich	1/1/94	NULL	1/1/94	NULL	5	income 0

The Claim State at this point is:

Personid	claimdate	claimplace	known	falsified	effective	endeff
000	1/1/94	Norwich	1/1/94	NULL	1/1/94	NULL

Phase 2: The claimant reports that his wife has had a baby and that they are going to move; this triggers a Change Report:

Personid	claimdate	claimplace	report date	report#	rep.by
1000	1/1/94	Norwich	1/4/94	1	claimant

This will result in an update of their existing Circumstances row and also trigger two new Circumstances rows:

Personid	claimdate	claimplace	known	falsified	effective	endeff	circ#	reason
1000	1/1/94	Norwich	1/1/94	NULL	1/1/94	3/4/94	4	address
1000	1/1/94	Norwich	1/4/94	NULL	15/3/94	NULL	1	child2 born
1000	1/1/94	Norwich	1/4/94	NULL	3/4/94	NULL	2	address change

The first row is an update of an existing row and the last two are new. There will also be updates and new rows in Claim State:

Personid	claimdate	claimplace	known	falsified	effective	endeff
1000	1/1/94	Norwich	1/1/94	NULL	1/1/94	15/3/94
1000	1/1/94	Norwich	1/4/94	NULL	15/3/94	3/4/94
1000	1/1/94	Norwich	1/4/94	NULL	3/4/94	NULL

The first line is an update; end effective date has gained a value; this is the date on which any of the person's circumstances changed as reported in this change report. The second two indicate that there will be one new claim state (as a result of acceptance that this is date of the birth of a child) until they move and another after they move.

Phase 3: the registrar has returned the birth certificate, which the Department will have referred to him, saying that it is fraudulent. Child 2 seems to be a figment of the applicant's imagination. (We offer this example for simplicity; there are many less dramatic reasons for changing belief about reported circumstances. Probably the most common is a simple mistake, on the part of DSS employees or the applicant). This results in another Change Report:

Personid	claimdate	claimplace	report date	report#	rep.by
1000	1/1/94	Norwich	20/4/94	1	registrar

Update the Circumstance row referring to child 2 and add a new row to Circumstances:

Personid	claimdate	claimplace	known	falsified	effective	endeff	circ#	reason
1000	1/1/94	Norwich	1/1/94	20/4/94	15/3/94	15/3/94	1	Child 2
1000	1/1/94	Norwich	20/4/94	NULL	15/3/94	NULL	1	No child 2

Again the updated row is shown first and the second is a new row. The effective time span for the circumstance of having Child 2 is now zero; it was never true. Circumstances are numbered within a change report so the new circ# is also 1. The claim state has also changed; two existing rows must be updated and two new rows, representing two new states, added. It is known that the claimstate starting on 15th March will end on 3rd April, when the couple move house, thus giving Claim State:

Personid	claimdate	claimplace	known	falsified	effective	endeff
1000	1/1/94	Norwich	1/4/94	20/4/94	15/3/94	15/3/94
1000	1/1/94	Norwich	1/4/94	20/4/94	3/4/94	3/4/94
1000	1/1/94	Norwich	20/4/94	NULL	15/3/94	3/4/94
1000	1/1/94	Norwich	20/4/94	NULL	3/4/94	NULL

A sample query on these data appears in the text.

On Temporal Grouping

James Clifford

Information Systems Department, Stern School of Business
New York, NY, USA

Albert Croker

Statistics and Computer Information Systems, Baruch College
New York, NY, USA

Fabio Grandi

Dipartimento di Elettronica Informatica e Sistemistica, Universitá di Bologna
Bologna, ITALY

Alexander Tuzhilin

Information Systems Department, Stern School of Business
New York, NY, USA

Abstract

In this paper we address some of the concerns that have been expressed regarding the practicality of the temporally-grouped, or history-oriented, data modeling approach. Specifically, we address the concern over the lack of an algebra for this paradigm, by presenting such an algebra. In addition, we examine the semantics of two notions, coalescing and restructuring, from the perspective of a comparison between the temporally grouped and temporally ungrouped paradigms.

1 Introduction

A large variety of extensions of the relational data model and query languages to include time have been proposed in recent years (see [9, 18, 19] for references to the growing body of literature on temporal databases). According to a fundamental structural property formalized in [1], all the proposals can be classified into two main categories: *temporally ungrouped* and *temporally grouped* models and languages. In temporally ungrouped models, the temporal representation is realized at extensional level, by means of timestamps added to data values as additional attributes to represent their temporal validity. In temporally grouped models, the temporal dimension is implicit in the structure of data representation: attributes are represented as *histories* considered as a whole and without the introduction of distinguished attributes. Attribute histories can be regarded as functions which map time into attribute domains.

The most important property of *temporally grouped* models and languages concerns their formal *expressiveness*, which has been shown [1] to be greater than the expressiveness of temporally ungrouped ones without the addition of an explicit, auxiliary mechanism for supporting temporal groups or "histories.". Moreover, it has also been shown [4] that history-oriented temporal query languages, providing a "grouped" point of view on data, can be more "natural" and friendly for human users as they support the concept of *history* as a first-class object of discourse.

A controversy regarding the two approaches was also brought up in the discussions of the *ARPA/NSF International Workshop on an Infrastructure for Temporal Databases*, held in Arlington in 1993. The main objective of the workshop was to establish a common foundation for the discipline of temporal databases and to develop a consensus grounding for further research and development. In a few words, while temporally grouped models appeared more attractive from a logical perspective (being more expressive and also user-friendly), temporally ungrouped models seemed more amenable to implementation at the state-of-the-art of commercial database technology, requiring almost minimal extensions of the 1NF relational model and SQL-92.

After the workshop, the definition of a system supporting temporal grouping has come together into the *history-oriented* entry of the "consensus glossary of temporal database concepts" [6]. According to the final glossary definition, a DBMS is said to be *history-oriented* if:

1. It supports history unique identification (e.g. via time-invariant keys, surrogates or OIDs);

2. The integrity of histories as first-class objects is inherent in the model, in the sense that history-related integrity constraints might be expressed and enforced, and the data manipulation language provides a mechanism (e.g., history variables and quantification) for direct reference to *object-histories.*

Both terms, temporally grouped and history-oriented, will be freely used when appropriate in the rest of the paper.

As another follow-up of the workshop standardization efforts, a committee was formed with the purpose of designing a temporal extension of the SQL-92 language. The committee, gathering people from both academia and industrial world, released a language specification, named TSQL2, in September 1994 [15, 16]. TSQL2 proposed a compromise solution between temporally grouped and temporally ungrouped approaches. Specifically, TSQL2 is provided with a *surrogate* data type [7] and special range variables [17]. Surrogates, which are system-generated identifiers, can be used to simulate the history identity inherent to a temporally grouped data model as shown in [1], but their correct management is left entirely up to the user in TSQL2. TSQL2 range variables can be used as history and version variables [4] in order to simulate history-oriented queries, but their correct use is not straightforward and still is up to the user. Rather than being more clear and readable, history-oriented TSQL2 queries may in fact be very complex and not very natural.

In spite of this, several objections to a temporally grouped approach have been raised. The principal objections will be considered and discussed in this work.

First, a history-oriented DBMS seems too far removed from an SQL-92-based relational system to be put into practice. For instance, even if a 1NF relational model with surrogates could be adopted, the standard relational algebra would be inadequate for defining certain necessary operations (e.g. there are difficulties in dealing with surrogates in Cartesian Products). Also temporally grouped extensions of SQL-92 require the introduction of the notions of history and temporal object at the language level; notions which are beyond the classical perspective of pure relational languages and would rather require features of an object-oriented approach.

Second, perhaps the most severe objection is just the fact that, although logic- or SQL-based languages have been defined, no algebra is available for grouped models yet. The most important consequence thereof is the lack of an effective operational core on which any real language implementation (query processing and optimization strategies) can be based.

Finally, while grouped models impose a structure on data tables, i.e., the history of stored data objects is the semantic criterion for grouping tuples, other temporal models and languages allow the restructuring of a table on an arbitrary set of columns. In particular, the restructuring operator [2], which has been considered a desirable language feature and has been generalized by the TSQL2 variable mechanism, has seemed to allow a change in the key of a temporal relation.

In this paper we try to make a step towards the resolution of the difficulties or objections that have been raised concerning the grouped approach. We will present a history-oriented extension of SQL language as an alternative to TSQL2. We will introduce an algebra for grouped models, on which our SQL extension can effectively be based, and sketch a temporal completeness proof for it. Finally, we will discuss the notions of regrouping and coalescing in the context of our approach.

2   An Algebra for Temporally Grouped Models

It is important to have an equivalent algebra for a query language or calculus because query evaluation is typically done by mapping a query into an equivalent algebraic expression. Therefore, we have developed an algebra for a temporally grouped model that is equivalent to the grouped calculus L_h [1], and we present it in this section. Because of the space limitations, we cannot describe the language L_h and assume that the reader is familiar with this language, as described in [1].

However, before describing a grouped algebra, we would like to point out some difficulties in developing this algebra. To illustrate our points, consider the following safe L_h query:

$$[e.A : t]R(e) \wedge t \in e.l \wedge \neg(\exists e')(\exists t')(Q(e') \wedge t' \in e'.l \wedge R(e) \wedge t \in e.l \wedge$$
$$e.A(t) = e'.B(t'))$$

where R and Q are temporally grouped relations, e and e' are tuple variables,

t and t' are temporal variables, $e.A : t$ is the target list, and $e.l$ is the lifespan of tuple e (the lifespan is the property of a tuple because the data model of L_h is homogeneous). Typically, when a calculus expression is mapped into the equivalent algebraic expression, this is usually done inductively on the number of operators in the calculus expression. However, if we do this with the L_h expression presented above, then the subformula

$$Q(e') \wedge t' \in e'.l \wedge R(e) \wedge t \in e.l \wedge e.A(t) = e'.B(t')$$

depends on two tuple variables (e and e') and two times (t and t'). This means that there cannot be any equivalent algebraic expression because such an expression would return the relation that has two time attributes in it and, thus, does not adhere to the data model of L_h.

For this reason, it has proven difficult to come up with a grouped algebra that it equivalent to the temporally grouped query language L_h which was proposed in [1] as part of the canonical temporally grouped historical relational model TG. (Historical, or valid-time [6] refers to the kind of time that is modeled by the temporal dimension, rather than the manner in which the temporal dimension is modeled. In this paper we do not specifically address another common temporal dimension of data, its transaction time.) To address this issue, we propose here a consistent extension to the data model $M_{TG} = (TG, L_h)$, and make small corresponding adjustments to its query language L_h as described in the next subsection.

2.1 An Inhomogeneous Historical Grouped Calculus L_{hi}

2.1.1 The Data Model TG_{hi}

In [1] the data model $M_{TG} = (TG, L_h)$ was presented, where TG is a canonical temporally grouped data model and L_h its associated query language. The calculus L_h is based on the data model $M_{TG} = (TG, L_h)$ that treats the domain of *all* of the attributes of a historical (or valid-time) relation as functions from time to values. In this paper we look at an extended data model, $M_{TG_{hi}} = (TG_{hi}, L_{hi})$, which considers two other types of domains for attribute values in addition to those of M_{TG}, i.e. temporal and atemporal (value-based) attributes. More formally, $M_{TG_{hi}} = (TG_{hi}, L_{hi})$ is a three-sorted data model, with sorts:

- $\mathcal{T}$: a non-empty domain of times.

- $\mathcal{V}$: a non-empty domain of values.

- $\mathcal{F}$: is a set of functions $F : \mathcal{T} \rightarrow \mathcal{V}$.

A *relation* in $M_{TG_{hi}}$ is defined similarly to a relation in M_{TG}, except it allows attribute values of all the three sorts, $\mathcal{T}$, $\mathcal{V}$, and $\mathcal{F}$, unlike the M_{TG} relations that allow only attribute values of sort $\mathcal{F}$. Attributes of sort $\mathcal{V}$ are used to model time invariant attributes, and attributes of sort $\mathcal{T}$ are used to model user-defined time.

EMPLOYEE			
NAME	*DOB*	*DEPT*	*SALARY*
Tom	8/15/51	$[0,4) \to$ Sales $[4,6] \to$ Mktg	$[2,3) \to$ 20K $[3,5) \to$ 30K $[5,6] \to$ 27K
Juni	2/28/61	$[2,6] \to$ Acctng	$[4,6] \to$ 28K
Ashley	5/25/59	$[1,3) \to$ Engrng $[3,4) \to$ Mktg $[5,6] \to$ Engrng	$[1,2) \to$ 27K $[2,4) \to$ 30K $[5,6] \to$ 35K

DEPARTMENT	
DEPT	*MGR*
$[0,6] \to$ Acctng	$[1,2) \to$ Paul $[2,5] \to$ Juni
$[0,6] \to$ Engrng	$[0,5) \to$ Wanda $[5,6] \to$ Ashley
$[0,6] \to$ Mktg	$[0,5) \to$ Tom
$[0,6] \to$ Sales	$[0,6] \to$ Sue

Figure 1: The Historical Grouped Relations **EMPLOYEE** and **DEPART-MENT**.

In addition to the three-sortedness extension, we relax the homogeneity assumption used in M_{TG}, which required that the lifespans of historical attributes in historical tuples must all be the same. In other words, if A and B are attributes of sort $\mathcal{F}$ in relation R then *lifespan(A)* is not necessarily equal to *lifespan(B)*. By relaxing this assumption, we make the data model of $M_{TG_{hi}}$ *inhomogeneous*.

To summarize, $M_{TG_{hi}} = (TG_{hi}, L_{hi})$ is a consistent extension of the data model $M_{TG} = (TG, L_h)$ proposed in [1]. The extensions make $M_{TG_{hi}}$ *multi-sorted* and *temporally inhomogeneous*.

Example 1 *Consider the following* **EMPLOYEE** *and* **DEPARTMENT** *relations. The first relation has the schema* **EMPLOYEE***(NAME, DOB, DEPT, SALARY), where attribute NAME has the sort $\mathcal{V}$, DOB has the sort $\mathcal{T}$, and DEPT and SALARY have the sort $\mathcal{F}$. The second relation has the schema* **DEPARTMENT***(DEPT, MGR), where attributes DEPT and MGR have the sort $\mathcal{F}$. Instances of both of these relations are presented in Figure 1. (Note that in these figures we use a shorthand notation for functions; for example, instead of specifying completely the function $\{< 0, Sales >, < 1, Sales >, < 2, Sales > < 3, Sales >\}$ we abbreviate the representation to $\{< [0,3), Sales >\}$ to save space.)*

$\square$

2.1.2 The Language L_{hi}

The language L_{hi} is a consistent extension of the language L_h; the straightforward language extensions address the extensions to the data model described above. First, L_{hi} is inhomogeneous, and, thus, the lifespan is a property of an individual attribute of sort $\mathcal{F}$. Therefore, a lifespan term in L_{hi} is of the form $e.A.l$, where e is a tuple variable, and A is an attribute of sort $\mathcal{F}$. Second, we extend L_h by making temporal terms to be not only temporal constants and variables but also terms of the form $e.A$, where A is an attribute of sort $\mathcal{T}$. Third, we extend L_h by making value terms to be not only value constants, domain variables, and expressions $e.A(t)$ for attributes A of sort $\mathcal{F}$, but also terms of the form $e.A$, where A is an attribute of sort $\mathcal{V}$.

Finally, the definition of an L_{hi} query is extended from that of L_h. An expression $[\alpha_1, \ldots, \alpha_n]\phi$ is an L_{hi} query if ϕ is an L_{hi} formula, and α_i, $i = 1, \ldots, n$, are expressions in one of the following forms. Either α_i is a free variable of sort $\mathcal{T}$ or $\mathcal{V}$ from ϕ, or it is an expression of the form $e.A : t$, where e is a free tuple variable from ϕ, A is an attribute of a relation of sort $\mathcal{F}$ associated with e, and t is a free variable of sort $\mathcal{T}$, such that $t \in e.A.l$. Moreover, only those variables appearing in α_i, $i = 1, \ldots, n$, are the free variables in ϕ. This definition says that the attributes in the answer to an L_{hi} query can be of any of the three sorts $\mathcal{F}$, $\mathcal{T}$, and $\mathcal{V}$. In contrast to this, the attributes in the answer to an L_h query are only of the sort $\mathcal{F}$. Furthermore, the notion of safety, as introduced in L_h, has to be adjusted in a straightforward way to account for these changes to L_h.

To summarize, both the data model and the query language of $M_{TG} = (TG, L_h)$ are special, restricted cases of their consistent extension $M_{TG_{hi}} = (TG_{hi}, L_{hi})$.

We now introduce some examples of L_{hi} queries. These examples are based on relations **EMPLOYEE** and **DEPARTMENT** presented in Figure 1.

Example 2 *The query "Find the names, dates of birth, salary and departmental histories of the people who worked at time 5 in the Accounting department" can be expressed in L_{hi} as*

$$[e.NAME, e.DOB, e.SALARY : t_1, e.DEPT : t_2]$$
$$\textbf{EMPLOYEE}(e) \wedge t_1 \in e.SALARY.l \wedge 5 \in e.DEPT.l \wedge$$
$$e.DEPT(5) = \text{``Accntg''} \wedge t_2 \in e.DEPT.l$$

Note that the answer to this query has attributes of all the three sorts $\mathcal{T}$, $\mathcal{V}$, and $\mathcal{F}$.

□

Example 3 *The query "What are the names of the managers for whom Tom has worked?" can be expressed in L_{hi} as*

$[e_1.NAME]$ **EMPLOYEE**$(e_1)\wedge$

$\quad\exists e_2 \exists t \exists d(\textbf{EMPLOYEE}(e_2) \wedge t \in e_2.DEPT.l \wedge$

$\qquad\textbf{DEPARTMENT}(d) \wedge t \in d.MGR.l \wedge t \in d.DEPT.l \wedge$

$\qquad e_2.NAME = Tom \wedge e_2.DEPT(t) = d.DEPT(t) \wedge$

$\qquad d.MGR(t) = e_1.NAME)$

□

2.2   An Inhomogeneous Grouped Algebra A_G

Having described the calculus L_{hi} and its data model, we are ready to present the corresponding algebra.

The grouped relational algebra, A_G, has five standard relational operators union, difference, Cartesian product, selection, and projection extended to the temporal domain. In addition, A_G contains two operators *tdom* and *vdom* that compute, respectively, the active temporal and value domains of a relation, and a timeslice operator. The operators of union, difference, Cartesian product, and projection are defined similarly to the standard relational case, and we use L_{hi} expressions to define them. Let R and Q be two L_{hi} relations.

1. *Union.* If R and Q are union-compatible, then $R \cup Q = \{e \mid R(e) \vee Q(e)\}$.
2. *Difference.* If R and Q are union-compatible, then

   $R - Q = \{e \mid R(e) \wedge \neg Q(e)\}$.
3. *Cartesian product.* $R \times Q = \{(e, e') \mid R(e) \wedge Q(e')\}$.
4. *Projection.* $\pi_{A_1,\ldots,A_k}(R) = \{e_1,\ldots,e_k \mid (\exists e)(R(e) \wedge \bigwedge_{i=1}^{k} e.A_i = e_i)\}$[1].

However, definition of selection is more involved in A_G than in the standard relational case.

5. *Selection.* Let $R(A_1, \ldots, A_n)$ be an L_{hi} relation. Then the syntax of selection is $\sigma_{F_1 \wedge \ldots \wedge F_m}(R)$ for $m \geq 1$, where each F_i is defined in one of the following ways:

a. $A_i =_f A_j$, where attributes A_i and A_j are of the sort $\mathcal{F}$, and $=_f$ is the equality operator for functions.

b. $A_i \theta_\tau A_j$ or $A_i \theta_\tau c$, where attributes A_i and A_j are of the sort $\mathcal{T}$, c is a constant of the sort $\mathcal{T}$, and θ_τ is a comparison operator $(=, >, \geq, <, \leq, \neq)$ for the temporal sort.

c. $\alpha_1 \theta_\nu \alpha_2$, where α_i ($i = 1, 2$) is either a constant of the sort $\mathcal{V}$, or an attribute of that sort, or an expression of the form $A(T)$, where A is an $\mathcal{F}$ attribute and T is a $\mathcal{T}$ attribute of R. Also, θ_ν is a comparison operator $(=, >, \geq, <, \leq, \neq)$ for the sort $\mathcal{V}$.

---

[1] If A_i is of sort $\mathcal{F}$, then the expression $e.A_i = e_i$ is not an L_h expression; rather, it is a macro stating that $e.A_i$ and e_i are equal as functions over time. More precisely, this means that the lifespans of $e.A_i$ and e_i are equal and for any time t in this lifespan $e.A_i(t) = e_i(t)$.

d. $A_i \in_\tau A_j.\tau$, where attribute A_i is of the sort $\mathcal{T}$, A_j is of the sort $\mathcal{F}$, and $\in_\tau$ is the membership operator for the temporal sort. In this expression, $A_j.\tau$ denotes the *domain* (lifespan) of the temporal attribute A_j.

e. $A_i \in_\nu A_j.\nu$, where attribute A_i is of the sort $\mathcal{V}$, A_j is of the sort $\mathcal{F}$, and $\in_\nu$ is the membership operator for the value sort. In this expression, $A_j.\nu$ denotes the *range* of the temporal attribute A_j.

If no confusion arises, we will drop the subscripts τ and ν in the comparison θ_τ, θ_ν and in the membership $\in_\tau$ and $\in_\nu$ operators and assume that their exact meanings can be judged from the context.

The meaning of $\sigma_F(R)$ is the set of tuples in R for which, when we substitute their values into the formula F replacing attributes appearing in F with the values of the tuples, F becomes true.

Moreover, the algebra A_G contains two additional "twin" operators *tdom* and *vdom* that compute, respectively, the active temporal and value domains of a relation.

6. *Active-domain* operators. Assume that $R(A_1, \ldots, A_n)$ has only attributes of sort $\mathcal{F}$. Then

$$tdom(R) \;=\; \{t \mid (\exists e)(R(e) \wedge \textstyle\bigvee_{i=1}^n t \in e.A_i.l)\}$$

If R also contains attributes of sort $\mathcal{T}$, then their values should also be included in $tdom(R)$. $vdom(R)$ is defined similarly to $tdom(R)$: if $R(A_1, \ldots, A_n)$ has only attributes of sort $\mathcal{F}$, then

$$vdom(R) \;=\; \{d \mid (\exists e)(\exists t)(R(e) \wedge \textstyle\bigvee_{i=1}^n (t \in e.A_i.l \wedge e.A_i(t) = d))\}$$

If R also contains attributes of sort $\mathcal{V}$, then their values should also be included in $vdom(R)$.

Note that operators $tdom(R)$ and $vdom(R)$ define mappings from relation R into a single attribute relation on the sorts $\mathcal{T}$ and $\mathcal{V}$ respectively.

Finally, the algebra A_G contains an additional *timeslice* operator that restricts the lifespans of attributes of sort $\mathcal{F}$. More specifically,

7. *Timeslice* operator. Let $R(A_1, \ldots, A_i, \ldots, T, \ldots, A_n)$ be an L_{hi} relation, where attribute A_i is of sort $\mathcal{F}$ and attribute T is of sort $\mathcal{T}$. Then

$$\tau_{A_i:T}(R) \;=\; \{e.A_1, \ldots, e.A_{i-1}, e.A_i : t, e.A_{i+1}, \ldots, e.A_n \mid R(e) \wedge t \in e.A_i.l \wedge$$
$$(\exists e')(R(e') \wedge e'.A_i = e.A_i \wedge t = e'.T)\}$$

This expression says that the timeslice operator $\tau_{A_i:T}(R)$ leaves all $\mathcal{F}$ attributes, except A_i, intact, groups together all the times T corresponding to the same instance of attribute A_i, restricts the lifespan of A_i to these grouped time instances, and projects the temporal attribute T out.

2.3 Equivalence of L_{hi} and A_G

When converting L_{hi} expressions into A_G, we map $R(e) \wedge t \in e.A.l$ into the A_G expression $\sigma_{S \in R.A.\tau}(R \times S)$, where $S = tdom(\pi_A(R))$. However, the conversion becomes ambiguous for the L_{hi} expression $R(e) \wedge Q(e) \wedge t \in e.A.l$ because it is not clear if $e.A$ should be mapped into $\pi_A(R)$ or $\pi_A(Q)$. To solve this problem and to make the mapping from L_{hi} to A_G expressions easier, we normalize L_{hi} formulas by replacing L_{hi} expressions of the form $R(e) \wedge Q(e) \wedge t \in e.A.l$ with

$(\exists e')(R(e) \wedge Q(e') \wedge e = e' \wedge t \in e.A.l)$. Similarly, we replace expressions of the form $R(e) \wedge Q(e') \wedge t \in e.A.l \wedge t \in e'.B.l$ with $(\exists t')(R(e) \wedge Q(e') \wedge t \in e.A.l \wedge t' \in e'.B.l \wedge t = t')$. This discussion motivates the following definition.

A safe L_{hi} expression ϕ is *normalized* if in every maximal conjunctive sub-formula of ϕ

- a tuple variable can appear in one and only one relation;

- every temporal variable belongs to one and only one lifespan.

Lemma 1 *Every safe L_{hi} formula can be converted to an equivalent safe normalized L_{hi} formula.*

Sketch of Proof: The proof is based on the observation that if a maximal conjunct of an L_{hi} formula is of the form $R(e) \wedge Q(e) \wedge \ldots$, then it is replaced with the expression $(\exists e')(R(e) \wedge Q(e') \wedge e = e' \wedge \ldots)$. Similarly, the L_{hi} expression $R(e) \wedge Q(e') \wedge t \in e.A.l \wedge t \in e'.B.l \wedge \ldots$ in a maximal conjunct is replaced with the expression $(\exists t')(R(e) \wedge Q(e') \wedge t \in e.A.l \wedge t' \in e'.B.l \wedge t = t' \wedge \ldots)$. □

Using this lemma, we can prove the main theorem of this section.

Theorem 2 *Safe L_{hi} calculus and the grouped algebra A_G are equivalent.*

Sketch of Proof: Since we defined the A_G operators using L_{hi} calculus, then it is clear that any A_G expression can be converted into an equivalent L_{hi} expression. To show that any safe L_{hi} query can be mapped into an equivalent A_G expression, first normalize the L_{hi} query. The crucial part in the proof of this theorem is to show how to map a maximal conjunctive subformula of an L_{hi} expression into A_G. To do this, consider a maximal conjunctive subformula in this query. Consider all the terms of the form $R_i(e_i)$ and of the form $t_j \in e_i.A_i.l$ in it. For each term $t_j \in e_i.A_i.l$ create a single-attribute relation $T_{R_{A_i}j} = tdom(\pi_{A_i.\tau}(R_i))$ (note that this is possible because the L_{hi} expression is normalized). Then take the Cartesian product of all the R_i's and $T_{R_{A_i}j}$'s and impose the following restrictions in the select operator on it. Each term $t_j \in e_i.A_i.l$ gives rise to the condition $T_{R_{A_i}j} \in R_i.A_i$. Each term $e_i.A_i = e_j.A_j$ gives rise to the condition $R_i.A_i =_f R_j.A_j$ in the selection. Each term $t_j = t'_j$, where $t_j \in e_i.A_i.l$ and $t'_j \in e'_i.A'_i.l$, gives rise to the condition $T_{R_{A_i}j} = T_{R'_{A'_i}j'}$. Finally, each term $e.A(t) = e'.A'(t')$ gives rise to the selection $R.A(T) = R'.A'(T')$, where T and T' are the single attribute relations of sort $\mathcal{T}$ corresponding to the terms $t \in e.A.l$ and $t' \in e'.A'.l$, and e and e' correspond to relations R and R' respectively. Finally, to convert the resulting relation to the form of the data model, every attribute A_i with an associated lifespan attribute T_{A_i} is timesliced to the set of times equal to the projection on attribute T_{A_i}.□

To illustrate how the conversion between L_{hi} and A_G works, we provide some examples. Since we expressed algebraic operators in terms of L_{hi} formulas above, we concentrate on mapping L_{hi} expressions to A_G. In the following examples, let $R(A)$ and $R(B)$ be two single attribute relations, where A and B have the sort $\mathcal{F}$.

Example 4 *The L_{hi} query*
$$[e.A : t](\exists e')(\exists t')(R(e) \wedge t \in e.A.l \wedge Q(e') \wedge t' \in e'.B.l \wedge e.A(t) = e'.B(t'))$$
has an equivalent A_G expression
$$\tau_{R.A:T_{R_A}} (\pi_{R.A,T_{R_A}} (\sigma_{T_{R_A} \in R.A.\tau \wedge T_{Q_B} \in Q.B.\tau \wedge R.A(T_{R_A}) = Q.B(T_{Q_B})}$$
$$(R \times Q \times T_{R_A} \times T_{Q_B})))$$
where $T_{R_A} = tdom(\pi_{A.\tau}(R))$ and $T_{Q_B} = tdom(\pi_{B.\tau}(Q))$ are temporal domains of A and B attributes in relations R and Q respectively.

$\square$

Example 5 *Consider the L_{hi} query*
$$[e.A : t]R(e) \wedge t \in e.A.l \wedge \neg(\exists e')(Q(e') \wedge t \in e'.B.l)$$
Before mapping it into A_G, we convert it into an equivalent L_{hi} query $[e.A : t]R(e) \wedge t \in e.A.l \wedge \neg(\exists e')(\exists t')(Q(e') \wedge t' \in e'.B.l \wedge R(e) \wedge t \in e.A.l \wedge t = t')$
which is equivalent to
$$\tau_{R.A:T_{R_A}} (\pi_{R.A,T_{R_A}} (\sigma_{T_{R_A} \in R.A.\tau} (R \times T_{R_A}) -$$
$$\pi_{R,T_{R_A}} (\sigma_{T_{R_A} \in R.A.\tau \wedge T_{Q_B} \in Q.B.\tau \wedge T_{R_A} = T_{Q_B}} (R \times Q \times T_{R_A} \times T_{Q_B}))))$$
where T_{R_A} and T_{Q_B} are defined as in Example 4.

$\square$

Example 6 *The L_{hi} query*
$$[e.A : t](\exists e')(\exists t')(R(e) \wedge t \in e.A.l \wedge Q(e') \wedge t' \in e'.B.l \wedge e = e')$$
has an equivalent A_G expression
$$\tau_{R.A:T_{R_A}} (\pi_{R.A,T_{R_A}} (\sigma_{T_{R_A} \in R.A.\tau \wedge T_{Q_B} \in Q.B.\tau \wedge R.A =_f Q.B} (R \times Q \times T_{R_A} \times T_{Q_B})))$$
where T_{R_A} and T_{Q_B} are defined as in Example 4.

$\square$

3 SQL Extension

Of the many proposals offered to extend the relational model for handling temporal information, the recent appearance of the TSQL2 language specification [15] is of considerable note. This specification is the result of a major collaborative effort whose goal to present a *standardized* temporal extension to the standard relational data model. Specifically, TSQL2 is presented as a temporally extended SQL-92, the current relational standard.

In the TSQL2 specification several goals were enunciated by the design committee as design guidelines. These guidelines addressed issues relating to the data model: support of a valid-time dimension, and based on homogeneous tuples; to the language: consistent extension of SQL-92, optional temporal support, and operators that do no give special semantics to explicit attributes; and to the implementation: implementable in some first normal form representational model, and have an efficiently implementable algebra that is an extension of the snapshot algebra. The thrust (both explicit and implicit) of these and many of the other features enunciated in the specification is that TSQL2 be a *true* or consistent extension of SQL-92 that defaults to SQL-92 when no temporal semantics are intended.

One consequence of this *upward compatibility* is that legacy applications need not be modified to accommodate a TSQL2-based database management system. This compatibility is achieved in the resulting TSQL2 proposal largely through the appending of additional clauses and sub-clauses to the SQL-92 syntax and by defining default semantics in the absence that is consistent with the SQL-92 clause that results by removing the TSQL2-specific clauses.

Although most of the features of TSQL2 are intended to directly support the formal incorporation of a temporal component to provide capabilities generally associated with database management systems, there is one feature of particular interest. The TSQL2 proposal includes provisions for the specification of a distinguished *surrogate* domain. This domain, and its associated attribute, provides a mechanism by which a user (application) can co-identify (i.e., recognize as forming a cohesive "group") a set of tuples, these having the same surrogate value. Used in this way, the surrogate is used as a grouping mechanism.

TSQL2 provides little in the way of support of a surrogate. It provides a way of associating a surrogate-based attribute with a relation (schema) and a mechanism for comparing for equality two surrogate values. Users are responsible for most other aspects pertaining to their management and administration.

As shown in [1] such a surrogate is necessary if a temporally ungrouped historical model is to have the expressiveness of a temporally grouped historical model. However, as is also shown, the effective management of surrogates is considerably complex. This complexity can be embedded in the semantics of the data language, the approach taken in [1], or, alternatively, left as a user task, effectively the approach of TSQL2.

The appeal of the temporally grouped approach to representing temporal data is due in part to its relationship to the goals, or at least the results of normalization in the standard relational model; that is, the ability to model a single instance of an object (entity or relationship) by a single tuple in a relation. Achieving this correspondence in a historical database where multiple values must be maintained for the attributes of an object requires some form of relaxation of the 1NF restriction. be used. Such an approach maintains the correspondence between a semantic "object" and a tuple, although it might increase the complexity required to implement such a model relative to that required to implement a 1NF model.

A temporally grouped historical relational extension represents one example of the desirability of a relationally-oriented model that supports complex objects. Recognition of this fact is evidenced by efforts currently underway to develop a new standard, SQL-3, that will provide a complex object modeling capability. The result of this effort may provide a modeling capability that is easily amenable to being extended to incorporate a historical dimension. More specifically, it may provide a sound basis upon which to build N1NF relations corresponding to the normative group model associated with the temporally grouped algebra that we describe in the next section.

Any SQL extension that is intended to query, or otherwise manipulate, a temporally grouped historical relational database must be able to accommodate the basic distinction between grouped and temporally ungrouped data models. In a temporally ungrouped model the temporal dimension is incorporated, explicitly or implicitly, through the addition of one or more *distinguished* temporal attributes. For each tuple, the value of these attributes indicates the period of *validity* of the data in the other attributes of the tuple. An SQL extension intended to accommodate such a temporally ungrouped historical model need only provide facilities for dealing with temporal attributes; the semantics of the tuple variables could remain largely unchanged from those of the standard SQL.

In a temporally grouped historical model a tuple represents the history of an entity (or relationship). More specifically, an attribute of a tuple is a history of the values assumed by that attribute. A history can thus be viewed as a pairing of traditional domain values and the times that those values are valid. This aspect of a temporally grouped historical model is what has to be accommodated by a grouped-based historical SQL extension. The following SQL-based SELECT statement provides such a capability:

```
SELECT attribute-target-list
FROM tuple/temporal variable declaration list
WHERE restriction predicate
```

The SELECT construct supports both the traditional tuple variable, and history-oriented temporal variables. As per the standard SQL, tuple variables are bound to relations, and range over the tuples of the relation to which they are bound. Temporal variables are bound to tuple variables, and range over the histories of tuples of the associated relation.

The FROM clause is used to declare both types of variables as well as to perform the necessary bindings. It has the form:

FROM rel_1 $t_1 : T_1$, rel_2 $t_2 : T_2$, $\ldots$

which declares tuple variable t_i and binds it to relation rel_n, and declares temporal variable T_i and binds it to tuple variable t_i. (Although not indicated, any number of tuple variables may be declared and bound to a single relation. Likewise any number of temporal variables can be declared and bound to a single tuple variable.)

The SELECT clause has the form:

SELECT tup-att-exp$_1$, tup-att-exp$_2$, $\ldots$, tup-att-exp$_n$

and as in the case of the standard SQL is used to specify the attribute values that are to be included in the resulting relation. tup-att$_i$ is of the form $t_i.A_i$ if the domain of A_i is of sort $\mathcal{V}$ or $\mathcal{T}$, and $t_i.A_i : T_i$ if its domain is of sort $\mathcal{F}$.

The WHERE clause plays the same role here as it does in the standard SQL; it specifies a predicate that is used to select those values, (tuple values and temporal values) over which the tuple and temporal variables range, that together satisfy the predicate.

Example 7 *Given the temporally grouped historical relation EMPLOYEE the query "Find the name and salary (histories) of all employees who worked in the Toy department at time 4" is expressed in SQL_{hi} as:*

```
SELECT E1.NAME, E1.Salary:T1
FROM EMPLOYEE E1:T1,T2
WHERE E1.DEPT(T2) = "Toy" AND T2 = 4
```

☐

In this example one tuple variable E1 was declared and bound to the relation EMPLOYEE, and two temporal variables, T1 and T2, were declared and bound to this tuple variable. The first, T1, since not otherwise constrained, was used to extract the complete histories of the SALARY attribute of EMP, and the second, T2, was used to reference the DEPT history value at the specified time.

Example 8 *The query "Find the names, dates of birth, salary and departmental histories of the people who worked at time 5 in the Accounting department" can be expressed in SQL_{hi} as:*

```
SELECT E1.NAME, E1.DOB, E1.SALARY:T1, E1.DEPT:T2
FROM EMPLOYEE E1:T1,T2
WHERE E1.DEPT(5) = ''Accntg''
```

☐

Finally,

Example 9 *"What are the names of the managers for whom Tom has worked?" can be expressed in in SQL_{hi} as:*

```
SELECT E1.NAME
FROM EMPLOYEE E1, E2:T1, DEPT D:T1
WHERE E2.NAME = ''Tom'' AND E2.DEPT(T1) = D.DEPT(T1) AND
             D.MGR(T1) = E1.NAME
```

☐

In the absence of temporal components, the grouped SQL SELECT statement described above reduces to a standard SQL-2 SELECT statement, and has the same semantics.

4 Some Semantic Issues Revisited

In this section we look at a number of semantic issues which are familiar and well-understood in the case of the static relational model, but which are more complex and appear to have generated some confusion in the temporal database literature when they have been extended to the case of temporal relations. In particular, we believe that it is worth revisiting the semantics of the operations of *coalescing* and *regrouping* in the context of the contrasts between the temporally ungrouped and temporally grouped modeling approaches.

Space precludes a discussion of the semantics of such notions in the temporal database domain as *functional dependency*, *relation key*, and *normalization*, upon which we believe that this distinction can also shed much light.

Coalescing

One notion that appears in a number of temporal data models is that of the "coalescing" of tuples. This concept is defined in the glossary as follows:

> The *coalesce* operation takes as argument a set of **value-equivalent** tuples and returns a single tuple which is **snapshot equivalent** with the argument set of tuples.

This definition relies on the auxiliary notion of value-equivalence:

> Informally, two tuples on the same (temporal) relation schema are *value equivalent* if they have identical non-timestamp attribute values.

This concept appears to have been introduced in [12] and it has reappeared in a number of other papers, including [10] (where it is called "compress") and [8].

The concept of coalescing is an artifact of temporal models which are 1NF, since it's function is to try to "merge" (or "coalesce") into a smaller number of tuples information about "the same object" which the 1NF constraint forces to be spread across a larger number of tuples. Furthermore, it appears to be relevant only to temporally ungrouped models using two timestamps, such as *StartTime* and *EndTime* as its timestamping mechanism. For example, the first two tuples in relation on the left, below, ought to be "coalesced", yielding the relation on the right.

A	B	StartTime	EndTime
a	b_1	1	2
a	b_1	3	5
c	b_2	3	6

A	B	StartTime	EndTime
a	b_1	1	5
c	b_2	3	6

Coalescing is an unnecessary (indeed, meaningless) operation in temporally grouped models. In M_g the information in the above relations would be represented as follows:

A	B
$1 \to a$	$1 \to b_1$
$2 \to a$	$2 \to b_1$
$3 \to a$	$3 \to b_1$
$4 \to a$	$4 \to b_1$
$5 \to a$	$5 \to b_1$
$3 \to c$	$3 \to b_2$
$4 \to c$	$4 \to b_2$
$5 \to c$	$5 \to b_2$
$6 \to c$	$6 \to b_2$

Furthermore, it is not clear under what circumstances the *coalesce* operator ought to be performed. Consider the following relation

EMPLOYEE	SALARY	StartTime	EndTime
a	30,000	1	2
a	35,000	3	5
c	35,000	6	7

and consider a query that projected this relation onto the *SALARY* column. Two different results are obtained depending on whether tuples are not coalesced (left) or are coalesced(right):

SALARY	StartTime	EndTime
30,000	1	2
35,000	3	5
35,000	6	7

SALARY	StartTime	EndTime
30,000	1	2
35,000	3	7

In a temporally grouped model, the information would be as shown on the left, and the result of the query as shown on the right. The issue of "coalescing" never arises.

EMPLOYEE	SALARY
$[1,2] \to a$	$[1,2] \to 30,000$
$[3,5] \to a$	$[3,5] \to 35,000$
$[6,7] \to c$	$[6,7] \to 35,000$

SALARY
$[1,2] \to 30,000$
$[3,5] \to 35,000$
$[6,7] \to 35,000$

Regrouping

A final semantic issue which needs to be clarified is that of the "regrouping" of a temporally grouped relation. This appears to be a virtually meaningless operation, except in certain cases that arise infrequently in practice. Consider the following relation in M_g with the key **EMP** serving as the basis for grouping:

EMPLOYEE		
EMP	*DEPT*	*SALARY*
1 → John 2 → John 3 → John	1 → Toy 2 → Toy 3 → Clothing	1 → 20K 2 → 25K 3 → 30K
1 → Henry 2 → Henry 3 → Henry	1 → Linen 2 → Linen 3 → Housewares	1 → 20K 2 → 30K 3 → 35K

Now, the operation of regrouping is supposed to take a temporally grouped relation, which is grouped by some attribute(s), and regroup it by some different attribute(s). Suppose we try to apply such an operation to the **EMPLOYEE** relation, and try to regroup it by the *SALARY* attribute.

There are several problems with this operation, as this example makes clear. First, if there is to be a regrouping on the attribute *SALARY*, there needs to be some basis for *forming* the new salary groups. Absent any other information, it must be that the basis for the regrouping is the salary *values*, and thus this operation will automatically impose a *time-invariant key constraint* on the resulting relation, which may or may not be appropriate for the application. We assume that this is the intended meaning of the operation, and hence the result is the following:

EMPLOYEE		
SALARY	*EMP*	*DEPT*
1 → 20K	1 → {John, Henry}	1 → {Toy, Linen}
2 → 25K	2 → John	2 → Toy
2 → 30K 3 → 30K	2 → Henry 3 → John	2 → Linen 3 → Clothing
3 → 35K	3 → Henry	3 → Housewares

A second problem, as this example clearly shows, the resulting object may not be a valid relation. In this case, for example, there are two employees who had the salary 20K at time 1, and so the resulting object must have a set of values for the remaining (non-grouping) attributes.

Finally, it is not at all clear what these new tuples represent. It might seem at first that they would represent "temporal portions of actual employee's salary histories." On closer examination, this turns out not to be the case. Consider the third tuple in the result: no employee had any such salary history. Thus the operation is problematic.

The classic example of this operation is the following **management** relation. According to [3], " Its key is **DEPT**. This key is possible because it is the key of the snapshots of the management relation." Thus, the notion of key here appears to be that of snapshot key, and the authors correctly point out that there is a case where such a regrouping operation might be useful.

management	
DEPT	*MANAGER*
$\Big[\ [11,49] \rightarrow Toys \ \Big]$	$[11,44] \rightarrow John$ $[45,49] \rightarrow Leu$
$[41,47] \rightarrow Clothing$ $[71,now] \rightarrow Clothing$	$[41,47] \rightarrow Tom$ $[71,now] \rightarrow Inga$
$[45,60] \rightarrow Shoes$	$[45,60] \rightarrow John$

In [3] this relation is restructured (the operation is not formally defined, but it is intuitively obvious and is the one we used, above) into the following "management-2" relation, with key **MANAGER**:

management-2	
MANAGER	*DEPT*
$\Big[\ [11,60] \rightarrow John \ \Big]$	$[11,44] \rightarrow Toys$ $[45,60] \rightarrow Shoes$
$[45,49] \rightarrow Leu$	$[45,49] \rightarrow Toys$
$[41,47] \rightarrow Tom$ $[71,now] \rightarrow Inga$	$[41,47] \rightarrow Clothing$ $[41,47] \rightarrow Clothing$

Notice first of all, as we pointed out above, that this restructuring operation, defined in terms of *equality of values*, incorporates the strong assumption that a Manager cannot change names and be considered the same Manager. It is also important to note, as [3] does, the underlying assumption at work here, "that *DEPT* and *MANAGER* functionally determine each other. In fact, without this assumption, no such restructuring is possible, as our SALARY example, above, demonstrated. For instance, consider the following relation, only slightly changed from this example:

management-3	
DEPT	*MANAGER*
$[11,49] \rightarrow$ Toys	$[11,44] \rightarrow$ John $[45,49] \rightarrow$ Leu
$[41,47] \rightarrow$ Clothing $[71,now] \rightarrow$ Clothing	$[41,47] \rightarrow$ Tom $[71,now] \rightarrow$ Inga
$[40,60] \rightarrow$ Shoes	$[40,60] \rightarrow$ John

Here, $DEPT \rightarrow MANAGER$ but not the inverse. It is clearly not semantically meaningful to restructure this relation, since it is not *about managers*, it is *about departments*. The result of an attempted restructuring would be the following:

management-4	
MANAGER	*DEPT*
$[11, 60] \rightarrow$ John	$[11, 39] \rightarrow$ Toys
	$[40, 44] \rightarrow$ {Toys,Shoes}
	$[45, 60] \rightarrow$ Shoes
$[45, 49] \rightarrow$ Leu	$[45, 49] \rightarrow$ Toys
$[41, 47] \rightarrow$ Tom	$[41, 47] \rightarrow$ Clothing
$[71, \text{now}] \rightarrow$ Inga	$[71, \text{now}] \rightarrow$ Clothing

This is not a valid relation in the model, since in general the value of the DEPT attribute may be set-valued. The reason that that in this case it is not possible to do the regrouping, is that $MANAGER \not\rightarrow DEPT$. So what exactly is this *regrouping* operation, and how general is it?

Note that when normalized, relations typically have the property that they represent information either about some real-world entity, or about an association (relationship) between or among some number of entities. In either case, it is the key attribute(s) which identify the thing being modeled, and its lifespan represents the maximal period of time during which information is known about the object. The other attributes are descriptive attributes which give additional, non-identifying information about the objects; the temporal dimension of this information is some subset (possibly all) of the lifespan of the object being modeled. In some cases these descriptive attributes are foreign keys, i.e., "references" to objects which are modeled in some other relation.

Consider, for example, the EMPLOYEE relation, which models employees with temporally grouped tuples. The notion of regrouping here can only apply to the non-key attributes, i.e., either to the attribute DEPT, which is a foreign key, or the attribute SALARY, which is not. In either case, there are problems. In the case of DEPT, where the operation might at first glance appear to make sense semantically, the operation, as we have seen, is only well-defined for the rare case when the 2 attributes are mutually FD ($DEPT \leftrightarrow EMP$), i.e., when the attribute to be regrouped on is itself a candidate key for the relation.

Thus, a regrouping operator for temporally grouped relations does not appear to be a useful one, and the lack of it is not a valid criticism of the temporally grouped approach to temporal relational databases. Should such an operation be deemed desirable, in the case of multiple candidate keys, its definition is straightforward and can be included in any temporally grouped relational data model.

5 Conclusions

In this paper we have addressed the two principal concerns that have been raised with respect to the temporally grouped, or history-oriented, approach to modeling temporal information in a temporal relational data model. Specifically, we presented an extension to the temporally grouped data model and query language proposed in [1], a data model and query language which is also quite similar to that proposed in [4]. These consistent extensions, motivated by the desire to define an equivalent algebraic query language, in fact provide greater modeling capability by allowing for the representation of three different sorts of information: constant values, times, and value histories. In addition, these extensions relax the temporal homogeneity requirement for the attributes of a given tuple. Having extended the data model and calculus in this fashion, we presented an equivalent algebraic query language, A_G,thereby addressing one of the major concerns about this approach.

In addition, we addressed a number of other semantic issues in the context of the temporally grouped/temporally ungrouped modeling distinction , and argued that in all cases the temporally grouped approach appears to have significant advantages.

Our conclusion is a strong recommendation that the effort to develop a temporal extension to the SQL-3 standard, dubbed TSQL3, be based upon the temporally grouped model so that it will better meet the modeling needs of temporal information.

References

[1] J. Clifford, A. Croker, A. Tuzhilin. On Completeness of Historical Relational Query Languages. *ACM Transactions on Database Systems*, 19(2):64–116, March 1994.

[2] S. Gadia. Weak Temporal Relations. *Proc. of ACM SIGACT-SIGMOD Symposium on Principles of Database Systems* (Cambridge, MA), March 1986.

[3] S.K. Gadia, S.S. Nair. Temporal Databases: A Prelude to Parametric Data. in *Temporal Databases: Theory, Design, and Implementation*, Benjamin/Cummings Publishing Co., Redwood City, CA, 1993.

[4] F. Grandi, M.R. Scalas, P. Tiberio. History and Tuple Variables for Temporal Query Languages, in [13].

[5] F. Grandi, M.R. Scalas, P. Tiberio. A History-oriented Temporal SQL Extension, to be presented at the *Second International Workshop on Next Generation Information Technologies and Systems* (Naharia, Israel), 1995.

[6] C.S. Jensen, J. Clifford, R. Elmasri, S.K. Gadia, P. Hayes, S. Jajodia (eds.), C. Dyreson, F. Grandi, W. Käfer, N. Kline, N. Lorentzos, Y. Mitsopoulos, A. Montanari, D. Nonen, E. Peressi, B. Pernici, J.F. Roddick, N.L. Sarda, M.R. Scalas, A. Segev, R.T. Snodgrass, M.D. Soo, A. Tansel. P. Tiberio, G. Wiederhold. A Consensus Glossary of Temporal Database Concepts, *ACM SIGMOD Record* 23:1, 1994.

[7] C.S. Jensen, R.T. Snodgrass. The Surrogate Data Type in TSQL2, A TSQL2 Commentary, in [14].

[8] C.S. Jensen, M.D. Soo, R.T. Snodgrass. Unifying Temporal Data Models via a Conceptual Model. *Information Systems*, 19(7):513–548, October 1994.

[9] E. McKenzie. Bibliography: Temporal Databases. *ACM SIGMOD Record*, 15(4):40–52, December 1986.

[10] S.B.Navathe, R.Ahmed. Temporal Extensions to the Relational Model and SQL. In *Temporal Databases: Theory, Design, and Implementation*, Benjamin/Cummings Publishing Co., Redwood City, CA, 1993.

[11] N. Pissinou, R.T. Snodgrass, R. Elmasri, I.S. Mumick, M.T. Özsu, B. Pernici, A. Segev, B. Theodoulidis and U. Dayal. Towards an Infrastructure for Temporal Databases: Report of an Invitational ARPA/NSF Workshop, *ACM SIGMOD Record* 23:1, 1994.

[12] R. T. Snodgrass. The Temporal Query Language TQuel. *ACM Transactions on Database Systems*, 12(2):247–298, July 1987.

[13] R.T. Snodgrass (ed.). *Proc. of the ARPA/NSF International Workshop on an Infrastructure for Temporal Databases*, Arlington (TX), 1993.

[14] R. T. Snodgrass (ed.). *The TSQL2 Temporal Query Language*, Kluwer Academic Publishers, 1995.

[15] R.T. Snodgrass, I. Ahn, G. Ariav, D.S. Batory, J. Clifford, C.E. Dyreson, R. Elmasri, F. Grandi, C.S. Jensen, W. Käfer, N. Kline, K. Kulkarni, T.Y.C. Leung, N. Lorentzos, J.F. Roddick, A. Segev, M.D. Soo, S.M. Sripada. TSQL2 Language Specification, *ACM SIGMOD Record* 23:1, 1994.

[16] R.T. Snodgrass, I. Ahn, G. Ariav, D.S. Batory, J. Clifford, C.E. Dyreson, R. Elmasri, F. Grandi, C.S. Jensen, W. Käfer, N. Kline, K. Kulkarni, T.Y.C. Leung, N. Lorentzos, J.F. Roddick, A. Segev, M.D. Soo, S.M. Sripada. A TSQL2 Tutorial, *ACM SIGMOD Record* 23:3, 1994.

[17] R.T. Snodgrass, C.S. Jensen. The From Clause in TSQL2, A TSQL2 Commentary, in [14].

[18] M.D. Soo. Bibliography on Temporal Databases. *ACM SIGMOD Record*, 20(1):14–23, March 1991.

[19] R. Stam and R. Snodgrass. A Bibliography on Temporal Databases. *Database Engineering*, 7(4):231–239, December 1988.

Time Series, a Neglected Issue in Temporal Database Research?

Duri Schmidt,
Angelika Kotz Dittrich,
Werner Dreyer
UBILAB,
Union Bank of Switzerland
Universitätsstrasse 84,
CH-8033 Zurich, Switzerland
phone ++41 1 234 21 47
fax ++41 1 234 65 18
{schmidt,dittrich, dreyer}
@ubilab.ubs.ch

Robert Marti

Informationssysteme,
ETH-Zentrum
CH-8092 Zurich,
Switzerland
phone ++41 1 632 72 60
fax ++41 1 632 11 72
marti@inf.ethz.ch

Abstract

With a few notable exceptions, it appears that the temporal database research community has largely neglected time series issues, believing that time series can be easily handled by temporal database management systems. In this paper, we take a different position. Time series management has special requirements concerning structural and functional aspects, time model, calendar system and query facilities. Temporal database management systems do not satisfy these requirements: mapping time series into snapshot and temporal relations is intricate, performance is problematic, functionality is only partly adequate, and the capability to organize time series into arbitrary groups is missing. A few commercial and research systems show interesting approaches, but more research is required to develop completely satisfying solutions.

1   Introduction

Time series are collections of observations made sequentially over time. They are important in many fields like banking or scientific research. Banks, for example, rely heavily on statistical analysis of time series in forecasts of economic variables such as inflation rates, interest rates or currency exchange rates, in portfolio management or in option and swap pricing. More and more data is used in such empirical investigations and hundreds of thousands of time series containing economic and financial data are currently available. Because of the large volume and intensive use of these time series, support by database management systems is essential.

At first glance, one might think that time series are just a special case of temporal data which can be managed easily by temporal database management systems (TDBMS). This view seems to be shared by most researchers working on temporal database issues. While TDBMS have received great attention, very few articles report about projects devoted to time series.

In this article, we take a different position by arguing that time series management systems (TSMS) markedly differ from TDBMS. We show that time series management has special requirements concerning data model, time model and functionality. In our analysis, we rely on the experiences we gained in the CALANDA time series management system project [2] [4]. The main emphasis of this paper is on the requirements of TSMS and the discussion of the shortcomings of TDBMS. Furthermore, we will shortly discuss four existing, interesting TSMS. The overview covers two research systems, i.e. our own system CALANDA [2] [4] and the system from the University of Berkeley [10] [1], and two commercial systems, i.e. FAME [5] and Illustra [6].

In section 1, we present the requirements of time series management. A short overview of TDBMS follows in section 2. Based on this, we explain the shortfalls of TDBMS for time series applications. In section 3 we shortly present four existing TSMS.

2   Requirements of time series management

In this chapter, we will put the emphasis on data model requirements of time series management because the shortcomings of temporal DBMS discussed later are mainly related to data model issues. There are of course further requirements that are not specifically related to time, concerning, e.g., user interface, global and private databases or data exchange, but these will not be elaborated here.

A data model for time series management must provide means to capture the following concepts: Multivariate time series, groups of time series, and calendars. A far more comprehensive discussion of the requirements can be found in [3].

2.1   Multivariate time series

The notion of time series must be at the center of the data model. A time series consists of a general description and a chronologically ordered sequence of observations. Henceforth, the general description will be called the header, the observations will be called the events.

Header data consists of common attributes characterizing the whole time series (e.g. in a stock price time series this might be the location of the stock exchange or the average price calculated over the whole series). Events model data collected over successive points in time - for example, the low, high, opening and closing price of a share for each trading day. Data fields in events

can have scalar types (numbers, strings etc.) or structured types (arrays of scalar types etc.).

With each time series, a calendar is associated which expresses the mapping between the events and their corresponding points in time. The calendar
defines the periodicity of regular time series or enumerates the time points for
irregular ones (for further remarks on calendars see 2.3 below).

Fig. 1 shows the structure of an example time series that records stock prices for a company "ABC Corp.". The header values are shown in the upper part
with attributes "Calendar", "Start date" etc. The attribute "Values" is a vector
of constants stored there for some analytical reason. The events show daily
prices consisting of the low price, the high price and an array of all prices (so-
called "ticks") per day.

Calendar:	business week
Start date:	1.1.1994
End date:	13.12.1994
Name:	ABC Corp.
Values:	23, 54, 48, 66

Date:	Low	High	Ticks
11.10.1994	77	85	79, 78, 77, 80, 83, 85
12.10.1994	80	84	84, 82, 80, 83
13.10.1994	82	86	84, 82, 83, 85, 86

Fig. 1: Example of a time series

An important aspect of time series analysis is the transformation of events
between different periodicities (e.g. transforming daily data to monthly data
and vice versa). The transformation depends on the kind of data represented by
an event value. Events may contain so-called stock values or flow values. A
stock value measures an amount available or observed at one point in time,
e.g., the number of securities in a portfolio or the price of a share. Stock values
can be differentiated further, e.g. they may measure the value observed at the
beginning or the end, the maximum, minimum or average value in a period. In
contrast, flow values measure a value accumulated over a period of time, like
the number of securities sold during a day or a cash flow. The different kinds of
values require different periodicity transformations. Take for example the transformation from daily to monthly periodicity: For the high selling price (a stock
value), the monthly value is the maximum of all daily values, for the closing
price (also a stock value) it is the value of the last day, and for the cash flow
it is the sum of all daily values.

As to functional requirements, the data model should provide the basic capabilities for creating, maintaining and accessing time series. Requirements on data access are especially demanding: The TSMS should not only be able to select data, but also preprocess (filter, transform) them for further analysis in more specialized application programs (such as statistics or graphical packages).

The data model must support the usual operations on atomic types as well as read and update access to structured types. Time series are usually subject to statistical evaluations in which matrix algebra plays a central role. Therefore, the TSMS should provide operations on arrays (vectors, matrices and even arrays of higher dimensions).

Important functions are the definition of time series, the manipulation of header and event data in time series, and the selection of data from time series. Another important capability is the derivation of new time series from existing ones, e.g. by computing the difference of two time series, calculating a moving average or aggregating events for a coarser granularity.

A TSMS must provide query capabilities tailored to time series. In the select condition, it should be possible to apply not only logical operations but also other arithmetic and time-related operations. The query optimizer should be able to handle such extended queries to achieve high performance for large time series bases.

The prevailing kind of access to time series data is along the time axis, i.e. usually consecutive events are selected from one time series. However, there is also the technique of cross-sectional analysis, where events of several time series are inspected at the same point in time. The data model must support efficient storage and access mechanisms for both cases with priority for the time dimension.

Time series management makes high demands on data quality. New raw data has to be checked for consistency with older events, outliers have to be detected, noise has to be filtered out, etc. The TSMS should offer operational facilities to express all these functions. To track the value of calibrated data back to the raw data, it is often necessary to retain the raw as well as the calibrated data. Old estimations have to be replaced by newer ones when new information is available, but one might like to retain the older data to review and improve the estimation process. This requires a versioning concept.

As analysts often define individual kinds of filters and transformations for time series, it is crucial that the set of operations of the TSMS should be extensible by the user.

2.2 Groups

In databases with a huge number of time series, detecting the data relevant to the interests of a user is an important issue. A useful way of facilitating this is to partition the set of time series into categories or groups according to various criteria (e.g. a set of share price series might be categorized along branches, country and/or size of the company). For that, a TSMS must support a flexible, powerful grouping mechanism. It is desirable that a group can recursively contain other groups, that elements can belong to more than one group and that participation in a group is by enumeration or by condition.

Similar to a time series, a group consists of two parts: a header with the general description and a member set. The header contains common attributes like the group name, number of members, or data derived from members (like the covariance matrix of some time series contained in that group). The member set contains all participating time series and subgroups. Fig. 2 shows an example group "Banks (Europe)" with four subgroups ("England", "France", "Germany", "Switzerland") and three time series ("number of banks", "number of private banks", "number of bankruptcies").

# of group members:	4
# of time series members:	3
Name:	Banks (Europe)
Source:	Profit & Loss
Comment:	Banks with more than 10000 employees

Members	
Groups	Time series
England	# of banks
France	# of private banks
Germany	# of bankruptcies
Switzerland	

Fig. 2: Example of a group

Operations are required to define groups, to manipulate and retrieve header data, to add, remove and select members. The manipulation of the member sets in various groups should be facilitated by set operations like intersection or union. One should also be able to apply operations to all members of a group without explicitly iterating over them. As with time series, functionality for groups should be extensible by the user.

2.3 Calendars

In time series management, an elaborate calendar system is obviously an important issue. Different time series may be based on different calendars, e.g. a calendar with five business days per week or a calendar with national bank holidays. Consequently, a TSMS must support a variety of calendars, taking into account various base calendars (like Gregorian calendar, Islamic calendar etc.), different granularity (like daily, weekly or quarterly calendars), business and non-business calendars and calendars with local holidays. For non-periodic time series, concepts like an ordinal calendar (just representing time units by natural numbers) and enumerated calendars (enumerating irregular sequences of dates) should be supported. Calendar-related functionality must include operations to define all these calendars, to transform time units between calendars, to scan calendars sequentially, to compare and do arithmetic calculations involving dates and time spans.

3 Temporal databases: a short overview

Over the last 15 years, many proposals to introduce concepts for elegantly dealing with the time-changing nature of information stored in databases have appeared in the literature. The starting point for most of these efforts has been the desire to keep the history of database contents instead of overwriting existing data values when new values became known, thereby generalizing the ubiquitous snapshot databases to temporal databases. (A comprehensive overview of research in the area of temporal databases can e.g. be found in [11].)

It was quickly discovered that there are different notions of time associated with data values, namely the time when data values are perceived to accurately model the real world (valid time) as opposed to the time when data values are actually stored in the database (transaction time). In the following, we will concentrate on valid time since this is usually the only relevant notion of time in time series bases.

A central issue in most research projects in temporal databases has been the development of general-purpose, declarative temporal query languages. Therefore, it is perhaps not surprising that — despite the well-know limitations of the relational data model — many of these proposals have been attempting to extend relational query languages more or less gracefully, culminating in the recent TSQL2 proposal [7]. (Besides, until very recently, only the relational model has had solid implementations on the market based on a more or less accepted industry standard.) These languages put an emphasis on the possibility to express rather complex queries. In particular, the coexistence of different facts plays an important role as evidenced by the temporal join operator.

Only recently have there been efforts to exploit the technology of extensible and object-oriented database systems (see e.g. [12] [8]). What is interesting to note is that these approaches attempt to avoid extending the query language with special syntax to deal with temporal semantics. Moreover, thanks to the relaxation of first normal form requirements, they typically associate time stamps with attribute values rather than with tuples as many of the relational extensions.

In the following, we will compare the requirements for the management of time series mainly with what is offered in relational approaches to temporal databases. However, we will mention object-oriented approaches where relevant.

4   Shortcomings of temporal database systems for time series applications

4.1   Structural aspects

In the following discussion of the structural aspects of temporal database models, it is sometimes difficult to clearly separate issues related to the conceptual level from issues related to the internal level. A major reason for these difficulties is that in practice the notion of (physical) data independence is essentially limited to the choice of how to index relations or classes. Non-trivial mappings from relations or classes of the conceptual schema to internal data structures are typically not possible.

As mentioned above, the majority of temporal data models are straightforward extensions of the relational data model in that tuples are associated with some sort of time stamp (mostly intervals). Hence, these data models inherit the well-known limitations of the relational model, in particular, the requirement of first normal form (1NF). This is inadequate since an atomic single-valued attribute which varies over time could naturally be viewed as one complex multi-valued attribute. Indeed, when adding the time-dimension to snapshot relations, a database designer often resorts to further decomposition of normalized relations in order to avoid the unnecessary repetition of those attribute values within a tuple which have not changed during an update. In an extreme case, temporal relations only consist of object-value pairs plus a time interval.

Even some of the more sophisticated temporal models which relax the requirement of 1NF are plagued by the absence of the possibility to store a set of data values in a given order and the absence of the notion of object identity. Indeed, the guarantee that an object identifier never changes during the lifetime of an object and that it will never be reused in the future is even more important in a temporal setting than in a non-temporal one.

In contrast to TSMS, temporal DBMS do not have a time series type as basic abstraction. Therefore, time series have to be modeled using a collection of snapshot and temporal relations. There are several solutions for the modeling of time series events with temporal relations. In the following, we will discuss the – according to our opinion – most instructive approaches.

Approach (a) is to represent every time series as a relation in its own right (see Fig. 3). This is a simple and efficient organization. However, because time series bases often consist of many thousands of time series and because in the relational model only one instance can exist per relation type, one would end up with many thousands of relations. Current TDBMS usually are not well suited for this since they are designed to work efficiently with hundred to thousand relations, but not with ten or hundred thousand. Furthermore, for every deletion and instantiation of a time series one would have to change the schema of the database which is cumbersome.

TS_5			
t	att 1	att 2	...
1	14	"x3"	...
2	36	"y7"	...

TS_11			
t	att 11	att 22	...
1	"uxs"	3.123	...
2	"dfwx"	45.121	...

Fig. 3: Sample temporal relations for the events of two time series. One temporal relation per time series.

Solution (b) is to define one relation per time series type (see Fig. 4). Because time series are usually read sequentially it makes sense to sort such a relation by time series identifier and by date. Normally, time series data is rarely updated except that new events are appended at the end. However, the above mentioned organization makes appends rather expensive. Not to sort the relation in this way makes appends cheap but sequential access rather expensive. Therefore, neither organization is really satisfying. With a clever primary organization of the relation and with the addition of indexes some of the drawbacks may be reduced. Unfortunately, usually only some operations benefit while others become more costly, and additional disk space is necessary.

Another drawback of solution (b) results from the problem that symbols are not first class objects in temporal DBMS. Time series names normally would be symbols. However, because symbols are not valid attribute types, they have to be modeled as strings. This leads to rather awkward queries and, annoyingly, one has always to qualify the selection criteria with the time series identifier. Additionally, for all manipulations one has to know the type of the time series because it defines the relation a time series is stored in.

A variation of this approach, which has more or less the same drawbacks, would be to put the instances of all time series types with the same tuple structure in the same relation. In this approach, it is even more difficult to find out in which relation the events of a specific time series are stored because one has to know which time series types are contained in the same relation.

TSType_X				
t	ts_id	att 1	att 2	...
1	"TS_5"	14	"x3"	...
2	"TS_5"	36	"y7"	...
1	"TS_9"	433	"afe"	...
2	"TS_9"	817	"bwr"	...

Fig. 4: Sample temporal relation for the events of multiple time series. One temporal relation per time series type.

In solution (c), only one temporal relation is used in a style similar to a universal relation. It contains all events of all time series (see Fig. 5). Normally, this approach is not feasible because it causes substantial waste of disk space.

TS_Events						
t	ts_id	att 1	att 2	...	att 11	...
1	"TS_5"	14	"x3"	...	null	...
1	"TS_9"	433	"afe"	...	null	...
...	...	...	...	...	...	...
1	"TS_11"	null	null	...	"uxs"	...

Fig. 5: Sample temporal relation for all events of all time series mode- led in a style similar to a universal relation.

Another implementation of (c) is solution (d) where the attribute names of the time series types are treated as data values rather than as part of the schema (i.e. as meta data). Fig. 6 shows how this relation is organized. Attributes for which the an event has no data value (e.g. TS_11 has no value for att1) are left out.

The queries with this organization are even more awkward to formulate than in approach (b), it still has a considerable space overhead, and events of multivariate time series may be rather expensive to retrieve because they are spread over multiple tuples.

TS_Events					
t	ts_id	att_name	int_value	str_value	...
1	"TS_5"	"att 1"	14	null	...
1	"TS_5"	"att 2"	null	"x3"	...
...	...	...	...	...	...
1	"TS_9"	"att 1"	433	null	...
...	...	...	...	...	...
1	"TS_11"	"att 11"	null	"uxs"	...

Fig. 6: Sample temporal relation for the events of all time series. Modeled also in a universal relation style but in a usually more space
efficient manner

For the header, there are similar modeling possibilities. Instead of temporal relations, snapshot relations are used. This situation seems to be less severe because the header can be represented as one tuple. However, in any case, a time series is spread over two relations, one containing the header data and the other containing the events. Additionally, even though the events of two time series may have the same structure their headers can have a different structure. In solution (b) this may make it even more difficult to know where the different parts of a time series are stored. Finally, the problems with symbols modeled as data values are the same.

So far, we have tacitly assumed that the event attributes are only simple values. According to our experience, it makes a lot of sense to allow arrays as attributes. Unfortunately, current TDBMS do not support array valued attributes. One could store arrays as BLOBs. However, in this case, no functionality is available to manipulate them.

A last point we want to discuss relates to the distribution of tasks between the user and the system. Because TDBMS do not know about time series they cannot take advantage of this a priori information to automatically optimize the physical data organization or offer a small adapted set of choices. The result is that the burden of optimizing the database is put on the user to a much larger degree than with a TSMS. Furthermore, the mapping of time series as described above is not trivial and burdens the user, too. Therefore, non-database experts have much more problems to design their time series bases and often need the help of specialists to succeed.

4.2   Time model

Temporal data models typically associate time intervals with the facts stored in the database, given that many data values remain constant over long periods of time. Time series instead have the property that data values are collected at specific points in time. These time points can either be completely enumerated or they occur according to some predefined pattern. As a result, the notion of a calendar is a crucial abstraction in time series applications, because it defines the mapping from time points to positions (indices) within a time series. Although TSQL2 [7] and MultiCal [9] support the definition of calendars by the user, the proposed facility mainly caters for multiple external representations of a given point in time. Moreover, their proposed internal time stamp formats which feature various internal bit fields are associated with an overhead which is not needed in most time series.

A related point is that operations such as the temporal join are often meaningless in collections of time series because the notion of "concurrent events" is often difficult if not impossible to define. In time series applications, the life span of a data value may be very short, as e.g. in some stock exchange applications. Indeed, some data values even change continuously. Therefore, the value of some quantity may be completely unknown except for the few sampling points represented in the database. Moreover, different time series may be associated with different, incompatible calendars.

4.3   Queries

Temporal databases are typically viewed as a collection of snapshot databases. As mentioned in section 3, a prevailing research topic has been the development of general-purpose, declarative temporal query languages based on the relational model and SQL, as epitomized by the TSQL2 proposal. Such languages emphasize the notion of inspecting a collection of snapshots, often interrelating different relations in complex ways. This generality is not needed in typical time series applications, however. Moreover, the sequential nature of time series often leads to queries which try to identify (sequential) patterns in time series. Again, temporal DBMSs do not provide adequate support for this type of query.

4.4   Functional aspects

In the requirements we stated that a TSMS should be able to transform time series in various ways. With this functionality, the data can be transformed in a central place without always loading it into a statistics program. Most of the transformations consist of the application of statistical functions like moving average and the like. Of course, much more complex operations can be applied in practice. Normally, TDBMS do not provide the possibility to implement user defined procedures or methods. Instead, TDBMS rely on a declarative language for data manipulation. These languages have severe restrictions which make it impossible to formulate the necessary statistical transformations.

Another issue concerns arrays. Because arrays are not part of the data model of current TDBMS, functions to execute computations with arrays are missing as well. However, statistical functions are often array manipulations. Therefore, even to carry out basic transformations, the data have to be extracted into some application and stored back into the database afterwards.

Calendar transformations are another area where TDBMS do not provide the right functionality. We do not deny that calendars play an important role in temporal databases as the basis for attributes of type date. However, even the efforts to introduce an elaborate calendar system into the relational model [9] do not take into account the special requirements of time series.

As explained in section 2.1, interpolation and extrapolation of time series between different periodicities is an essential issue. With respect to interpolation, TDBMS use assume that the value of an attribute at a time t which is different from the sampling points is always the last value recorded prior to time point t (i.e. the value $v(t)$ during an interval $[a, b)$ is constant and equals $v(a)$. It is not possible to choose any other interpolation function (like linear or spline functions etc.) Fig. 7 illustrates this discrepancy between TDBMS and TSMS.

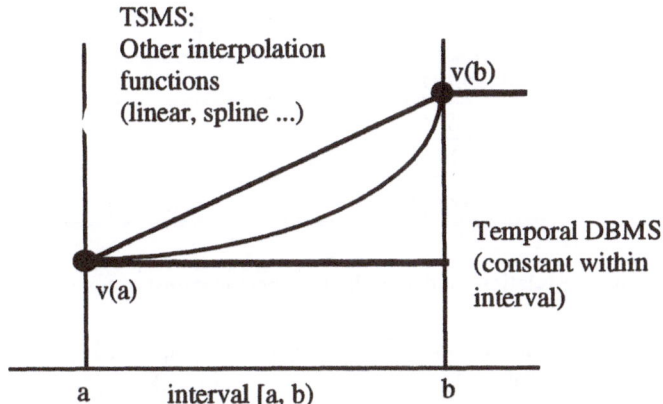

Fig. 7: Different approaches to interpolation in TDBMS and TSMS

For extrapolating time series, a large variety of aggregation functions are needed - more than just the ones predefined in TDBMS. In addition, the user should be able to extend this functionality. Beside specifying the transformation for every single query or procedure, the TSMS should also support static attribute properties denoting the aggregation type (e.g. a time series attribute should always be summed or averaged when extrapolating). All these features are not available in current TDBMS.

4.5 Groups

Existing temporal data models do not provide explicit group concepts. Hence, an implementation of groups has to rely on the structuring capabilities of the underlying non-temporal model. Much like time series, groups can be mapped to relations only very inefficiently and with limited functionality. For the modeling of group headers, the same arguments apply as for time series headers (see above). To represent the members of groups, there are two possibilities.

Possibility (a) stores the member identifiers in one relation per group, including a flag to distinguish time series from group members as shown in Fig. 8. (Without the flag attribute, extra joins would be needed to find out what kind of object a member_i references.) This solution has similar drawbacks as solution (a) for events in section 4.1, namely large number of relations and frequent schema changes. Furthermore, it is not possible to formulate a single closed SQL query such as "Which groups contain time series TS_1?" because one would first have to query the system catalog for all relation names which correspond to groups and then issue a query looking for the members of the group for each relation name found.

Grp_1	
member_id	kind_of_member
"TS_5"	TS
"TS_11"	Grp
"Grp_2"	TS

Fig. 8:   Sample relation modeling the member relationship for one group

Solution (b) uses one common relation for all groups with grp_id as an attribute (see Fig. 9). With a large number of groups, this solution yields one large relation. For this relation, a similar tradeoff can be observed as with described for time series. If the relation is sorted, inserts will be very costly. If it is not sorted, groups will be scattered across the relations with tuples stored far apart.

With both solutions, there are general drawbacks: Data pertaining to one group (header and members) have to be stored in different relations. The transitive closure of a group (i.e. all members reachable via its subgroups) cannot be computed as the relational model does not support recursive queries. Apart from the structural shortcomings, there is also the lack of user extensible functionality for groups.

members		
grp_id	member_id	kind_of_member
"Grp_1"	"TS_5"	TS
"Grp_1"	"TS_11"	TS
"Grp_1"	"Grp_2"	Grp
"Grp_2"	"TS_10"	TS

Fig. 9: Sample relation containing the member relationships for all groups

5   Overview of existing DBMS for time series management

With respect to the practical relevance of time series data, the number of commercial and even prototype systems in this field is rather low. To our knowledge, there are currently only four systems (2 commercial and 2 prototype) which provide database functionality for time series. In the following, a short overview and comparison of these systems will be given.

5.1   TSMS developed at University of Berkeley

At University of Berkeley, a research prototype for time series management has been developed based on extended relational technology [10] [1]. The system uses POSTGRES as the implementation base. The underlying model supports simple time series and the aggregation of time series for one semantic entity. Each time series is modeled as an n-ary vector and described by a set of additional information items like frequency, exception set, life span etc. Each time series is associated with a calendar with a variety of calendars being definable. Queries and manipulation of time series are supported by extensions to the relational operations. There is a predefined set of operators for special computations on time series like the transformation from one frequency to another. Within the framework of the extensible RDBMS, the user can add functions for individual kinds of computations, e.g. specific interpolation or extrapolation operators. A further specialty of this system is the use of rules involving time series data.

5.2 Illustra TimeSeries DataBlade

The commercial system Illustra is an extensible RDBMS following in the lines of POSTGRES. Illustra users are offered a number of optional so-called "DataBlades" for special types of applications, one of these being the "TimeSeries DataBlade" [6]. This data blade offers a relational framework for time series analysis with concepts similar to those of the Berkeley system described above. It supports two new data types, namely time series and calendar. Time series can be multivariate, i.e. consist of an arbitrary number of recorded attributes. Time series can have various granularities and be associated with different calendars. There is no aggregation or grouping mechanism in Illustra to structure the set of time series. Access to data is based on an SQL extension, which allows to combine time series and other relational data in one query. In addition to the general SQL facility, about 40 predefined functions are supplied, e.g. to aggregate time series, compute a time lag, clip a predefined interval etc. Further analysis functions can be defined by the user by ways of the abstract data type feature of the RDBMS.

5.3 FAME

Another commercial system is FAME from FAME Software Corporation, a subsidiary of Citybank [5]. FAME is not based on the relational model nor any other known modeling paradigm, but uses a proprietary approach. Data objects available in FAME are scalars, univariate time series and computed time series described by formulas. Time series may be defined with various frequencies from seconds up to multiples of a year. Each time series is described by a standard header with information like frequency, first and last date recorded and aggregation type (summed, averaged etc.). FAME offers powerful specialized functionality for statistical evaluation and forecasting (linear regression, Box-Jenkins, moving average, Monte Carlo Analysis and many others). In that sense, it is rather a statistics package than just a DBMS. There are also a number of functions to produce graphical output and reports in various formats. Import from and export to a variety of file formats is supported. FAME is a very comprehensive system as to calculations on and presentation of time series. Query capabilities consist in finding data objects by name (including a wild card facility) and retrieving events by time stamp. Time series can be grouped by so-called name lists (e.g. all time series related to earnings could be named "*.earnings", where * is a wild card for the name of each company).

5.4 CALANDA

CALANDA is a special-purpose DBMS for time series management currently under development at Union Bank of Switzerland. CALANDA offers data management functionality directly targeted at economists and financial analysts who will be able to use the system with their domain-specific knowledge about time series only.

CALANDA has an object-oriented data model with special root classes to model time series and groups of time series. All the usual object-oriented features like inheritance, method definition, overloading etc. are supported for these classes. CALANDA supports multivariate time series with an arbitrary number of attributes per event. Beside simple attribute domains, multidimensional array types are an important modeling instrument for statistical applications. Each time series consists of a sequence of events and a header which is a record with a user-defined attribute structure. There are predefined operations for filtering of time series, frequency transformation, array manipulation etc. Of course, the user can extend this functionality by defining his or her own methods. For that purpose, CALANDA offers a computationally complete data manipulation language for operator definition and retrieval. However, in contrast to FAME, CALANDA is not supposed to replace statistical packages but to provide sound DBMS functionality.

Groups are supported as a flexible instrument for categorizing and aggregating time series. The - often huge - set of time series can be structured by building up a directed acyclic graph which can be used for navigation, querying and set operations. Grouping is not restricted to time series that describe one semantic entity, but can be applied to any set of time series that fulfill common criteria (e.g. all time series of securities which are currently above/below a market index, all time series of companies in a given country and so forth). CALANDA offers extensive calendar functionality providing date arithmetic, holidays, business weeks, calendar transformation etc. Because CALANDA is targeted at end-users, it offers a graphical user interface (GUI) that resembles spreadsheets or 4GL tools for relational DBMS. Interoperability mechanisms for coupling CALANDA to other kinds of DBMS are currently under development.

CALANDA has been implemented using the class library ETOS which is a seamless integration of the ODBMS ObjectStore and the application framework ET++ [13]. ETOS provides persistent storage of objects, basic database functionality including transactions, queries on collections, handling of databases etc. as well as a complete framework for the development of applications with graphical user interfaces. On top of this infrastructure layer, a customized layer has been realized which consists of the CALANDA kernel and the components of its GUI. Thus, CALANDA relies on the data management facilities of an ODBMS, tailoring it to the specific structural, operational and user interface needs of time series management.

Fig. 10 gives a comparative overview of the systems summing up their most important features. As the system from University of Berkeley and the Illustra TimeSeries DataBlade have very similar functionality, they are presented in the same column.

System	FAME	Berkeley System / Illustra TSDB	CALANDA
data model	proprietary	extended relational	object-oriented
time series	univariate with simple values	multivariate with simple values and defined data types	multivariate with simple values and n-dim arrays
grouping	simple name lists	–	acyclic directed group graph
functionality	poor DBMS functionality rich set of statistical functions	extended RDBMS funct. some predefined functions	full ODBMS funct. predefined functions
extensibility	user-defined functions	extensible (C functions)	easy to extend user defined methods, inheritance, overloading
queries	poor	extended SQL	special query operations
user interface	command line, proprietary 4GL	(embedded) SQL, C	GUI, C++ interface, API

Fig. 10: Comparison of DBMSs for time series management

6   Conclusion

In this paper we have shown that time series databases differ considerably from what is usually understood by temporal databases. We have presented the special requirements with respect to the structure and functionality of multivariate time series, groups and calendars that must be supported in a time series management system. Current temporal databases are dominated by relational technology and are intended to solve the problem of managing historical instead of just snapshot data. With respect to time series, a number of shortcomings can be observed regarding logical and physical structure, time model, queries and functionality. Relations are not well suited to handle time series and groups, retrieval along the time axis is poor, operational support for filtering and transformation is missing etc.

As we have shown, there are currently only very few systems that try to solve the problem. At our site, we are currently developing the CALANDA time series system which is based on object-oriented technology. Our early experiences with that system have shown that it meets well the needs of time series analysts for easy modeling and powerful manipulation of time series. Relevant applications are e.g. large stock databases with historical security prices or macro economic databases with statistical data on countries, industry groups and the like.

For future developments, we wonder whether temporal database management systems and time series management systems will meet. There are certainly a number of common points which have to be solved in both kinds of systems. At present, we observe that the development of systems diverges. It will be an interesting research perspective to find out whether it is feasible to come up with a system that can handle all kinds of time-related aspects or whether special-purpose systems are needed.

References

[1]   R. Chandra, A. Segev: Managing Temporal Financial Data in an Extensible Database. Proc. of the 19th VLDB Conf., Dublin 1993, pp. 302-313.

[2]   W. Dreyer, A. Kotz Dittrich, D. Schmidt: An Object-Oriented Data Model for a Time Series Management System. Proceedings of the 7th International Working Conference on Scientific and Statistical Database Management (SSDBM'94), Charlottesville, Virginia, Sep. 1994, pp. 186-195.

[3]   W. Dreyer, A. Kotz Dittrich, D. Schmidt: Research Perspectives for Time Series Management Systems. ACM SIGMOD Record Vol. 23, No. 1, March 1994, pp. 10-15.

[4]   W. Dreyer, A. Kotz Dittrich, D. Schmidt: Using the CALANDA Time Series Management System. Proc. ACM SIGMOD Intl. Conf., San Jose 1995, p. 489.

[5]   FAME Software Corporation: User's Guide to FAME, 1990.

[6]   Illustra Information Technologies, Inc.: Illustra TimeSeries DataBlade, technical information 1994.

[7]   R. Snodgrass et al.: TSQL2 Language Specification. ACM SIGMOD Record Vol. 23, No. 1, March 1994, pp. 65-86.

[8]   R. Snodgrass: Temporal Object-oriented Databases: A Critical Compari-
        son. In W. Kim (ed.): Modern Database Systems, The Object Model, In-
        teroperability, and Beyond, Addison Wesley, 1995, chapter 19, pp. 386-
        408.

[9]   M. Soo, R. Snodgrass: Mixed Calendar Query Language Support for
        Temporal Constants. TempIS Technical Report 29, Computer Science
        Department, University of Arizona, Tucson, 1992.

[10]   A. Segev, A. Shoshani: A Temporal Data Model Based on Time Sequen-
        ces. In [11], chapter 11, pp. 248 - 269.

[11]   A. Tansel et al. (eds.): Temporal Databases, Theory, Design, and Im-
        plementation. Benjamin Cummings, 1993.

[12]   G. Wuu, U. Dayal: A Uniform Model for Temporal and Versioned Ob-
        ject-oriented Databases. In [11], chapter 11, pp. 230-247.

[13]   A. Weinand, E. Gamma: ET++ – a Portable, Homogeneous Class Library
        and Application Framework. In W.R. Bischofberger, H.-P. Frei (eds.):
        Computer Science Research at UBILAB: strategy and projects, procee-
        dings of the UBILAB conference, Zurich 1994. Universitätsverlag Kon-
        stanz, 1994, pp. 66-92.

V. Implementation Issues for Temporal DBMSs

Access Methods for Bi-Temporal Databases

Anil Kumar   Vassilis J. Tsotras [+]
Depts. of Electr. Eng. and Computer Science
Polytechnic University, Brooklyn, NY 11201
{akumar, tsotras} @photon.poly.edu

Christos Faloutsos [*]
AT&T Bell Labs
Murray Hill, NJ 07974
christos@research.att.com

Abstract

While much work has recently appeared in literature on access methods for transaction-time databases, not much has been done for indexing bitemporal databases, i.e., databases that incorporate both transaction and valid time dimensions. In this paper we first discuss the issues involved in addressing general bitemporal queries and then propose two general approaches in solving such queries. For simplicity we present our findings in relation to the so-called bitemporal pure-timeslice query. However our methodology applies to more complex bitemporal queries. The first approach reduces bitemporal queries to partial persistence problems for which an efficient method is then designed. Using this approach we introduce a new access method for the bitemporal pure-timeslice query, the *Bitemporal Interval Tree*. The second approach "sees" bitemporal data objects as consisting of two intervals, a valid-time and a transaction-time interval. It then divides bitemporal data objects in two categories according to whether the right endpoint of the transaction time interval is known, and uses a different, R*-tree based organization, for each category. In this paper we present the advantages and disadvantages of these approaches. In addition we compare them through simulation with a straightforward approach that "sees" the intervals associated with a bitemporal object as one rectangle that is stored in a single R*-tree.

1. Introduction

Conventional databases have been designed to capture the most recent data of the modeled reality. As new data values become available through updates, the existing data values are removed from the database. Hence, such databases capture only a snapshot of reality and have been called *snapshot* databases. While they serve some applications well, conventional databases are not sufficient for applications that require past and/or future data. What is needed is a *temporal* database that supports the storage and querying of time varying information. Two orthogonal time dimensions have been proposed in literature in order to represent temporal evolution: the *valid* and *transaction* times [1].

According to [2], "the valid time of a fact is the time when the fact is true in the modeled reality". Transaction time refers to the time when a new value is posted to the database by a transaction. A temporal database is categorized as transaction-time, valid-time or bitemporal, according to which temporal dimension(s) it supports.

A transaction-time database conceptually keeps timeslices of the database indexed

[+] This work was partially supported under ARPA Contract No. DAAH01-94-C-R116 and by the New York State Science and Technology Foundation as part of its Center for Advanced Technology program.

[*] On leave from Dept. of Comp. Science, Univ. of Maryland, College Park, MD20742. This work was partially supported by the Institute of Systems Research and by NSF under Grants No. EEC-94-02384, IRI-8958546 and IRI-9205273, with matching funds from Empress Software Inc. and Thinking Machines Inc.

by transaction time. Hence it can rollback the database to some previous state as of some past transaction time. Transaction times are consistent with the serialization order of transactions and thus they are system generated and are monotonically increasing. Since it is impossible to change the past, transaction times cannot be changed; therefore, there is no way to correct errors in past tuples. Since the transaction time dimension represents the history of a database activity rather than real world history, a transaction-time database could roll back to an incorrect previous timeslice. A valid-time database on the other hand, maintains the entire history of an enterprise as best known now; i.e. it stores the current knowledge about the past. If errors are discovered in this history, they are corrected by modifying the database. When a correction is applied, previous values are not retained and therefore it is not possible to view the database as it was in the past.

Clearly both temporal dimensions are needed in order to accurately model reality. In bitemporal databases one can query tuples that are valid at some (valid) time, as seen at some other (transaction) time; hence, the history of retroactive/proactive changes can be completely captured. While much work has been done recently on access methods that support one time axis ([3, 4, 5, 6, 7, 8, 9, 10, 11, 12, 13, 14, 15, 16, 17, 18, 19, 20]; for a recent comparison of such methods see [21]), not much has been done for bitemporal indexes, i.e., methods that support both transaction and valid time on the same index.

In this paper we present two methodologies to design efficient bitemporal indexes. Both of our approaches take advantage of the specifics of time evolution, in particular the properties that valid time may not be in order, but transaction time is always in increasing order. Work reported in the transaction-time literature has shown that exploiting the characteristics of time evolution leads to better indexing for transaction-time databases. This is to be contrasted with one obvious solution to bitemporal queries that considers each time attribute simply as a separate dimension on a multidimensional access method (like an R*-tree).

Section 2 summarizes the desirable properties of a good temporal access method and discusses previous approaches to single-time access methods. Section 3 elaborates on the bitemporal environment and its queries. Section 4 describes some straightforward approaches to the bitemporal pure-timeslice query, and section 5 presents our solutions to the problem. Simulation results appear in section 6, while section 7 presents open problems for further research.

2. Performance Characteristics and Previous Work

Any access method used to organize time-evolving data is characterized by the following costs: *space* (the space consumed by the method's data structures in order to keep such data), *update processing* (the processing needed to update the method's data structures for data changes) and *query time* (the time needed to solve a temporal query).

All three costs are functions of three basic parameters: the answer size a, the number of changes n and the page (block) size b. The answer size a is the number of objects satisfying the query predicate. The number of changes n corresponds to the total number of valid-time changes that occur in a bitemporal evolution (thus n is also an upper bound to the number of transaction-time updates since at a given transaction a number of valid-time updates is processed in general). It represents the minimal information needed by any index to perform errorless reconstruction of time-varying data. A valid-time change corresponds to either the insertion, deletion or modification of a valid-time interval. Regarding the third parameter, we assume that every secondary memory access transmits one page of b records and this counts as one I/O.

There are two desirable properties for an efficient access method: *index pagination* and *data clustering*. Index pagination deals with the issue of how well index nodes of a method are paginated. Data clustering is achieved if records that are "logically" related for a given query can also be stored physically close; then the query is optimized as fewer pages are accessed.

A variety of temporal access methods have been proposed in recent years. All of the previous approaches support a single time axis; in addition the usual assumption is that time is always increasing and updates are always applied on the latest state, i.e., the past is not changed. These are characteristics of a transaction-time evolution, so we first discuss transaction-time support. In a transaction-time database, it is implicitly assumed that when a change happened in the real world it updated the database instantly.

One of the first transaction-time queries addressed was the *pure-key* query, i.e., find all previous values (the history) of a given key [3, 4]. Another transaction-time query is the *pure-timeslice* query. A set of objects evolves over time and at each time instant an object may be added or deleted. The query is to find the set's state (i.e., the objects contained in the set) as of some time t. The more general query is the *range-timeslice* problem, where the predicate includes a condition on the objects' key space, i.e., find the objects that were "alive" at t and whose keys are in range k. (Obviously, the time predicate can instead of a time instant be a time interval).

A number of methods have been proposed to solve the pure-timeslice problem [8, 10, 13, 15, 17]. These methods keep the time evolution separate from the key space and are thus more efficient for pure-timeslice queries than range-timeslice queries. To answer range-timeslice queries the whole timeslice is first computed and then objects outside the requested range are eliminated. In another approach, the whole range is divided into predefined ranges and the requested range-timeslice is computed by finding timeslices of the predefined ranges that cover the query range. To better address range-timeslice queries a method must combine the time and key spaces (on the other hand, combining time-key spaces means that this method requires logarithmic update time). Range-timeslice queries are addressed in this way by [6, 9, 11, 12, 16].

A common approach in transaction-time access methods is that a temporal object is associated with an interval $[t_1, t_2]$, where t_1 represents the transaction time this object was created, or transaction birth time, and t_2 represents that time this object was deleted, or transaction deletion time. This interval represents the object's (transaction) lifetime. Recall that in transaction-time databases, there is an implicit assumption that when an object is created in the real world it is inserted in the database at the same time instant. Initially, when an object is inserted, its (transaction) birth time t_1 is known, but its (transaction) deletion time t_2 is yet unknown. So typically, this object is inserted in the database with an interval of the form: $[t_1, now)$ where *now* is a variable representing the current time. If later on this object is deleted, its (transaction) lifetime interval is updated to the appropriate deletion time.

To summarize, a transaction time database can be "thought of" as an evolving collection of objects. At each transaction time, objects are added, deleted or modified (assuming that objects have attributes that can be modified). Object deletions or modifications do not discard previous objects; rather such updates are "logical". A query is in general specified by some time predicate (usually a single time instant, but intervals are also possible) and maybe some key (attribute) predicate.

A valid-time database on the other hand represents the history as best known now. Thus, conceptually, a valid-time database can be "thought of" as a collection of valid time intervals. Intervals are added, deleted or modified. When an interval is deleted (or modified), the old object is not retained in the database. Hence, if a data structure is used to represent a valid-time database, this data structure should support dynamic addition and deletion of intervals (in any order). A valid-time query is specified in a similar way as a transaction-time query.

The simplest query would be to find all valid-time intervals that intersect a given valid time instant. This problem is known in literature as the *dynamic interval management* problem [22]. The best main-memory solution for this problem is the *priority search tree* data structure [23], yielding $O(k)$ space, $O(\log_2 k)$ update processing per change (for interval addition/deletion) and $O(\log_2 k + a)$ query time, where k corresponds to the number of intervals in the structure when the query is asked and a is the size of the answer (number of intervals intersecting the given time). It has been proved that this is optimal in the main memory environment.

For a disk based environment, one could use an R-tree [24] to dynamically insert or delete intervals. While such an approach may be practical for many data distributions, it is an interesting problem to find a method that can guarantee good worst case performance. Recall that while R-trees would use $O(k/b)$ space and $O(\log_b k)$ time for interval insertion, interval deletion and search can in the worst case be $O(n/b)$ (since when searching for an interval, one has to follow all nodes overlapping this interval, whether or not these nodes actually contain it). It is an open problem whether dynamic interval management on secondary storage can be achieved optimally, i.e., in $O(k/b)$ pages, $O(\log_b k)$ update time and $O(\log_b k + a/b)$ query time [25]. More recently, [26] address this and similar problems however no optimal solution is yet known.

Some of the single time-axis methods have also been proposed as supporting (some notion of) valid time. Since the requirement that the past does not change is a transaction-time application requirement and not a data structure requirement, in general any access method used to support transaction time databases could be used for valid time databases. The main difference however is in the performance, since valid-time cannot assume the increasing characteristics of transaction time.

Among the single time axis approaches, the work in [12, 14] falls in between transaction and valid time databases. This method associates with each temporal object an interval whose both endpoints are known and uses the SR-tree (a variation of an R-tree [24]) to store and query such intervals. The method is optimized towards insertions of intervals and searches. Deletions of intervals may be problematic since some intervals are split in many segments, which makes their update more difficult. However, as it is mentioned in [14] such interval deletions would correspond to "revising" the history, hence they are not critical for an index for historical data. This is the case for transaction time databases. In addition, data objects could be added in the SR-tree only after both of their transaction-time endpoints are known. Hence, newly inserted objects whose intervals have "unknown" right endpoints would have to be kept in a separate structure (such structure is not described but it could be a variation of an R-tree). If intervals were inserted in the SR-tree structure as $[t_1, now)$ where now is a very large number, the performance would degrade for two reasons: excessive overlapping, and frequent deletions (which are needed when a $[t_1, now)$ interval is updated to $[t_1, t_2)$).

If the interval associated with each object corresponds to the object's valid time interval, the SR-tree could be used for valid time databases. However, in this environment deletions of intervals are possible, hence intervals would have to be physically deleted from the structure frequently.

Recently, other kinds of temporal queries have appeared in literature [27, 28]. They are reciprocal in nature to the ones we examine here: given a pattern and a time series (a transaction time evolution), a typical query asks for all those times that a similar pattern appeared in the series. The search involves some distance criterion that qualifies when a pattern is similar to the given pattern. The distance criterion guarantees no false dismissals (false alarms are eliminated afterwards). Whole pattern matching [27] and sub-matching [28] queries have been examined.

We proceed by describing the bitemporal environment in more detail.

3. The Bitemporal Environment and its Queries

To better clarify the subtle differences between the two time dimensions consider keeping the history of a company's contracts. A contract is of the form: (c, I), where c is the contract identifier and I is the contract duration interval. Interval I corresponds to an interval on the valid time axis. This contract information is recorded on a database at some transaction time t that is orthogonal to interval I. (According to [29] this example will create a *bitemporal-state* table). Assume that when a new contract is recorded at t, an indelible ink printout is created that contains the intervals of all contracts the company ever had, together with the new one; this printout is stamped with t. The indelible ink means that no corrections can be applied on it after time t. The printout represents a history timeslice (denoted as $ht(t)$) as it contains the history of the company's contracts as best known at time t (this representation is taken from [1]).

It is possible that at a later transaction time $t' > t$, some previously recorded contract interval is found to be erroneous (for example, a contract was shorter/larger in reality than what was recorded, or should have never been recorded) or a proactive/retroactive change modifies the interval of some recorded contract to a new one. As a result a new history timeslice is printed, stamped with time t' that reflects these changes. This new printout $ht(t')$ will contain all unchanged contracts from $ht(t)$ plus the modified contracts. Thus, $ht(t')$ is the contract history as it is best known at time t'. A valid-time database would only store and query the latest $ht(t')$.

However, $ht(t)$ represents some past, but useful, knowledge we had about the company. The evolution of the company is best represented by a bitemporal database which retains and thus can query all ht's. A bitemporal database can be "visualized" as a series of history timeslices $ht(t)$, where each timeslice is marked by transaction time t, and consists of a collection of valid time intervals (Figure 1). Since changes (error corrections, updates, new intervals etc.) are applied to the most current printout and result to a new printout $hs()$, the transaction-time dimension always increases. No transaction can update a printout with smaller transaction time. In contrast, any interval on the current printout can be corrected or updated, to create the next printout. This is why transaction time changes are said to be in increasing order, while valid-time changes can be out of order (but always on the latest $ht(t)$).

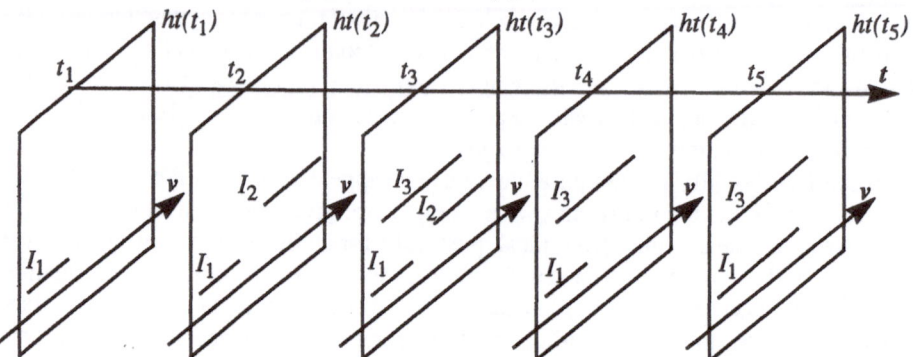

Fig. 1: A conceptual view of a bitemporal database. The t-axis corresponds to transaction time, while the v-axis is for valid times. At transaction time t_1 interval I_1 is added to form $ht(t_1)$; then at t_2 and t_3 intervals I_2 and I_3 are added in historical timeslices $ht(t_2)$ and $ht(t_3)$ respectively. At t_4 interval I_2 is deleted, while at t_5 interval I_1 is modified.

It is important to note the orthogonality of the two dimensions in this example: the (transaction) time at which a new historical timeslice is created is in general irrelevant to the intervals reported on it, which can be earlier, current or later than this time (especially since future contracts can also be recorded).

While conceptually the above evolution is represented as a series of history timeslices, if a bitemporal database were to physically store all these timeslices it would soon run out of space. Thus it is important to invent access methods that support such bitemporal evolutions without having to physically store each ht.

For the purpose of presenting our methodologies we will concentrate on the simplest of the bitemporal queries, the *bitemporal pure-timeslice* query (in short BPT) which is defined as: "for a transaction time t and a valid time v find all intervals that were intersecting v as of t". An example of a BPT query is: "find all the company contracts that were valid on January 1, 1994, as best known on November 1, 1993". The history timeslice on Nov. 1, 1993 contains all contracts known as of that time; this includes past, current or future contracts. From all these, the query retrieves only the contracts that would be valid on Jan. 1, 1994.

In principal, the bitemporal pure-timeslice query is different than the single-axis (transaction time) pure-timeslice query (as described in section 2) in the sense that the later keeps the evolution of a set of objects and should address queries on this set, while the former keeps the evolution of a set of intervals and must address queries on these intervals. Similarly, the bitemporal pure-timeslice is different than the dynamic interval management problem (which addresses queries in a valid-time database) since it keeps and can address queries among many history timeslices instead of just one.

A more complex bitemporal query is the *bitemporal range-timeslice query*: "find all the company contracts that were valid on January 1, 1994 and had contract id's in range k, as best known on November 1, 1993". In general a bitemporal query is of the form: "for a transaction time interval T, a valid time interval I and a key range R, find all objects in range R who intersected interval I during transaction times in T". A large collection of bitemporal queries appears in [29].

4. Straightforward Approaches to Bitemporal Queries

We proceed with the description of five obvious, but inefficient (for various reasons) ways to address the Bitemporal Pure-Timeslice (in short BPT) query. Similar solutions hold for the more complex bitemporal queries. Let each $ht(t)$ be organized by some data structure that supports interval intersection queries and dynamic additions, deletions or modifications of intervals (this data structure could be some type of a balanced tree like an R-tree, etc.) The obvious approaches are:

(1) One could explicitly store at each transaction time the whole timeslice of the valid-time history, i.e., for every transaction time t simply store $ht(t)$ and its data structure (in our example this corresponds to the printout created at each transaction time). Then each $ht(t)$ is accessed by some index on the transaction times. The main disadvantage of this solution is the space and update requirements. Since consecutive timeslices are taken, the space grows to $O(n^2/b)$ pages. Similarly, the update processing at each transaction is high: $O(n/b)$ time is needed for storing the $ht(t)$ (assuming that the data structure of each $ht(t)$ uses only linear space to the number of intervals in $ht(t)$).

(2) Suppose that whenever a transaction updates the database for an interval insertion, deletion or modification, the transaction time together with the change are stored on a sequential log. If storing a single update takes $O(1)$ time (by appending it on the end of the log) this method has minimal updating and uses minimal $O(n/b)$ space. However, answering a BPT query requires $O(n/b)$ time as the whole log may have to be searched serially until the appropriate transaction time t is found.

(3) In a hybrid approach, suppose that timeslices are stored every l-th transaction and in addition the entire update sequence between subsequent timeslices is kept. Answering the BPT query for transaction time t and valid time v implies first accessing (and querying for v) the stored $ht(t')$ with the largest t' such that $t' \leq t$, and then reading through the updates until a transaction with time larger that t is found. Depending on the choice of l this hybrid method behaves like one of the other two methods, i.e., it causes a blow-up either in space or in query time.

(4) This approach "represents" objects by some multidimensional "bounding box". A multidimensional spatial access method is used that treats transaction and valid times as two distinct dimensions. Observe however that transaction time intervals cannot be bounded when inserted in the structure since their right endpoint is unknown at insertion. Hence, when an object with valid-time interval I is inserted in the database at transaction time t, it is accompanied by a transaction-time "lifespan" of the form [t, *now*], where *now* is a variable that represents the current transaction time. Thus *now* extends to "infinity" or "forever". If this object is deleted or modified at some time t'', ($t'' > t$) its lifespan becomes [t, t'']. In this case an actual deletion (from real world) is represented as a "logical" deletion in the database, since this object remains physically stored but with a different lifespan. An object will thus be represented by a rectangle in the two-dimensional space. (In the more general bitemporal range-timeslice queries, we would have used an additional dimension for the object key space). The BPT query is then translated to finding all rectangles that include the query

point (t, v) as it is depicted in Figure 2.

Putting intervals in "bounding boxes" by extending their right endpoint to "infinity" or "now" deteriorates the performance of such an index because of extensive overlapping. This will become apparent from our simulation results where a single R*-*tree* [30] was used as the multidimensional spatial access method. While the R-tree (and its variants) is a robust data structure that can address a number of problems quite efficiently, temporal problems have crucial characteristics that if incorporated in the structure, could provide for better access methods.

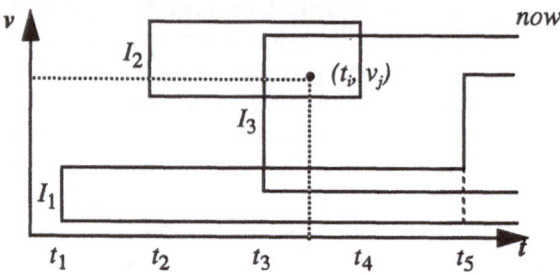

Fig. 2: The two-dimensional (valid and transaction axis) representation of the problem. The evolution of Fig.1 is depicted, as it is at time $t > t_5$. The modification of interval I_1 at time t_5 creates the ending of the initial rectangle for I_1 and the insertion of a new extended rectangle from t_5 to *now*. Similarly, interval I_3 remains unchanged after its insertion, so it extends up to *now*. A query for (t_i, v_j) is now a point.

(5) Suppose that bitemporal data is indexed on a single time dimension (transaction or valid). For example, the valid time interval of an object could be considered as a special attribute (tuple) and based on its transaction time behavior the object is placed in a (single time axis) access method. Then a BPT query is answered in two steps: first all objects existing at transaction time t are found and then the valid time interval of each such object is checked whether it includes valid time v. Alternatively, we could have a structure that keeps all valid-time intervals ever inserted in the database. Each such interval is accompanied by an attribute tuple corresponding to its transaction time lifespan. Then to answer a BPT we will first find all objects with intervals containing valid time v and then discard those objects whose transaction time lifespan does not contain t. Clearly, both variations are not efficient.

5. Two Methodologies for solving Bitemporal Queries

In designing efficient access methods for bitemporal queries we should take into consideration the specifics of the evolution in each time dimension. As we have argued, valid-time evolution should support dynamic insertion and deletion of intervals in any order. We assume for simplicity that interval modification is represented by the old interval being deleted, followed by a new interval being inserted. On the valid time axis both valid-time endpoints are known. This represents the knowledge from the real world. Thus we may even insert a valid time interval like: $(-\infty, \infty)$, since this is the knowledge we had at the time of insertion. On the other hand, since transaction time has a meaning only after something has happened (in our case only after some update to the database was made), transaction time is monotonically increasing and the future on this axis is not known.

In the rest we present two methodologies for solving bitemporal queries that take into advantage the above characteristics of time dimensions. The first approach (section 6) reduces a bitemporal problem into a partial persistence problem, for which an access method is then designed. The second approach divides bitemporal objects in two categories according to whether the right endpoint of the transaction time interval extends to infinity, and uses a different, R*-tree based organization, for each category. We term this approach the 2-R tree method (section 7). We present both approaches for the BPT query. We also compared our approaches with the straightforward, single R-tree approach (in short 1-R tree). The partial-persistence approach guarantees logarithmic worst case query time and update processing for the BPT, in the expense of extra copies per object (the overall space however is still linear to the number of changes in the evolution). In comparison, the 1-R and 2-R tree use minimal space (only one copy per object) but their average update and query processing are larger than the corresponding times of the partial-persistence approach. The 2-R method has asymptotically less update but larger query time than the 1-R method. The choice of which methodology to use depends on the application characteristics.

6. Bitemporal Queries and Partial Persistence

We begin this section by relating the bitemporal pure-timeslice (BPT) problem to the notion of persistence [31]. A data structure is called *persistent* if a change applied to it creates a new version of the data structure while the previous version is still retained and can be accessed. Otherwise, if old versions are discarded the structure is termed *ephemeral*. Partial persistence implies that only the newest version can be modified (i.e., changes are applied only to the newest version), while in full persistence every version can be modified.

Partial persistence "suits" nicely with transaction time. In a transaction-time or in a bitemporal database, changes are always applied on the latest database state. The difference between a transaction-time database and a bitemporal database is that in the former the database state is a relation (a set of point-objects), while in the latter it is a history timeslice *ht()* (a set of interval-objects). Then, accessing the past reduces into making the structure that represents the database state partially persistent.

The structure used to represent the database state depends on what queries we need to answer. In a transaction-time database for example, we can represent the state using a hashing function (for "find all objects" queries) or a B-tree structure ("find all objects with keys in a given range"). [31] shows how to make any linked main-memory data structure partially (or fully) persistent. In a database environment we have to worry about I/O, thus pagination and data-clustering are major issues. These issues were efficiently addressed for transaction-time databases in [6, 11, 16, 17].

The state of a bitemporal database (a given *ht*) should be represented by a data structure that supports dynamic interval addition/deletion. By "viewing" a bitemporal query as a partial persistence problem, we obtain a <u>double</u> advantage. First we disassociate the valid-time requirements from the transaction-time ones. If we can use a well paginated data structure that supports dynamic insertions/deletions of intervals then the valid time support is provided from this structure while the transaction time support is achieved by making this structure partially persistent (and well paginated). Second, changes are always applied on the latest state of the structure and they last until updated (if ever) at a later transaction time. As a result, no transaction time lifespan $[t, now]$ is needed. Recall that this was the major disadvantage of the straightforward approach based on two-dimensional bounding (since it results to large rectangle overlapping).

We therefore need to find a good dynamic, ephemeral data structure for representing each individual state ht and make it partially persistent and well-paginated. Ideally this structure should also be space efficient (given the time-evolving environment). For the BPT query we only need a data structure that can support dynamic additions/deletions of intervals and interval intersection queries. This is again the *dynamic interval management* problem (since each ht on its own is a valid-time database), and there are various main-memory dynamic data structures which solve it: the Interval Tree [32], the Segment Tree [33], the Priority Search Tree [23]. We decided to start with the Interval Tree. The Priority Search Tree could be another good candidate and we plan to try it in the future. We did not choose the Segment Tree since it needs more than linear space (for n interval changes it uses $O(n\log_2 n)$ space) and therefore its bitemporal counterpart could only increase the overall space.

We propose a new method for answering BPT queries, the *Bitemporal Interval Tree*. Our method assumes that queries involving valid time instants are "focused" on a known set $U' = U \cup \{-\infty\} \cup \{\infty\}$. Without loss of generality we can assume that U is an ordered set of integers, i.e., $U = \{1, 2,..., V\}$. The special elements $-\infty$ and ∞ denote the "fromever" and "forever" notions of the valid time axis. Focusing on a set U' of valid times means that our method will be more efficient when answering bitemporal queries involving instants from this set. This assumption has no influence on the valid time intervals that can be accommodated in our method. Our method stores valid time intervals whose either both, or one, or none endpoint is from U'. Queries on valid time instants outside U' will still be answered, but their performance is not guaranteed. Focusing on a valid set appears in many applications where we are mainly interested for some well-defined valid-time period. In addition, it is usually the case that the focus of interest moves to higher valid times (since in many real applications valid time intervals tend to move towards higher values as transaction time increases). One property of our method is that extending U can be performed without reorganizing intervals that have both endpoints in the previous set U.

The Bitemporal Interval Tree has $O(\log_b V + \log_b n + a)$ query time I/O's, $O((n+V)/b)$ space and the update time is logarithmic. As mentioned above, the stated query performance is guaranteed for bitemporal predicates of the form (t, v) where $v \in U'$. We proceed with subsection 6.1 that introduces the basic ideas of the Interval Tree while in 6.2 we present an overview of the Bitemporal Interval Tree.

6.1 The Interval Tree

The crucial characteristic of an Interval Tree [32] is that it transforms the interval intersection problem into a number of range search problems. Let S be a set of n intervals with endpoints from set U; that is: $S = \{[l_i, r_i); l_i, r_i \in U, l_i < r_i, 1 \le i \le n\}$. An Interval Tree for S, with respect to set U, consists of a (backbone) full binary tree T with V leaves and a number of doubly-linked lists (Figure 3). Each leaf is labeled with one element from U. Each non-leaf node u is assigned value $val(u)$ that serves as a split key which will direct the search from node u to its subtrees. Every interval $[l, r)$ from S is associated to a single non-leaf node u of the tree where u is the node that contains l and *r* in its left and right subtrees respectively [34]. The intervals associated to a particular node *u* are kept in two doubly-linked lists: $L(u)$ and $R(u)$, where $L(u)$ ($R(u)$) keeps the intervals in increasing (decreasing) order of their left (right) endpoints. For fast insertion/deletion, each list is implemented with a balanced binary tree (not shown in Fig.3).

Inserting an interval [*l*, *r*) in the Interval Tree is easy: starting from the root of *T*, locate the first node *u* such that $l < val(u) < r$. Then insert *l* into $L(u)$ and *r* into $R(u)$. Searching for *u* would at most need to go down a path of the interval tree, thus it takes $O(log_2 V)$. Inserting in each list takes at most $O(log_2 n)$ time (at worst all intervals may end up at the same node). Deleting an interval is done in a similar way. Since every interval from *S* is kept in a single node *u* the space used by all the lists is $O(n)$. In addition, the Interval Tree uses $O(V)$ space for the backbone binary search tree.

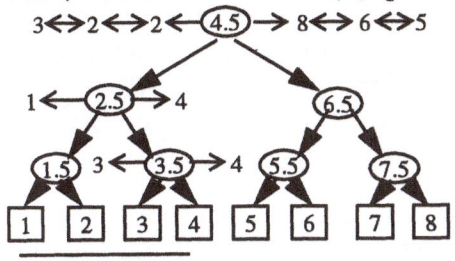

Fig.3: An Interval Tree with $U = \{1,..., 8\}$ and $n = 5$ intervals. The *value* of each node is shown inside the node. The left/right lists for the root node contain the endpoints of (2,6), (2,8) and (3,8).

Given a query *v*, if *a* denotes the number of intervals from *S* that intersect *v*, then the query is answered in $O(log_2 V + a)$ time (number of comparisons). Let *p* be the path in *T* from the root to the leaf labeled *v*. For every node u_i in *p* the algorithm checks whether $v < val(u_i)$ or $v > val(u_i)$. If $v < val(u_i)$ then *v* emanates from the left subtree of u_i and all intervals assigned to u_i have right endpoints *r* that extend *v* (*r*>*v*). Each such interval would intersect query *v*, if and only if, its left endpoint *l* is before *v* (*l*<*v*). However these left endpoints already exist in increasing order in list $L(u_i)$ and hence the algorithm simply has to traverse list $L(u_i)$ starting from the first endpoint and reading all of them until the endpoint greater than *v* is found. All such endpoints correspond to intervals that belong to the answer since they intersect *v*. No more endpoints need to be read from this list since by construction they correspond to intervals that start after *v*. Each of the $log_2 V$ lists of path *p* traversed by a query is called a *qualifying* list for this query.

6.2 The Bitemporal Interval Tree

The Bitemporal Interval Tree can be "visualized" as a method that keeps the evolution of an Interval Tree over transaction time. For the purpose of including all possible valid times, the backbone structure of the Interval Tree is first enhanced with nodes representing the special elements $-\infty$ and ∞, and, two sets U_+ and U_-, that "contain" the finite elements that are greater/less than the maximum/minimum element of *U* respectively. This backbone structure appears in Figure 4. The idea is similar: each node will accommodate the intervals whose leftpoint emanates from the node's left subtree and the rightpoint extends to this node's right subtree. Each of U_+ and U_- is simply a node, i.e., there is no subtree under these nodes (this is the meaning of "focusing": since we have focused on set *U*, intervals falling inside *T* are classified in detail and hence queries on U will be answered efficiently).

Unless we extend the focus area (we will discuss such extensions later), the backbone structure of Figure 4 does not change as transaction time proceeds. What actually changes are the lists associated with each node in the structure. If all these lists were made partially persistent then to answer a BPT query with predicate (t,v) we need to search the backbone tree of Figure 4 for value v and in each node visited we need to "rollback" the left or right list in the state it had at transaction time t. Then v is searched on the past state of such lists. While this is a correct high-level description of how our method works, it is a simplification.

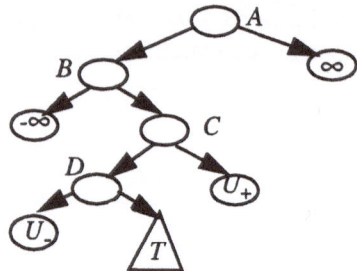

Fig.4: The full backbone structure of the Bitemporal Interval Tree. Node U_+ (U_-) will accommodate intervals whose both ends are in U_+ (U_-). Subtree T corresponds to a full binary tree for the set $U = \{1, 2,..., V\}$.

There are various problems we have to address: First, we have to provide efficient list pagination. Second, rolling back each list on the path separately would produce $O\left(\log_b V \cdot \log_b n + a\right)$ query time instead of $O\left(\log_b V + \log_b n + a\right)$ I/O's (for queries (t,v) where $v \in U'$). Third, we have to paginate the whole structure of our method.

We note that if the query predicate (t,v) is on $v \notin U'$ (i.e., v belongs to U_+ or U_-) the query time becomes $O\left(\log_b n + e/b\right)$. The $O\left(\log_b n\right)$ component is for rolling back the list associated with node U_+ or U_- to transaction time t and the $O(e/b)$ component is for searching this list. If e corresponds to the number of elements this list had at time t, at worst all such elements have to be checked but not all contribute to the answer.

For simplicity, we concentrate on an Interval Tree with backbone T (i.e., we will concentrate on valid intervals with endpoints from U), however, the techniques described are applied to the whole backbone structure of figure 4.

6.2.1 Partially persistent and fully paginated ordered lists

We proceed by considering a single list from the Interval Tree and show how to make it well paginated and partially persistent. Let X be an ephemeral list of ordered elements. There is a pointer to the top element of the list and each element has a *next* pointer to its right sibling in the list. The elements are kept in increasing order starting from the top of the list. Adding or deleting an element from X corresponds to finding the position of this element in X and performing the action. If X is to become partially persistent, previous states of X are retained while updates are applied on the latest state of it. Hence the list state becomes a function of time and $X(t)$ is the ordered sequence of elements the list had at time t. The query is defined as: given (transaction) time t, find the elements in $X(t)$ that were less than some value v (valid time).

This problem is a *special* case of a more general (transaction-time) *range-timeslice* query, that asks for the elements a set had at some t and in a given range of keys $[v_1, v_2]$. Various efficient access methods have been proposed [6,11,16] for this problem.

The Multi-Version B-tree (MVB tree, in short) [16] creates a partially persistent B$^+$-

tree. This method optimally solves the general range-timeslice problem using $O(n/b)$ space, $O(\log_b m)$ amortized update per change and $O(\log_b n + a/b)$ query time. Here, n represents the total number of elements ever added or deleted in the set. Variable m denotes the size of the current set when an update takes place and a represents the answer size. The TSB tree [6] is more space efficient, however it can guarantee worst case query performance only when the set evolution is described by additions of new data or updates on existing data. For deletions, a special "marker" is used on deleted records. For the interest of creating a method that always guarantees its performance, we have used the splitting policies of [16]. As it will be seen from the simulation results, this increases the space of our method. We plan to experiment also with the TSB tree splitting policies, which will result to less space.

Observe however, that there is a crucial <u>difference</u> between the way we want to traverse a list and the way the MVB (or the TSB) tree answers range queries. If the MVB tree was used to represent each evolving list, the list data are on leaf pages of the MVB structure. The MVB (or the TSB) structure however does not provide pointers connecting its leaf pages. The reason is simple: the logical sibling of a data page (i.e., the next page on the list) may vary over time since $X(t)$ is dynamic. For its queries, the MVB (or the TSB) tree does not need sibling pointers. This is because the search for a range query starts from the root of the structure and proceeds down the structure (in a top/down fashion). If we were to use this approach in our application, we would always have to search each list starting from the root of its MVB (or TSB) structure. This would at best result in $O(\log_b V \cdot \log_b n + a)$ query time, since we need to spent $O(\log_b n)$ I/O's going down the MVB (or TSB) structure of <u>each</u> qualifying list.

In our environment we need to access the pages that contain the elements of list $X(t)$ in order, starting from the beginning of the list. To solve this problem we still facilitate the splitting/merging policies that the MVB (or the TSB) methods use for their data pages, but we introduce an auxiliary structure that keeps these pages on a "conceptual" list $PX(t)$. At time t, $PX(t)$ connects in order all the pages that have elements from $X(t)$. In addition, for updating purposes, we use an ephemeral B^+ tree as a secondary index that keeps the alive elements of the most current X and pointers to the list pages where these elements' records are actually stored.

Hence, instead of dealing with list element insertion/deletions (i.e., $X(t)$), we deal with page insertions/deletions in the list of pages $PX(t)$. When an element is added/deleted from $X(t)$ the ephemeral B^+ tree will provide us with the page of $PX(t)$ that this update has to be performed. Then the update is performed using the MVB (or TSB) splitting/merging policies. If at t a page is copied (or time split), the original page is considered "deleted" and is taken off $PX(t)$. The new page is considered as an addition to list $PX(t)$. A page deletion is not physical but logical since the past is retained. The problem is thus transformed into making the list of pages $PX(t)$ partially persistent.

In [35] we describe a method that makes $PX(t)$ partially persistent and behaves as following: each page insertion/deletion takes $O(1)$ *amortized* time, the whole space used is $O(k/b)$ (where k is the total number of page insertions/deletions in PX's evolution) and the first a pages of $PX(t)$ are accessed in $O(\log_b k + a)$ I/Os. Observe that k is itself bounded by $O(n/b)$. Our method uses a variation of the *backward updating* technique [19] that was initially introduced in [36, 37] for main memory data structures solving computational geometry problems.

6.2.2 Paginating and Querying the Bitemporal Interval Tree

It remains to discuss how the overall Bitemporal Interval Tree is paginated, how queries are reduced to $O\left(\log_b V + \log_b n + a\right)$ and how the space becomes $O((n+V)/b)$. Consider one node of tree T. The history of its two lists will be kept individually using the method described in the previous section. If each such list is to be accessed separately, a bitemporal query (t, v) would be answered by first searching through T for v to find the "qualifying" lists and then "rollback" to t the histories of each qualifying list. There are $\log_2 V$ qualifying lists that will be rolled back using $O\left(\log_b n\right)$ I/O's per list. To avoid the numerous searches in list histories we propose to synchronize the list histories using backward updating. The technique is now implemented on tree paths.

As mentioned earlier, our assumption on "focusing" on set U implies that the backbone binary tree T does not change over time and thus it can be paginated easily. What changes with time are the lists assigned in each node. Suppose that T is paginated in a straightforward way: starting from the root of T each page is assigned a subtree of equal size $(O(b))$. Hence, a new multiway tree PT of pages is created (Figure 5). Every page of PT is thus "responsible" for the nodes of a subtree of T. Inside each page of PT we have two kinds of objects: *node* records that correspond to the nodes of the binary tree T, and *pointer* records that correspond to pointers to children pages in PT.

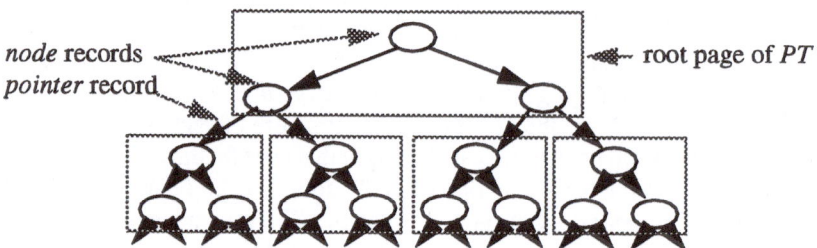

Fig.5: An example of the pages of tree PT. Each page is "responsible" for a subtree of nodes from the binary tree T.

A page in the PT tree can be considered as evolving over time through the changes that occur on the node records for which this page is responsible for. The space of each PT page has two portions. A "reserved" portion that keeps the original objects this page stores *(node* and *pointer* objects) and an "extra" space of size qb $(2/b < q < 1)$ for changes that occur in these objects. Consider a leaf page A of PT and assume that at some transaction time t, A's extra space becomes "full" with changes (for a leaf page these changes are due only to node record changes). Then a new copy of A is created. This new copy has its reserved portion full of current data, while its extra portion is empty. The parent page B of A in the PT tree should also be updated and so on. This is performed by changing B's *pointer* that was pointing to A to point to the new copy of page A. Therefore, pointer objects inside a page can change, too. These changes are also stored in the extra space of the parent page and can similarly cause the parent page to be copied if its extra space becomes full.

There is still a minor problem: we may access all first pages for everyone of the $\log_2 V$ qualifying lists associated in a path, however, not all of them may provide answer. To avoid such page accesses, in each page together with pointer records we keep the first element of each list pointed by the page. As a result, the Bitemporal Interval

Tree solves a BPT query in $O(\log_b V + \log_b n + a)$ I/O's: $O(\log_b n)$ I/O's to find the root of $PT(t)$, $O(\log_b V)$ I/O's to traverse the path down the $PT(t)$ tree, and, a to find the answer. At worst, each list accessed contributes only one interval to the answer, but no data page without at least one answer will be accessed.

While we can achieve good pagination of the $PT(t)$ structure, we should avoid using a full page per node's list if this list has not enough history (changes) to occupy a full page. This would result in $O(V + n/b)$ space as in the worst case there may be $O(V)$ such lists in T. To deal with this problem the lists that have less than $O(b)$ changes are kept all together in a B-tree like structure. Special care is needed for the pointers from the PT structure to this B-tree as time proceeds [35].

We conclude the description of the Bitemporal Interval Tree with a discussion on extending the "focus" on the valid time dimension. In practical applications as transaction time proceeds, we may want the focus on valid time to proceed, too. Extending the focus in that case would mean moving V towards larger values, currently assigned to node U_+, and thus increasing the height of tree T. Assume that at some transaction time t the focus is extended to $V' > V$. This implies that queries (v', t') where $1 \le v' \le V'$ and $t \le t'$ will now have guaranteed performance. In case that we want to guarantee query performance for the same queries but going all the way to the past of transaction time (i.e., even for $t' < t$) the intervals that have been previously assigned to nodes C and U_+ (Fig.4) would have to be re-assigned. However, intervals that have been already assigned to T will not have to be re-assigned. It is an interesting open problem to find an I/O optimal access method for the bitemporal pure-timeslice query that can also dynamically change its valid-time universe.

7. Dividing Bitemporal Objects on Transaction Time

In this section we present a second methodology for addressing bitemporal queries. One of the disadvantages of using a single R-tree to keep bitemporal objects (as in Figure 2) is the large overlapping due to the "mix" of rectangles with known right endpoint and those extending to *now*. This affects update processing. For example, when at some transaction time t_2 an interval I which was "born" at t_1 is "deleted" a search for I is first performed, the rectangle for I that extends to *now* is physically deleted and a new rectangle for I that extends from t_1 to t_2 is inserted. The physically deleted rectangle of I (extending from t_1 to *now*) presents an extra "burden" to the structure for as long as it is in the R-tree. It affects updating because it extends to *now* and it is probable that will contain or intersect many other intervals especially if its valid time length is large, causing overlapping which in turn degrades the performance of the tree.

Therefore we propose using two different R-trees that keep bitemporal objects according to their right transaction time endpoint. When I is "born" at t_1 it is first inserted at the *front* R-tree. The front R-tree keeps all intervals for which the right transaction endpoint is unknown (i.e., extending to *now*). The *back* R-tree keeps the valid intervals with known transaction lifetime. When I is "deleted" at t_2 it is physically deleted from the front R-tree and is inserted as a rectangle of height I from t_1 to t_2 on the back R-tree (figure 6). Hence, the back R-tree need to only support insertions of rectangles. In the front R-tree a bitemporal object is represented as an interval that is perpendicular to the transaction axis. Such objects are inserted in increasing transaction time, however deletions can happen everywhere in the transaction axis.

Using two R-trees will asymptotically decrease update processing as overlapping is reduced only among the intervals of the front R-tree. A query about *(v,t)* is answered with two searches. The back R-tree is searched for all rectangles that contain point *(v,t)*. However transaction time creates a different problem: every interval in the front R-tree that has been inserted at transactions before *t* has to be checked for including valid time *v*. Hence, the front R-tree is searched for all intervals that intersect a horizontal interval at height *v* extending from *t* all the way until the beginning of transaction time. Many such intervals may not contain *v* and thus will not contribute to the answer.

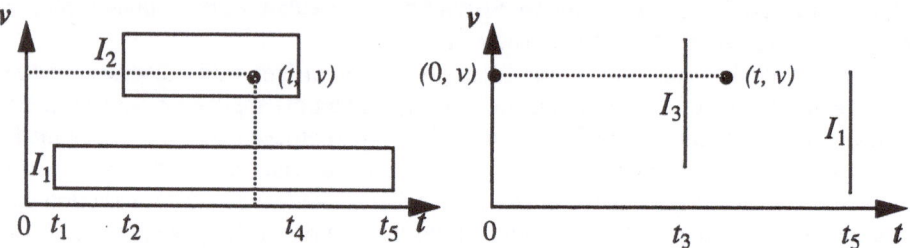

Fig. 6: In the two R-tree methodology, bitemporal data is divided according to whether the right transaction endpoint is known. The scenario of Fig. 2 is presented here. The left 2-dimensional space is stored in the *back* R-tree while the right in the *front* R-tree.

8. Performance Analysis

We compared through simulations the presented methodologies, i.e., the Bitemporal Interval Tree (BIT) and the two R-tree method (2-R) against the straightforward approach that uses a single R-tree (1-R). An R*-tree implementation [30] was used to implement each R-tree. The page size chosen for the simulations was 932 bytes. To compare the performance of the three structures we selected 8 data files, each containing 60000 updates (about 35000 inserts of valid time intervals and 25000 deletes).

To create a data file, the valid time intervals are first chosen. The starting point of a valid interval is selected randomly (with a uniform distribution) anywhere in set $U = \{1,..., 1024\}$ and the ending point was chosen uniformly within a range of K of the first point. Different values of K have been chosen for the different data files. Simulations numbered 1 through 7 have K equal to 5, 100, 200, 400, 500, 700 and 1000, respectively. Hence, as the simulation number increases, the average size of valid time intervals increases. Data for simulation number 8 has been created differently: valid interval endpoints are randomly selected within set U.

We then proceed with the transaction time evolution. We have assumed that at each transaction time exactly one update occurs. Hence there are 60000 transaction times. The simulations have been setup to start with about 4000 inserts, i.e., in each of the first 4000 transaction times a valid time interval is picked randomly for insertion (from the valid time intervals created above). This is done in order to get a structure with reasonable number of intervals before carrying out the deletes. At each transaction time with probability 0.7 we do a random insertion while with probability 0.3 we delete randomly one of the inserted intervals. Each data file also contains 10000 bitemporal puretimeslice queries. Each *(v,t)* query is selected by choosing the valid time *v* randomly with a uniform distribution within set U and the transaction time *t* randomly with a uniform distribution within the overall transaction space.

Firstly we compared the three algorithms for the average number of pages accessed for each update. The simulation results appear in Figure 7. The BIT method accesses about the same average number of pages for each update irrespectively of the data distribution; this is expected from the theoretical analysis of the BIT method since updating always follows a path of logarithmic size. Updating is based only on the interval being inserted/deleted. When an interval is deleted the only information given is the valid time interval (i.e, the interval's transaction birth time is not known). The R-tree methods first perform a search to find where the deleted interval is and then the actual deletion occurs. The number of pages accessed by the 1-R and 2-R approaches increases as the value of K increases. This is due to the overlapping created: intervals are wider and hence more pages are accessed during deletions. The 2-R method, is asymptotically better since searching the front R-tree for an interval to be deleted is more efficient (there are less overlapping intervals in the structure than in the 1-R case).

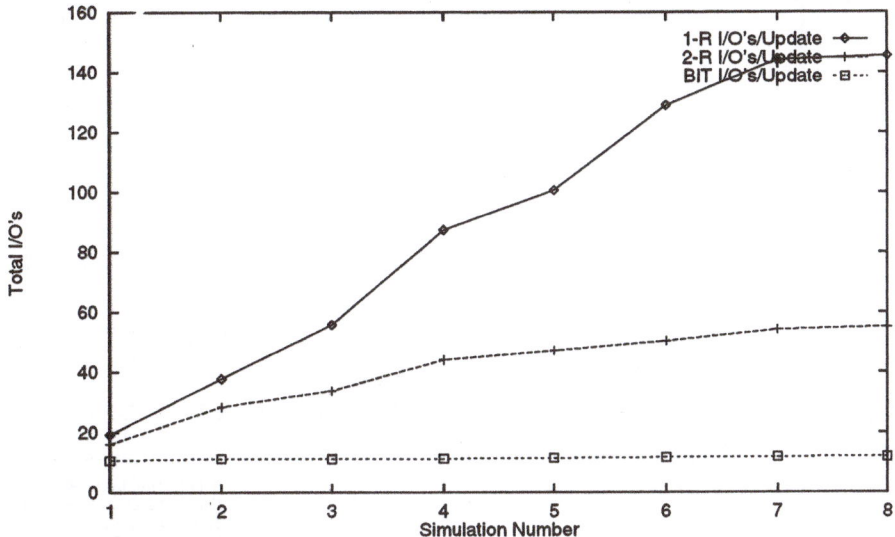

Fig. 7: Average number of I/O's per update in the BIT, 1-R and 2-R methods.

The space consumed per data file by each method appears in Figure 8. The 1-R approach as expected has the best overall space utilization. The 2-R method also uses one copy per bitemporal object, however the page utilization is slightly less. The implementation of the BIT method we used in the simulations needs about 3.6 to 4.8 times the number of pages needed for the 1-R tree method and about 3.1 to 4.3 times the number of pages needed for the 2-R tree method. It should be noted that most of the pages used in the BIT structure are used to store the lists of the interval tree nodes. Hence the overall space of the BIT can be reduced if instead of using the MVB spliting/merging policies [16] we use the data page policies of the TSB [6]. We did not implement the TSB policies but we have estimated the space requirement if using them. It appears to be about 3.2 times of the 1-R tree method and about 2.7 times of the 2-R tree method.

We also compared the query time performance of the three methods. Figure 9 shows the number of pages accessed per query averaged over 10000 random bitemporal pure-timeslice queries, for each of the data files. As the simulation number increases the average number of answers also increases (on the average there are 37, 700, 1300, 2500, 3000, 3800, 4900 answers/query for simulations #2 through #8 respectively). The BIT method gives the best performance of the three methods for all simulations. The 1-R tree method searches a larger number of pages since the data clustering is not optimal due to the overlap between the intervals stored in the different data pages. The 2-R tree method performs the worst of all. It was noted from the experiments that a large number of data pages is accessed in the front R-tree in this method (now a query may have a long transaction time dimension extending all the way to the past, and thus may access a large number of data pages with no answer).

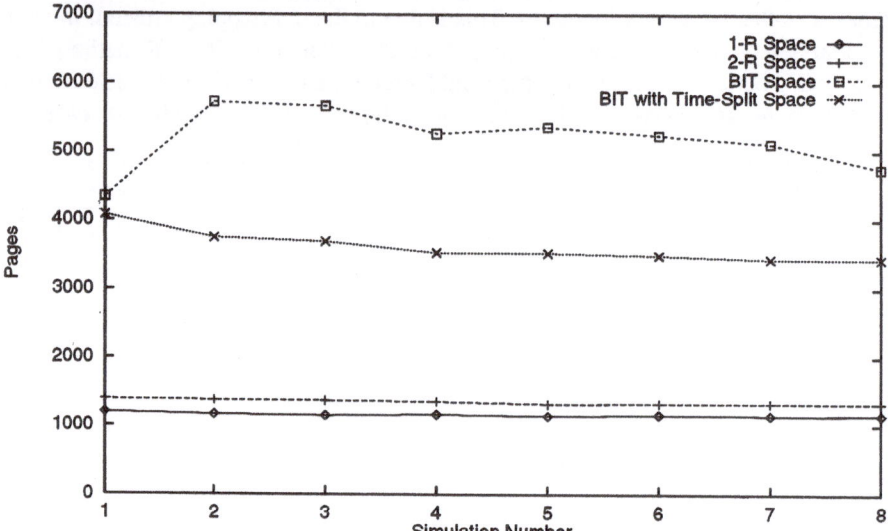

Fig. 8: Number of pages used in BIT, BIT with TSB (estimate only), 1-R, and 2-R methods.

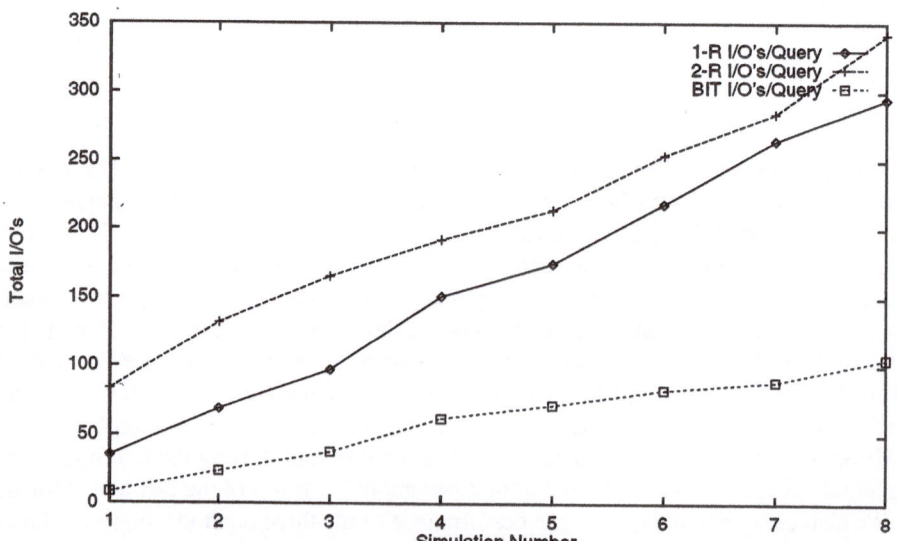

Fig. 9: Average number of I/O's per query in the BIT, 1-R and 2-R methods.

To summarize, the R-tree based methods clearly use less space since each data object appears only once. In addition, these methods are robust in the sense that they can support more dimensions, making range-timeslice bitemporal queries an easy extension. While the BIT method uses more copies per object (the space still being linear to the total number of updates) its average update processing and query times are better (and guaranteed even in the worst case). The choice of which approach to use is a space/time trade-off. For range-timeslice bitemporal queries we have been working with a partially persistence R-tree. Then the transaction-time behavior is addressed from persistence, allowing the R-tree to deal only with valid time intervals.

9. Conclusions

In this paper we have addressed the problem of designing efficient access methods for bitemporal queries. We have introduced two methodologies in designing such methods. The first methodology translates the bitemporal query into a partial persistence problem and then designs a method for the equivalent problem. This approach led to the Bitemporal Interval Tree for the bitemporal pure-timeslice query. This index is well paginated and provides good guaranteed worst case performance. The second methodology divides bitemporal objects in two categories, according to their transaction time behavior. In our implementations a separate R*-tree was used to store data in each category. We compared our approaches with a straightforward approach that keeps bitemporal objects in a single R*-tree. The R*-tree based methods use limited space, since each data object is kept only once. The Bitemporal Interval Tree uses more space (however still linear to the number of objects). The R*-tree based methods have update processing that depends greatly on the average size of the valid time intervals. In contrast, update processing in the Bitemporal Interval Tree is independent of that. Finally, the Bitemporal Interval Tree provides the best query performance among all methods. It remains an interesting open problem to find the I/O optimal solution for the bitemporal pure-timeslice query. We are currently researching more complex bitemporal queries (i.e., queries that include key ranges) using a partially persistent R* tree.

Acknowledgment

We would like to thank B. Seeger for kindly providing us the R* and MVB-tree codes.

References:

[1]   R. Snodgrass, I. Ahn. Temporal Databases. IEEE Computer,Vol.19,No.9, pp 35-42, 1986.

[2]   C.S. Jensen, editor et al. A Consensus Glossary of Temporal Database Concepts. ACM SIGMOD Record, Vol. 23, No. 1, pp. 52-64, 1994.

[3]   V. Lum, P. Dadam, R. Erbe, J. Guenauer, P. Pistor, G. Walch, H. Werner, J.Woodfill. Designing DBMS Support for the Temporal Database. Proc. ACM SIGMOD, pp 115-130, 1984.

[4]   I. Ahn, R. Snodgrass. Performance Evaluation of a Temporal Database Management System. Proc. ACM SIGMOD, pp 96-107, 1986.

[5]   M. Stonebraker. The Design of the Postgres Storage System. Proc. 13th Conference on Very Large Databases, pp 289-300, 1987.

[6]   D.Lomet, B.Salzberg.Access Methods for Multiversion Data. Proc. ACM SIGMOD,pp315-324, 1989.

[7]   D. Lomet, B. Salzberg. The Performance of a Multiversion Access Method. Proc. ACM SIGMOD, pp 353-363, 1990.

[8]   A. Segev, H. Gunadhi. Event-Join Optimization in Temporal Relational Databases. Proc. 15th Conference on Very Large Databases, pp 205-215, Aug. 1989.

[9]   Y. Manolopoulos, G. Kapetanakis. Overlapping B+ Trees for Temporal Data. Proc. of 5th JCIT Conf.,

Jerusalem, Israel. Oct.22-25, pp 491-498, 1990.

[10] R. Elmasri, G. Wuu, Y. Kim. The Time Index: An Access Structure for Temporal Data. Proc. 16th Conference on Very Large Databases, Aug. 1990.

[11] S. Lanka, E. Mays. Fully Persistent B$^+$ Trees. Proc. ACM SIGMOD, pp 426-435, 1991.

[12] C. Kolovson, M. Stonebraker. Segment Indexes: Dynamic Indexing Techniques for Multi-dimensional Interval Data. Proc. ACM SIGMOD, pp 138-147, 1991.

[13] C.S. Jensen, L Mark, N. Roussopoulos. Incremental Implementation Model for Relational Databases with Transaction Time. IEEE Trans. on Knowledge and Data Engineering, Vol. 3, No 4, pp 461-473, 1991.

[14] C. Kolovson. Indexing Techniques for Historical Databases. In A.Tansel, J. Clifford, S.K. Gadia, S. Jajodia, A. Segev, and R. Snodgrass (eds.), Temporal Databases: Theory, Design, and Implementation, Benjamin/Cummings, pp 418-432, 1993.

[15] T.Y.C. Leung, R.R. Muntz. Stream Processing: Temporal Query Processing and Optimization. In A.Tansel, J.Clifford, S.K.Gadia, S.Jajodia, A.Segev, and R.Snodgrass(eds.), Temporal Databases: Theory, Design and Implementation, Benjamin/Cummings, pp 329-355, 1993.

[16] B. Becker, S. Gschwind, T. Ohler, B. Seeger, P. Widmayer. On Optimal Multiversion Access Structures. Proceedings of Symposium on Large Spatial Databases, 1993. Published in Lecture Notes in Computer Science, Vol 692, pp. 123-141, Springer-Verlag (1993).

[17] V.J. Tsotras, N. Kangelaris. The Snapshot Index, an I/O-Optimal Access Method for Snapshot Queries. CATT-Tech. Report 93-68, Polytechnic University, Dec.1993. Also appears at the Information Systems, An International Journal, Vol. 20, No. 3, pp 237-260, 1995.

[18] H. Shen, B.C. Ooi, H. Lu. The TP-Index: A Dynamic and Efficient Indexing Mechanism for Temporal Databases. Proc.10th IEEE Intern. Conf. on Data Engineering, 1994.

[19] V.J. Tsotras, B. Gopinath, G.W.Hart. Efficient Management of Time-Evolving Databases. Accepted at the IEEE Trans. on Knowledge and Data Engineering, 1994.

[20] G.M. Landau, J.P. Schmidt, V.J. Tsotras. On Historical Queries along Multiple Lines of Time Evolution. To appear at the VLDB Journal, 1995.

[21] B. Salzberg, V.J. Tsotras. A Comparison of Access Methods for Time-Evolving Data. Submitted for publication; available as a technical report from Polytechnic University (CATT-TR-94-81), or, Northeastern University (NU-CCS-94-21), 1994.

[22] Y.J. Chiang, R. Tamassia. Dynamic Algorithms in Computational Geometry. Proceedings of IEEE, Special Issue on Computational Geometry, Vol 80, No 9, pp 362-381, 1992.

[23] E.M. McCreight. Priority Search Trees. SIAM Journal of Computing, Vol.14, No 2, pp 257-276, 1985.

[24] A. Guttman.R-Trees: A Dynamic Index Structure for Spatial Searching. Proc. ACM SIGMOD, 1984.

[25] P.C. Kanellakis, S. Ramaswamy, D.E. Vengroff, J.S. Vitter. Indexing for Data Models with Constraints and Classes. Proc. ACM PODS, pp 233-243, 1993.

[26] S. Ramaswamy, S. Subramanian. Path Caching: a Technique for Optimal External Searching. Proc. 13th ACM PODS, pp 25-35, 1994.

[27] R. Agrawal, C. Faloutsos, A. Swami. Efficient Similarity Search in Sequence Databases. Proc. FODO Conference, 1993.

[28] C. Faloutsos, M. Ranganathan, Y. Manolopoulos. Fast Subsequence Matching in Time-Series Databases. Proc. ACM SIGMOD, pp 419-429, 1994.

[29] R.Snodgrass et.al. TSQL92 Language Specification.ACM SIGMOD Rec.Vol 23, No1, pp65-86, 1994.

[30] N. Beckmann, H.P. Kriegel, R. Schneider, B. Seeger. The R*-tree: An efficient and Robust Access Method for Points and Rectangles. Proc. ACM SIGMOD, pp 322-331, 1990.

[31] J.R. Driscoll, N. Sarnak, D. Sleator, R.E. Tarjan. Making Data Structures Persistent. J. of Comp. and Syst. Sci., Vol 38, pp 86-124, 1989.

[32] H. Edelsbrunner. A new Approach to Rectangle Intersections, Part I&II. Int. Journal of Computer Mathematics, Vol. 13, pp 209-229, 1983.

[33] J.L. Bentley. Algorithms for Klee's Rectangle Problems. Computer Science Department, Carnegie-Mellon University, Pittsburgh, 1977.

[34] H. Samet. The Design and Analysis of Spatial Data Structures. Addison-Wesley, 1989.

[35] A.Kumar, V.J. Tsotras, C. Faloutsos. On designing Access Methods for Bitemporal Databases. Polytechnic University Tech. Report (CATT-TR-95-85), 1995.

[36] B.Chazelle. Filtering Search: a new approach to query answering. Proc.24th IEEE FOCS,1983.

[37] R. Cole. Searching and Storing Similar Lists. J.of Algorithms, Vol 7, pp 202-220. 1986.

Transaction Support in a Temporal DBMS

Costas Vassilakis
Department of Informatics, University of Athens
Panepistimiopolis, TYPA buildings, 15771, Athens, Greece

Nikos Lorentzos
Agricultural University of Athens
Iera Odos 75, 11855, Athens, Greece

Panagiotis Georgiadis
Department of Informatics, University of Athens
Panepistimiopolis, TYPA buildings, 15771, Athens, Greece

Abstract

Transactions are a significant concept in database systems, facilitating functions both at user and system level. However transaction support in temporal DBMSs has not yet received enough research attention. In this paper, we present techniques for incorporating transaction support in a temporal DBMS, which is implemented as an additional layer to a commercial RDBMS. These techniques overcome certain limitations imposed by the underlying RDBMS, and avoid excessive increment of the log size.

1 Introduction.

Transactions are an important feature of database systems. At user level, transactions are the unit of *integrity* ([1]), allowing the database to go from a valid state to another passing from an invalid state, provide the ability to undo erroneous changes, and provide an atomic, "all-or-nothing" abstraction ([2]), which makes programming tasks easier. At system level transactions constitute the unit of *sharing* ([1]), and *recovery*. For example, locks acquired during a session are released at the end of the active transaction and after a system failure the database can be restored to its state, at a COMMIT point.

In this paper, we present techniques for incorporating transactions in a layered temporal DBMS ([3]). The temporal DBMS uses an interval extended relational model ([4]), for temporal data representation. VT-SQL ([5]), a consistent extension to SQL89, is its data definition and manipulation language. Data are timestamped at tuple level, and valid time relations are coalesced. The temporal DBMS is split in two layers, the lower one being a commercial RDBMS (INGRES), which is used for data storage and retrieval. The kernel of the RDBMS has been extended, to support an additional data type, DATEINTERVAL, as well as operations on this type. The upper layer is the *temporal engine*, coded in C and embedded SQL, which supports the valid time semantics. One component in this layer is VT-RA, a Valid Time Relational Algebra. Figure 1 illustrates the overall temporal RDBMS architecture.

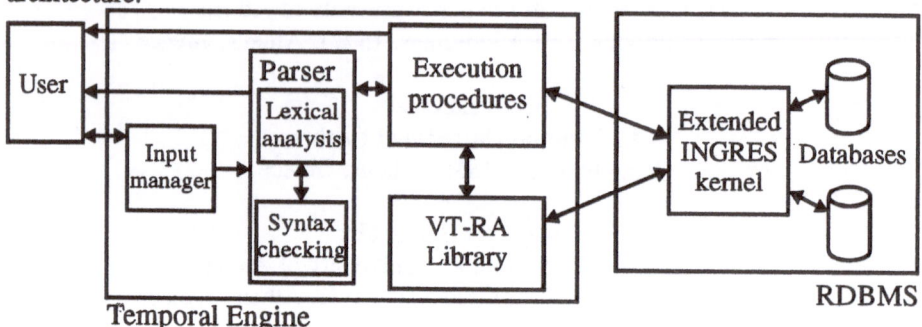

Figure 1 - Temporal RDBMS architecture

Transaction support in such a layered temporal RDBMS cannot rely on the support offered by the RDBMS for two reasons:

1. In many cases, the temporal engine must create temporary tables to store intermediate results (e.g. the table holding the updated tuples in the execution of the UPDATE statement or the table holding the result of the extended SELECT, in the execution of the INSERT statement, according to the algorithms presented below). However, in some DBMSs (e.g. ORACLE), issuing a DDL statement, such as CREATE TABLE or DROP TABLE, introduces an implicit commit point ([6]), so changes to the database state made before that point, cannot be undone using a ROLLBACK statement. Other DBMSs (e.g. Sybase) disallow the usage of DDL statements within multi statement transactions ([7]).

2. Writing results to intermediate tables is logged (as all modification operations are). Since, the execution procedures of the VT-SQL statements produce substantial amount of intermediate results, the size of the log space increases considerably. Thus, techniques should be developed to reduce log space requirements.

The rest of this paper is organised as follows: In section 2, the Valid Time Relational Algebra is presented, in brief. In section 3, the syntax and semantics of VT-SQL are described. Section 4 presents the algorithms used for the DML statements, in order to provide transaction support. Section 5 addresses protection and crash recovery issues arising from the techniques described in section 4. The last section concludes and outlines future work.

2 Valid time relational algebra.

The design of the temporal RDBMS has been based on Valid Time Relational Algebra (VT-AL) ([4]), a consistent extension to Codd's algebra ([8]). New data types have been introduced for the representation of time, namely DATE and DATEINTERVAL. Date literals have the format YYYY-MM-DD, which is a more readable form of the ANSI standard. DATEINTERVAL values are denoted as $[d_i, d_j)$, where d_i and d_j are dates, and d_i is before d_j. A DATEINTERVAL value contains all dates from d_i and up to, but not including d_j. VT-RA defines transformations between the representations of time (points and intervals), new predicates for interval comparison, as well as extended UNION and EXCEPT operations, which are applicable to relations containing attributes of type DATE and/or DATEINTERVAL. These operations are described briefly in the following paragraphs. A detailed presentation can be found in [4] and [9].

2.1 Fold.

Let R be a relation whose schema is $(A_1, A_2, ..., A_n)$. When R is folded on column A_i (denoted as FOLD[A_i] (R)), where the domain of A_i is of a DATE or DATEINTERVAL type, all its tuples whose A_j columns have identical values $\forall j \neq i$, and their A_i columns can merge (i.e. are overlapping or adjacent), are replaced in the resulting relation by a single tuple with the same values in the A_j columns $\forall j \neq i$, but its i-th component is formed by the *merging* of the i-th components of these tuples. For example, if SALARY is any of the relations in figure 2, then FOLD[Time] (SALARY) yields the relation in figure 3.

The FOLD operation may apply to multiple columns. This is denoted by FOLD [$A_{i_1}, A_{i_2}, ..., A_{i_n}$] (R), and is equivalent to folding relation R on column A_{i_1}, then on column A_{i_2} and so on up to column A_{i_n}.

SALARY

Name	Amount	Time
John	10K	d1
John	10K	d2
...	...	...
John	10K	d4
John	10K	d10
...	...	...
John	10K	d14
Alex	12K	d1
...	...	...
Alex	12K	d19

SALARY

Name	Amount	Time
John	10K	[d1, d3)
John	10K	[d2, d5)
John	10K	[d10, d15)
Alex	12K	[d1, d10)
Alex	12K	[d10, d15)
Alex	12K	[d15, d18)
Alex	12K	[d16, d20)

(a)   (b)

Figure 2 - Two valid time relations

SALARY

Name	Amount	Time
John	10K	[d1, d5)
John	10K	[d10, d15)
Alex	12K	[d1, d20)

Figure 3 - A valid time relation

2.2 Unfold.

When a relation R is unfolded on attribute A_i (denoted as UNFOLD $[A_i]$ (R)), where the domain of A_i is of a DATE or DATEINTERVAL type, each tuple $(t_1, ..., t_{i-1}, t_i, t_{i+1}, ..., t_n)$ of R is replaced in the resulting relation by a family of tuples $(t_1, ..., t_{i-1}, t_{i_j}, t_{i+1}, ..., t_n)$, where each t_{i_j} is a date included in t_i (as a trivial case, a date is considered to include only itself). For example, if SALARY is the relation in figure 3, then UNFOLD[Time] (SALARY) yields the relation in figure 2(a). An UNFOLD may apply to multiple columns; this is denoted by UNFOLD $[A_{i_1}, A_{i_2}, ..., A_{i_n}]$ (R), and is equivalent to unfolding relation R on column A_{i_1}, then on column A_{i_2} and so on up to column A_{i_n}.

2.3 Normalise.

The NORMALISE operation can be applied to multiple columns of type DATE or DATEINTERVAL. It is denoted by NORMALISE $[A_{i_1}, ..., A_{i_n}]$ (R), and is semantically equivalent to FOLD $[A_{i_1}, ..., A_{i_n}]$ (UNFOLD $[A_{i_1}, ..., A_{i_n}]$ (R)). The NORMALISE operation is thus introduced for notational convenience.

2.4 PUnion.

The PUNION operation can be applied to two union-compatible relations and operates on multiple columns of type DATE or DATEINTERVAL. Two relations R and S are union-compatible if:
1. The number of columns in R is the same as the number of columns in S and
2. Column R_i is type-compatible with column S_i, $\forall$ i.

The PUNION operation of two relations R and S is denoted by R PUNION $[A_{i_1}, ..., A_{i_n}]$ S and is equivalent to applying NORMALISE $[A_{i_1}, ..., A_{i_n}]$ to the result of R UNION S. For example, if a relation S has a single tuple,

$$(John, 10K, [d3, d12))$$

and SALARY is the table in figure 3, then the result of SALARY PUNION [Time] S consists of the two tuples

(John, 10K, [d1, d15))
(Alex, 12K, [d1, d20))

2.5 PExcept.

The PEXCEPT operation can be applied to two union-compatible relations and operates on multiple columns of type DATE or DATEINTERVAL. The PEXCEPT operation of two relations R and S is denoted by R PEXCEPT $[A_{i_1}, ..., A_{i_n}]$ S and is equivalent to applying the FOLD $[A_{i_1}, ..., A_{i_n}]$ operation to the result of the

UNFOLD $[A_{i_1}, ..., A_{i_n}]$ (R) EXCEPT UNFOLD $[A_{i_1}, ..., A_{i_n}]$ (S)

operation. For example, if a relation S consists of the two tuples

(John, 10K, [d10, d15))
(Alex, 12K, [d10, d15))

and SALARY is the table in figure 3, then SALARY PEXCEPT [Time] S consists of the tuples

(John, 10K, [d1, d5))
(Alex, 12K, [d1, d10))
(Alex, 12K, [d15, d20))

Tables which require the use of PUNION (PEXCEPT) for data insertion (deletion) rather than UNION (EXCEPT) are called *normalised.*

3 VT-SQL syntax and semantics.

The DDL statements of VT-SQL are the same as in SQL, except for the CREATE TABLE statement, which has been extended to allow for the specification of the primary key of a valid time table (see section 3.2, below). In the following paragraphs, therefore, the syntax and semantics of the VT-SQL DML statements is presented. A complete presentation of the VT-SQL syntax and semantics, can be found in [5]. In the syntax, which follows, terms enclosed in brackets ([]) are optional; braces ({}) are used for items that may be repeated zero or more times; parentheses are used for grouping, and single quotes are used for parentheses which must be typed literally; capitals indicate reserved words and italics are used for user-provided values.

3.1 The Select statement.

The VT-SQL syntax for the SELECT statement is

```
extended-select
[(UNION | UNION ALL | EXCEPT) [ResultColumnList]
[extended-select]
[ORDER BY ResultColumn [ASC | DESC]
         {, ResultColumn [ASC | DESC]}]
```

The *extended-select* is defined as

```
sql-select
[REFORMAT AS [(FOLD | UNFOLD) columnList
             {(FOLD | UNFOLD) columnList}]
[NORMALISE ON ResultColumnList]
```

(Note that another version of UNFOLD, namely UNFOLD ALL, is also described in [9] but has been omitted here, for brevity reasons.) An *extended-select* is executed by evaluating its *sql-select* part, and then applying the REFORMAT/NORMALISE operations specified by the corresponding clauses. If the VT-SQL select statement includes a second *extended-select*, then the result of each of the two *extended-select* is computed, and a VT-RA operation is applied to them, in order to evaluate the final query outcome (this presumes that the schemata of the results of the two *extended-selects* are union-compatible). The UNION keyword specifies that either the VT-RA PUNION or the standard UNION operation should be applied, depending on whether the keyword UNION is followed by a column list or not, respectively. In the former case, the column list specifies the columns on which the PUNION operation will normalise the final result; these columns must be of type DATEINTERVAL or DATE. The ALL keyword may follow the UNION keyword, indicating that duplicate occurrences of result tuples should be retained. Analogously, the EXCEPT keyword specifies that either the PEXCEPT or EXCEPT operation must be applied, depending on whether the keyword is followed by a column list or not. Finally, the ORDER BY clause follows the SQL89 specification.

3.2 The Insert statement.

The syntax of the VT-SQL INSERT statement is identical with that of the SQL INSERT, except one case: If the tuples to be inserted are specified by a query, this query may be an *extended-select*. When data are inserted in a non-normalised table, the semantics of the INSERT statement are identical with the semantics of its SQL counterpart. If, however, the tuples are inserted into a normalised table, then an ordinary insertion takes place, followed by a NORMALISE operation on the appropriate columns.

The concept of the key of a table has been extended to normalised relations. Thus, the key of SALARY, in figure 3, is <Name, Time-p>. This means that SALARY may never contain two tuples, $t1$ and $t2$, which satisfy both (i) t1.Name = t2.Name and (ii) t1.Time and t2.Time are two dateintervals which have at least one date in common. We say that SALARY preserves the uniqueness of the primary key *at a date level*.

If the key of a normalised relation R has been defined and a piece of data, which is to be inserted, has already been recorded in R, then the transaction is aborted. For example, consider SALARY, in figure 3, with key <Name, Time-p>. If we issue the command

```
INSERT INTO SALARY
VALUES ('John', 10K, '[d4, d10)')
```

the insertion will fail, because John's salary for date $d4$ is already in SALARY. This implementation convention is an extension of that in standard SQL.

3.3 The Delete statement.

A PORTION clause has been added to the DELETE statement, which may be used when deleting data from a normalised table. If the PORTION is present in a DELETE statement, it designates the valid time period to which the deletion applies. If the PORTION clause is not specified, the deletion applies to whole tuples. For example, after the execution of the command

```
DELETE FROM SALARY
PORTION Time = '[d3, d12)'
WHERE Name = 'John'
```

then SALARY, in figure 3, will consist of the tuples

$$(John, 10K, [d1, d3))$$
$$(John, 10K, [d12, d15))$$
$$(Alex, 12K, [d1, d20))$$

3.4 The Update statement.

When updating a non-normalised table, UPDATE behaves exactly as in SQL. If, however, the table is normalised, the update is followed by a NORMALISE operation on the appropriate columns. Analogously to the DELETE statement, the UPDATE of a normalised table may contain a PORTION clause, which specifies the valid time period to which the update is applied. For example, the command

```
UPDATE SALARY
PORTION Time = '[d3, d5)'
SET Name = 'Tom'
WHERE Name = 'John'
```

will result in that SALARY, in figure 3, will consist of the tuples

(John, 10K, [d1, d3))
(John, 10K, [d10, d15))
(Tom, 10K, [d3, d5))
(Alex, 12K, [d1, d20))

Again, if the table preserves the uniqueness of the primary key *at a date level*, the transaction is aborted if the update may result in a table, which violates this uniqueness.

4 Transaction support.

Transaction support can be facilitated in a layered temporal RDBMS by having the temporal engine connected *twice* to the RDBMS, thus opening two sessions, the *user session* and the *system session*. User tables are always accessed (both for reading and writing) through the user session. The system session is used in order to issue to the RDBMS the DDL statements which create or drop the temporary tables, as well as the DML statements which insert or modify data in these tables. Data in the temporary tables can be read by both the user and the system session.

Different sessions to the RDBMS have independent commit modes, i.e. statements issued through a session do not affect the commit status of other sessions. Locking also takes place at session level, i.e. objects locked in shared or exclusive mode by one session are not available for update or access to other sessions, so care must be taken that the locking scheme does not lead to deadlocks.

In the following paragraphs, the usage of the two sessions, as well as the locking schemes employed, to provide full transaction support, are described in detail.

4.1 The Select statement.

Three cases are considered for the evaluation of the SELECT statement (for a complete description, see [3]):

1. If the SELECT statement does not imply the application of operations not supported by the RDBMS (i.e. REFORMAT, NORMALISE, PUNION and PEXCEPT operations), the temporal engine opens a cursor through the user session, for the user query. The result tuples are fetched through this cursor and presented to the user.

2. If the user query consists of only one *extended-select* then the following steps are taken:

   A. A temporary table is created through the system session, whose schema matches the schema of the table resulting from the *sql-select*. A cursor is opened through the user session for the *sql-select* part of the user query.

   B. The cursor opened in step (A) is used to fetch the result tuples, which are inserted into the temporary table through the system session. When all result tuples have been inserted into the temporary table, the system session commits, emptying its log space.

C. The REFORMAT and NORMALISE clauses are executed from within the system session. As soon as each operation stated in each clause completes, the temporary table holding the results of the previous step is dropped through the system session, and the system session commits.

D. The tuples contained in the final temporary table are fetched through the system session, and forwarded to the user. When all data has been exhausted, the final temporary table is dropped through the system session, and the system session commits.

3. If the user query consists of two *extended-select* statements, combined by a UNION, EXCEPT, PUNION, PUNION ALL or PEXCEPT operation, then the following procedure is used:

A. Steps (A)-(C) of case 2 are performed to evaluate each of the *extended-select* statements, storing the results in intermediate tables.

B. The UNION, EXCEPT, PUNION, PUNION ALL or PEXCEPT operation is applied through the system session to the intermediate tables produced in step (A), and the results are stored in a temporary table. Upon operation completion, the intermediate tables produced in step (A) are dropped through the system session, and the system session commits.

C. The tuples contained in the temporary table created in step (B) are fetched through the system session, and forwarded to the user. Finally, the temporary table is dropped through the system session, and the system session commits.

The execution procedure described above for the SELECT statement does not introduce any implicit commit points for the user session and does not expand the user session log file (only the system session's log is expanded, but only transiently, as it is truncated at the system session's commit points). Furthermore, since the user tables are handled by the user session and all temporary tables are accessed through the system session, no deadlock problems are introduced.

4.2 The Insert statement.

Insertions issued against non-normalised tables, can directly be forwarded for execution, through the user session, to the underlying RDBMS. The algorithm employed for data insertion in a normalised table R considers four distinct cases, (i)-(iv), below. In the sequel, the columns of any table R will be denoted as R_{c1}, R_{c2}, ..., R_{cN}, R_{vt}, with R_{vt} being the column storing the valid time of the tuple. Columns not participating in the primary key -which includes all the columns from R_{c1} through R_{cN} if no primary key is defined on the table- will be denoted as R_{nonKey}, and columns participating in the primary key -except for R_{vt}- will be referenced as R_{key}.

Case (i): *The values to be inserted are specified by means of the VALUES clause, and no primary key is defined on the table.*

The temporal engine opens a cursor *ins_cur* on the target relation through the user session, selecting all tuples which are *value equivalent* to the insertion tuple (i.e. each column in R_{nonKey} is equal to the corresponding column in the insertion tuple) and have overlapping or adjacent valid times. Each qualifying tuple is deleted from the target relation through cursor *ins_cur* (for which the fetched tuple is current), and the valid time of the insertion tuple is replaced by the union of its current value and the timestamp of the deleted tuple (the union of two adjacent or overlapping dateintervals is a dateinterval containing all time points in both arguments). Finally, the insertion tuple is appended to the target relation, through the user session.

In this case, all interaction with the RDBMS is performed through the user session, so no deadlock problems are introduced. Furthermore, changes to the database state are almost minimal, so log size increment is kept low (the minimum changes would be deleting all the selected value equivalent tuples except the last one, whose timestamp should be updated to the coalescing of the timestamps of all the selected value equivalent tuples.

Case (ii): *The values to be inserted are specified by means of the VALUES clause, and a primary key has been defined on the table.*

The algorithm starts off with one insertion tuple, holding the values specified in the VALUES clause. A *savepoint Save1* is created for the user session (the name of the savepoint is actually a unique, system-generated string), and a cursor *ins_cur* is opened on the target table, through the user session, selecting all tuples for which all the columns in R_{key} have values equal to the values of the corresponding table in the insertion tuple, and their valid times are adjacent or overlapping to the timestamp of the insertion tuple. For each tuple that is fetched through the cursor, the following checks are made:

1. If the valid time of the fetched tuple is overlapping with the valid time of the insertion tuple, then the INSERT statement violates primary key uniqueness. The user session is rolled back to the savepoint created at the beginning of the algorithm, by issuing a

```
ROLLBACK TO Save1
```

statement through the user session, and further processing is aborted.

2. If all columns in R_{nonKey} of the fetched tuple have values equal to the corresponding columns of the insertion tuple, then the fetched tuple is deleted from the target table, through cursor *ins_cur*, and the valid time of the insertion tuple is replaced by the union of its former value and the value of the fetched tuple's valid time.

3. In all other cases, i.e. if any column in R_{nonKey} of the fetched tuple is not equal to the corresponding column of the insertion tuple, the algorithm continues with the next tuple.

When no more tuples can be fetched through the cursor, the insertion tuple is appended to the table, through the user session.

Remarks about locking problems and log size increment for the previous case (in which no primary key is defined), hold for this case too.

Case (iii): *The values to be inserted are specified by means of an extended-select query, and no primary key has been defined on the table.*

The *extended-select* is evaluated as described in subsection 4.1, and the result is stored in a temporary table (if the query can directly be supported by the RDBMS, a cursor is opened through the user session, fetching the result tuples, which are stored in a temporary table, through the system session; if the query consists of an SQL SELECT, followed by a REFORMAT and/or a NORMALISE clause, then only steps (A) to (C) are performed). The temporary table holding the result of the *extended-select* will be denoted as *T1* (its name is actually a unique, system-generated string). Subsequently, the temporal engine opens a cursor on table *R* through the user session, selecting all tuples which can be coalesced with any tuple in *T1*, i.e. tuples for which every column in R_{nonKey} has value equal to the corresponding column in $T1_{nonkey}$ and the value of R_{vt} is overlapping or adjacent to the value of $T1_{vt}$. Since tuple fetching through this cursor implies access to table *T1*, which will be dropped afterwards through the system session, it is important that this access does not place any locks on the tuples of *T1*. This is accomplished by issuing a statement

```
SET LOCKMODE ON TABLE T1 WHERE READLOCK = NOLOCK;
```

through the user session, prior to opening the cursor (this command is an INGRES extension to SQL89 ([10]); the syntax in other DBMSs may be different). Each qualifying tuple is fetched into memory, and deleted from the target table, through the user session, and subsequently inserted through the system session in table *T1*. Afterwards, the system session is used to perform a normalisation operation on table *T1*, each tuple of the FOLD operation's result is fetched into memory through the system session, and inserted into the target table through the user session. Finally, the temporary tables are dropped through the system session, and the system session commits.

This algorithm does not present deadlock problems, since when the user session accesses the temporary tables, created and altered through the system session, it does so without requiring or imposing any locks. During these accesses, the system session is quiescent, so no concurrency problems are introduced, due to absence of locks. Finally, the only changes made through the user session are the deletions of the tuples that can be coalesced with any of the insertion tuples, plus the actual insertion of the resulting tuples in the target table, keeping log size increment at reasonable levels.

Case (iv): *The values to be inserted are specified by means of an extended-select query, and a primary key has been defined on the table.*

A *savepoint* is introduced for the user session, the *extended-select* is evaluated and the results are stored in a temporary table, as described for the previous case. Afterwards, the temporal engine renounces its locking rights for the user session on table *T1* by issuing a statement

```
SET LOCKMODE ON TABLE T1 WHERE READLOCK = NOLOCK;
```

through the user session; the same session is used to open a cursor, on the join of the target table and *T1*, selecting those tuples for which all columns in R_{Key} have values equal to the corresponding columns of table *T1* and R_{vt} is overlapping or adjacent to $T1_{vt}$. For each one of these tuples, all columns of table *R*, and columns in $T1_{nonKey}$ and $T1_{vt}$ are fetched into the main memory, and the following checks are made:

1. If the values of R_{vt} and $T1_{vt}$ are overlapping, the insert operation is aborted, due to the presence of duplicate keys; the database is rolled back to the savepoint introduced at the beginning of the algorithm execution, and further processing is aborted.

2. If the values of R_{vt} and $T1_{vt}$ are adjacent, and all columns in R_{nonKey} have values equal to the corresponding columns in $T1_{nonKey}$, the current tuple of the target table is deleted, through the user session, and subsequently inserted into $T1$, through the system session (the values are currently into the main memory, so they can be inserted immediately).

3. In all other cases, the fetched tuple is ignored.

When this process completes, the system session commits, and a cursor is opened on table $T1$, through the system session, fetching all the fields of each row, sorted on columns $T1_{key}$, $T1_{vt}$, $T1_{nonkey}$, in that order. The first row is fetched and marked as *working tuple*, and the algorithm proceeds as follows:

1. The next tuple is fetched through the cursor. If data has been exhausted, *working tuple* is inserted into the target table through the user session and the algorithm continues with step (5), otherwise the fetched tuple is marked as *current tuple*, and the algorithm continues with step (2).

2. If either the value of any of the columns in $T1_{key}$ is different in *working tuple* and *current tuple* or the values of $T1_{vt}$ in the two tuples are neither overlapping nor adjacent, then *working tuple* is inserted into the target table through the user session, *current tuple* replaces *working tuple* and step (1) is performed again.

3. If the values of $T1_{vt}$ in *working tuple* and *current tuple* are overlapping (note that at this step the values of these two tuples on $T1_{key}$, are equal), then the operation produces duplicate keys; the database is rolled back to the savepoint introduced at the beginning of the algorithm execution and further processing is aborted.

4. If the value of any of the columns in $T1_{nonKey}$ is different in *working tuple* and *current tuple*, then *working tuple* is inserted into the target table through the user session and *current tuple* replaces *working tuple*; otherwise, $T1_{vt}$ in working tuple is replaced by the union of its former value and the value of $T1_{vt}$ in the *current tuple* and *current tuple* is discarded and control passes to step (1).

5. Temporary tables are dropped through the system session and the system session commits.

The remarks made about the absence of deadlocks and log size increment for the previous case, hold for this case too.

In some RDBMSs (e.g. Ingres) locking control statements, such as *SET LOCKMODE* can be issued only at the beginning of a multi-statement transaction. If this is the case, then the default read locking mode of the user session should be set to 'no locking', when the session is opened, and the user should use the *SET LOCKMODE* command, to specify the tables to which read access should result to locking. Note that this modification does not result to loss of locking capabilities, but to a change of default behaviour.

4.3 The Delete statement.

If the PORTION clause is not specified in the DELETE statement, the request is directly forwarded to the underlying RDBMS for execution, through the user session. If, however, the PORTION clause is specified, the following actions are taken, in order to satisfy the user request: The temporal engine opens, through the user session, a cursor on the target table, selecting the rows matching the criteria stated in the WHERE clause and having valid times overlapping with the period specified in the PORTION clause (denoted as *period*, hereafter). For each selected tuple, the values of all fields along with the value of *period* are fetched into main memory, and one of the following actions is taken:

1. If the value of *period* is a superinterval of the value of R_{vt}, then the tuple is deleted from the target table, through the user session.
2. If the difference R_{vt} - *period* yields exactly one interval (i.e. the time points included in R_{vt} but not in *period* are consecutive and, consequently, can be represented by a single DATEINTERVAL value) then the value of R_{vt} of the current tuple is set to R_{vt} - *period*, through the user session.
3. If the difference R_{vt} - *period* yields two intervals, *diff1* and *diff2*, the value of R_{vt} of the current tuple is set to *diff1*, and a new tuple is appended to the target table, for which columns R_{c1}, ..., R_{cN} are equal to the values of the corresponding columns in the current tuple, whereas the value of column R_{vt} is equal to *diff2*. Both the value change and the tuple insertion are performed through the user session.

Since the whole interaction is performed through the user session, the algorithm is deadlock free. The changes made to the database state are also kept to an absolute minimum, resulting in the minimum increment to the log size.

4.4 The Update statement.

If the UPDATE statement is applied to a non-normalised table, the UPDATE can directly be forwarded for execution to the underlying DBMS. If, however, the target table is normalised, then the following cases are considered:

Case (i): *The table has no primary key, and the PORTION clause is not specified.*

The temporal engine opens a cursor on the target table, through the user session, selecting tuples qualifying with respect to the WHERE clause. For each selected tuple, all columns are fetched into memory, and the new values for the fields referenced in the SET clause are computed; the selected tuple is deleted from the table, through the user session, and a tuple containing the updated values is stored in a temporary table, through the system session (the table will be denoted as *update_temp* and is created through the system session). When all qualifying tuples have been fetched, the system session commits, and the algorithm described for case (iii) in subsection 4.2 is employed to insert the tuples of *update_temp* into the target table (obviously, the step involving the execution of the *extended-select* is not performed; table *T1* mentioned in subsection 4.2 is actually the *update_temp* table, produced in the previous step).

No deadlock problems are introduced through this algorithm, since the user session is used to access the user table, and subsequently a deadlock-free insertion algorithm is used. Log size increment is kept low, since every tuple update maps to one deletion and one insertion through the user session (actually, more deletions can be performed, if some updated tuple can be coalesced with some tuple which is not updated).

Case (ii): *The table has no primary key and the PORTION clause is specified.*

The temporal engine opens a cursor on the target table through the user session, selecting the tuples which qualify with respect to the WHERE clause and for which the value of R_{vt} overlaps with the value of the period specified in the PORTION clause. For each qualifying tuple, all the original values of the columns, the new values for the columns to be updated and the value of the period in the PORTION clause (denoted as *period*, hereafter)are fetched into main memory. Depending on the values of R_{vt} and *period*, one of the actions (1)-(3) described in subsection 4.3 is performed, in order to delete the updated portion of the tuple from the target table. After the designated information has been removed, a tuple is inserted through the system session into a temporary table *update_temp* (which will have been created through the system session). The values of the columns of this tuple are determined using the following algorithm:

1. If the column appears on the left hand side of an assignment in the SET clause, then the value of the corresponding right hand side expression is used.
2. If the column is not updated, then its original value is used, except for column R_{vt}, for which the value of the *expression* appearing in the PORTION clause is used.

When all qualifying rows have been dealt with, the rows in *update_temp* are inserted in the target table using the algorithm described in subsection 4.2 for case (iii). (The step of evaluating the *extended-select* is skipped and *update_temp* replaces *T1*.)

Remarks made on the absence of deadlocks for the previous case, hold for this case too. Log size increment is also kept low, with every update mapping to either one tuple deletion and one insertion or one update and one insertion or one update and two insertions, depending on the portion of the tuple which will be updated.

Case (iii): *The table has a primary key and the PORTION clause is not specified.*

The algorithm employed for case (i) can be used here, modified so that a *savepoint* is introduced for the user session at the beginning of the operation, and the resulting tuples are inserted into the target table using the algorithm for inserting data in a table for which a key is defined (case (iv) of the INSERT statement, with the necessary amendments: The step of evaluating the *extended-select* is skipped, *update_temp* replaces *T1* and the savepoint introduced at the start of the operation is used when the database should be rolled back due to primary key uniqueness violation). Remarks on the absence of deadlocks and log size increment for case (i) hold for this case too.

Case (iv): *the table has a primary key and the PORTION clause is specified.*

The algorithm described for case (ii) can be used for this case, modified so that a *savepoint* is introduced for the user session at the beginning of the operation, and the resulting tuples are inserted in the target table using the algorithm for inserting data in a table for which a key is defined (case (iv) of the INSERT statement, with the necessary amendments). Remarks on the absence of deadlocks and log size increment for case (ii) hold for this case too.

5 Protection and crash recovery.

This section presents techniques for dealing with protection and crash recovery issues, arising from the algorithms presented in section 4. A protection scheme which prevents ad-hoc modification of temporary tables is presented in section 5.1, and an algorithm for removing temporary tables which remained in the database because of a system crash is described in section 5.2.

5.1 Protection scheme for temporary tables.

The correctness of data contained in temporary tables is a crucial point for the successful completion of the operations described in the previous sections. Thus, it is important to prevent users from modifying the contents of temporary tables. User access to these tables must also be avoided, as locks may be placed, which can lead to substantial delays (e.g. the system session will have to wait until these locks are released, before dropping the table) or even deadlocks.

In general, the life span of temporary tables is limited and, actually, users ignore the names of temporary tables, so the probability of user access is limited. However, it is possible that during the evaluation of a complex query or in a period of increased system load, some user acquires information about the name of a temporary table (by querying an RDBMS system catalogue) and access it or modifies it, by issuing a query. Temporary tables can be protected from unauthorised access using the following technique:

1. A special user id, e.g. *temporal*, is created in the RDBMS, and the CREATE TABLE privilege is granted to this user id for every database handled by the RDBMS. The system session is opened under this special user id, using the IDENTIFIED BY clause of the embedded SQL connect statement.
2. If a temporary table must be accessed through the user session, this access is preceded by the command sequence

```
GRANT SELECT ON TempTable TO UserName
COMMIT
LOCK TABLE TempTable IN EXCLUSIVE MODE
```

which is issued through the system session. (If a LOCK TABLE statement is not available, the same effect can be accomplished by setting the locking granularity of the system session to table level, its read access locking mode to exclusive and accessing a single tuple of the temporary table through it). *TempTable* is the name of the temporary table which must be accessed by the user session, and *UserName* is the user id under which the user session is opened. The SELECT privilege is revoked as soon as the user session completes the necessary access, by issuing the statements

```
REVOKE SELECT ON TempTable FROM UserName
COMMIT
```

through the system session.

3. After each COMMIT point of the system session, all existent temporary tables, on which the SELECT privilege is granted, are locked in exclusive mode.

Using a different user id for the system session protects the temporary tables from unauthorised modifications, since none of the INSERT, DELETE and UPDATE privileges are granted by default to user ids different than the table creator. Read access to the temporary tables is limited to the period during which it is absolutely necessary and, when it is permitted, the table is locked in exclusive mode by the system session. Thus, this access has to be done in the "no lock" fashion employed by the user session, which eliminates any delay or deadlock possibility.

5.2 Removing remnant temporary tables.

It is possible that, during the execution of a query, requiring the creation of intermediate tables, either some temporal engine or the RDBMS or the computer system, on which any of these programs are executed, crashes. Since the system session commits its results with temporary tables present in the database, the RDBMS considers these tables permanent and will try to preserve them through system crashes. Therefore, a method must be provided, to remove these tables from the database. One of the following three approaches can be followed:

1. A *naming convention* can be adopted for the temporary tables, e.g. their name should always start with the string tt_temp. When the RDBMS recovers from a crash, a program can be invoked by the database administrator, which drops all tables whose name starts with this specified string (the names can be determined by querying the RDBMS system catalogues). Users should be warned about this policy, so they will not create a table which might be removed by this procedure.

2. If the special user id, under which the system sessions are opened, is not used for other reasons, then upon crash recovery the database administrator can execute a program, which destroys all tables owned by the special user id.

3. A special table can be introduced, which can be used by the temporal engine to store the names of the temporary tables currently present in the database. A temporary table should then be registered in this catalogue *before* the CREATE TABLE statement, which creates this temporary table, is issued to the RDBMS. The registration should be removed only after the corresponding DROP TABLE statement has been issued (data insertion and deletion in the catalogue is performed through the system session). Upon crash recovery, a program is invoked, which removes from the database all tables registered in this catalogue.

6 Conclusions - Future Work.

In this paper, we presented techniques for supporting transactions in a layered temporal DBMS. The techniques presented exploits the transaction support features of the underlying RDBMS, using a second connection to it, through which operations on temporary tables are performed. Care is also taken, so that no deadlock problems are introduced, as locking is done at session level.

Future work includes support for multiple interval granularities, multiple valid time dimensions, as well as multi-user extensions.

Acknowledgement: We would like to thank the reviewers for their constructive comments.

7 References.

1.   Date C. J. An introduction to database systems, Vol. II. Addison-Wesley Publishing Company, 1985.
2.   Tanenbaum A. S. Modern operating systems. Prentice Hall Inc. 1992.
3.   01 Pliroforiki, University of Athens, Agricultural University of Athens, Information Dynamics. ESPRIT III Project 7224 (ORES) Deliverable D4.1. Implementation of valid time SQL, April 1994.
4.   Lorentzos N. The interval extended relational model and its application to valid time databases. In: Temporal databases: theory, design and implementation. Clifford J, Snodgrass R. et al (Ed.). Benjamin Cummings, 1993, pp. 67-91.
5.   01 Pliroforiki. ESPRIT III Project 7224 (ORES) Deliverable D2. Specification of valid time SQL, April 1993.
6.   ORACLE Corporation. SQL language reference manual (for version 6.0), 1990.
7.   Sybase Inc. Transact SQL user's guide (for release 4.2), 1990.
8.   Codd E. F. A relational model of data for large shared data banks. Communications of the ACM, 1990; 13(6):377-387.
9.   01 Pliroforiki, UMIST. ESPRIT III Project 7224 (ORES) Deliverable C3. Specification of valid time formalism. April 1993.
10.   Ingres Corporation. Ingres SQL and ESQL reference manual (for release 6.4), 1991.

On Schema Versioning
in Temporal Databases

Cristina De Castro   Fabio Grandi   Maria Rita Scalas

C.I.O.C.-C.N.R. and D.E.I.S., Università di Bologna

Bologna, Italy

Abstract

The support of schema versioning has been considered only to a limited extent in the literature on temporal databases. In particular, solutions were proposed so far for the management along transaction-time of schema versions, to be used as different interfaces on the same temporal data.

In this paper we investigate the distinct functionalities of new solutions for schema versioning along *valid-* and *transaction-time* in a temporal relational environment. The support of schema versioning implies operations both at intensional and extensional levels. Two distinct design solutions (*single-* and *multi-pool*) are presented for the management of extensional data in the presence of schema versioning. Moroever, a further distinction is introduced to define *synchronous* and *asynchronous* versioning of data and schemas.

The proposed solutions differ in the semantics and in the possible operations they support. The mechanisms for the selection of data through a schema version is strictly related to the particular schema versioning solution, and has also influences on the data definition and manipulation languages at user-interface level. We also show how the temporal language TSQL2, originally designed to support transaction-time schema versioning, can accordingly be extended.

1   Introduction

Two time dimensions are usually considered in temporal databases [17, 18]: *transaction-time*, which tells when an event is recorded in a database, and *valid-time*, which tells when an event occurs, occurred or is expected to occur in the real world [7]. According to the temporal dimensions they support, temporal databases can be classified as *monotemporal* (transaction- or valid-time), *bitemporal* or *snapshot*. Transaction-time DBs record all the versions of data inserted, deleted or updated in successive transactions (current and non current versions). Valid-time DBs maintain the most recently inserted versions of data, each relative to a distinct valid-time interval (current versions, forming the present historical state). Bitemporal DBs support both transaction and valid-time and thus maintain all the valid-time versions recorded in successive transactions (present and past historical states). Snapshot DBs do not support time: they maintain only the most recently inserted (current) version. A DB in which relations with more than one temporal format (e.g. snapshot, valid-time and bitemporal relations) coexist can also be called *multitemporal* [1].

When a *schema change* is applied to a traditional database, the current schema is usually substituted by a brand new version. The data corresponding to the past schema are lost or restarted according to the new schema if the database supports *schema evolution*. In both cases, a portion of intensional information may be no longer available together with the corresponding piece of extensional information. In order to avoid information loss, the concept of *schema versioning* has been introduced [7, 12]. In current literature [5, 10, 11, 13], several proposals have been made for the maintainance of schema versions along *transaction time* whereas the necessity for the support of schema versioning along *valid time* is still debated. We also studied transaction-time schema versioning in a multitemporal environment in [2].

In [3, 4], we considered the notion of schema versioning along valid-time which will be further emphasized in this paper. Whereas transaction-time schema versioning is sufficient for any *on-time* schema change, that is schema changes effective when applied, or for applications for which the exact time of application of a schema change is not crucial (this seems to be the case of most CAD/CAM/CIM applications), valid-time schema versioning is made necessary by database applications requiring *retro-* or *pro-active* schema changes. It can be noticed that retroactive changes are quite common in databases, both concerning extensional and intensional data. Like valid-time databases have been introduced to accomodate retroactive changes of extensional data, valid-time schema versioning is necessary to allow also retroactive changes of intensional data. For instance, retroactive changes of intensional data can be enforced by changes in laws with retroactive effects (e.g. new encoding rules requiring more digits can be stated for social security numbers today, but effective from 1/1/1996) or, even more likely, they can be a consequence of *deferred updates* (e.g. the new encoding rules are stated and effective now but the corresponding schema change will be applied to the database only next month). Also proactive changes of intensional data are possible in consequence of particular design choices (i.e. in *what-if* analysis during development or maintainance of database applications), and require valid-time schema versioning to be supported. Advanced database application may also require bitemporal schema versioning, when not only must retro- and pro-active schema changes be managed but it is also necessary to *keep track* of them in the database (e.g. for auditing purposes). As it happens to extensional updates in bitemporal databases, this is only possible by means of schema versioning along both time dimensions.

Moreover, as far as the extensional aspects of schema versioning are concerned, we consider two distinct solutions for the management of data and show how each solution works in reply to schema changes, queries or updates. In the following, by the term *data pool* we denote a repository for extensional data. The solutions for organization and management of data pools are presented and discussed at logical level. The paper intends to present some possible solutions and show their main properties. Physical design issues are not faced here, since physical design parameters need further study on storage occupation, depending not only on the operations allowed but also on the workload, in terms of selections, updates and frequencies of the different kinds of operations allowed on the data in the presence of schema versioning. The topic deserves by itself a detailed study, also involving space and time complexity and thus feasibility, that will be subject of a separate future work.

The two solutions we consider are [3]:

- **Single-Pool Solution** The data corresponding to all schema versions are maintained into a single data pool.

- **Multi-Pool Solution** Distinct data pools are maintained for distinct schema versions [2, 15].

The single-pool solution is consistent with the solution adopted in [13] in [19] for schema evolution and schema versioning along transaction-time.

Another degree of freedom in data management, which takes place when extensional and intensional data are versioned along the same temporal dimension(s), gives rise to the following distinction [3]:

- **Synchronous Management** In this type of management, *the temporal pertinence of a schema version must include the temporal pertinence of the corresponding data* along the common temporal dimensions. In this case, data are stored, retrieved and updated always through the schema version having the same temporal pertinence along the common temporal dimension(s).

- **Asynchronous Management** In this case the temporal pertinence of a schema version and the temporal pertinence of the corresponding data are completely independent. Data can thus be retrieved and updated through any schema version, whose validity is independent of the validity of data also along common temporal dimension(s).

In all the schema versioning proposals published in literature, asynchronous versioning seems to be adopted. As a matter of fact, the schema version to be used for data access can be specified independently from the time pertinence of data and separate linguistic tools are provided to this purpose in query language extensions. For instance, in the TSQL2 [13, 19] query:

```
SELECT * FROM REL
    WHERE VALID(REL) OVERLAPS DATE '1980-01-01'
    SCHEMA DATE '1990-01-01'
```

can be used to retrieve (extensional) data valid on 1/1/80 from the relation **REL** using the current schema version as of 1/1/90. Since there is no correlation between the time pertinence of data and schemas, we must be in the presence of "asynchronous" management in order to express (and answer) such a query. In this case (e.g. if **REL** is a valid-time relation), the asynchronous management is guaranteed, in a natural way, by the *orthogonality* of the time dimensions. As a matter of fact, we always have asynchronous management between *different* time dimensions. But assume that **REL** is a transaction-time relation, transaction-time schema versioning is still used, and consider the following query:

```
SELECT * FROM REL
    WHERE TRANSACTION(REL) OVERLAPS DATE '1980-01-01'
    SCHEMA DATE '1990-01-01'
```

Well, this is a legal query only in the case of synchronous management, because different transaction times are to be used for the selection of data and schema (and it seems to be a correct TSQL2 query). In our opinion, synchronous management for transaction-time repesent a very hybrid solution which strains the semantics of transaction-time. It should be kept in mind that reference to transaction-time in the past has the meaning of a *rollback* operation, bringing back the database to a past state of its life. Therefore, the states in which the extensional and the intensional parts of the database can be brought back should be consistent. This is the reason for which synchronous management for transaction-time schema versioning is mandatory in our approach. If an application requires asynchronous management of data and schemas, valid-time schema versioning should be employed. Since no special constraints are enforced by the semantics of valid time, valid-time schema versioning can either be synchronous or asynchronous.

The rest of the paper is organized as follows: in Section 2 we present the single- and the multi-pool solutions, both in the synchronous and asynchronous case and show how they work in valid- and in transaction-time schema versioning. The differences are discussed also on the basis of some examples. Section 3 is devoted to the query language extensions and semantics in the considered environment. The use of different schema versions to manipulate data is illustrated on the basis of the features of each type of extensional management. Examples are provided in order to show how different results can be obtained in the presence of different schema versioning solutions.

2 Schema Versioning

In this section we introduce valid-time, transaction-time and bitemporal schema versioning, and describe mechanisms for their support and management. The operations on schema versions and the corresponding data are illustrated by means of figures and examples. More details can be found in [3].

The data definition language must be extended in order to support all kinds of schema versioning. We show how the TSQL2 temporal extension of SQL-92 [14, 19] could be upgraded to this purpose. TSQL2 is already designed to support schema transaction-time schema versioning [13]. Its data definition language is provided with the **CREATE** and **ALTER** statements [16], for the creation and modification of a table, respectively.

The statement:

CREATE TABLE $<$ table name $> <$ table elements $>$
    $<$ temporal definition $>$

allows the definition of a new table named $<$ table name $>$, where $<$ table elements $>$ defines the non temporal attributes of the table and $<$ temporal definition $>$ specifies the temporal format of the table (type of data versioning). For instance, the statement:

CREATE TABLE REL$(a_1 : d_1, a_2 : d_2, a_3 : d_3)$
    AS VALID AND TRANSACTION

defines a bitemporal table with non temporal attributes a_1, a_2, a_3. The domains of such attributes are d_1, d_2, d_3, respectively. For the sake of simplicity, domains will be omitted in the following. The TSQL2 statement **ALTER TABLE** allows a change to be effected on a relation schema.

In a multitemporal environment, schema changes should also include the change of the table temporal format [2, 3, 16]. To this end, **ADD** or **DROP** clauses with **VALID** or **TRANSACTION** specification must be used. For instance, the statement:

```
ALTER TABLE REL
    DROP TRANSACTION
```

changes the temporal format of table **REL** from bitemporal to valid-time. In transaction-time schema versioning, a **CREATE** or **ALTER** statement always concerns the current schema version, thus, no time for the new schema (version) can be specified: the implicit transaction-time pertinence of the schema change is always [NOW, UC], and cannot be changed by the user. The symbol UC has the meaning of "until changed" and is used to timestamp only current data (not changed yet). On the contrary, in valid-time or bitemporal schema versioning, a new clause is introduced to allow the user to specify the validity of the schema change. Therefore, in our extension, the **CREATE** and **ALTER** statements are augmented with a **VALID** clause [3]. For instance, the statement:

```
ALTER TABLE REL
    ADD COLUMN a₆ : d₆
    VALID PERIOD '[t'-t"]'
```

requests the creation of a new schema version valid in $[t', t'']$ for relation **REL**, where attribute a_6 is added.

2.1 Valid-Time Schema Versioning

In all the prospected solutions, management of *intensional data* does not present new or peculiar difficulties. In valid-time schema versioning, system catalogues are implemented by means of valid-time relations, whose tuples correspond to schema versions. The tuple timestamps represent the validity of each schema version. Therefore, the management of intensional data in response to a schema change in valid-time schema versioning reduces to the update of a valid-time relation. The only difference (and complication) from transaction-time versioning is that more than one schema versions may be interested by a single change. As a matter of fact, whereas in transaction-time versioning only the current schema version is affected by the change [2], in valid-time versioning all the schema versions totally or even partially overlapped by the validity of the change are affected. An comprehensive example is given in Fig. 1, which illustrates at intensional level the schema change "**DROP COLUMN** a_5" with validity $[t', t'']$. The situations before and after the change are shown in Figg. 1a and 1b, respectively. Among all the schema versions, two are partially overlapped by $[t', t'']$. The version relative to $[t_1, t_2]$ is unaffected, because it does not contain the attribute a_5, and so it remains unchanged. The schema version relative to $[t_4, t_5]$ is partially overlapped and actually affected by the

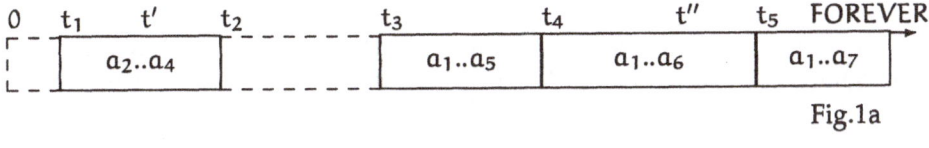

Fig.1a

```
ALTER TABLE REL
DROP COLUMN a5
VALID PERIOD '[t'-t"]'
```

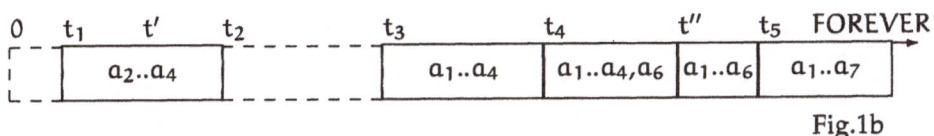

Fig.1b

Figure 1: Situation before (1a) and after (1b) the schema change "**DROP COLUMN** a_5" with validity $[t', t'']$.

change. This version is thus split into two portions: the non-overlapped portion maintains all its old attributes $a_1..a_6$, whereas the overlapped portion loses the attribute a_5 becoming $(a_1..a_4, a_6)$. The schema version relative to $[t_3, t_4]$ is also affected and totally overlapped, thus a_5 is dropped from this version.

Furthermore, the only difference between single- and multi-pool versioning at intensional level is that, in the latter case, pointers to the new data pool(s) must be stored in the catalogues (see [3] for details).

As far as extensional data management is concerned, the different strategies qualify the single- versus the multi-pool solution.

2.1.1 Single-Pool Solution

The single-pool consists of a repository where all the extensional data are stored according to a global schema (*completed schema* in [14]), which includes all the attributes introduced so far by successive schema changes. If a schema change is destructive, such as the drop of an attribute or the restriction of a domain, the change can only be recorded in the catalogues, since no data can be discarded from the single-pool. On the contrary, if a change adds an attribute, a temporal dimension or extends a domain, the whole data pool is converted to the new format. Note that if the change concerns a domain, the attribute must be extended to the largest one defined so far. If the change of a domain produces a new domain incompatible with the old one (e.g. when changing an attribute CODE from numeric to alphabetic), two attributes must be maintained, with the same name as seen by the user, but corresponding to different domains and belonging to different schema versions as recorded in the catalogues. Since the change of temporal format is also allowed, if a schema change adds new temporal dimensions the whole data pool must be converted to the enlarged temporal format, using the temporal conversion maps defined in [1], as shown in [2]. Data are thus maintained according to the largest schema and in the largest temporal format so far defined and only the catalogues maintain the history of the changes. This solution does not minimize the data space relative to to each schema version.

The considerations above are not meant to be a complete solution for the management of a single pool, but just outline some features and problems of such a choice. A complete solution should deal with the problem of the integration of schema changes and thus *compatibility* of schema versions in all the possible cases. Furthermore, a complete taxonomy should include schema changes involving more than one relation, such as the merging of two schemas. Due to the large amount of issues presented in this paper, it is not possible to deal with all of their features in a single work.

As an example, Tabb.1–3 respectively show the evolution of the single pool of the snapshot table Employee(EMP-NAME, ADDRESS) before and after the schema changes of conversion to the valid-time format and successive addition of the attribute PHONE. The first change is supposed to span from 1985, some update activity concerning the Employee Jones occurs between the two changes and, in 1995, the attribute PHONE is added.

EMP-NAME	ADDRESS
Brown	London
Jones	Edinburgh
Rossi	Rome
Matisse	Paris

Table 1: Single-pool for Employee before the schema changes.

EMP-NAME	ADDRESS	VALID TIME
Brown	London	{1985..FOREVER}
Jones	Edinburgh	{1985..FOREVER}
Rossi	Rome	{1985..FOREVER}
Matisse	Paris	{1985..FOREVER}

Table 2: Single-pool for Employee after the addition of transaction-time.

EMP-NAME	ADDRESS	PHONE	VALID TIME
Brown	London	NULL	{95..FOREVER}
Jones	Edinburgh	NULL	{80..87}
Jones	New York	4040404	{89..FOREVER}
Rossi	Rome	NULL	{95..FOREVER}
Matisse	Paris	NULL	{95..FOREVER}

Table 3: Single-pool for Employee after the addition of PHONE.

In the single-pool solution, two pieces of information are necessary: the current structure of the single pool (all the attributes defined so far and the largest temporal format) and the structure and temporal format of each schema version. The original structure and temporal format of data in each schema version can thus be reconstructed using the catalogue information.

There are no differences between the synchronous and the asynchronous case as far as schema changes are concerned.

2.1.2 Multi-Pool Solution

The multi-pool solution requires the creation of as many data pools as the number of schema versions. Consider again Fig.1 and suppose each schema version along valid-time corresponds to a data pool of its own. The data pools underlying unaffected schema versions, totally or partially overlapped, are left untouched. For instance, this is the case of the schema version relative to $[t_1, t_2]$, which does not contain the attribute a_5. For each affected and totally overlapped schema version a new data pool substitutes the previous one (e.g. schema version $[t_3, t_4]$); a new data pool is created for each partially overlapped and affected schema version (e.g. the portion $[t_4, t'']$ of schema version $[t_4, t_5]$), and a copy of the old pool remains connected to each of the non-overlapped portions of the original schema (e.g. the portion $[t'', t_5]$ of schema version $[t_4, t_5]$).

One of the main differences between the single- and the multi-pool solution is the following: a schema change applied to several schema versions produces different results on the different versions. This does not cause substantial differences in the intensional management, but the extensional management must be differentiated on each data pool.

2.1.3 Asynchronous Multi-pool solution for valid-time schema versioning

In this case, each data pool is formatted according to the corresponding schema version. Therefore, when a new data pool is started the tuples are copied from the initial affected pool, according to the change applied to the previous schema.

2.1.4 Synchronous Multi-pool solution for valid-time schema versioning

The synchronous management of the multi-pool solution is achieved by restricting the validity of data (if any) in each new pool to its intersection with the schema version validity (due to synchronous versioning, the validity of all data in the pool must be contained in the validity of the pool itself). Note that the above restriction might cause a loss of information on the original validity lifespan of extensional data.

For instance, suppose the schema version of Employee in Tab.4 to be valid in the whole valid-time universe {0..FOREVER} and a schema change to occur, which adds the attribute PHONE in the interval $[t', t''] = [90, \text{FOREVER}]$. The multi-pool synchronous management produces Tabb. 5–6. It can be noticed that some tuples (e.g. (Jones, New York, {89..FOREVER})) may be replicated in both new versions with the valid-time interval split in two parts according to synchronous management. Another example is shown in Fig. 2: the left portion of Fig. 2 illustrates the synchronous management of a valid-time table in the presence of valid-time schema versioning in the multi-pool and in the single-pool solution. Note that, in the presence of a single schema version, the single- and the multi-pool coincide. According to a change which overlaps the schema version SV1 on $[t_2, t_3]$, a further schema version SV2, composed of the attributes a_1, a_2, a_3, is created. In the multi-pool, the insertion of SV2 produces a new data pool and the original tuples are split according to their validity and partitioned between the two pools. In the single-pool, no actual split is effected on the content of the data pool. The right portion of Fig. 2 shows an example for the asynchronous case. If the same schema change which adds a_3 is applied in the asynchronous case, no split of data validity must be performed. In this case, the single-pool coincides with the new data-pool and no data duplication is performed. It must be noticed that, in valid-time schema versioning, historical continuity of data "across the pools" is guaranteed only by their synchronous management. On the contrary, the asynchronous management may cause continuity along valid-time to be violated. These are characteristics of the two types of management.

EMP-NAME	ADDRESS	VALID TIME
Brown	London	{95..FOREVER}
Jones	Edinburgh	{80..87}
Jones	New York	{89..FOREVER}
Rossi	Rome	{95..FOREVER}
Matisse	Paris	{95..FOREVER}

Table 4: Portion [0..FOREVER] of the multi pool of Employee before the addition of PHONE.

EMP-NAME	ADDRESS	VALID TIME
Jones	Edinburgh	{80..87}
Jones	New York	{89..90}

Table 5: Portion [0..90] of the multi pool of Employee after the addition of PHONE.

EMP-NAME	ADDRESS	PHONE	VALID TIME
Brown	London	NULL	{95..FOREVER}
Jones	New York	NULL	{90..FOREVER}
Rossi	Rome	NULL	{95..FOREVER}
Matisse	Paris	NULL	{95..FOREVER}

Table 6: Portion [90..FOREVER] of the multi pool of Employee after the addition of PHONE.

2.2 Transaction-Time Schema Versioning

If transaction-time schema versioning is supported, schema changes concern only the current schema version and the versioning can only be synchronous, since transaction-time does not allow retroactive or proactive changes. In this case, the catalogues are defined and managed as transaction-time tables as shown in [2].

SYNCHRONOUS MULTI-POOL

FROM	TO	a_1	a_2	
t_1	t_3	k_1	v_1	
t_2	t_3	k_2	v_2	

data pool
SV1 (t_1, t_3)

FROM	TO	a_1	a_2
t_1	t_2	k_1	v_1

data pool
SV1 (t_1, t_2)

				a_3
t_2	t_3	k_1	v_1	–
t_2	t_3	k_2	v_2	–

data pool
SV2 (t_2, t_3)

ASYNCHRONOUS MULTI-POOL

FROM	TO	a_1	a_2	
t_0	t_4	k_1	v_1	
t_2	t_6	k_2	v_2	

data pool
SV1 (t_1, t_3)

FROM	TO	a_1	a_2
t_0	t_4	k_1	v_1
t_2	t_6	k_2	v_2

data pool
SV1 (t_1, t_2)

				a_3
t_0	t_4	k_1	v_1	
t_2	t_6	k_2	v_2	–

data pool
SV2 (t_2, t_3)

SYNCHRONOUS SINGLE-POOL

FROM	TO	a_1	a_2	a_3
t_2	t_3	k_1	v_1	–
t_2	t_3	k_2	v_2	–

ASYNCHRONOUS SINGLE-POOL

FROM	TO	a_1	a_2	a_3
t_0	t_4	k_1	v_1	–
t_2	t_6	k_2	v_2	–

Figure 2: Synchronous and asynchronous valid-time schema versioning in the multi- and single-pool solutions.

MANAGER	DEPT	SALARY	TRANS. TIME
Matisse	Food	1000	{80..90}
Matisse	Toys	1500	{91..92}
Matisse	Clothing	2000	{93..UC}
Jones	Food	900	{73..83}
Jones	Clothing	1800	{84..UC}

Table 7: Transaction-time relation Dept-Mgr.

MANAGER	DEPT	SALARY	TRANS. TIME
Matisse	Food	1000	{80..90}
Matisse	Toys	1500	{91..92}
Matisse	Clothing	2000	{93..94}
Jones	Food	900	{73..83}
Jones	Clothing	1800	{84..94}

Table 8: Archived pool of Dept-Mgr after the change.

MANAGER	DEPT	TRANS. TIME
Matisse	Clothing	{94..UC}
Jones	Clothing	{94..UC}

Table 9: Current pool of Dept-Mgr after the change.

2.2.1 *(Synchronous) Single-pool solution for transaction-time schema versioning*

As far as the extensional level is concerned, all the tuples of the current data pool must be converted to the enlarged format, as described for valid-time versioning.

2.2.2 *(Synchronous) Multi-pool solution for transaction-time schema versioning*

In this case, a separate data pool, even if archived, must be maintained for each transaction-time schema version. The management of extensional information requires two distinct phases: the start of a new data pool followed by the archiving of the previous one. The format of the new data pool consists of all and only attributes contained in the new schema version. Again, such attributes may be temporal (timestamps). The initialization of the new pool also requires the retrieval of data from the old one. This solution requires only the current tuples of the old pool to be copied into the new one. This choice is done according to the semantics of synchronous versioning, which does not allow modifications of non-current tuples, even if, from a logical point of view, they could also be contained in the data pool of the current schema version.

If the change does not alter the temporal format of data, the selection is effected as follows: if the tuples of the old pool are snapshot or valid-time, they are all copied into the new data pool (all current data). If they contain transaction-time, only the current tuples (whose transaction timestamp includes the present time) are copied into the new data pool.

If the change concerns the temporal format of the table, a copy of the tuples in the old pool is first converted to the desired temporal format; among the resulting tuples, all and only the current ones are actually copied into the new data pool [3, 4].

After the initialization of the new pool, the old one is archived: if data in the source pool are snapshot or valid-time, they remain unaltered, and they are implicitly archived by the archiving of their schema version, i.e. the user knows that such data can be not anymore current since they belong to an archived schema version. If data contain transaction-time, the current tuples are archived by setting the enpoint of their timestamp to the present transaction-time, NOW, of the schema change.

For example, consider the transaction-time relation Dept-Mgr in Tab.7 and suppose that the following schema change occurs: the attribute SALARY is dropped at NOW = 1994. The after situation in the single pool is unaltered, since no data can be discarded from it. The drop of the attribute can only be recorded in the catalogues. As far as the multi-pool is concerned, the archived pool and the new one are shown in Tabb. 8–9. Note that the current tuples only are copied into the current pool.

2.3 Bitemporal Schema Versioning

Bitemporal schema versioning allows the maintainance of all the valid-time schema versions as inserted in successive schema changes. A schema change performed at transaction-time NOW with validity $[t', t'']$ can only concern the current and overlapped bitemporal schema versions. The management of bitemporal schema versioning at intensional level is equal to the update of a bitemporal relation [6]. Fig. 3 shows the bitemporal counterpart of the example in Fig. 1.

As far as operations on extensional data are concerned, the management of the single-pool solution is substantially the same as discussed in synchronous or asynchronous valid-time schema versioning and (synchronous) transaction-time schema versioning. In the single-pool, when a schema change is applied, the whole data pool is converted to the "enlarged" format of the new schema version. In the multi-pool, it is necessary to initialize as many data pools as the number of new schema versions obtained by applying the change to the current ones. When a partially or totally overlapped schema version is affected, a data pool is started for each affected portion determined by the valid-time interval of the schema change. The current tuples are copied into the new pool, according to the rules of transaction-time schema versioning. In the case of asynchronous versioning, the valid-time pertinence (if any) of the tuples is not furtherly modified. In the case of synchronous versioning, it is restricted to that of the corresponding schema version. All the data pools corresponding to affected schema versions must be archived. For the sake of brevity, bitemporal schema versioning is sketched here as the "merging" of valid- and transaction-time schema versioning, without a description of bitemporal single- versus multi-pool management. More details on extensional data management can be found in [4]. An early study on bitemporal schema versioning, which adopted a synchronous multi-pool solution, can also be found in [15].

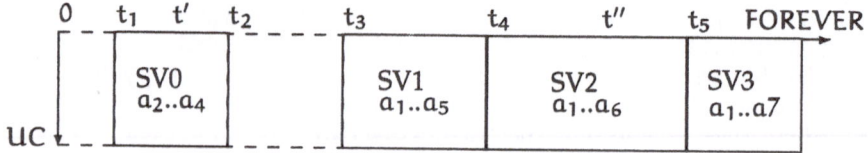

ALTER TABLE REL
DROP COLUMN a_5
VALID PERIOD '[t'-t'']'

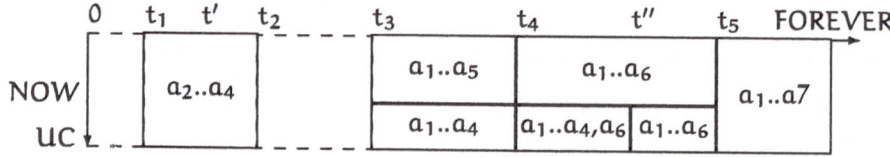

Figure 3: Bitemporal Schema versioning: situation before and after a schema change performed at NOW and valid in the interval [t', t''].

3 Data Manipulation

In this section we show which extensions are required to the query language in a system supporting one of the proposed schema versioning solutions.

3.1 Data Retrieval

The TSQL2 data manipulation statements (the **SELECT** statement and the modification statements) are provided with a **SCHEMA** clause in order to support schema version selection [13]. Therefore, TSQL2 is designed to work in a system supporting, in our terminology, asynchronous single-pool transaction-time schema versioning. It can be noticed that this particular solution is not permitted in our approach when the table is transaction-time or bitemporal, since transaction-time versioning cannot be asynchronous. The TSQL2 **SELECT** statement has a **SCHEMA** clause devoted to transaction-time specification for schema version selection. The same syntax of TSQL2, but with different semantics, can be used in our proposal only for valid-time schema selection in asynchronous schema versioning. In (synchronous) transaction-time schema versioning, no **SCHEMA** clause is allowed, since the same transaction-time specifications used for data selection (contained in the **WHERE** clause) are also used for schema selection. Also in synchronous valid-time schema versioning no **SCHEMA** clause is allowed, since the valid-time specifications in the **WHERE** clause are used for both schema and data selection.

In valid-time schema versioning, synchronous and asynchronous management deeply differ as to schema selection mechanisms. In the synchronous management, the temporal conditions on data valid-time, if any, specified in a **WHERE** clause for extensional data are to be used also for schema selection, whereas any possible schema can be specified in case of asynchronous management. For instance, consider the following query and suppose that the bitemporal table **REL** is subject to asynchronous valid-time schema versioning:

```
SELECT * FROM REL
    WHERE VALID(REL) OVERLAPS DATE '1980-01-01'
        AND TRANSACTION(REL) FOLLOWS DATE '1990-01-01'
    SCHEMA PERIOD '[1975-01-01 - 1985-01-01]'
```

The processing of this query uses all the schema versions of **REL** whose validity overlaps the interval [1/1/75, 1/1/85]. Among all the data corresponding to such schemas, the query retrieves the data whose validity overlaps 1/1/80 and whose transaction-time interval follows 1/1/90. If more than one schema version are valid in the interval [1/1/75, 1/1/85], as many "copies" of data are retrieved as many schema verions are found. The management is different in case of the multi- or the single-pool: in case of multi-pool solution, a distinct data pool corresponds to each selected schema version and, thus, data are retrieved in the format they are stored in each pool. In case of single-pool, all the data are stored in the same "enlarged" format and, thus, a filtering phase (including conversion of temporal format) is required in order to adapt retrieved data to the different schema versions involved: the data are returned according to the distinct schema versions. If synchronous versioning is also adopted, the filtering phase must restrict the time pertinence of retrieved data, along the same temporal dimension(s) used for synchronous versioning, to be completely contained within the temporal pertinence of the corresponding schema version.

3.2   Data Modification

The same considerations made for the retrieval statements can be extended to update operations. In transaction-time schema versioning, updates only concern current data and act through the current schema version, thus a **SCHEMA** clause is not allowed. The same applies to synchronous valid-time versioning. In asynchronous valid-time versioning, a **SCHEMA** clause can be used in **INSERT, DELETE, UPDATE** statements in order to specify the validity of the schema version(s) which must be used for data modification.

In case of synchronous versioning, the temporal pertinence of appended data is always restricted to be contained, along the temporal dimension(s) of synchronous versioning, in the temporal pertinence of the corresponding schema version.

We try now to evaluate by means of some examples how the single- and the multi-pool solutions differently behave in case of valid-time and transaction-time schema versioning.

3.2.1   *Updates in valid-time schema versioning*

Consider Fig. 4a and Fig. 4c which show the multi- and the single-pool of a valid-time relation whose schema is versioned along transaction-time. Suppose that the versioning is asynchronous and that the following updates are applied:

- Update v_2 to v_{10} using SV1.

- Update v_2 to v_{20} using SV2.

The results are shown in Fig. 4b for the multi-pool and in Figg. 4d–4e for the single-pool. Note that in the multi-pool the final result does not depend on the execution order of the updates, since the data pools are actually separated (Fig. 4c). If the same operations are performed on the single-pool, the result depends on the execution order of the updates (see Figg. 4d–4e).

3.2.2   Updates in transaction-time schema versioning

Tabb.7 and 9 show respectively the single- and the current pool of Dept-Mgr. In both solutions, the current schema version is Dept-Mgr(MANAGER, DEPT, TRANS.TIME). Suppose Jones becomes manager in department Jewellery and this is recorded at NOW = 1995. The before and after situations are shown in Tab.10 (single-pool) and Tab.11 (multi-pool). Note that in the single-pool, which still contains the dropped attribute SALARY, the new tuple a NULL SALARY value. Thus, depending on which solution is adopted, the same transaction produces two different results.

MANAGER	DEPT	SALARY	TRANS. TIME
Matisse	Food	1000	{80..90}
Matisse	Toys	1500	{91..92}
Matisse	Clothing	2000	{93..UC}
Jones	Food	900	{73..83}
Jones	Clothing	1800	{84..95}
Jones	Jewellery	NULL	{95..UC}

Table 10: Single-pool of the transaction-time relation Dept-Mgr after update.

MANAGER	DEPT	TRANS. TIME
Matisse	Clothing	{94..UC}
Jones	Clothing	{94..95}
Jones	Jewellery	{95..UC}

Table 11: Current pool of Dept-Mgr after update.

A snapshot table composed by the attributes (a_1, a_2, a_3) is shown in Fig. 5; suppose the following operations are performed: drop of attribute a_2, update of tuple (k_4, x_4) to (k_4, x_5) and re-add of attribute a_2. Fig. 5a1,5a2,5a3 and 5b show the results of such updates in the multi-pool and in the single-pool respectively. The successive re-add of the same attribute does not reconstruct the tuple values according to the original copies, but to the most recent copy of the data pool. In the multi-pool the "new" added attribute is filled up with nulls, whereas the single-pool simple still retrieves the values v_1, v_2, v_3, v_4 as proper of the latest schema version, as they were before the dropping of a_2.

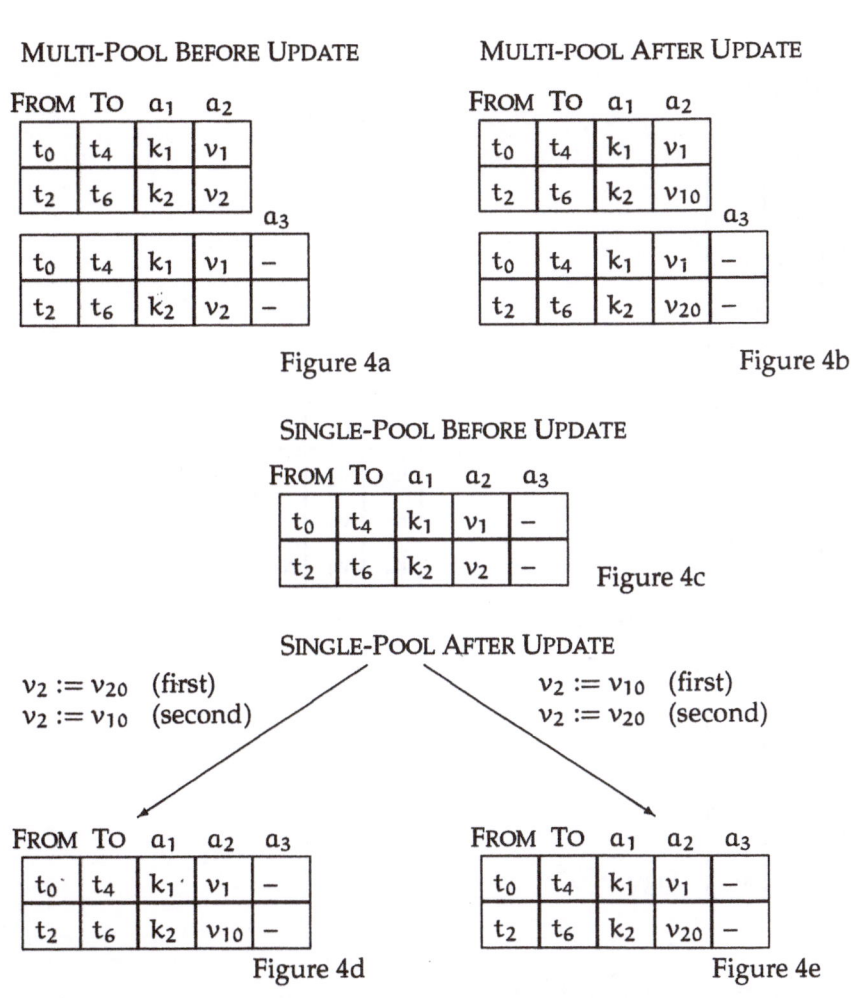

Figure 4: Asynchronous valid-time schema versioning: different results in the multi- and the single-pool.

MULTI-POOL

a_1	a_2	a_3
k_1	v_1	–
k_2	v_2	–
k_3	v_3	–
k_4	v_4	x_4

Figure 5a1

SINGLE-POOL

a_1	a_3
k_1	–
k_2	–
k_3	–
k_4	x_4

Figure 5a2

a_1	a_2	a_3
k_1	v_1	–
k_2	v_2	–
k_3	v_3	–
k_4	v_4	x_5

Figure 5b

a_1	a_2	a_3
k_1	–	–
k_2	–	–
k_3	–	–
k_4	–	x_5

Figure 5a3

Figure 5: Transaction-time schema versioning.

4 Conclusions

In this paper we provided a study of valid- and transaction-time schema versioning. Our goal was to introduce different solutions for the management of schema versioning. We proposed two distinct storage solutions: single- and multi-pool. A further distinction has been made between synchronous and asynchronous versioning.

The different design solutions have been principally compared on the basis of their semantic properties, since a detailed analysis of storage, maintainance and query processing costs was beyond the scope of this paper. In conclusion, the single-pool solution avoids data duplication, even if it requires an enlargement of the data format required for storage. On the contrary, the multi-pool requires the duplication of the current portion of data in transaction-time schema versioning, and duplication of the whole affected pool(s) in case of valid-time schema versioning. Anyway, the multi-pool solution allows several independent evolutions of data, each one relative to a specific schema version, whereas a single copy is maintained in the single-pool. Furthermore, the single-pool forces data to be converted according to the desired schema version at query processing time.

Future work will be devoted to a more complete comparison of the proposed solutions in terms of system performance, taking into account distinct application requirements and workloads.

References

[1] DE CASTRO C., GRANDI F., SCALAS M.R.: "Semantic Interoperability of Multitemporal Relational Databases", in *Entity-Relationship Approach - ER '93*, Lecture Notes in Computer Science, Vol. 823, Springer-Verlag, 1994.

[2] DE CASTRO C., GRANDI F., SCALAS M.R.: "Management of Schema Versions in Multitemporal Relational Databases", Proc. 2nd Italian Conference on Advanced Database Systems (SEBD '94), Rimini, Italy, June 1994 (*in Italian*).

[3] DE CASTRO C., GRANDI F., SCALAS M.R.: "Schema Versioning for Multitemporal Relational Databases", C.I.O.C.-C.N.R. Tech. Rep. No. 100, Bologna, Italy, July 1994.

[4] DE CASTRO C., GRANDI F., SCALAS M.R.: "Extensional Data Management in Multitemporal Relational Databases Supporting Schema Versioning", Proc. 3rd Italian Conference on Advanced Database Systems (SEBD '95), Ravello, Italy, June 1995.

[5] DADAM P., TEUHOLA J.: "Managing Schema Versions in a Time-Versioned Non-First-Normal-Form Relational Database", Proc. Datenbanksysteme in Büro, Technik und Wissenschaft, GI-Fachtagung, Darmstadt, Germany, April 1987.

[6] GRANDI F., SCALAS M.R., TIBERIO P.: "A History-oriented Data View and Operation Semantics in Temporal Relational Databases", C.I.O.C.-C.N.R. Tech. Rep. No. 76, Bologna, Italy, January 1991.

[7] JENSEN C., CLIFFORD J., ELMASRI R., GADIA S.K., HAYES P., JAJODIA S. (editors), DYRESON C., GRANDI F., KAFER W., KLINE N., LORENT-ZOS N., MITSOPOULOS Y., MONTANARI A., NONEN D., PERESSI E., PERNICI B., RODDICK J.F., SARDA N.L., SCALAS M.R., SEGEV A., SNODGRASS R., SOO M.D., TANSEL A., TIBERIO P., WIEDERHOLD G.: "A Consensus Glossary of Temporal Database Concepts", ACM SIGMOD RECORD, Vol. 23, No. 1, March 1994.

[8] JENSEN C.S., SOO M.D., SNODGRASS R.T.: "Unification of Temporal Relations", Proc. 9th IEEE International Conference on Data Engineering (ICDE '93), Vienna, Austria, April 1993.

[9] KLINE N.: "An update of the Temporal Database Bibliography", ACM SIGMOD RECORD, Vol.22, No. 4, December 1993.

[10] MCKENZIE E., SNODGRASS R.: "Schema Evolution and the Relational Algebra", Information Systems, Vol. 15, No. 2, 1990.

[11] RODDICK J.F.: "SQL/SE - A Query Language Extension for Databases Supporting Schema Evolution", ACM SIGMOD RECORD, Vol. 21, No. 3, September 1992.

[12] RODDICK J.F.: "Schema Evolution in Database Systems - An Annotated Bibliography", ACM SIGMOD RECORD, Vol. 21, No. 4, December 1992.

[13] RODDICK J.F., SNODGRASS T.: "Schema Versioning Support', in [19], ch. 22.

[14] SNODGRASS R.T., AHN I., ARIAV G., BATORY D., CLIFFORD J., DYRE-SON C.E., ELMASRI R., GRANDI F., JENSEN C.J., KAFER W., KLINE N., KULKARNI K., CLIFF LEUNG T.Y, LORENTZOS N., RODDICK J.F., SEGEV A., SOO M.D., SRIPADA S.M.: "TSQL2 Language Specification", ACM SIGMOD RECORD, Vol.23, No.1, March 1994.

[15] SCALAS M.R., CAPPELLI A., DE CASTRO C.: "A Model for Schema Evolution in Temporal Relational Databases", Proc. of 7th IEEE European Computer Conference (CompEuro '93), Paris Evry, France, May 1993.

[16] SNODGRASS R.T., JENSEN C.S., GRANDI F.: "Schema Specification", in [19], ch. 11.

[17] SOO M.: "Bibliography on Temporal Databases", ACM SIGMOD Record, March 1991.

[18] TANSEL A., CLIFFORD J., GADIA V., JAJODIA S., SEGEV A., SNOD-GRASS R.T. (eds.), Temporal Databases: Theory, Design and Implementation, The Benjamin/Cummings Publishing Company, Redwood City, CA, 1993.

[19] SNODGRASS R.T. (editor), AHN I., ARIAV G., BATORY D., CLIFFORD J., DYRESON C.E., ELMASRI R., GRANDI F., JENSEN C.J., KÄFER W., KLINE N., KULKARNI K., CLIFF LEUNG T.Y., LORENTZOS N., RAMAKRISHNAN R., RODDICK J.F., SEGEV A., SOO M.D., SRIPADA S.M., *The TSQL2 Temporal Query Language*, Kluwer Academic Publishers, Norwell, MA, 1995.

VI. Potpourri

A Temporal Foundation of Video Databases

Rune Hjelsvold, Roger Midtstraum, and Olav Sandstå

Norwegian Institute of Technology

Trondheim, Norway

Abstract

Audio and video data represent streams of data with inherent temporal properties. In this paper we consider a video database as a collection of partial ordered sets where temporal relationships exist between elements from the same *video stream*. Video production introduces dependencies between different time coordinate systems. In this paper we give a formal definition of the contents of a video database. We also define *mapped video object sets* and operations on such sets that can be used for querying the temporal properties of video data and that can be used for mapping video objects between different time coordinate systems. At last, we illustrate how the proposed foundation can be used in searching and browsing.

1 Introduction

Traditional data types such as numbers, texts and graphics take static values - i.e., their values do not change unless explicitly updated. Conventional database systems were designed to maintain the most recent values and the change of the database values over time is not explicitly maintained. On the other hand, temporal databases are addressing the needs to maintain past, present, and future data [20]. Video data are inherently temporal - although not in the traditional sense; the contents of a video screen are dynamically changing when video data are displayed to the user.

Technically, video data can be considered as a *stream* of images (called *frames*) displayed to the user at a constant *frame rate* (measured in frames per second - *fps*[1]). Much of the research on video databases is concerned with the problems of guaranteeing constant frame rates and audio/video synchronization.

Video information is, however, more complex than just a stream of frames. As noted by Gibbs et al. [4], one piece of video may be temporally derived from another piece of video - e.g., when a sequence from a video recording is used in a video document. At the same time, several pieces of video may be combined into a document by defining the temporal relations between these pieces. Figure 1 illustrates these concepts. The main goal of our research is to develop database support for modelling, searching and browsing of video data.

---

[1] Some typical frame rates are 24 fps (cinematic film), 25 fps (PAL - the European video standard), and 30 fps (NTSC - the American/Japanese video standard).

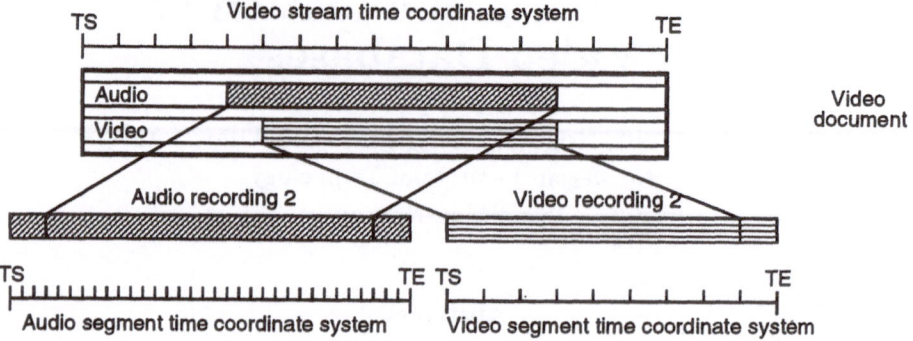

Figure 1: Temporal Relations between Video Documents and Stored Segments

As discussed in [9, 10], a video database should support applications and users in sharing video information. In a shared environment the same piece of video may be used in several video documents. The traditional way to cope with this type of information sharing is to make a separate copy of the video for each document. When digital video is managed by a computer one can create virtual video documents [15, 14] and, thus, avoid making copies of video and meta-data to save storage space and preserve database consistency [8].

Since video is a complex data type we have argued [11] that a video database should provide a generic data model which captures the most important properties of video data such as video document composition, video document structuring and contents indexing. It should also provide a set of well-defined operations that can be used in video data browsing and querying. The purpose of this paper is to present a video database foundation that gives a formal definition of the contents of a video database and that defines operations for querying the temporal properties of video data.

This paper is organized as follows: In Section 2 we discuss the importance of time for interpreting video information. Section 3 presents the mathematical definition of the the contents of video databases. In Section 4 we present (temporal) operations that apply to video data and collections of such data. The operations are based on temporal database research and we discuss how the proposed operations differ from temporal data operations. Sections 5 and 6 discuss how the operations can be used to provide browsing and querying capabilities while Section 7 concludes the paper.

2 The Role of Time in Video Composition

The very first film makers noticed that temporal composition (in film theory called *montage*) was at least as important as spatial composition - i.e., how the scene space is organized (in film theory called *mise en scène*). During a series of experiments and studies in the last half of the 1920s, Soviet film makers [7] found that the meaning of a piece of film was heavily influenced by the surrounding parts (i.e., its context). Sergei M. Eisenstein, for instance, showed "the fact that two film pieces of any kind, placed together, inevitably combine into a new concept, a new quality, arising out of the juxtaposition" [7]. Eisenstein illustrates this by a small example: "For example, take a grave, juxtaposed with a woman in mourning weeping beside it, and scarcely anybody will fail to jump to the conclusion: a widow." [7]

The Soviet film makers identified three main steps in film creation - time considerations play the major role in two of these steps:

> *Pudovkin offers a sort of formula: Film creation equals (1) what is shown in the shots, (2) the order in which they appear, and (3) how long each is held on the screen. [7]*

It is, therefore, necessary to establish a context - i.e., adding pieces of video - for the user to interpret a single piece of video correctly. For instance, to ensure that the user interprets the woman mentioned in the previous example as a widow, the video showing her should be preceded by video showing the grave. Handling contexts is an important feature of a shared video base since the interpretation of video data is depending strongly on its context.

In a different paper [12] we have proposed explicit handling of contexts and defined three different contexts for a piece of video. The *primary* context is the context established in one specific video document as a result of the *montage*. Information derived from the primary context will be closely related to the document into which a piece of video is used, but it will not generally be relevant for other documents - i.e., contexts - into which the same piece of video is used.

The single recording that a piece of video is part of, constitutes its *basic* context. Information derived from the basic context will be valid for a piece of video independent from any primary context into which it may appear - e.g., information about the location for recording and information about persons or objects shown in the frames. (This type of information has been called *sensory indexes* by Rowe et al. [18].)

When retrieving information regarding a specific video document it may also be useful to consider other documents into which the same piece of video has been used. These documents constitute the *secondary* context seen from one specific document's perspective.

3 Video Data

A video database will store different types of information as shown in the data model presented in [11]. In this paper we will define a video database as a collection of sets where the elements of each set are elements of the same type. We are using an object-oriented approach so each element is identified by a unique object identity. Objects may be complex with attributes that are objects on their own. Below we give a short description of the different object types which are relevant for this paper:

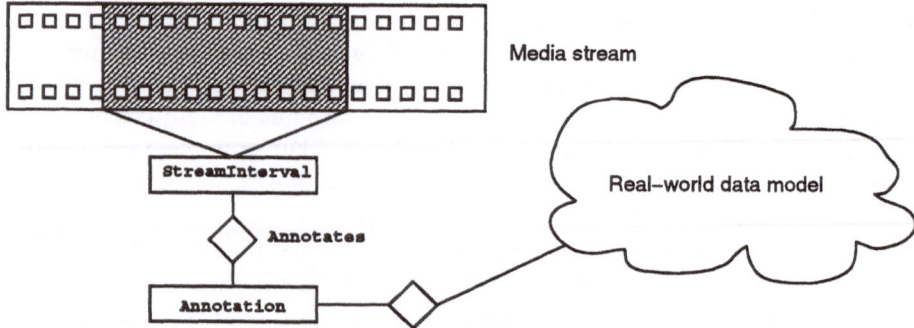

Figure 2: Linking a Real-World Model to Stream Intervals

- **Stored Media Segments:** Audio and video data which are generated during recording are stored as separate media segments.

- **Video Streams:** Video documents are composed from pieces of stored media segments. A video document represents a logical stream of video data that may not be explicitly stored.

- **Media Streams:** Media streams are a generalization of stored media segments and video streams.

- **Stream Interval:** A stream interval represents a contiguous sequence from a media stream that is explicitly identified.

- **Video Content Indexes/Annotations:** For browsing and querying purposes there is a need to relate entities from a real-world model to pieces of video. As shown in Figure 2 this relation can be established via an annotation object that identifies the stream interval of interest and that is linked to an element of a real-world model.

- **Video Document Structure:** Video documents can - as other more traditional documents - have a certain structure [9]. This structure can be represented by a set of structural components where each component identifies a stream interval.

3.1 Media Streams and Video Time Systems

As other data, video data can be related to real time - e.g., date and time for production (recording and editing). In this paper, however, we are concerned with the time systems defined by video streams and stored media segments and the relation between these time systems. Digital audio and video represent data with a discrete time system [4] - e.g., the unit of time in PAL video is 1/25th of a second while the unit of time in CD audio is 1/44100th of a second.

Contrary to real time, there is no total ordering of time in a video database. Each media stream *ms* defines its own time coordinate system uniquely identified by a stream identity (*ms.SID*). Each media stream defines the absolute start (*ms.TS*) and end (*ms.TE*) times for the time coordinate system and the size of each time unit (*ms.TimeUnitSize*). The collection of media streams is denoted MS_Set.

Figure 1 illustrates how these time coordinate systems relate to each other. Generally, audio and video are digitized with different frequencies since video usually is digitized at 5-30 Hz while audio usually is digitized at 8-44 kHz. As a consequence, the time unit in a video stream may be different from the time unit of the stored segments used in the composition. This is shown in the figure.

3.2   Stream Intervals

A stream interval identifies a contiguous part of a media stream. It is an element of the *StreamInt_Set* and has the following definition:

$StreamInt = (oid, MS\_ref, TS, TE)$ where

$$TS \leq TE \wedge$$
$$\exists ms \in MS\_Set \ (MS\_ref = ms \wedge ms.TS \leq TS \wedge ms.TE \geq TE)$$

From the definition it can be noted that:

- A stream interval may be part of either a stored media segment or a video document which it refers to via *MS_ref*.

- The size of a stream interval is at least one time unit and its start and end times are within the range defined by the referred media stream.

3.3   Stored Media Segments

In addition to the attributes inherited from media streams, a stored media segment has a *Type* attribute that gives the type and format of the stored segment - e.g., MPEG-1 video - and a *MediaData* attribute that contains the actual media data.

3.4   Video Streams

Each video stream has a *Tracks* attribute which defines a set of tracks of a single medium and a *Composition* attribute that defines how the video stream is composed.

AV_Clips are the building blocks in a video stream composition. Each AV_Clip represents an interval of an audio/video recording (stored media segment) and all AV_Clips in a video stream share a common time-line in a way similar to the approach used in QuickTime [2]. This means that we assume that stored segment time values are bound to video stream time coordinate systems during production.

In our work we have deliberately chosen a two-level approach where each AV_Clip is mapped to an audio or a video recording and cannot be an interval from another (virtual) video stream. We then avoid unnesting of an arbitrary number of levels during replay and querying. In addition, this allows the distinctions that we have made between primary, basic and secondary contexts. The opposite choice has been taken in OVID [17] and by Duda et al. [6] to give the authors of video/multimedia documents greater flexibility in reusing composite components and in handling document dependencies. The AV_Clip is a member of the *AV_Clip_Set* and is defined as follows:

$$AV\_Clip = (oid, VS\_SI, Track, SMS\_SI) \text{ where}$$
$$VS\_SI, SMS\_SI \in StreamInt\_Set \land$$
$$\exists vs \in VS\_Set \ (VS\_SI.MS\_ref = vs \land Track \in vs.Tracks) \land$$
$$\exists sms \in SMS\_Set \ (SMS\_SI.MS\_ref = sms \land Track.Type = sms.Type)$$

From the definition it can be noted that:

- The AV_Clip refers to a stream interval from a stored media segment (*SMS_SI*).

- The AV_Clip also refers to the corresponding stream interval within the video stream itself (*VS_SI*).

- The AV_Clip must be part of a track of the same media type.

Now, we can define a video stream's composition:

$$vs.Composition = \{ \ avc \in AV\_Clip \mid avc.VS\_SI.MS\_ref = vs \ \}$$

3.5 Content Indexing

As shown in Figure 2 annotations provide the means for relating real-world entities such as persons, objects and locations or free text descriptions to stream intervals. This way of indexing arbitrary pieces of video contents has been inspired by T.G.A. Smith [19].

An annotation is a member of the *Annot_Set* and can be defined as:

$$Annot = (oid, a_1, a_2, ..., a_m, SI\_ref) \text{ where}$$
$$SI\_ref \in StreamInt\_Set \land a_1, ..., a_m \text{ are type specific attributes}$$

From the definition it can be noted that:

- Different types of annotations may have a different number of attributes but annotations of all types identify a stream interval where the annotation is valid.

- The stream interval may refer to a stored media segment for sensory content indexing or a video stream for topic content indexing [18].

3.6   Structure

In a video database there are two main types of meta-data related to a video stream, content indexes and video document structure. We have proposed a video document structure that allows the user to organize the contents of a video document in a hierarchical structure (inspired by film theory [16]) of shots, scenes, sequences, and compound units [11]. One important aspect of structural components is that they may represent contexts for interpreting video data at various levels of granularity - e.g., a shot represents a context of finer granularity than a sequence.

A structural component is a member of the *Struct_Set* and can be defined as:

$$StructComp = (oid, Type, a_1, a_2, ..., a_m, SI\_ref) \text{ where}$$
$$SI\_ref \in StreamInt\_Set \land \exists vs \in VS\_Set \ (SI\_ref.MS\_ref = vs) \land$$
$$Type \in \{cu, seq, scene, shot\} \land a_1, ..., a_m \text{ are type specific attributes}$$

From the definition it can be noted that:

- Video structures are related to video streams only and not to stored media segments. This stems from the assumption that structures are created during editing.

- Four different types of structural components are defined.

4   Basic Video Operations

In the following subsections we will discuss different types of operations that may be applied to video objects and sets of such objects.

4.1   Stream Interval Functions and Operations

In this subsection we will present functions and operations that apply to stream intervals. A stream interval represents a set of time values and, thus, variants of the set operations *intersection, union*, and *difference* can be applied to stream intervals.

Interval Intersection
The interval intersection operation (*) creates and returns a stream interval representing the intersecting part of two stream intervals if this exist (which also means that the two stream intervals have to be from the same media stream). If x and y are two intersecting stream intervals $z = x * y$ has the following properties:

$$z.MS\_ref = x.MS\_ref \land z.TS = \max(x.TS, y.TS) \land z.TE = \min(x.TE, y.TE)$$

Interval Concatenation
The interval concatenation operation (+) creates and returns a stream interval

representing the concatenation of two stream intervals if the two stream intervals constitute one, contiguous stream interval. If x and y are two concatenating stream intervals $z = x + y$ has the following properties:

$$z.MS\_ref = x.MS\_ref \wedge z.TS = \min(x.TS, y.TS) \wedge z.TE = \max(x.TE, y.TE)$$

Lower Interval Difference

The difference between two intervals may, in the case where the first input interval encloses the other, result in two piecewise contiguous intervals. Since a stream interval is defined to be one, contiguous interval we have chosen to define two variants of the difference operator, which return the lower and upper part of the resulting interval, respectively. The lower interval difference $(-_<)$ creates and returns a stream interval representing the part of a stream interval appearing before the other interval, if such a part exist. If x and y are two stream intervals from the same video stream and $x.TS < y.TS$ then $z = x -_< y$ returns a non-empty interval which has the following properties:

$$z.MS\_ref = x.MS\_ref \wedge z.TS = x.TS \wedge z.TE = \min(x.TE, y.TS - 1)$$

Upper Interval Difference

The upper interval difference $(-_>)$ creates and returns a stream interval representing the part of a stream interval appearing after the other interval, if such a part exist. If x and y are two stream intervals from the same video stream and $x.TE > y.TE$ then $z = x -_> y$ returns a non-empty interval which has the following properties:

$$z.MS\_ref = x.MS\_ref \wedge z.TS = max(x.TS, y.TE + 1) \wedge z.TE = x.TE$$

4.2   Mapped Video Object Set Operations

In the previous subsection we studied operations on individual stream intervals. In this subsection we will discuss operations that apply to sets of video objects. The members of these sets are called *mapped video objects* because of their structure: *(Obj_ref, Interval)*. *Obj_ref* is the identity of an video object that will have a stream interval attribute. *Interval* is also a stream interval which can be associated with the video object that may be different from the stream interval over which the object is defined. The rest of this subsection and the next subsection will explain the use of the mapped video object set.

Set and Relational Operations

Set theoretic operations such as intersection, union, and difference are defined in the normal way. Relational operations such as selection and projection [3] are also defined on mapped video object sets:

Selection: $\sigma_P(A) = \{a \mid a \in A \wedge P(a)\}$
Projection: $\pi_Y(A) = \{a[Y] \mid a \in A\}$

where P is a boolean predicate defined over attributes of the elements of A.

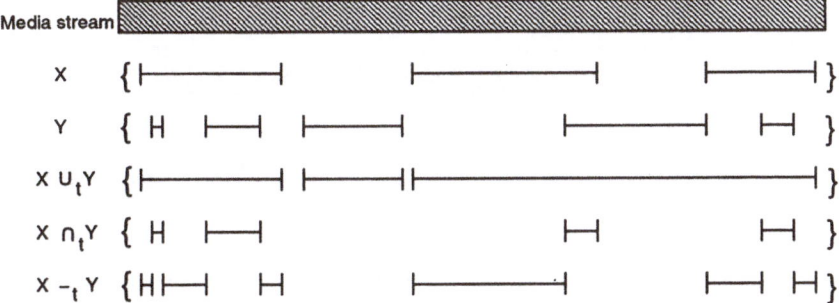

Figure 3: Video Stream Set Operations

The temporal set operations defined in this section are different from the ones defined by Clifford and Crocker [5], in which case only merge-compatible tuples - i.e., tuples where attributes other than the time attributes have pairwise equal values - are merged. The reason for defining the operations this way will become more apparent when discussing querying in Section 6. Figure 3 exemplifies how the *Interval* part of some mapped video objects are combined with temporal set operations.

Temporal Merge Operations

The first operation, *tMerge*, is a unary operation that combines all stream intervals that intersect into longer, non-intersecting intervals. The operation can be defined as:

$$tMerge(X) = \; Y \text{where } \forall x \in X (\exists y \in Y(x.Interval \text{ WITHIN } y.Interval \wedge \\ \nexists z \in Y(z.Interval \text{ INTERSECTS } y.Interval \; \wedge \; z \neq y)))$$

Interval Set Union

Stream interval set union, $\cup_t$, returns the union of stream intervals from the two input sets after merging intersecting stream intervals. The operations can be defined as:

$$X \cup_t Y = tMerge(X \cup Y)$$

Interval set intersection

Stream interval set intersection, $\cap_t$, returns the stream intervals constituting the pairwise intersection between the elements of the two input sets. The operation can be defined as:

$$X \cap_t Y = \; \{(NULL, x.Interval * y.Interval) \mid x \in X \wedge y \in Y \wedge \\ x.Interval \text{ INTERSECTS } y.Interval\}$$

Interval set difference

Stream interval set difference, $-_t$, returns the subintervals from stream intervals

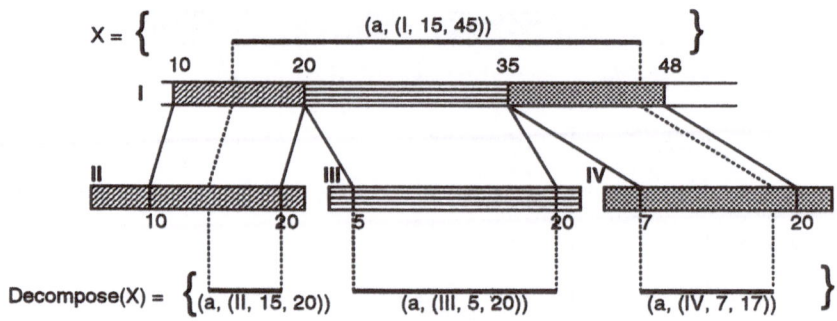

Figure 4: The *Decompose* Operation

in the first input set after removing all subintervals intersecting at least one
stream interval from the second set. The operations can be defined as:

$$X -_t Y = \quad Z \text{ where } \forall z \in Z(\exists x \in X(z.Interval \text{ WITHIN } x.Interval)\wedge$$
$$\nexists y \in Y(y.Interval \text{ INTERSECTS } z.Interval)\wedge$$
$$\nexists v \in Z(v \text{ INTERSECTS } z \wedge v \neq z))\}$$

Filter Operations

Allen has shown that there are 13 (disjunct) relationships that can exist between
two temporal intervals [1] that can be evaluated by comparing start and end
times for the intervals [13]. Other relationships, such as INTERSECTS can also
be defined. Because a video database contains several different time coordinate
systems, we have to add the condition that two stream intervals have to be
from the same stream before a time interval relationship can exist.

The filter operator, *tReduce*, returns a set of objects from an *originating set*
that have a given temporal relationship to at least one of the elements from a
filter set. Let X and Y be two mapped video object sets and let P be a boolean
predicate returning *true* if a given relationship exists. Then we define

$$tReduce(X, Y, P) = \{x \in X | \exists y \in Y(P(x.Interval, y.Interval))\}$$

4.3 Context Mapping Operators

The operators in this subsection map objects from one time coordinate system
onto another. A mapping operation does not affect the *Obj_ref* part of a
mapped video object while the *Interval* part after the operation gives the
interval of time onto which the object is mapped.

The *Decompose* operator which is illustrated in Figure 4 maps the objects
in the input set onto the corresponding stored media segments. If an element
in the input set is already related to a part of a stored media segment, the
element will be copied without changes to the output set. If an an element in
the input set is related to a part of a video stream, the element will be mapped
onto the stored media stream(s) from which the corresponding stream interval

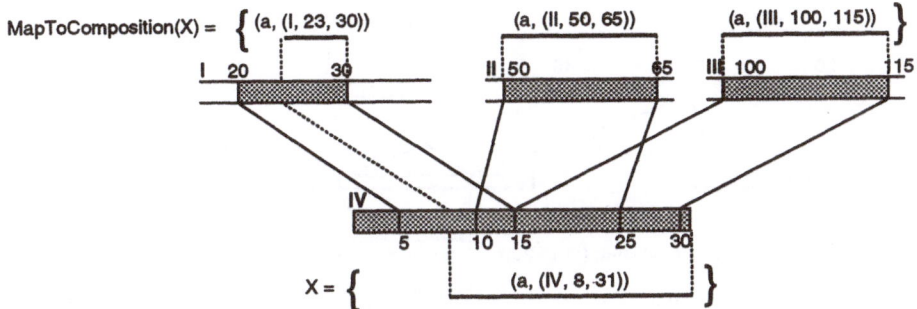

Figure 5: The *MapToComposition* Operation

is composed. In Figure 4 *I* is a video stream and *II*, *III*, and *IV* are stored media segments.

The *MapToComposition* operator maps objects in the opposite direction - i.e., from the time coordinate systems of stored media segments to video streams. If an element in the input set is related to a video stream, the element will be copied without changes to the output set. If, on the other hand, the element is related to a stored media segments, the element will be mapped onto all video streams which uses parts of the stream interval in its composition. This is illustrated in Figure 5.

The *MapToStream* operator maps objects onto one specific video stream. All elements in the input set related to the specified "target" video stream given as input to the operator will be copied to the output set. If an element in the input set is related to a different video stream, the element will not be copied to the output set. If an element in the input set is related to a stored media segment, it will be mapped to the given video stream if possible. The *MapToStream* is similar to *MapToComposition* except that only objects referring to the given stream will be present in the result. If, for instance, *X* is as given in Figure 5 the result from mapping *X* to stream *I* would be: $MapToStream(X, I) = \{ (a, (I, 23, 30)) \}$

5   Contents Browsing

A user of a video database who are watching or working with a video document may wish to get more information about the video material than can actually be seen in the pictures and heard from the sound. The user may, for instance, want to know the names of the persons shown, the name of the location where the video was recorded and the time of recording. To address this kind of needs the database system should support browsing of content indexes related to a video document.

Since annotations can be made in different contexts, browsing can also be done in different contexts. By browsing the *primary* context the user will get

306

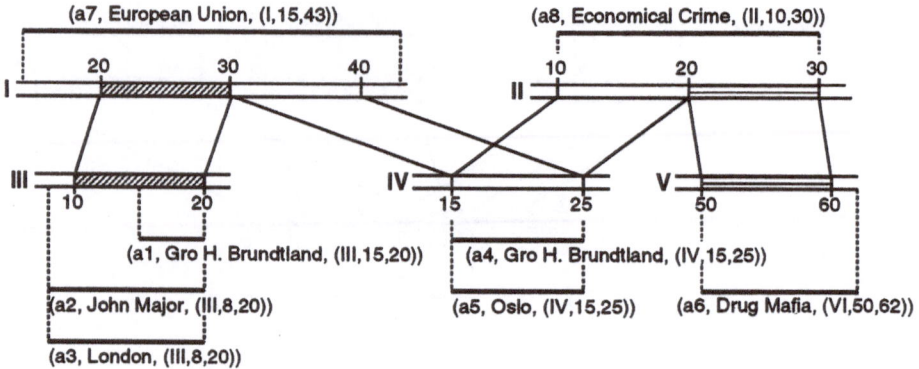

Figure 6: The Video Intervals and Annotations used in our Examples

all annotations related to the topic of a video document - i.e., all annotations related to that specific document. By browsing the *basic* context the user will get all annotations related to the stored media segments used in the document's composition - e.g., annotations related to persons, objects or locations seen in the video recording. By browsing the *secondary* context the user will get annotations applied to other video documents using some intersecting parts of the video document's stored media segments.

5.1 Browsing Primary Context

The most fundamental scope of contents browsing is to browse the annotations that are directly related to a virtual video (or a stored media segment). Browsing primary context means retrieving every annotation that is directly associated with a particular stream interval. Assume the stream *interval of interest* is given by the interval *ThisInterval*. Then, formally, the set of relevant annotations is given by:

$$\{\ (a, a.Interval * ThisInterval)\ |\ \exists a \in Annot\_Set \wedge$$
$$a.Interval\ \text{INTERSECTS}\ ThisInterval\ \}$$

This set gives the object identifiers of all the annotations defined for some part of *ThisInterval* and, for each annotation, the specific part of *ThisInterval* where the annotation is valid. One can implement a `GetPrimaryAnn` function which will return the set of relevant annotations. The function must be called with *ThisInterval* as parameter and will return the set of all annotations intersecting the given interval.

The following example may clarify this concept: Assume that five different stream intervals are defined in a video database as shown in Figure 6. The first two media streams (*I* and *II*) are video streams, while the other (*III*, *IV* and *V*) are stored media segments. Annotations are related to both the basic and

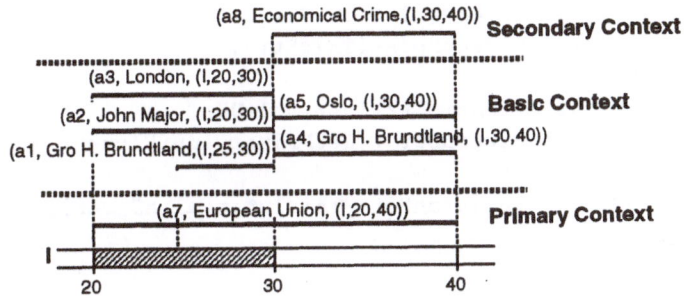

Figure 7: The Stream Interval of Interest and the Valid Annotations

primary contexts. The set of annotations is called AS and its elements are:

$\{\ (a1, Gro\ H.\ Brundtland, (III, 15, 20)),\ (a2, John\ Major, (III, 8, 20)),$
$(a3, London, (III, 8, 20)),\ (a4, Gro\ H.\ Brundtland, (IV, 15, 25)),$
$(a5, Oslo, (IV, 15, 25)),\ (a6, Drug\ Mafia, (V, 50, 62)),$
$(a7, European\ Union, (I, 15, 43)),\ (a8, Economical\ Crime, (II, 10, 30))\ \}$

Let $(I, 20, 40)$ be the value of *ThisInterval*. The result from applying the function `GetPrimaryAnn` on interval I is: $\{\ (a7, (I, 20, 40))\ \}$ which is the only annotation in the primary context of *ThisInterval*. This is illustrated in Figure 7 which also shows how the annotations from the basic and the secondary contexts can be mapped onto *ThisInterval*.

5.2   Browsing Basic Context

Often it is interesting to get the content of the stored media segments that are used in a the composition of a virtual video stream - i.e., the basic content for the virtual video stream interval.

The way of doing this is to decompose the *ThisInterval* into the corresponding stored media stream intervals by using the *Decompose* operation presented in Section 4.3. This returns a set of stored media segments, and by applying the operation given in the previous subsection on each of these we get a set of basic annotations. The problem is that these annotations are no longer defined in the primary context of the original video stream and they have to be mapped to this context. The *MapToStream* operation defined in Section 4.3 will do this kind of mapping.

Pseudo code for function `GetBasicAnn` for an interval *ThisInterval* can look like this:

```
GetBasicAnn(StreamInt ThisInterval) : AnnotationSet
BEGIN
  Res = {};
  ThisSet = {};
```

```
INSERT (NULL, ThisInterval) INTO ThisSet;
BasicCtxtInterval = Decompose(ThisSet);
BasicAnnSet = {};
FOR EACH Element IN BasicCtxtInterval DO
  BasicAnnSet = BasicAnnSet + GetPrimaryAnn(Element.Interval);
ENDFOR;
Res = MapToStream(BasicAnnSet, ThisInterval.MS_ref);
RETURN res;
END;
```

By taking the union of the result from `GetPrimaryAnn` and `GetBasicAnn` the user will get annotations from both the primary and the basic context.

Continuing the example from the previous subsection we first have to decompose *ThisInterval*. This decomposition gives the set of basic contexts:

$$\{ (NULL, (III, 10, 20)), (NULL, (IV, 15, 25)) \}$$

Performing the `GetPrimaryAnn` on each of these stored media segments we get the basic annotations:

$$\{ (a1, (III, 15, 20)), (a2, (III, 10, 20)), (a3, (III, 10, 20)),$$
$$(a4, (IV, 15, 25)), (a5, (IV, 15, 25)) \}$$

These are the basic annotations for the virtual video interval. But before the result can be presented to the user the annotations have to be mapped to the primary context of *ThisInterval*:

$$\{ (a1, (I, 25, 30)), (a2, (I, 20, 30)), (a3, (I, 20, 30)),$$
$$(a4, (I, 30, 40)), (a5, (I, 30, 40)) \}$$

5.3   Browsing the Secondary Context

The two previous subsections showed how to browse the content that is directly valid for a video document. But since our model support sharing of video, users may sometimes want to get information that is related to other use of the same basic material (i.e., the secondary context).

The browsing process is similar to the one used for browsing the basic context except for one additional mapping. We do not want to make this discussion more comprehensive that necessary and will only illustrate the browsing algorithm through the example.

Again, we start by decomposing *ThisInterval* to have it mapped to basic contexts. From this we can get the corresponding intervals from the secondary context by applying the `MapToComposition` operation which will give us the following set:

$$\{ (NULL, (I, 20, 30)), (NULL, (I, 30, 40)), (NULL, (II, 10, 20)) \}$$

The two first elements are part of *ThisInterval* and, thus, part of the primary context, so we only use the last stream interval when searching for annotations.

The function `GetPrimaryAnn` used on the latter interval gives the set of annotations from the secondary context: $\{ (a8, (II, 10, 20)) \}$

Before presenting this set to the user, we have to map the element to the primary context by first decomposing it to the basic context and then map it to the stream interval of interest:

$Decompose(\{ (a8, (II, 10, 20)) \}) = \{ (a8, (IV, 15, 25)) \}$
$MapToStream(\{ (a8, (II, 10, 20)) \} , I) = \{ (a8, (I, 30, 40)) \}$

By using set operations on this set and the sets from the previous subsections the user can further specify the amount of meta-data he or she wants to browse.

5.4   Browsing of Structure

Assume that a user of a television news archive wants to browse through a collection of television news to have a quick impression of their contents. Fast forward replay has been the traditional way to do this kind of browsing. The structure information can be used to generate a table of contents and allow the user to, for instance, directly jump to one given news item or one specific scene within a news item. The structure information can also be used to give the user a description of the context into which a piece of video has been used - e.g., when pieces of video have been retrieved in content-based queries.

6   Video Querying

While browsing allows a user to get all information (in the database) related to a specific piece of video, querying makes it possible to formulate some conditions and then retrieve only the video material that have the desired properties.

Since the focus of this paper is on continuous media and not on data modelling as such, we can limit our data model of the mini-world to very simple annotations which have only a name attribute and structural components that have only a type attribute. A more thorough discussion of application domain models related to video databases can be found in [10] and in [18]

The space limitations do not allow a discussion of every aspect of querying in our model. Rather we will give some motivating examples of different complexity to show how the basic concepts and operations can be utilized in query formulation and query processing.

6.1   Simple Queries

The simpler queries are the queries where it is sufficient to use the selection operator only. Assume that AS is the set of annotations as defined in Section 5. Then we can formulate queries which retrieves the set of stream intervals where the Norwegian Prime Minister Gro H. Brundtland can be seen (S_1), and

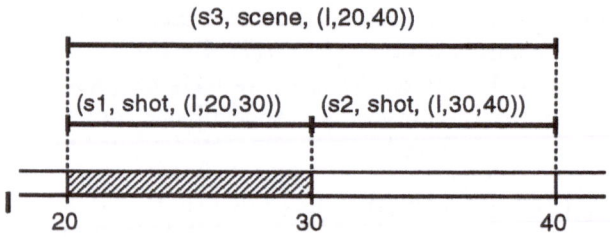

Figure 8: Structure Information for Part of the Video stream with SID = I

the set of stream intervals where the British Prime Minister John Major can be seen (S_2):

$$S_1 = \sigma_{Name = 'Gro\ H.\ Brundtland'}(AS) = \{\ a1,\ a4\ \}$$
$$\pi_{oid,Interval}S_1 = \{\ (a1,(III,15,20)),\ (a4,(IV,15,25))\ \}$$

$$S_2 = \sigma_{Name = 'JohnMajor'}(AS) = \{\ a2\ \}$$
$$\pi_{oid,Interval}S_2 = \{\ (a2,(III,8,20))\ \}$$

6.2 Queries With Operations on Sets of Stream Intervals

Queries where we only use the selection operator do not allow us to formulate conditions which involve operations on stream intervals. One example of such a query is the need to find stream intervals related to both John Major and Gro H. Brundtland (S_3).

$$S_3 = \pi_{oid,Interval}S_1 \cap_t \pi_{oid,Interval}S_2 = \{\ (NULL,(III,15,20))\ \}$$

If we want to find the stream intervals with John Major or Gro H. Brundtland or both, S_4 will provide the answer.

$$\begin{aligned} S_4 &= \pi_{oid,Interval}S_1 \cup_t \pi_{oid,Interval}S_2 \\ &= \{\ (NULL,(III,8,20)),\ (NULL,(IV,15,25))\ \} \end{aligned}$$

It is also possible to find the stream intervals with Gro H. Brundtland which are not related to John Major (S_5).

$$S_5 = \pi_{oid,Interval}S_1 -_t \pi_{oid,Interval}S_2 = \{\ (NULL,(IV,15,25))\ \}$$

6.3 Explicit Control of the Granularity of the Result

The structure defined for video streams can be used to control the granularity of the query results. Rather than getting the smallest possible stream intervals fulfilling the conditions we can make queries which return structural components of the requested type.

Suppose that we have a set of structural components as defined in SS (see also Figure 8):

$$SS = \{ (s1, shot, (I, 20, 30)), (s2, shot, (I, 30, 40)), (s3, scene, (I, 20, 40)) \}$$

Assume that we want to retrieve all scenes which in some way are related to Gro H. Brundtland:

```
BEGIN
  GroSet = SELECT(AS,Name='Gro H. Brundtland'); // S1
  Scenes = SELECT(SS,Type=scene);                // {(s3,(I,20,40))}
  Res = tReduce(Scenes,GroSet,INTERSECTS*);      // {(s3,(I,20,40))}
  RETURN Res;
END;
```

In the filter operation we have used a variant of the INTERSECTS called INTERSECTS* that implicitly maps the originating and filter sets to the primary contexts before performing the filtering. If the sets had not been mapped, tReduce operation would have returned an empty set because the elements of GroSet and Scenes are all from different contexts.

6.4 Complex Queries

Imaging a video database which contains material from television news. A researcher may then want to know if material related to economical crimes have been used in scenes which are related to the European Union. If the annotations are made within the same context we can search as follows:

```
BEGIN
  Scenes = SELECT(SS,Type=scene);                   // {(s3,(I,20,40))}
  EUSet = SELECT(AS,Name='European Union');         // {(a7,(I,15,43))}
  ECSet = SELECT(AS,Name='Economical Crime');//      {(a8,(II,10,30))}
  Res = tReduce(Scenes,EUSet,INTERSECTS*);          // {(s3,(I,20,40))}
  Res = tReduce(Res,ECSet,INTERSECTS*);             // Empty
  RETURN Res;
END;
```

As the example shows, we will not find the relevant scenes if the annotations are made in different contexts which both use the same part of some stored media segments. To be able to retrieve such scenes we have utilize the power of the context mapping operations and to process the query as shown below.

```
BEGIN
  Scenes = SELECT(SS,Type=scene);                        // {(s3,(I,20,40))}
  EUSet = Decompose(SELECT(AS,Name='European Union'));
      // { (a7,(III,10,20)), (a7,(IV,15,25)) }
  ECSet = Decompose( SELECT(AS,Name='Economical Crime') );
      // { (a8,(IV,15,25)), (a8,(V,50,60)) }
  Res = tReduce(Scenes,EUSet,INTERSECTS*);          // {(s3,(I,20,40))}
```

```
Res = tReduce(Res,ECSet,INTERSECTS*);        // {(s3,(I,20,40))}
RETURN Res;
END;
```

7 Conclusion and Further Work

In this paper we have developed a temporal foundation for modelling, searching, and browsing of video data. We have shown that the results achieved by the temporal database community are useful when developing database support for video data but we have also shown that video data put forward new requirements that need extended functionality.

The main reason for the new requirements is that a video database constitutes partial ordered time systems. Thus, all operations have to care about the argument's time coordinate systems. In addition, video composition creates dependencies between different time coordinate systems and operations have to be provided to map objects between time coordinate systems. The mapping operations that we have proposed supports such mappings in a consistent way.

In video database queries the user will often ask for objects having a given temporal relation to other objects. The proposed filter operation provides a useful tool for formulating such queries.

The set operations are defined over mapped video object sets. By this we have provided a homogeneous way to operate on sets of stream intervals, sets of video objects and sets of video objects mapped onto a different time coordinate system.

We feel that our research has shown that the temporal database community can contribute to video/multimedia database research and we will encourage temporal database researchers to study video and multimedia databases as a special type of temporal databases that need their contributions.

To demonstrate and to evaluate our research we are developing a video database framework called VideoSTAR (Video STorage And Retrieval) [11]. The research reported in this paper has been the basis for developing a video query algebra interface to VideoSTAR [12] which is now running on our prototype system.

As a further activity we will evaluate the VideoSTAR framework by implementing real video databases on top of the framework. A part of this evaluation is to evaluate the video query algebra and the expressiveness of the underlying foundation. As a further research one should also look into efficiency and optimization problems and one should try to develop a declarative query language that can utilize the power of the video query algebra.

References

[1] J.F. Allen. Maintaining Knowledge about Temporal Intervals. *Communications of the ACM*, November 1983.

[2] Apple Computer, Inc. *QuickTime*. Inside Macintosh. Addison-Wesley Publishing Company, 1993.

[3] P. Atzeni and V. De Antonellis. *Relational Database Theory*. The Benjamin/Cummings Publishing Company, Inc., 1993.

[4] C. Breiteneder, S. Gibbs, and D. Tsichritzis. Modelling of Audio/Video Data. In *Proceedings of the 11th International Conference on the Entity-Relationship Approach*, Karlsruhe, Germany, October 7-9 1992.

[5] J. Clifford and A. Crocker. The Historical Relational Data Model (HRDM) Revisited. In A.U. Tansel et al., editors, *Temporal Databases: Theory, Design, and Implementation*, chapter 1. The Benjamin/Cummings Publishing Company, Inc., 1993.

[6] A. Duda, R. Weiss, and D.K. Gifford. Content-Based Access to Algebraic Video. In *Proceedings of the International Conference on Multimedia Computing and Systems*, Boston, MA, May 1994.

[7] J.C. Ellis. *A History of Film*. Prentice Hall, 3rd edition, 1990.

[8] R. Hjelsvold. Sharing and Reuse of Video Information. In *Proceedings of the ACM Multimedia'94 Conference Workshop on Multimedia Database Management Systems*, San Francisco, California, October 1994.

[9] R. Hjelsvold. Video Information Contents and Architecture. In *Proceedings of the 4th International Conference on Extending Database Technology*, Cambridge, UK, March 28-31 1994.

[10] R. Hjelsvold and R. Midtstraum. Modelling and Querying Video Data. In *Proceedings of the 20th VLDB Conference*, Santiago, Chile, September 1994.

[11] R. Hjelsvold and R. Midtstraum. Databases for Video Information Sharing. In *Proceedings of the IS&T/SPIE Symposium on Electronic Imaging Science and Technology, Conference on Storage and Retrieval for Image and Video Databases III*, San Jose, CA, February 1995.

[12] R. Hjelsvold, R. Midtstraum, and O. Sandstå. Searching and Browsing a Shared Video Database. To be presented at the First Internation Workshop on Multimedia Database Management Systems, to be held in Blue Mountain Lake, NY, August 1995.

[13] T.Y.C. Leung and R.R. Muntz. Stream Processing: Temporal Query Processing and Optimization. In A.U. Tansel et al., editors, *Temporal Databases: Theory, Design, and Implementation*, chapter 14. The Benjamin/Cummings Publishing Company, Inc., 1993.

[14] T.D.C. Little et al. A Digital On-Demand Video Service Supporting Content-Based Queries. In *Proceedings of ACM Multimedia 93*, Anaheim, USA, August 1993.

[15] W.E. Mackay and G. Davenport. Virtual Video Editing In Interactive Multimedia Applications. *Communications of the ACM*, 32(7), 1989.

[16] J. Monaco. *How to Read a Film. The Art, Technology, Language, History and Theory of Film and Media.* Oxford University Press, 1981.

[17] E. Oomoto and K. Tanaka. OVID: Design and Implementation of a Video-Object Database System. *IEEE Transactions on Knowledge and Data Engineering*, 5(4), 1993.

[18] L.A. Rowe, J.S. Boreczky, and C.A. Eads. Indexes for User Access to Large Video Databases. In *Proceedings of the IS&T/SPIE Symposium on Electronic Imaging Science and Technology, Conference on Storage and Retrieval for Image and Video Databases II*, San Jose, CA, February 1994.

[19] T.G.A. Smith. If You Could See What I Mean... Descriptions of Video in an Anthropologist's Notebook. Master's thesis, MIT, 1992.

[20] A.U. Tansel et al. *Temporal Databases - Theory, Design and Implementation.* The Benjamin/Cummings Publishing Company, Inc., 1993.

Querying Historical Data in IBM DB2 C/S DBMS Using Recursive SQL

T.Y. Cliff Leung

IBM Santa Teresa Lab.

San Jose, CA 95141, USA

Hamid Pirahesh

IBM Almaden Research Center

San Jose, CA 95120, USA

Abstract

Many applications handle time-varying data. In this paper, we discuss how existing features of IBM DB2 for AIX Version 2 can be used to support this type of applications efficiently, in terms of both storage and query evaluation [1]. We discuss several temporal data models, the trade-offs among these models, and how one can formulate so-called "as of" or "time-slice" queries in these models. We also show how "time-coalesce" operation can be expressed directly in SQL. In all these features, the recursive SQL capability supported by DB2 plays a crucial role. While DB2 lacks many temporal features proposed in the literature, we show to what extent existing features of a commercial DBMS, such as DB2, can be used to provide some advanced supports for time-varying data.

1 Introduction

Historical data analysis is a very important component in many advanced application areas. Example applications include inventory control and decision support in traditional business environments, and complex system performance monitoring using trace data. This type of analysis can provide valuable information by querying entity history. There has been active research in temporal database systems for more than a decade [12, 9], and recently TSQL2 has been designed by a group of experts in this community [10, 11].

While there is no direct temporal support in commercial relational DBMSs, such as DB2, that many researchers have been seeking, relational DBMSs support time, date and timestamp data types which can be exploited in storing temporal information. Scalar functions are also provided to extract time fields such as year, month and hour. Although users or DBAs have to maintain historical data themselves, historical data can still be stored and queried in database, just like any other types of data.

Many temporal data models have been proposed in the literature [7, 9, 5]. In this paper, we discuss how users can implement the "classic" data model [7]. In the classic approach, one can augment a non-temporal table with a pair of timestamp columns which store the start time and end time for each tuple. We show how one can formulate as of queries in this model.

One of the major problems in the classic temporal data model is that historical databases can grow quickly and tremendously in size due to update operations. For example, if a database initially has 10G bytes data and every

---

[1] IBM DB2 for OS/2 has the same functionality as DB2 for AIX [3]. In this paper, we simply refer to them as DB2 for brevity.

tuple is updated 10 times over a period of time, the database becomes 100G bytes. This poses a serious performance problem for queries and updates. To address this concern, we present several alternative data models in this paper. In these data models, update operations append to historical tables only the *updated* information instead of the entire tuple of current information at the time of update. This strategy is very effective in reducing the storage overhead when the historical table has many columns but only very few columns are modified by update operations.

A key question in these alternative data models is whether we may store less information than the classic data model. For example, it is important to formulate a time-join query in SQL in these alternatives to preserve the SQL orthogonality. In this paper we show that not only do these approaches require less storage space, there is also no information loss compared with the classic data model. In other words, how historical data is actually stored can be encapsulated as far as querying is concerned. The benefit of such encapsulation comes at the expense of processing some temporal queries such as **as of** queries. However, we show that one can formulate optimized **as of** queries using recursive SQL.

The **time-coalesce** operation, which returns a set of non-overlapping or non-adjacent time periods, is an important operation that is not supported in traditional relational DBMS. We show how one can express this operation using recursive SQL. The benefit of such feature is that the query result can be directly used as a derived table in the from clause of a complex query, again preserving the SQL orthogonality.

The organization of this paper is as follows. In Section 2, we discuss how a classical temporal data model [7] can be implemented using a relational DBMS, and describe several **as of** queries. Recursive SQL queries will be introduced briefly in Section 3. We present in Section 4 an incremental-forward data model which keeps the initial data values intact while appending only the changes. We describe how **as of** queries can be formulated using recursive SQL. In Section 5 we discuss an incremental-backward data model which keeps the current version of data and the changes over time. The support for **time-coalesce** operation will be discussed in Section 6. Finally Section 7 presents the conclusions.

2   Historical Data, Updates, and Queries

In this section, we show how users can implement a classical historical data model [7] in a relational DBMS. We discuss several update operations and historical queries. Without loss of generality, we assume that the time granularity is date.

We consider the following generic non-temporal table T: the column KEY is the primary key. Initially on 01/01/1995 (January 1, 1995), there are only two tuples:

```
create table T (KEY int not null primary key, C1 int, C2 int);
```

```
T (1, 10, 100)
T (2, 10, 100)
```

Consider the following sequence of updates since 01/01/95:

```
On 1/4/1995,  C1 was updated to 20  for KEY=1.
On 1/6/1995,  C1 was updated to 30  for KEY=2.
On 1/7/1995,  C2 was updated to 200 for KEY=1.
On 1/10/1995, C1 was updated to 20  for KEY=2.
```

There are several ways of structuring and storing this data. One commonly known approach uses a pair of timestamp columns for storing the time period of each tuple — tuple-timestamping [7, 9]. We refer to it as a *time-interval* approach as it uses a pair of timestamp columns to represent time intervals. In this approach, we can "temporalize" the table T, which is an existing populated table, by issuing alter commands:

```
alter table T add column TS date not null with default
              add column TE date
              drop primary KEY;
alter table T add primary key (KEY, TS);
alter table T add constraint ts_te check (TE is null or TS<TE);
```

The first alter command augments the table with a pair of timestamp columns to represent a time interval [TS,TE) where TS is the start time and TE is end time [2]. Several additional constraints are also added to the table:

- The primary key for the altered table is composed of the KEY and TS columns.

- The default value for the column TS is 01/01/0001, which can also be used to represent the "beginning" of the time line.

- The default value for the column TE is null. This is, we intentionally overload the use of null to represent the value "now + 1 day" which means "don't know until further notice" [3].

- One cannot store null in the TS column as we do not store a tuple which contains unknown start time.

- The constraint (ts_te) enforces the fact that a time period must start earlier than it ends: for each tuple, its TE value must be greater than its TS value or the TE value is null.

Instead of altering an existing table, one can equivalently create a historical table using a create statement:

```
create table T_int (KEY int not null, C1 int, C2 int,
              TS date not null with default, TE date,
              primary key (KEY, TS),
              constraint ts_te check (TE is null or TS < TE));
```

---

[2]In this paper, we do not distinguish the treatment of valid times and transaction times with respect to querying. Unless otherwise stated, we refer these columns to as valid time columns.

[3]It has been argued that now is very special and thus it is not desirable to overload the use of any other data value (such as null) to mimic now [2].

KEY	C1	C2	TS	TE
1	10	100	01/01/1995	01/04/1995
1	20	100	01/04/1995	01/07/1995
1	20	200	01/07/1995	NULL
2	10	100	01/01/1995	01/06/1995
2	30	100	01/06/1995	01/10/1995
2	20	100	01/10/1995	NULL

Table 1: T_int: Historical version of table T using *time-interval* approach

We list in Table 1 the tuples after all updates have been applied. For example, the first tuple represents the fact <KEY=1, C1=10, C2=100> during the period [01/01/1995, 01/04/1995), and the third tuple represents the fact <KEY=1, C1=20, C3=200> during the period from 01/07/1995 until further notice. In this data model, all tuples with a null value in the TE column are considered as the current version. When a current tuple is updated, say the tuple with KEY=1 on 01/20/1995, the TE column of the third tuple is modified from null to 01/20/1995 and then a corresponding new tuple is inserted. In other words, users have to *explicitly* perform the necessary modification and insertion operation in their applications. Insertion of a tuple with a new KEY value is straightforward — insert a new tuple with the date of insertion in the TS column and null in the TE column. Deletion of an existing current tuple simply sets the TE column from null to the date of operation.

With the full history of updates stored in a table, one can ask many interesting historical queries. For example, one can join two historical tables based on overlapping time periods of two tuples — intersect-join or time-join. In this paper, we are more interested in finding out a snapshot of a historical table at a particular time point, i.e., the so-called **as of** queries:

Case 1: What are the data values as of January 6, 1995?

```
select KEY, C1, C2, '01/06/1995' as "AS OF TIME"
from   T_int
where  TS <= '1995-01-06' and
       '1995-01-06' < case when TE is null
                          then current date + 1 day else TE end
```

This query, applied on Table 1, returns two tuples:

```
KEY            C1            C2           AS OF TIME
-----------   -----------   -----------   ----------
           1            20           100 01/06/1995
           2            30           100 01/06/1995
```

In this query, we use a **case** expression when the TE column is involved in a comparison because of possibly null values. In SQL, a relational operator (such as "<") is evaluated as false in presence of null. Since we intentionally overload the use of null in the TE column to represent **now + 1 day**, one can obtain the actual value by substituting null with "current date + 1 day" using a **case** expression. Recall that a time period [TS, TE) ends at TE and thus we use the "<" operator in the **where** clause.

Case 2: What are the current version of data values (i.e., as of now)?

```
select KEY, C1, C2, current date as "AS OF TIME"
from   T_int
where  TE is null
```

This query, which was executed on 02/27/1995, returns:

KEY	C1	C2	AS OF TIME
1	20	200	02/27/1995
2	20	100	02/27/1995

Note that this is a simplified version of the previous **as of** query.

Case 3: What are the earliest version of data values?

```
select KEY, C1, C2, TS
from   T_int t1
where  TS = (select min(TS)
             from   T_int t2
             where  t1.KEY = t2.KEY)
```

This query returns:

KEY	C1	C2	TS
1	10	100	01/01/1995
2	10	100	01/01/1995

Let us now describe another alternative which uses a single timestamp column. We refer to it as the *time-point* approach. Using the above example, one can create the following table:

```
create table T_pt (KEY int not null, C1 int, C2 int,
                   TS date not null with default,
                   primary key (KEY, TS));
```

where the TS column represents the start time of the tuple until a *new* tuple with same KEY value is inserted to the table. We show in Table 2 the table after all updates have been applied.

There are pros and cons of adopting the *time-interval* approach versus the *time-point* approach as follows:

1. The *time-point* approach, i.e., using a single timestamp column, requires less storage space because the end time column (TE) is not stored in the table. Furthermore, there is no inherit problem with storing the data value now because the end time is *not* stored. However, this approach

KEY	C1	C2	TS
1	10	100	01/01/1995
1	20	100	01/04/1995
1	20	200	01/07/1995
2	10	100	01/01/1995
2	30	100	01/06/1995
2	20	100	01/10/1995

Table 2: T_pt: Historical version of table T using *time-point* approach

has a problem of representing the fact that an object is no longer valid — this can be easily modeled in the *time-interval* approach using a time period.

2. Updates in the *time-point* approach are much more efficient because only a new tuple is inserted instead of a modification followed by an insertion. Furthermore, it is not necessary to retrieve the latest version of the tuple with the same KEY value. In other words, the update really operates in the append-only mode. This is especially important for operational databases because the performance impact would be minimal.

3. In the *time-point* approach, some of the above **as of** queries are slightly more complex and in fact, they are often less efficient to execute because the corresponding TE value is not stored. For example, in order to obtain the current version of data, one has to ask:

```
select KEY, C1, C2, TS
from   T_pt t1
where  TS = (select max(TS)
             from   T_pt t2
             where  t1.KEY = t2.KEY)
```

In summary, there are differences in modeling capability between the *time-interval* and the *time-point* approach. There is also a major tradeoff between update efficiency and storage requirement versus ease of expressing **as of** queries and their efficiency. However, both approaches share a common drawback, namely an update essentially inserts a new tuple of comparable size into the database! That is, given that there are initially n tuples and on the average tuples are updated m times, the table size becomes approximately $m \times n$ of the initial size. This eventually creates a serious performance problem for both updates and querying [1]. To address this concern, we consider several alternative approaches in storing historical data. Particularly, we are interested in reducing the storage requirement and yet the above **as of** queries can still be executed efficiently. Furthermore, it is essential that we can perform time-join. In other words, in these data models, we ought to be able to produce the full history of updates as shown in Table 1 using SQL query. In designing these alternative data models, the SQL orthogonality is an important criterion.

3   Recursive SQL

In this section, we describe the recursive query capability in DB2. A major building block in formulating a recursive SQL is the use of *common table expression* (CTE). A common table expression defines a result table that can be used in any from clause in a select query that follows the CTE definition. Consider the following example.

```
with DT (c1, c2) as (select c1, c2 from T where c1>10)
   select * from DT a, DT b where a.c1=b.c1;
```

The with clause, which is a SQL standard language construct, creates a common table expression, named DT, which is used twice in the from clause of a subsequent select query. DT contains all tuples from table T whose C1 value is greater than 10. An important behavior of a common table expression is that each use of the common table expression shares the same result, and thus the self join in the query uses the same content of DT.

Formulating recursive queries relies upon the use of CTE — recursion occurs when the CTE is referenced within the definition of the CTE itself. Let us illustrate this using a simple relation which stores manager-employee relationship:

```
mgr_emp(manager, employee)
```

```
mgr_emp(Ed,     Tom)
mgr_emp(Tom,    Paul)
mgr_emp(Tom,    Steve)
mgr_emp(Paul,   Jay)
mgr_emp(Steve,  Linda)
mgr_emp(Ed,     Jo)
```

The following query lists all the employees who report to Tom directly and indirectly:

```
with DT (employee) as
   (select employee                    /* base case */
    from   mgr_emp
    where  manager = 'Tom'
   union all
    select e.employee                  /* recursive case */
    from   mgr_emp e, DT t
    where  t.employee = e.manager)
select *
from   DT;
```

The recursive SQL is composed of a union of a base case and a recursive case. The base case computes all the employees who report directly to Tom. The result is stored in the common table expression (DT). In the recursive part, we join the base table (mgr_emp) with DT to compute the staffs who report directly to the managers stored in DT, and we store the result of this computation, again, in DT. This recursive computation continues until no new rows are inserted into DT. For this query, the answer set is: {Paul, Steve, Jay, Linda}. Note that for cyclic data, a recursive SQL may lead to an infinite loop.

4 Incremental-Forward Model

In this section, we present an alternative data model which essentially keeps the initial tuples intact and inserts only the incremental information [4]. We discuss only the *time-interval* approach; the corresponding version of *time-point* approach can be obtained in a similar fashion.

In the incremental-forward model, the delete and insert operations remain the same as the classic data model described in Section 2, but for each update operation to an existing tuple with a value k in its KEY column, we:

- set the TE column of the existing tuple to the date of update operation;

- insert a new tuple with:

  - k as the KEY column value,
  - the date of the update operation as the new TS value,
  - new data values for the updated columns, and
  - nulls for other columns.

Consider the first update in our example — C1 was updated to 20 for KEY=1 on 1/4/1995, the user performs:

```
modify: <1, 10, 100, 01/01/1995, 01/04/1995>
insert: <1, 20, NULL, 01/04/1995, NULL>
```

Note that the C2 column of the inserted tuple is set to null. In other words, all newly inserted tuples due to *update* operations contain only the incremental information. After all updates have been applied to our example, the table becomes [5]:

```
T_delta_fwd (1, 10,   100, 01/01/1995, 01/04/1995)
T_delta_fwd (1, 20,   NULL, 01/04/1995, 01/07/1995)
T_delta_fwd (1, NULL, 200, 01/07/1995, NULL)
T_delta_fwd (2, 10,   100, 01/01/1995, 01/06/1995)
T_delta_fwd (2, 30,   NULL, 01/06/1995, 01/10/1995)
T_delta_fwd (2, 20,   NULL, 01/10/1995, NULL)
```

The major advantage of this data model is that the table size does not grow proportionally with the rate of update operations because storing null requires much less space than regular data values. This approach is especially attractive when the historical table has many columns but only a few columns are updated at a time. The disadvantage of this data model is that formulating some *as of* queries is more complicated. For example, in order to obtain the data values as of 01/06/95, conceptually one would have to retrieve the initial data values and "roll" forward in time using all the updated values until 01/06/95. With this difficulty, a key requirement is whether one can re-construct the content as shown in Table 1. There are two reasons for this requirement. First, it is extremely desirable to perform time-join with other historical tables and

---

[4] This data model is somewhat similar to the "Backlog" approach proposed in [4], and the "after-image" in recovery log [13].

[5] We rename the table as T_delta_fwd for our discussion purpose.

this requires the full-history content. Note that this re-construction process ought to be achieved via SQL constructs or extensions; otherwise, the result cannot be used as a derived table in other part of SQL query. Second, it is equally desirable to use all as of queries listed in Section 2 without any changes. Fortunately this re-construction process can be done using a recursive SQL query and furthermore, a view using this query can be created (e.g., by a DBA) and all as of queries can use the view directly.

Case 0: What is the full history of updates?

```
create view T_int (KEY, C1, C2, TS, TE) as
     (select i.*                             /* base part */
      from   T_delta_fwd i
      where  i.TS = (select min(j.TS)
                     from   T_delta_fwd j
                     where  j.KEY=i.KEY)
      union all
      select j.KEY, coalesce(j.C1, k.C1), coalesce(j.C2, k.C2),
             j.TS, j.TE                       /* recursive part */
      from   T_delta_fwd j, T_int k
      where  j.TS=k.TE and j.KEY=k.KEY);

select * from T_int; /* retrieve full-history content */
```

In the above recursive query, the base part retrieves all initial tuples with the earliest start time. The recursive part effectively rolls forward in time by matching tuples from DTR whose end time equal the start time of tuples in T_delta_fwd with the same KEY value. The construct coalesce outputs the first argument if it is not null, otherwise the second argument is output [6] [6]. That is, the recursive part outputs old column values unless there was an update to the columns. A simple "select *" query now returns the tuples as shown in Table 1.

Let us digress here to address the query performance. We note that there is a correlated subquery in the base case of the recursion, and evaluating correlated subqueries can be very slow. In order to speed up its processing, one can create an index on <KEY, TS> columns in *ascending* order as follows.:

```
create unique index idx1 on T_delta_fwd(KEY, TS);
```

In fact, DB2 automatically creates such index because <KEY, TS> is the primary key of the table. With this index, processing the subquery becomes very fast because it requires index access only. For each correlation value of the KEY column, a sequence of TS data values will be fed to the min aggregate function. Since the index was created in ascending order of KEY and TS values, this sequence of TS values is also in ascending order. For the min aggregate, only the first TS value is needed. In other words, only one row is needed for the aggregate function!

The use of the above view encapsulates how the historical data is stored and thus relieves the burden on users and applications. However, the full-history

---

[6]The construct coalesce(x,y) is defined as "case when x is not null then x else y end". It is different from time-coalesce operator to be discussed in a Section 6.

content must be materialized each time the view is used and this can have some performance impact on the as of queries. In the following, we discuss how one can formulate optimized versions of the as of queries, again using recursive SQL queries [7].

Case 1: What are the data values as of January 6, 1995?

```
with DTR (KEY, C1, C2, TS) as
     (select KEY, C1, C2, TS                    /* base part */
      from   T_delta_fwd i
      where  i.TS = (select max(TS)
                     from   T_delta_fwd j
                     where  j.KEY=i.KEY and j.TS<='1995-01-06')
      union all
      select i.KEY, coalesce(j.C1, i.C1), coalesce(j.C2, i.C2),
             i.TS                               /* recursive part */
      from   T_delta_fwd i, DTR j
      where  (j.C1 is null or j.C2 is null) and j.KEY=i.KEY and
             i.TS = (select max(k.TS)
                     from   T_delta_fwd k
                     where  k.KEY=i.KEY and k.TS<j.TS))
select KEY, max(C1) as C1, max(C2) as C2, /* main query */
       '01/06/1995' as "AS OF TIME"
from    DTR
group by KEY
```

In this query, one may think that we obtain the initial data values and roll forward in time using the updates until we pass 01/06/1995. However, the above query does exactly the opposite in that we start with the tuple in proximity of 01/06/1996 and roll *backward* in time until we obtain all non-null data values. The base part retrieves the tuples with the latest updates as of 01/06/1996. The recursive part then continues going backward in time until all the fields are retrieved (i.e., they are all non-nulls) or we have reached the earliest version. This is achieved by the construct coalesce. That is, the recursive part continues to obtain the previous version tuples only if some data fields are nulls. Finally in the main query, all tuples generated by the common table expression are grouped on the KEY column. We note that there is at most one unique non-null C1 value in each KEY group. The max aggregate functions essentially eliminate null in the C1 column in each group, and return the only unique non-null value. The same argument applies to the C2 column.

Like in the view approach (Case 0), the recursive query contains correlated subqueries. Using a similar idea in the view approach, one can create an index on <KEY, TS> columns in *descending* order to speed up its processing.

```
create index idx2 on T_delta_fwd(KEY desc, TS desc);
```

Again, processing the subquery requires accessing only this index. The reason for creating an index in descending order is that evaluating the max aggregate

---

[7]It is highly desirable that an optimizer can take the use of the view in the as of queries and transform it into the optimized versions, but currently DB2 optimizer is not capable to perform such optimization.

function becomes very fast: the data stream of TS values from the index access is in the descending order and thus only the first value is needed.

Case 2: What are the current version of data values (i.e., as of now)?

```
with DTR (KEY, C1, C2, TS) as
     (select KEY, C1, C2, TS
      from   T_delta_fwd i
      where  i.TS = (select max(j.TS)
                     from   T_delta_fwd j
                     where  j.KEY=i.KEY and j.TE is null)
      union all
      select i.KEY, coalesce(j.C1, i.C1), coalesce(j.C2, i.C2),
             i.TS
      from   T_delta_fwd i, DTR j
      where  (j.C1 is null or j.C2 is null) and j.KEY=i.KEY and
             i.TS = (select max(k.TS)
                     from   T_delta_fwd k
                     where  k.KEY=i.KEY and k.TS<j.TS))
 select KEY, max(C1) as C1, max(C2) as C2,
        current date as "AS OF TIME"
 from   DTR
 group by KEY
```

Note that this is a slightly variation of the last as of query.

Case 3: What are the earliest version of data values?

```
select KEY, C1, C2, TS
from   T_delta_fwd i
where  i.ts = (select min(ts)
               from   T_delta_fwd j
               where  j.KEY=i.KEY)
```

This query is the same as the one in Section 2.

5 Incremental-Backward Model

The idea of the incremental-backward model is very similar to the incremental-forward model, except that the current version of a tuple always keep all its latest data values. For each update operation to an existing tuple with a value k in its KEY column, we:

- insert a new tuple with the current version of data values, as in the classic data model.

- modify the existing tuple:
    - set the TE column to the date of update operation, and
    - except the KEY column, set all unmodified columns to null.

Consider the first update in our example — C1 was updated to 20 for KEY=1 on 1/4/1995, the user performs:

```
modify: <1, 10, NULL, 01/01/1995, 01/04/1995>
insert: <1, 20, 100,  01/04/1995, NULL>
```

Note that the C2 column in the original tuple is set to null. That is, in order to retrieve the initial data values of a tuple, conceptually one would have to obtain the current version and apply all the updates backward in time. The benefit of such model compared with the incremental-forward model is that retrieving the current version is very efficient — all current data values are readily available in a single tuple of which the TE value is null. Using the same example in the previous section, the following shows the result table after all update operations have been applied:

```
T_delta_bwd (1, 10,   NULL, 01/01/1995, 01/04/1995)
T_delta_bwd (1, NULL, 100,  01/04/1995, 01/07/1995)
T_delta_bwd (1, 20,   200,  01/07/1995, NULL)
T_delta_bwd (2, 10,   NULL, 01/01/1995, 01/06/1995)
T_delta_bwd (2, 30,   NULL, 01/06/1995, 01/10/1995)
T_delta_bwd (2, 20,   100,  01/10/1995, NULL)
```

Like in the forward-incremental data model, one can create a view which returns the full-history content and, again, all previously mentioned as of queries can use this view without changes. Similarly, one can also formulate optimized versions for the as of queries for performance reason. We list these queries below.

Case 0: What is the full history of updates?

```
create view T_int (KEY, C1, C2, TS, TE) as
    (select *                              /* base part */
     from   T_delta_bwd
     where  TE is null
   union all
     select j.KEY, coalesce(j.C1, k.C1), coalesce(j.C2, k.C2),
            j.TS, j.TE                     /* recursive part */
     from   T_delta_bwd j, T_int k
     where  k.TS=j.TE and k.KEY=j.KEY);

select * from T_int; /* retrieve full-history content */
```

In this view, the base part of the recursion retrieves all current versions of tuples. The recursive part joins tuples from the common table expression (DTR) and the base table (T_delta_bwd) based on the condition that the end time of the tuple from the base table equals the start time of the tuple from DTR with the same KEY value. That is, the recursive part retrieves the previous version by rolling backward in time. The recursion stops when all earliest versions have been retrieved.

Case 1: What are the data values as of January 6, 1995?

```
with DTR (KEY, C1, C2, TS) as
  (select KEY, C1, C2, TS
   from   T_delta_bwd i
   where  i.TS = (select max(j.TS)
                  from   T_delta_bwd j
                  where  j.KEY=i.KEY and j.TS<='1995-01-06')
  union all
    select i.KEY, coalesce(j.C1, i.C1), coalesce(j.C2, i.C2), i.TS
    from   T_delta_bwd i, DTR j
    where  (j.C1 is null or j.C2 is null) and j.KEY=i.KEY and
           i.TS = (select min(k.TS)
                   from   T_delta_bwd k
                   where  k.KEY=i.KEY and k.TS>j.TS))
  select KEY, max(C1) as C1, max(C2) as C2,
         '01/06/1995' as "AS OF TIME"
  from   DTR
  group by KEY
```

Case 2: What are the current version of data values (i.e., as of now)?

```
select KEY, C1, C2, current date as "AS OF TIME"
from   T_delta_bwd
where  TE is null
```

Note that this query is much more efficient to execute!

Case 3: What are the earliest version of data values?

```
with DTR (KEY, C1, C2, TS) as
  (select KEY, C1, C2, TS
   from   T_delta_bwd i
   where  i.TS = (select min(j.TS)
                  from   T_delta_bwd j
                  where  j.KEY=i.KEY)
  union all
    select i.KEY, coalesce(j.C1, i.C1), coalesce(j.C2, i.C2), i.TS
    from   T_delta_bwd i, DTR j
    where  (j.C1 is null or j.C2 is null) and j.KEY=i.KEY and
           i.TS = (select min(k.TS)
                   from   T_delta_bwd k
                   where  k.KEY=i.KEY and k.TS>j.TS))
  select KEY, max(C1) as C1, max(C2) as C2, min(TS) as TS
  from   DTR
  group by KEY
```

6   Time-coalesce Operation

In the previous sections, we showed the power of recursive SQL in formulating as of queries. In this section, we further show its usefulness in formulating time-coalesce operator [6, 8]. We refer to this operator as time-coalesce in order to avoid the confusion with the construct coalesce that we discussed earlier. The input to this operator is a bag of time periods and the output from this operator is a bag of disjoint time periods.

To illustrate the usefulness of this operator, let us consider a work_on table which stores the information on an m-to-n relationship between employee and project. One can ask how long a particular employee has worked on *any* project. To answer this query, one has to apply a time-coalesce operation to obtain a set of non-overlapping or non-adjacent time periods because an employee could have worked on more than one projects at the same time. To illustrate the idea further, we consider the following generic time interval table:

```
intv_table (KEY int, TS date, TE date)

intv_table (1, 01/01/1995, 01/10/1995)
intv_table (1, 01/01/1995, 01/10/1995)
intv_table (1, 01/15/1995, 01/20/1995)
intv_table (2, 01/01/1995, 01/10/1995)
intv_table (2, 01/06/1995, 01/15/1995)
intv_table (2, 01/15/1995, NULL)
intv_table (3, 01/01/1995, 01/13/1995)
intv_table (4, 01/01/1995, NULL)
```

If the time-coalesce operation is applied on each group of tuples of the same KEY value, one would obtain the following:

```
KEY         TS          TE
----------- ----------- -----------
          1 01/01/1995 01/10/1995
          1 01/15/1995 01/20/1995
          2 01/01/1995 NULL
          3 01/01/1995 01/13/1995
          4 01/01/1995 NULL
```

Ideally a DBMS should provide a runtime support for this operator. To the best of our knowledge, this is not available in any commercial relational database systems. However, one can express the time-coalesce operation using a recursive SQL query as shown in Figure 1.

In the recursive query, the base part allows us to keep non-overlapping time periods such as the tuple with KEY=4 above. The first recursive part forms new time periods by combining adjacent periods or overlapping ones where the tuple from the base table (intv_table) has an earlier start time than the tuple from the common table expression. The second recursive part is the "asymmetric" version of the first recursive part — the tuple from the common table expression has an earlier start time. Finally, in the main query, we remove those time periods which are contained in another period. Like in our previous queries, case expressions are used to handle nulls in the TE column.

```
with DTR (KEY, TS, TE) as
  (select KEY, TS, TE                /* base part */
   from   intv_table
  union all
   select i.KEY, i.TS, j.TE          /* 1st recursive part */
   from   intv_table i, DTR j
   where  ((i.TS<j.TS
             and j.TS<case when i.TE is null
                      then current date else i.TE end
             and case when i.TE is null
                  then current date else i.TE end <
                  case when j.TE is null
                  then current date else j.TE end)
            or
            i.TE=j.TS)
            and j.KEY=i.KEY
  union all
   select i.KEY, i.TS, j.TE          /* 2nd recursive part */
   from   intv_table j, DTR i
   where  ((i.TS<j.TS
             and j.TS<case when i.TE is null
                      then current date else i.TE end
             and case when i.TE is null
                  then current date else i.TE end <
                  case when j.TE is null
                  then current date else j.TE end)
            or
            i.TE=j.TS)
            and j.KEY=i.KEY)
select distinct i.KEY, i.TS, i.TE        /* main query */
from   DTR i
where not. exists
 (select 1
  from   DTR j
  where  i.KEY=j.KEY and
         ((j.TS<=i.TS and
           case when i.TE is null
            then current date else i.TE end <
           case when j.TE is null
            then current date else j.TE end)
          or
          (j.TS<i.TS and
           case when i.TE is null
            then current date else i.TE end <=
           case when j.TE is null
            then current date else j.TE end)))
```

Figure 1: An SQL query for computing time-coalesce operation

It should be emphasized that the performance of this query is certainly not as good as the approach using appropriate runtime support. The benefit of being able to express such query is that one can use the result of the query as a derived table in other from clause, or one can create a view for other use. Hence, SQL orthogonality is preserved.

7 Conclusions

In this paper, we described how users can store historical data in relational DBMSs such as DB2 and formulate as of queries using recursive SQL, case expression, and coalesce construct. We also described how time-coalesce operation can be done, again, using recursive SQL and case expression. Although relational DBMS is far from being a temporal DBMS according to the definition in [7], these language constructs do provide a powerful mechanism for users to store, manipulate and query historical data with reasonable performance.

Acknowledgement

We thank the anonymous reviewers for their comments on the paper.

References

[1] I. Ahn and R. Snodgrass. *Performance evaluation of a temporal database management system.* In **Proc. of the ACM SIGMOD Int. Conf. on Management of Data**, pages 96–107, May 1986.

[2] J. Clifford, R. Snodgrass, T. Isakowitz, and C. Jensen. *NOW in TSQL2.* In **TSQL2 Commentary**, 1994.

[3] IBM. **Database 2 AIX/6000: SQL References**, 1995. Forthcoming.

[4] C. Jensen, L. Mark, and N. Roussopoulos. *Incremental Implementation Model for Relational Databases with Transaction Time.* **IEEE Trans. on Knowledge and Data Engineering**, 3(4):461–473, December 1991.

[5] C. Jensen and R. Snodgrass. *The TSQL2 Data Model.* In **TSQL2 Commentary**, 1994.

[6] E. McKenzie and R. Snodgrass. *Supporting Valid Time in an Historical Relational Algebra: Proofs and Extensions.* Technical Report TR 91-15, University of Arizona, Tucson, Dept. of Computer Science, August 1991.

[6] J. Melton and A. Simon. **Understanding the new SQL: A Complete Guide.** Morgan Kaufmann, 1993.

[7] R. Snodgrass and I. Ahn. *A Taxomony of Time in Databases.* In **Proc. of the ACM SIGMOD Int. Conf. on Management of Data**, pages 236–246, May 1985.

[8] R. Snodgrass and C. Jensen. *The From Clause in TSQL2.* In **TSQL2 Commentary**, 1994.

[9] A. Tansel, J. Clifford, S. Gadia, S. Jajodia, A. Segev, and R. Snodgrass. **Temporal Databases: Theory, Design, and Implementation**. Benjamin/Cummings, 1993.

[10] R. Snodgrass et. al.. *A TSQL2 Tutorial*. **The ACM SIGMOD Record**, 23(3), September 1994.

[11] R. Snodgrass et. al.. *TSQL2 Language Specification*. **The ACM SIGMOD Record**, 23(1), March 1994.

[12] M. Soo. *Bibliography on Temporal Databases*. **The ACM SIGMOD Record**, 20(1):14–23, March 1991.

[13] J. Ullman. **Principles of Database Systems**. Computer Science Press, Rockville, MD, Second Edition, 1982.

[14] ISO_ANSI. *ISO-ANSI Working Draft: Database Language SQL2 and SQL3; X3H2; ISO/IEC JTC1/SC21/WG3*, 1993.

Composite Temporal Events in Active Databases: A Formal Semantics

Iakovos Motakis

Department of Computer Science, U.C.L.A.

Los Angeles, California

Carlo Zaniolo

Department of Computer Science, U.C.L.A.

Los Angeles, California

Abstract

Active databases must support rules triggered by complex patterns of composite temporal events. This paper proposes a general method for specifying the semantics of composite event specification languages. The method is based on a syntax-directed translation of the composite event expressions into $Datalog_{1S}$, whose formal semantics is then used to define the meaning of the original event expressions. We show that the method is applicable to languages such as ODE, Snoop and SAMOS that are based respectively on the formalisms of Finite State Machines, Event Graphs and Petri Nets. The proposed method overcomes various problems and limitations affecting such formalisms.

1 Introduction

A new generation of database systems supports active rules for the detection of events occurring in the database and the triggering of induced actions. In many applications, the simple-event detection mechanisms found in commercial systems, such as Ingres, Oracle or Sybase, are not sufficient; complex sequences of events must instead be detected as the natural precondition for taking actions and firing rules [9]. Sophisticated research prototypes have in fact been implemented recently to provide this capability— an incomplete list of such systems includes [9, 13, 10, 4]. These systems feature composite event detection mechanisms, which are based on formalisms such as Finite State Automata [12], Petri Nets [11], or Event Graphs [3].

The problem of formally specifying the semantics of active rules remains largely unsolved. Indeed, giving a formal semantics to active database behavior presents a challenge even when only simple events are involved. For composite event expressions, this problem becomes even more complex, inasmuch as the issues of temporal databases and active rule languages are now combined and intertwined [17]. This issue must be resolved if trustworthyness is expected from systems incorporating this advanced capability.

In this paper we propose a general method for defining the semantics of composite event specification languages. The method is based on a syntax-directed translation of the composite event expressions into $Datalog_{1S}$, whose formal semantics is then used to define the meaning of the original event expressions.

We first demonstrate the method by giving a complete definition of the Event Pattern Language (EPL). EPL, the language of an active database system designed and implemented at UCLA provides the capability of detecting, reasoning and acting upon complex patterns of events that evolve over time. Then, we explain how our method can be applied to ODE [13], Snoop [4] and SAMOS [10], in order to formally define the intuitive and/or operational semantics of the composite event specification languages of these systems. Furthermore, we point out their differences along with some problems and limitations of theirs, which often follow from their implementation frameworks.

The method proposed in this paper matches and surpasses the capabilities of the formalisms used in the past, in terms of (a) defining precisely the intuitive semantics of different language characteristics, including *event attributes, negation, simultaneous events and parameter contexts*, and (b) ease of mapping to correct execution semantics. Therefore, we obtain a general method for defining the semantics of such languages, and a useful tool for comparing their constructs and their expressive power.

Because of space limitations, explicit time events are not discussed in this paper. However, these can also be incorporated in our method using the approach discussed in [15].

2   The EPL Language

In the rule-based syntax of EPL, sequences of goals specify sequences of events; each goal can correspond to either (i) a basic event, or (ii) a (possibly negated) basic event qualified by condition predicates, or (iii) a composite event constructed using sequences, repetitions, conjunctions, disjunctions and negations of other (possibly composite) events. EPL is implemented as a portable frontend to active relational databases supporting simple event detection. Two versions of EPL have been developed, the first in $\mathcal{LDL}++$ [1] and the second in CLIPS [16].

2.1   EPL Programs

An EPL program is organized in *modules*, which can be compiled and enabled independently. The *events declaration section* of a module defines the set of relevant basic event types, monitored by the module. A *basic event type* is denoted as :

```
insert(Rname), delete(Rname), update(Rname),
```

where Rname is the name of a database relation.

EPL rules are specified in a module's *rules section*. Each rule has a name, which is unique within its module. A rule's body (head) corresponds to an event (action). Example 1 demonstrates an EPL module with one rule. In all examples, we use the following bank accounts relation.

```
ACC(Accno, Owner, Type, Balance)
```

Example 1 *An EPL module with a rule that keeps track of large withdrawals from savings accounts.*

```
begin AccMonitor
   monitor  insert(ACC), update(ACC), delete(ACC);
   LargeWithdrawal:
     update( ACC(X),
                X.Type = "Savings", X.old_Balance-X.new_Balance > 100000 )
   -> write( "Large withdrawal from account %d at time %s \n",
                X.Accno, asctime( X.evtime) ).
end.
```

The `AccMonitor` module keeps track of all the modifications in the `ACC` relation. Rule `LargeWithdrawal` specifies a *qualified basic event*. Such an event has the form:

$$evtkind(\ Rname(X),\ < condition-expression >\ ),$$

where `X` denotes the tuple of relation `Rname`, that has been inserted, deleted or updated. For *update* events, EPL makes available to the programmer both the new and the old contents of the updated tuple. The prefixes `new` and `old` are used to distinguish between them. When no prefix is specified, the new contents are assumed.

The attribute `evtime`, which is attached to a basic event's tuple variable contains the time the event occurred. The < condition-expression > is built using the standard arithmetic and comparison operators and the logical connectives AND, OR and NOT.

Actions: There are three kinds of actions : (a) Write actions, (b) SQL commands and (c) Operating system calls.

In all cases, the format of the action specifier is similar to that of the *printf* statement in the C language. The action's arguments are taken from tuple variables defined by basic events in the rule's body.

Negated Events: A (qualified) basic event may be negated. Consider for instance the following rule, as part of the module `AccMonitor`:

```
NoUpdateOn00201:
      ! update( ACC(X), X.Accno = 00201 )
      -> write("any event but an update on 00201")
```

This *negated qualified basic event* will be satisfied by the occurrence of *any* basic event of the types monitored by the `AccMonitor` (including possible insertions and deletions), except for an update of account 00201.

2.2   EPL Language Constructs

So far, we have been concerned with *basic events*, which may be qualified or negated.

The power of EPL follows from its ability to specify composite events. We distinguish between *event expressions* (also called *event types*) and *event instances*. An event expression `E` is specified using the EPL language, where an event instance of `E` consists of a sequence of basic events that participated in the satisfaction of `E`. In the sequel, we will refer to *events* when the distinction is clear from the context. We will also use the term *event occurrence*, to refer to the time instant when an event expression is satisfied (an instance of this event expression is completed).

Composite event expressions are defined as follows:

Definition 1 *Let $E_1, E_2, ..., E_n$, $n > 1$, be EPL event expressions (maybe composite themselves). The following is also an EPL event expression :*

1. *$(E_1, E_2, ..., E_n)$: a sequence consisting of an instance of E_1, immediately followed by an instance of E_2, ..., immediately followed by an instance of E_n.*
2. *$* : E$: a sequence of zero or more consecutive instances of E.*
3. *$(E_1 \& E_2 \& ... \& E_n)$: A conjunction of events. It occurs when all events $E_1, ..., E_n$ occur simultaneously.*
4. *$\{E_1, E_2, ..., E_n\}$: A disjunction of events. It occurs when at least one event among $E_1, ..., E_n$ occurs.*
5. *$!E$: It occurs when not any instance of E occurs.*

A number of additional (derived) constructs may be defined in terms of the basic ones (see also [12]). Some of these are :

- *any $\equiv$ The disjunction of all basic events (of the types monitored). It occurs every time such an event occurs.*
- *$[E_1, E_2, ..., E_n] \equiv (E_1, * : any, E_2, * : any, ..., * : any, E_n)$. Relaxed sequence. It consists of an instance of E_1, followed later by an instance of E_2, ..., followed later by an instance of E_n.*
- *$prior(E_1, E_2) = [E_1, any] \& E_2$. An occurrence of E_2 follows an occurrence of E_1 (i.e., an instance of E_1 is completed prior to the completion of an instance of E_2)*
- *$first(E) \equiv (E \& ![E, any])$: It occurs, when the first instance of E occurs.*

Note that in an instance of $[E_1, E_2]$, the first basic event in the instance of E_2 must follow an occurrence of E_1, where in $prior(E_1, E_2)$, this is not required.

In addition to the above, a composite event may have attributes, which are derived from the attributes of its component basic events. Attribute semantics and scope rules are described in the next section. Examples of EPL composite events follow.

Example 2 *Report transfers of large amounts, from a customer's savings account to his/her checking account.*

```
LargeTransfer:
  ( update(ACC(X),
            X.Type = "Savings", X.old_Balance-X.new_Balance > 100000),
    update(ACC(Y),
            Y.Type = "Checking", Y.Owner = X.Owner,
            Y.new_Balance-Y.old_Balance = X.old_Balance-X.new_Balance) )
  -> write("Large Transfer of %s \n", X.Owner)
```

We assumed here, that a transfer transaction results in an immediate sequence of updates. The condition expression of the second update can refer to the tuple variables of both basic events.

Example 3 *Report the cases where two large deposits are made to an account, without any intervening withdrawal from it.*
```
Good Customer:
    ( update(ACC(X), X.new_Balance-X.old_Balance > 100000),
      *:! update(ACC(Y),
                  Y.Accno = X.Accno, Y.new_Balance < Y.old_Balance),
      update(ACC(Z),
                  Z.Accno = X.Accno, Z.new_Balance-Z.old_Balance > 100000)
    -> write("Good Customer: %s \n", X.Owner)
```

Example 4 *(Relaxed Sequence) Identify cases of customers who opened a Savings account, after they had closed another one before.*
```
WellcomeBack:
    [ delete(Acc(X), X.Type = Savings),
      insert(Acc(Y), Y.Type = Savings, Y.Owner = X.Owner) ]
    -> write("Customer %s is back \n", X.Owner)
```

Quite often, we need to find the *first* instance of an event F following an instance of another event E. Below, we express such an event pattern using the definition of the **first** derivative construct. This demonstrates the negation of a composite event and a conjunction.

Example 5 *If an account's balance drops to zero, report the next deposit to it, as well as the time elapsed.*
```
ActiveAgain:
    [ update(ACC(X), X.Balance = 0) ,
      ( update(ACC(Y), Y.Accno = X.Accno, Y.Balance > 0)  &
      ! [update(ACC(Z), Z.Accno = X.Accno, Z.Balance > 0),  any] ) ]
   -> write("Account %d is active again, after so much time: %s \n",
              X.Accno, asctime(Y.Time - X.Time) )
```

3 Semantics of EPL

We first introduce the notion of *event histories*, against which the EPL expressions are evaluated. The *global event history* is a series of *basic events*, that is ordered by time of occurrence (timestamp) and can be obtained from a system log. It can be represented by the relation hist(EventType, RelName, TimeStamp), where each tuple records a basic event occurrence and contains its type (insert, delete, or update), the name of the relation upon which it occurred, and the time of the occurrence.

Since an EPL expression is evaluated with respect to a particular module, a separate *event history* must be obtained for each such module. Focusing now on one module, we assume that a relation evt_monit(EventType, TableName) is kept for it, that records the basic event types the module monitors. Then, our module's *event history* is defined by the following stratified *Datalog* rules:

```
hist_monit(nil, nil, 0000, 0.)
hist_monit(E, R, T2, s(J)) ←    hist_monit(_, _, T1, J),
                                 hist(E, R, T2), evt_monit(E, R),
                                 ¬between(T1, T2).
between(T1, T2) ←    hist(E, R, T), evt_monit(E, R), T1 < T,  T < T2.
```

In this way, an *event history* can be defined for each module of interest. For instance, the following table contains a brief example event history for module `AccMonitor`:

hist_monit	EventType	TableName	TimeStamp	Stage
	nil	nil	0000	0
	upd	ACC	1423	1
	upd	ACC	1425	2
	ins	ACC	1430	3
	ins	ACC	1502	4

Observe that a sequence number, called *stage* has been introduced. The stage sequence defines an ordered structure on the distinct timestamps, that allows us to express properties of composite events that are based on the *relative order* of occurrence of their component basic events, as opposed to absolute time properties. Thus, the stage is the unit of time (*chronon*) in our model. Absolute time properties of events can also be expressed using their timestamps.

Different *event occurrence granularities* can be handled. At the "smallest database operation" granularity, every new insertion, deletion, or update creates a new stage. However, if "transaction boundaries granularity" is assumed, then each committed transaction creates a new stage, and all the basic events that occurred within this transaction are recorded in its stage, timestamped with the transaction's commit time. Basic events that share a sequence (stage) number are called *simultaneous* and are further discussed in Section 3.5.

Using this model, the fundamental concept of an *immediate sequence* of basic events corresponds to the occurrence of such events at successive stages.

These observations lead naturally to the use of $Datalog_{1S}$ as a formal basis for defining the semantics of EPL rules. $Datalog_{1S}$ [2] is a temporal language that extends *Datalog*, by allowing every predicate to have at most one temporal argument (constructed using the unary successor function s), in addition to the usual data arguments. The temporal argument in our case is the *stage* column in the event history.

As most active relational databases do, we further assume that for each DB table, there are three relations accumulating the inserted, deleted and updated tuples, together with their timestamps. For inserts into ACC for instance, we have the relation `ins_ACC(Accno, Owner, Type, Balance, Timestamp)`. The `del_ACC` table has a similar format, while for updates, we must record both the old and new values:

`upd_ACC(Accno_old, Accno_new, Owner_old, Owner_new, ... Timestamp)`

3.1 Event Satisfaction

We can now define the meaning of arbitrary EPL event expressions, through the notion of *satisfaction* of such expressions.

We start with qualified basic events. For instance, the satisfaction of the event `E = ins(ACC(X), X.Type = "Savings")` is defined as follows:

$$\text{ins\_ACC(Accno, Owner, Type, Bal, Time, J)} \leftarrow$$
$$\text{hist\_monit(ins, "ACC", Time, J),}$$
$$\text{insertedACC(Accno, Owner, Type, Bal, Time).}$$
$$\text{sat}_E\text{(Accno, Owner, Type, Bal, Time, J)} \leftarrow$$
$$\text{ins\_ACC(Accno, Owner, Type, Bal, Time, J),} \quad \text{Type} = \text{"Savings".}$$

The predicate `ins_ACC` describes the history of occurrences of `insertedACC`; for each occurrence of this event type, `ins_ACC` contains a tuple with its attribute bindings and the stage of the occurrence.

In general, a qualified basic event is represented as $E = $ `evtkind(R(X), q(X))`, where `q` denotes the event's condition expression, which can refer to the attribute values of tuple variable `X`. The rule template for the *satisfaction predicate* of such an event is:

$$\texttt{sat}_E(\texttt{X}, \texttt{J}) \leftarrow \texttt{evtkind\_R(X, J)}, \quad \texttt{q(X)}$$

The concept of "an event *immediately following* another event" can also be expressed. Take for instance, the immediate sequence of Example 2, which is represented as:

$$F = (\ \texttt{upd(ACC(X)}, \texttt{q}_1\texttt{(X))}, \ \texttt{upd(ACC(Y)}, \texttt{q}_2\texttt{(X, Y))}\ )$$

Its semantics is defined by the following three $Datalog_{1S}$ rules (from now on, unless otherwise indicated, variables will denote tuples):

Example 6
$$\begin{aligned}
\texttt{sat}_1(\texttt{X, J}) &\leftarrow & \texttt{upd\_ACC(X, J)}, \quad \texttt{q}_1\texttt{(X)}.\\
\texttt{sat}_2(\texttt{X, Y, s(J)}) &\leftarrow & \texttt{upd\_ACC(Y, s(J))}, \quad \texttt{sat}_1(\texttt{X, J}), \quad \texttt{q}_2\texttt{(X, Y)}.\\
\texttt{sat}_F(\texttt{X, Y, J}) &\leftarrow & \texttt{sat}_2(\texttt{X, Y, J}).
\end{aligned}$$

The first qualified basic event occurs at stage J, if an update on relation `ACC` is recorded at this stage and condition q_1 is satisfied. The second update on `ACC` must then occur at the next stage `s(J)` and condition q_2 must be satisfied (observe that q_2 can refer to the tuple variable `X` defined by the first basic event, in addition to `Y`). The third rule is a *copy-rule*, inasmuch as the satisfaction of composite event F coincides with that of $\texttt{sat}_2$.

There exists a natural mapping from EPL expressions to $Datalog_{1S}$. Thus, to formally define the meaning of an EPL expression, we only need to define a procedure which derives an equivalent set of $Datalog_{1S}$ rules for that expression. The resulting set of rules has a well-established formal semantics (model-theoretic and fixpoint-based) [2]. To formalize the translation, we represent EPL expressions by their parse trees, using the following prefix notation:

1. $seq(E_i, E_j) \equiv (E_i, E_j).$[1]
2. $*seq(E_i, E_j) \equiv (*E_i, E_j).$[2]
3. $and(E_i, E_j) \equiv E_i \ \& \ E_j.$
4. $or(E_i, E_j) \equiv \{E_i, E_j\}.$
5. $neg(E) \equiv !E.$

Example 7 *The EPL expression*
$$(\texttt{upd(A(X)}, \texttt{qa(X))}, \ * : (* : \texttt{ins(B(Y)}, \texttt{q}_b\texttt{(X, Y))}, \ \texttt{del(C(Z)}, \texttt{q}_c\texttt{(X, Z)))}, \ \texttt{upd(D(V)}, \texttt{q}_d\texttt{(X, V)))}$$

The parse tree for the expression of Example 7 is shown in Figure 1. The nodes of the tree are numbered according to the postorder traversal sequence.

Each node `i` corresponds to a subevent E_i, and the *satisfaction predicate* of E_i is denoted as $\texttt{sat}_i$. For a subevent expression, its *satisfaction predicate* contains one tuple for each distinct (in terms of variable bindings and stage) occurrence of this subevent.

---

[1] $(E_1, E_2, \ldots, E_{n-1}, E_n) = seq(E_1, seq(E_2, \ldots, seq(E_{n-1}, E_n) \ldots))$. Similarly for the relaxed sequence, the conjunction and the disjunction constructs.

[2] We use the binary construct `*seq` in place of the $* :$ EPL construct, so that the representation is more compact and easier to follow. This is not restricting, since $* : E \equiv *seq(E, \varepsilon)$, where $\varepsilon \equiv$ no event.

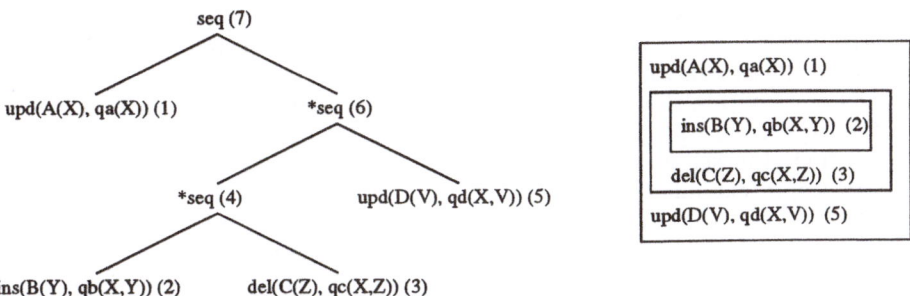

Figure 1: An EPL expression with Immediate and Star Sequences

3.2   The Translation Procedure

As demonstrated by the last translation example, for a composite EPL expression, the $Datalog_{1S}$ rules must model (i) the transmission of variable bindings according to the scope rules of the various constructs, so that variables can be matched and conditions can be checked, and (ii) the temporal precedences among the various subevents.

Table 1 describes how this information is derived for each basic EPL construct (formally it defines a simple attribute grammar for syntax-directed translation).

EvtType E	PPS	EVar(E)	IVar
$evt(R(X))$	—	X	—
$seq(F,G)$	$PPS(F) = PPS(E)$ $PPS(G) = F$	$EVar(F) \cup$ $EVar(G)$	$IVar(F) = IVar(E)$ $IVar(G) = IVar(E) \cup$ $EVar(F)$
$*seq(F,G)$	$PPS(F) = F \cup PPS(E)$ $PPS(G) = F \cup PPS(E)$	$EVar(G)$	$IVar(F) = IVar(E)$ $IVar(G) = IVar(E)$
$or(F,G)$	$PPS(F) = PPS(E)$ $PPS(G) = PPS(E)$	$\emptyset$	$IVar(F) = IVar(E)$ $IVar(G) = IVar(E)$
$and(F,G)$	$PPS(F) = PPS(E)$ $PPS(G) = PPS(E)$	$EVar(F) \cup$ $EVar(G)$	$IVar(F) = IVar(E)$ $IVar(G) = IVar(E)$
$neg(F)$	$PPS(F) = PPS(E)$	$\emptyset$	$IVar(F) = IVar(E)$

Table 1: An attribute grammar for syntax-directed translation from EPL to $Datalog_{1S}$.

For each subevent Q of an EPL event E, the second column in Table 1 defines the *Possible Predecessors Set* of Q, denoted as PPS(Q). A subevent P is a possible predecessor of Q within E, if in an instance of E, the satisfaction of P can *immediately* precede the first basic event of an instance of Q (i.e., the instance of Q can begin at the next stage). Because of disjunctions and the star operator, a particular subevent may have many possible predecessors.

For example, consider the immediate sequence event: E = seq(F,G). F is the only possible predecessor of G; but the set of possible predecessors of F depends on which events may precede E—i.e., F inherits E's possible predecessors.

The remaining two columns of Table 1 describe the scope rules for variables in EPL. The third column shows the set of *exported variables* of an EPL expression. These are variables defined in the expression (variables appearing in basic events within this expression), whose scopes extends past the satisfaction of the expression. The fourth column contains for each subevent Q of an EPL expression, the set of variables *imported* into Q (variables defined outside Q, whose scopes extends to Q).

Again, for E = seq(F,G), the set of variables exported from E is the union of the variables exported from F and G. On the other hand, E might have imported some variable names from previous events and if so, these are also passed down to F and G. In addition to variables inherited by E, variables imported into G include those exported from F.

Event Type E	Datalog$_{1S}$ Rule Templates
Qual. Basic Event $evt(R(X),\ Cond)$	*for each* $P \in PPS(E)$ $sat_E(IV, X, s(J)) \leftarrow evt\_R(X, s(J)),\ sat_P(IV, \_, J),$ $Cond(IV, X)$
$seq(F(X), G(Y))$	$sat_E(IV, X, Y, J) \leftarrow sat_G(IV, X, Y, J)$
$*seq(F(X), G(Y))$	$sat_E(IV, Y, J) \leftarrow sat_G(IV, Y, J)$
$or(F(X), G(Y))$	$sat_E(IV, J) \leftarrow sat_F(IV, X, J)$ $sat_E(IV, J) \leftarrow sat_G(IV, Y, J)$
$and(F(X), G(Y))$	$sat_E(X, Y, IV, J) \leftarrow sat_F(IV, X, J),\ sat_G(IV, Y, J)$
$neg(F(X))$	*for each* $P \in PPS(E)$ $sat_E(IV, s(J)) \leftarrow any(s(J)),\ sat_P(IV, \_, J),$ $\neg sat_F(\_, s(J))$
ε	*for each* $P \in PPS(E)$, $sat_E(IV, J) \leftarrow sat_P(IV, \_, J)$

Table 2: *Datalog*$_{1S}$ rule templates for the basic constructs of EPL.

Using the information of Table 1, the generation of the actual rules is simple as shown in Table 2. Observe that except for basic events, X and Y denote *sets* of exported variables defined in various subevents, where IV denotes the *set* of imported variables into a particular event type E. The anonymous variable _ has replaced all variables that must be kept local.

The first row of this table deals with qualified basic events having some possible predecessors (the case of a basic event with no possible predecessors is trivial). Such an event E is satisfied at stage s(J), when: (1) a possible predecessor of E was satisfied at stage J, (2) E occurs at stage s(J), and (3) The condition of E is satisfied. Example 6 illustrates this translation.

The rules for disjunction and conjunction are apparent. Observe that in a conjunction, all the variables defined in its conjuncts are exported, where in a disjunction, none of the variables defined in its disjuncts is exported. The rule for *negated events* is explained in Section 3.6.

Note also, that the variables of a satisfaction predicate consists of the union of its exported variables, plus the variables imported into it.

3.3 Immediate and Star Sequences

Having illustrated how immediate sequences are handled, we move on to the case of star sequences, which is somewhat more complicated.

Consider e.g., the EPL expression E = (F, G, *:H, K). Obviously, PPS(G) = {F}. However, because of the star operator, an instance of H might immediately follow either an occurrence of G, or a previous occurrence of H. Therefore, PPS(H) = {G,H}. Similarly, an instance of K may immediately follow either an occurrence of G (zero instances of H after G), or the last occurrence of H and thus, PPS(K) = {G,H}. Variables defined in a *star* subexpression are not exported to subexpressions that follow. The fourth row of Table 1 provides the formal details.

Example 7 shows a more complicated case, where *star* subexpressions are nested. Referring to Figure 1 and using Table 1, we get:

$$PPS(7) = \emptyset$$
$$PPS(1) = PPS(7) = \emptyset$$
$$PPS(6) = \{1\}$$
$$PPS(4) = \{4\} \cup PPS(6) = \{1,4\}$$
$$PPS(5) = \{4\} \cup PPS(6) = \{1,4\}$$
$$PPS(2) = \{2\} \cup PPS(4) = \{1,2,4\}$$
$$PPS(3) = \{2\} \cup PPS(4) = \{1,2,4\}$$

The variable scopes for this example have been visualized in Figure 1 using contours. Basic events are listed in order of their appearance in the EPL expression and all basic events in the same *star* subexpression are enclosed within the same contour. The condition of a basic event E can refer to all variables whose scopes extends to this event. Using this information and the *PPS* sets of the basic events, the following $Datalog_{1S}$ rules are derived for Example 7:

$$sat_1(X, J) \leftarrow upd\_A(X, J), \ q_a(X).$$
$$sat_2(X, Y, s(J)) \leftarrow ins\_B(Y, s(J)), \ sat_1(X, J), \ q_b(X, Y).$$
$$sat_2(X, Y, s(J)) \leftarrow ins\_B(Y, s(J)), \ sat_2(X, \_, J), \ q_b(X, Y).$$
$$sat_2(X, Y, s(J)) \leftarrow ins\_B(Y, s(J)), \ sat_4(X, \_, J), \ q_b(X, Y).$$
$$sat_3(X, Z, s(J)) \leftarrow del\_C(Z, s(J)), \ sat_1(X, J), \ q_c(X, Z).$$
$$sat_3(X, Z, s(J)) \leftarrow del\_C(Z, s(J)), \ sat_2(X, \_, J), \ q_c(X, Z).$$
$$sat_3(X, Z, s(J)) \leftarrow del\_C(Z, s(J)), \ sat_4(X, \_, J), \ q_c(X, Z).$$
$$sat_4(X, Z, J) \leftarrow sat_3(X, Z, J).$$
$$sat_5(X, V, s(J)) \leftarrow upd\_D(V, s(J)), \ sat_1(X, J), \ q_d(X, V).$$
$$sat_5(X, V, s(J)) \leftarrow upd\_D(V, s(J)), \ sat_4(X, \_, J), \ q_d(X, V).$$
$$sat_6(X, V, J) \leftarrow sat_5(X, V, J).$$
$$sat_E(X, V, J) \leftarrow sat_6(X, V, J).$$

Consider for instance $E_2 = ins(B(Y), q_b(X, Y))$. This basic event may immediately follow an occurrence of basic event E_1, or another occurrence of E_2 (because of the innermost star), or an occurrence of a star subsequence E_4 (because of the outermost * iteration).

The satisfaction predicates for the seq and *seq nodes are defined through *copy-rules*. These predicates are not needed, unless such a node is a possible predecessor of some basic event, as is the case of E_4. However, we have included them in our presentation for clarity reasons.

As demonstrated in this example, EPL scope rules are implemented, by passing variables through the satisfaction predicates, to the conditions of all the basic events within the scope of the variables.

3.4 Any and Relaxed Sequences

In section 2.2, EPL derivative constructs such as **any**, **prior**, and **relaxed sequences** were defined in terms of the basic constructs. Thus, a translation into $Datalog_{1S}$ need not be given explicitly. Yet, a direct translation is often desirable, as it leads to much more efficient implementation. For instance, **any** need not be defined as the disjunction of all basic events in the module of interest, but can be simply derived as follows:

$$\text{any}(J) \leftarrow \text{hist\_monit}(\_, \_, \_, J)$$

A relaxed sequence is treated similarly to an immediate sequence; e.g. the rules of Table 1 for an immediate sequence remain intact in the case of a relaxed sequence. The only difference is that in $[F, G]$, an instance of G may start at some stage later, but not necessarily immediately after an occurrence of F. By using an *auxiliary predicate* has_sat_1, the relaxed sequence

$$E = [\ \text{upd}(\text{ACC}(X), q_1(X)),\ \text{upd}(\text{ACC}(Y), q_2(X, Y))\ ],$$

can be translated into the following rules:

$$
\begin{aligned}
\text{sat}_1(X, J) &\leftarrow & \text{upd\_ACC}(X, J),\ q_1(X) \\
\text{has\_sat}_1(X, J) &\leftarrow & \text{sat}_1(X, J) \\
\text{has\_sat}_1(X, s(J)) &\leftarrow & \text{any}(s(J)),\ \text{has\_sat}_1(X, J) \\
\text{sat}_2(X, Y, s(J)) &\leftarrow & \text{upd\_ACC}(Y, s(J)),\ \text{has\_sat}_1(X, J),\ q_2(X, Y)
\end{aligned}
$$

3.5 Conjunction and Simultaneous Events

A *conjunctive event* $E = (F\ \&\ G)$ occurs at a stage where both F and G occur. The instances of F and G that cause E to be satisfied may have different starting stages. F and G are *evaluated independently of each other* (in parallel).

Using the conjunction construct, we can express sequences based on event occurrences, as opposed to event instances that follow each other. An example is the definition of **prior**, which is repeated here (variables are included):

$$E(X, Y) = \text{prior}(F(X), G(Y)) = (\ [F(X), \text{any}]\ \&\ G(Y)\ )$$

Assuming that the rules for $F(X)$ and $G(Y)$ have been generated and that an auxiliary predicate has_sat_F is defined as in the previous section, the satisfaction predicate of E is defined as:

$$\text{sat}_E(X, Y, s(J)) \leftarrow \text{sat}_G(Y, s(J)),\ \text{has\_sat}_F(X, J)$$

Conjunction can also be used to handle *simultaneous* events. Consider e.g.

$$E = (\ \text{upd}(A(X)),\ (\ \text{ins}(B(Y))\ \&\ \text{del}(C(Z))\ )\ ),$$

This composite event occurs when the first basic event is immediately followed by the simultaneous occurrence of the last two basic events. Its translation follows:

$$
\begin{aligned}
\text{sat}_1(X, J) &\leftarrow & \text{upd\_A}(X, J) \\
\text{sat}_2(X, Y, J) &\leftarrow & \text{ins\_B}(Y, s(J)),\ \text{sat}_1(X, J) \\
\text{sat}_3(X, Z, J) &\leftarrow & \text{del\_C}(Z, s(J)),\ \text{sat}_1(X, J) \\
\text{sat}_E(X, Y, Z, J) &\leftarrow & \text{sat}_2(X, Y, J),\ \text{sat}_3(X, Z, J)
\end{aligned}
$$

Eventhough simultaneous events have not been discussed in previous approaches, there are many cases where this functionality is desired. As discussed in the beginning of section 3, this is necessary when *transaction boundaries granularity* must be modeled. Simultaneous events may also occur in a distributed or multiprocessor environment.

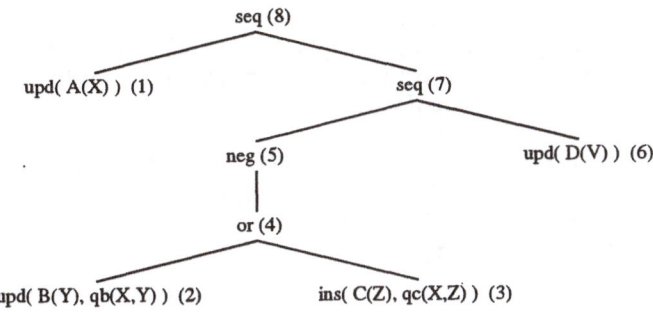

Figure 2: An EPL expression with a negated subevent

3.6 Negation

Handling negation of arbitrary composite events has been problematic in most of the previous approaches, which therefore support only limited forms of negation.

Using $Datalog_{1S}$, the semantics of general negation can be easily defined. For instance, for the negated qualified basic event
E = !ins(ACC(X), X.Type = "Savings"), we have (using domain variables):

$$sat_F(Accno, Owner, Type, Bal, Time, J) \leftarrow$$
$$ins\_ACC(Accno, Owner, Type, Bal, Time, J), \ Type = \text{``Savings''}$$
$$sat_E(J) \leftarrow \quad any(J), \ \neg sat_F(\_, \_, \_, \_, \_, J).$$

The second rule expresses the fact that E occurs at every stage where *some* basic event occurs, but F does not occur. Referring to the **hist_monit** table, E occurs at every stage, except stage 3, where an insertion of a savings account is recorded.

As these rules show, the variables defined inside a negated event are not exported outside it. This restriction ensures the safety and domain-independence of EPL expressions.

The general case is similar. The second rule above can still be used for the negated event E = !F, where F is an arbitrary event. Note that at every stage that sat_E is satisfied, we have the occurrence of a different instance of E, and thus, every such instance has *single stage duration*.

The following example illustrates how negated composite events are handled. This example also demonstrates a disjunctive event.

Example 8 *The EPL expression for Figure 2.*
(upd(A(X)), ! {upd(B(Y), q_b(X, Y)), ins(C(Z), q_c(X, Z))}, upd(D(V)))

The satisfaction of the negated event E_5 (at a stage where neither E_2, nor E_3 occur) must intervene the occurrences of basic events E_1 and E_6.

Since a negated event instance has *single stage duration*, negated events are treated similarly to basic events, as far as *ordering* is concerned. Namely, one rule of the form shown in Table 2 is created for each of the possible predecessor of a negated event. In this example, the only possible predecessor of the negated event E_5 is E_1.

The $Datalog_{1S}$ rules for Example 8 follow:

$$\begin{aligned}
\text{sat}_1(X, J) &\leftarrow & \text{upd\_A}(X, J). \\
\text{sat}_2(X, Y, s(J)) &\leftarrow & \text{upd\_B}(Y, s(J)),\ \text{sat}_1(X, J),\ q_b(X, Y). \\
\text{sat}_3(X, Z, s(J)) &\leftarrow & \text{ins\_C}(Z, s(J)),\ \text{sat}_1(X, J),\ q_c(X, Z). \\
\text{sat}_4(X, J) &\leftarrow & \text{sat}_2(X, Y, J). \\
\text{sat}_4(X, J) &\leftarrow & \text{sat}_3(X, Z, J). \\
\text{sat}_5(X, s(J)) &\leftarrow & \text{any}(s(J)),\ \text{sat}_1(X, J),\ \neg\text{sat}_4(\_, s(J)). \\
\text{sat}_6(X, V, J) &\leftarrow & \text{upd\_D}(V, s(J)),\ \text{sat}_5(X, J). \\
\text{sat}_7(X, V, J) &\leftarrow & \text{sat}_6(X, V, J). \\
\text{sat}_E(X, V, J) &\leftarrow & \text{sat}_7(X, V, J).
\end{aligned}$$

The rule for E_5 expresses the fact that E_5 occurs at the stage immediately following E_1's occurrence, if neither E_2, nor E_3 occur at this stage.

E_1 is considered to be a possible predecessor of E_2 and E_3 as well. Generally, in a sequence expression of the form $(F, !G)$, the subexpression G is evaluated with respect to the basic event history starting right after the satisfaction of F. Using Table 1, we get for instance:
$\text{PPS}(2) = \text{PPS}(4) = \text{PPS}(5) = \text{PPS}(7) = \{1\}$

4 Application to Other Systems

One of the most appealing characteristics of the proposed method is its generality, whereby it can be used for the formal definition of the concepts appearing in previous systems.

For the case of ODE, this is straightforward, since most of the language constructs in EPL and ODE are the same. The most important difference is that, in ODE, the *relaxed sequence* is a basic construct and the *immediate sequence* is a derivative one. Thus, the semantics of ODE can be defined by a syntax-directed translation from ODE expressions into $Datalog_{1S}$ rules, similar to that used for EPL. [3]

Such translation procedures can also be defined for Snoop and SAMOS's language, that have a somewhat different flavour from EPL and ODE. One of their differences is that the meaning of the sequence of two events E_1 and E_2 is equivalent to the meaning of $\text{prior}(E_1, E_2)$ in EPL and ODE.

Because of space limitations we cannot be exhaustive and in our discussion, we focus instead on concepts which are fundamental and distinguishing. Specifically, for Snoop, we focus on its novel concept of parameter contexts and we exemplify how this can be incorporated in our method. For SAMOS, we give a very detailed example of how we can formally define the execution semantics of Petri Nets, which have been used for its implementation. For an extended treatment of Snoop and its parameter contexts, the reader is referred to [15].

4.1 Parameter Contexts

The *parameters contexts* introduced in Snoop can be used to detect and compute the parameters of composite events in different ways, and thus, they can be very useful in precisely matching the semantics of a wide range of applications

---

[3] The definition of disjunction in ODE seems to be problematic. In [12], only conjunction is defined as a primitive construct, while disjunction is defined through negation, via De Morgan's law. This is a problem in the presence of variables and also when disjunctions with multiple-stage duration are concerned (a negative event has always single stage duration).

[4]. The general semantics of EPL and ODE correspond to the *unrestricted context* of Snoop.

For two of Snoop's parameter contexts, we show how to extend our method, in order to adopt them. We use a *relaxed sequence* example, since the various parameter contexts arise essentially by different interpretations of such sequences.

Example 9 *The EPL expression* E(X,Y,Z) = [A(X),B(Y),C(Z)], *and the event history:* $\ldots, A(1), \ldots A(2), \ldots, B(1), \ldots C(1), \ldots B(2), \ldots C(2)$, *where* A,B,C *denote basic events with parameters* X,Y,Z *respectively.*

In the *unrestricted context*, all the instances of E are detected. These are: $[A(1), B(1), C(1)]$, $[A(2), B(1), C(1)]$, $[A(1), B(1), C(2)]$, $[A(2), B(1), C(2)]$, $[A(1), B(2), C(2)]$, $[A(2), B(2), C(2)]$.

- **Recent Context.** In this context, at each stage of the history, only the most recent occurrences of the events (primitive or composite) are considered. The following instances of E are detected in the recent context: $[A(2), B(1), C(1)]$ and $[A(2), B(2), C(2)]$.

  We can enforce this parameter context by defining a predicate last_sat$_F$(X, J), for each Snoop subexpression F(X). In the last_sat$_F$, for a particular stage J, X denotes the set of parameter bindings of the *last* occurrence of F, *before or at* this stage. The following stratified $Datalog_{1S}$ rules define the semantics of our example EPL expression, in the recent context:

$$\text{sat}_1(X, J) \leftarrow \quad A(X, J)$$
$$\text{last\_sat}_1(X, J) \leftarrow \quad \text{sat}_1(X, J)$$
$$\text{last\_sat}_1(X, s(J)) \leftarrow \quad \text{any}(s(J)), \text{ last\_sat}_1(X, J), \neg\text{sat}_1(\_, s(J))$$

$$\text{sat}_2(X, Y, s(J)) \leftarrow \quad B(Y, s(J)), \text{ last\_sat}_1(X, J)$$
$$\text{last\_sat}_2(X, Y, J) \leftarrow \quad \text{sat}_2(X, Y, J)$$
$$\text{last\_sat}_2(X, Y, s(J)) \leftarrow \text{any}(s(J)), \text{ last\_sat}_2(X, Y, J), \neg\text{sat}_2(\_, \_, s(J))$$

$$\text{sat}_E(X, Y, Z, s(J)) \leftarrow \quad C(Z, s(J)), \text{ last\_sat}_2(X, Y, J)$$

- **Chronicle Context.** In the chronicle context, when a composite event E is satisfied, its parameter bindings are obtained from the oldest *unused* occurrences of its component events, that satisfy the precedence requirements of E (*unused* implying that the same basic event occurrence can participate in *at most one* instance of a particular composite event).

  Thus, the two instances of E that would be detected in the chronicle context are: $(A(1); B(1); C(1))$ and $(A(2); B(2); C(2))$.

  A way to express the chronicle context semantics using $Datalog_{1S}$ is illustrated in the next section, since as it is explained there, the execution semantics of Petri Nets correspond to this parameter context.

4.2 SAMOS and Petri Nets

The most distinguishing feature of SAMOS is its event detection mechanism, which is based on *coloured Petri Nets* [6]. A *coloured Petri Net* is an extended version of a classical Petri Net, that allows the flow of parameter bindings

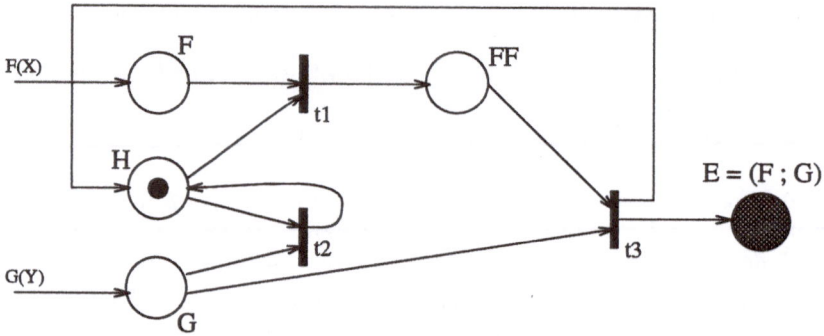

Figure 3: The Petri Net for the expression E = (F ; G).

through it. In this way, the parameter passing within a composite event instance can be modeled. For a detailed description of how Petri Nets can be used for the detection of composite events, the reader is referred to [11]. Here we focus on the example of Figure 3 borrowed from [10], which illustrates the basic concepts. The figure shows the initial state of the Petri Net, where a token is contained in the *auxiliary place* H.

This Petri Net accepts as input the occurrences of events F and G. Every such occurrence corresponds to a new token inserted into the Petri Net; this token contains the parameter bindings of the event occurrence. An output token is created when an occurrence $F(x)$ is matched with an appropriate occurrence $G(y)$. The output token containing the parameter bindings (x, y) is deposited into the output place E and a new occurrence of E is signaled. Right after that, this output token is removed from the Petri Net.

At a particular point in time, the tokens of the unmatched occurrences of F are contained in places F and FF. In particular, FF contains the token of the oldest among these occurrences, where F contains the tokens for the rest of them. These different tokens are distinguished by their *colours*. Specifically, a token corresponding to an occurrence of F is *coloured* with an integer denoting the *order* of this occurrence among all the occurrences of F in the event history (this can be obtained by a method similar to that defining the *stage* of a basic event in the event history).

An occurrence of G is ignored, if there is not any token (occurrence) in FF to be matched with; observe how this is achieved by using the *auxiliary place* H. However, an occurrence $G(y)$ that finds a token $F(x)$ in FF is matched with it (this is achieved by firing the gate t3) and the occurrence of $E(x, y)$ is then signaled. After that, H becomes active again (it contains a token) and if there are any tokens in F, the token of the *oldest* unmatched occurrence of F is passed to FF (through the firing of gate t1), so that it can be matched with the next occurrence of G. Note that this behaviour corresponds to the *chronicle* parameter context discussed in the previous section. The execution semantics of our Petri Net is best illustrated by an example, such as the one of Table 3.

Since, places F and FF are *coloured*, the colours (order numbers) of their tokens are shown as well. Place H is also coloured and the colour of its token is N+1, if N occurrences of E have been signaled so far (and thus, the first N occurrences of F have been used).

In coloured ordinary Petri Nets there is not inherent measure of time, or

Event	H	F	FF	G	E
	1	-	-	-	-
$G(y_a)$	1	-	-	y_a	-
t_2 fires	1	-	-	-	-
$F(x_a)$	1	$(x_a,1)$	-	-	-
t_1 fires	-	-	$(x_a,1)$	-	-
$F(x_b)$	-	$(x_b,2)$	$(x_a,1)$	-	-
$G(y_b)$	-	$(x_b,2)$	$(x_a,1)$	y_b	-
t_3 fires	2	$(x_b,2)$	-	-	(x_a,y_b)
t_1 fires	-	-	$(x_b,2)$	-	-
$G(y_c)$	-	-	$(x_b,2)$	y_c	-
t_3 fires	3	-	-	-	(x_b,y_c)

Table 3: An execution sequence of the Petri Net in Figure 3.

model of time flow. Thus, ordinary Petri Nets make it possible to describe *what* happens, but not *when* it happens [6]. Aiming at resolving this issue, an extension of ordinary Petri Nets, called *synchronized* Petri Nets, has recently been proposed. They enable the modeling of systems whose evolutions are time dependent and where the succession of system *states* must be clearly and deterministically described. The *state* of a Petri Net is defined by the assignment of tokens to places.

In a synchronized Petri Net, gate firings are synchronized to external events and they obey a particular partial order defined by the structure of the Petri Net. An external event triggers a sequence of gate firings that occur in one or more *steps*, until the Petri Net reaches a *stable state*. This is exemplified in Table 3.

We now demonstrate how $Datalog_{1S}$ can be used to capture the execution semantics of a synchronized Petri Net. We assume that the occurrences of basic events are *non-simultaneous*, as required by Petri Nets (this is in fact a limitation of theirs). The following $Datalog_{1S}$ program defines the execution semantics of the Petri Net in Figure 3.

$$
\begin{aligned}
&\text{in\_F}(X, N, J) \leftarrow && F(X, N, J) \\
&\text{in\_F}(X, N, s(J)) \leftarrow && \text{any}(s(J)),\ \text{in\_F}(X, N, J),\ \neg t_1(X, N, s(J)) \\[4pt]
&\text{in\_H}(1, 0) && \\
&\text{in\_H}(N, s(J)) \leftarrow && \text{any}(s(J)),\ \text{in\_H}(N, J),\ \neg t_1(\_, N, s(J)),\ \neg t_2(\_, N, s(J)) \\
&\text{in\_H}(N, J) \leftarrow && t_2(\_, N, J) \\
&\text{in\_H}(N + 1, J) \leftarrow && t_3(\_, \_, N, J) \\[4pt]
&\text{in\_G}(Y, J) \leftarrow && G(Y, J) \\
&\text{in\_G}(Y, s(J)) \leftarrow && \text{any}(s(J)),\ \text{in\_G}(Y, J),\ \neg t_2(Y, \_, s(J)),\ \neg t_3(\_, Y, \_, s(J)) \\[4pt]
&\text{in\_FF}(X, N, J) \leftarrow && t_1(X, N, J) \\
&\text{in\_FF}(X, N, s(J)) \leftarrow && \text{any}(s(J)),\ \text{in\_F}(X, N, J),\ \neg t_3(X, \_, N, s(J)) \\[4pt]
&\text{sat}_E(X, Y, J) \leftarrow && t_3(X, Y, \_, J) \\[4pt]
&t_1(X, N, s(J)) \leftarrow && \text{in\_F}(X, N, J),\ \text{in\_H}(N, J) \\
&t_2(Y, N, s(J)) \leftarrow && \text{in\_G}(Y, J),\ \text{in\_H}(N, J) \\
&t_3(X, Y, N, s(J)) \leftarrow && \text{in\_FF}(X, N, J),\ \text{in\_G}(Y, J)
\end{aligned}
$$

An *order parameter* N for the occurrences of basic event F has been introduced. A different predicate is defined for each place and each gate.

Consider for instance the rules for place F. The first rule says that the token for the *N-th* occurrence of F is deposited into the place of F, at the stage of that occurrence. The second rule says that the token of *colour* N (corresponding to the *N-th* occurrence of F) is contained in place F at stage s(J), if it is contained there at stage J and gate t1 is not enabled at stage s(J), which would cause that token to be removed.

On the other hand, the rule for a gate expresses the fact that if all its inputs become active at stage J, then the gate is enabled at stage s(J). An output token is created from information passed from the inputs of gate t3 and it is deposited into the place for E — see the rules for t3 and sat$_E$.

The *component by component* translation described above can produce a lengthy set of rules. Moreover, note that we have lost the direct correspondence between basic event occurrences and stages, which we have assumed in the previous sections.

We can solve these problems by providing a much simpler set of $Datalog_{1S}$ rules, that still models precisely the execution semantics of our example Petri Net and also maintains the one-to-one correspondence between external basic events and stages. This is achieved by folding the sequence of stages (states) in Table 3 into the one in Table 4.

In the new table, each external basic event creates only one new stage. This stage is defined by (a) the tokens residing at the regular places F and FF, at the end of the *sequence of firings* originated by the basic event, and (b) the token (if any) deposited into the output place E, during this sequence of firings.

Event	F	FF	E
	-	-	-
$G(y_a)$	-	-	-
$F(x_a)$	-	$(x_a,1)$	-
$F(x_b)$	$(x_b,2)$	$(x_a,1)$	-
$G(y_b)$	-	$(x_b,2)$	$(x_a y_b,1)$
$G(y_c)$	-	-	$(x_b y_c,2)$

Table 4: The simplified stage sequence for the execution sequence of Table 3.

The following $Datalog_{1S}$ rules defines the sequence of stages in Table 4:

$$\text{in\_F}(X, N, s(J)) \leftarrow F(X, N, s(J)), \text{in\_FF}(\_, \_, J)$$
$$\text{in\_F}(X, N, s(J)) \leftarrow \text{any}(s(J)), \text{in\_F}(X, N, J), \neg\text{in\_FF}(X, N, s(J))$$

$$\text{in\_FF}(X, N, s(J)) \leftarrow F(X, N, s(J)), \neg\text{in\_FF}(\_, \_, J)$$
$$\text{in\_FF}(X, N+1, s(J)) \leftarrow \text{in\_F}(X, N+1, J), \text{sat}_E(\_, \_, N, s(J))$$

$$\text{sat}_E(X, Y, N, s(J)) \leftarrow G(Y, s(J)), \text{in\_FF}(X, N, J)$$

Note that no predicate is needed for auxiliary place H. Also, no predicate is needed for G, since an occurrence of G is either immediately matched with an occurrence of F, or it is "dumped". As a result, we obtain a much simpler set of rules that still defines precisely the execution semantics of our example Petri Net.

Eventhough these rules are not stratified, they are locally stratified and XY-*stratified* [19]; therefore they can be evaluated in an incremental and efficient manner. To see that, observe that the computation of the contents of in_F and in_FF at stage J can be followed by the computation of the contents of in_FF at stage s(J), which can then be followed by the computation of the contents of in_F at stage s(J). This order of evaluation (prescribed by the XY-stratification of the program) leads to an efficient fixpoint, which is triggered by each basic event occurrence and terminates in a fixed number of steps.

5 Related Work

There has been no generally accepted approach to the definition of semantics and to the implementation of event detection mechanisms for composite event specification languages; each system employs a different formalism.

We consider first the familiar model of Finite State Machines (FSMs), which is the implementation framework of ODE. Eventhough FSMs provide an easy-to-understand model that is suggestive of efficient implementation, they suffer from two major limitations, as follows:

1. FSMs do not support variables. It is suggested in [12] that parameter-ized events are handled by creating several instances of an FSM, one for each set of partial variable bindings of the composite event that the FSM implements (detects). The resulting model surrenders the initial simplicity and intuitive appeal of FSMs, without providing a fail-proof formalism. In particular, the semantics of negation when attributes are involved remains a problem.

2. Since FSMs are inherently sequential, simultaneous events cannot be handled, unless transitions based on combinations of events are allowed. But even if simultaneous events are disallowed, constructs such as conjunction can only be modeled by an exponentially increasing size of states in an FSM. This is because the FSM for $E = E_1 \wedge E_2$ is built by constructing the cross-product of the FSMs for E_1 and E_2 [14]. Instead, in EPL, the fact that the two conjuncts are evaluated *in parallel* and *independently* from each other leads to the generation of a number of rules that equals the sum of the numbers of rules generated for the two conjuncts, plus an extra rule for the conjunction condition.

Petri Nets solve the problem of exponential blow-up in FSMs, by allowing concurrent processing. Also, coloured Petri Nets cater for the handling of parameterized composite events. However, there are still some limitations. Simultaneous events cannot be handled. Also, it is not clear how the semantics of general negation (as defined in EPL) can be captured by Petri nets. The composite event detection mechanism of Snoop, which is based on Event Graphs, [3] suffers from these limitations as well.

Another concept, whose formal definition is missing in previous approaches is that of *event histories* and the *succession of states* in the system. This becomes necessary when introducing simultaneous events. Finally, all previous approaches are limited to operational specifications, where our logic-based approach has a declarative nature.

Our method has similarities to Chomicki's work on the efficient detection of violations of dynamic integrity constraints [5], which is not however directly related to general active database systems. Integrity constraints are expressed in Temporal Logic. Another difference of [5] from our work is that *condition-action* rules are used, which are re-evaluated at each stage, in an incremental, *history-less* way. This is contrasted to our *event-driven* rules.

6 Conclusions and Future Work

In this paper, we have proposed a general method for the definition of the semantics of composite event languages, such as those used in active temporal databases. Whereas different formalisms were used in the past for different languages, we have shown here that the same formalism can be used to define the concepts of every language. As a result, the task of comparing and understanding the differences and similarities of the languages is simplified.

Besides generality, another advantage of the proposed approach is that event histories, simultaneous events, variables and their scopes, parameter contexts, negation, conjunction and disjunction can all be part of the same model. $Datalog_{1S}$ is a most natural tool for defining the semantics of event languages, due to its ability to model both the temporal and logical aspects of queries.

From an implementation standpoint, the produced sets of rules can be efficiently evaluated in an incremental and history-less manner.

This paper leaves several issues to further research. For instance, the issue of comparing the expressive power of different composite event languages is one that deserves much more attention than it has received so far. In this respect, $Datalog_{1S}$ provides a sound formal basis, due to the fact that its formal semantics is well-understood and its expressive power w.r.t. to other languages (temporal or otherwise) has been previously characterized [2].

A related issue is to compare the effectiveness of different temporal reasoning formalisms in expressing the semantics of active temporal languages. For instance, composite event expressions could also be translated into Temporal Logic [8], or a temporal logic programming language, such as Templog [2], or SimTL [18]. In many cases, this yields a very natural formal definition of the semantics such expressions. For instance, the following *Future Temporal Logic* formula defines the meaning of the EPL expression $E = (A, *:(*:B, C), D)$, which has a form similar to that of example 7:

$$E = A \text{ next } ((B \text{ until } C) \text{ until } D)$$

On the other hand, $Datalog_{1S}$ is normally more conducive to effective operational semantics than Temporal Logic formulas. Thus, one might prefer to use $Datalog_{1S}$, or alternatively, to derive efficient operational semantics by translating Temporal Logic formulas into $Datalog_{1S}$, a mapping discussed in [2]. Finally, the optimization of operational semantics presents many opportunities for significant improvements and interesting research.

References

[1] N. Arni, K. Ong, S. Tsur, and C. Zaniolo. LDL++: A second generation deductive database system. submitted for publication.

[2] M. Baudinet, J. Chomicki, and P. Wolper. Temporal Deductive Databases. In A. Tansel et al., editor, *Temporal Databases: Theory, Design and Implementation*, chapter 13, pages 294–320. Benjamin/Cummings, 1993.

[3] S. Chakravarthy, V. Krishnaprasad, E. Anwar, and S. K. Kim. Anatomy of a composite event detector. Technical Report CIS TR-93-039, University of Florida, December 1993.

[4] S. Chakravarthy, V. Krishnaprasad, E. Anwar, and S. K. Kim. Composite events for active databases: Semantics, contexts and detection. In *Proceedings of the 20th VLDB Conference*, pages 606–617, September 1994.

[5] J. Chomicki. History-less checking of dynamic integrity constraints. In *Proceedings of the International Conference on Data Engineering*, pages 557–564, 1992.

[6] R. David. *Petri Nets and Grafcet: Tools for modeling discrete event systems*. Prentice Hall, New York, 1992.

[7] U. Dayal, E.N. Hanson, and J. Widom. Active Database Systems. In W. Kim, editor, *Modern Database Systems*. Addison Wesley, 1995.

[8] E. Emerson. Temporal and Modal Logic. In Jan van Leeuwen, editor, *Handbook of Theoretical Computer Science*, volume B, chapter 16, pages 995–1072. Elsevier/MIT Press, 1990.

[9] U. Dayal et al. The HiPAC Project: Combining active databases and timing constraints. *ACM-SIGMOD Record*, 17(1):51–70, March 1988.

[10] S. Gatziu and K. R. Dittrich. Events in an object-oriented database system. In *Proceedings of the First Intl. Conference on Rules in Database Systems*, pages 23–39, September 1993.

[11] S. Gatziu and K. R. Dittrich. Detecting composite events in active databases using petri nets. In *Proceedings of the 4th Intl. Workshop on Research Issues in Data Engineering: Active Database Systems*, pages 2–9, 1994.

[12] N. H. Gehani, H. V. Jagadish, and O. Shmueli. Composite event specification in active databases: Model and implementation. In *Proceedings of the 18th VLDB International Conference*, pages 327–338, 1992.

[13] N. H. Gehani, H. V. Jagadish, and O. Shmueli. Event specification in an active object-oriented database. In *Proceedings of the ACM SIGMOD International Conference on Management of Data*, pages 81–90, 1992.

[14] D. Harel, A. Pnueli, J. P. Schmidt, and R. Sherman. On the formal semantics of statecharts. In *Proceedings of the 2nd IEEE Symposium on Logic in Computer Science*, pages 54–64, 1987.

[15] I. Motakis and C. Zaniolo. Composite Temporal Events in Active Database Rules: A Logic-Oriented Approach. submitted for publication.

[16] NASA, Lyndon Johnson Space Center, Software Technology Branch. *CLIPS 6.0 Reference Manual*, June 1993.

[17] N. Pissinou, R. Snodgrass, R. Elmasri, I. Mumick, M. Ozsu, B. Pernici, A. Segev, B. Theodoulidis, and U. Dayal. Towards an infrastructure for temporal databases. *ACM-SIGMOD Record*, 23(1), March 1994.

[18] A. Tuzhilin. Applications of Temporal Databases to Knowledge-based Simulations. In A. Tansel et al., editor, *Temporal Databases: Theory, Design and Implementation*, chapter 23. Benjamin/Cummings, 1993.

[19] C. Zaniolo. A unified semantics for active and deductive databases. In *Proceedings of the 1st International Workshop on Rules in Database Systems*, pages 271–287, 1993.

VII. Panels

PANEL
Whither TSQL3?

Panel Chair: Richard T. Snodgrass, University of Arizona

Panelists:
James Clifford, Stern School of Business, New York University
Umeshwar Dayal, Hewlett-Packard Labs
Arie Segev, University of California, Berkeley

TSQL2 was designed to be a minimal extension of SQL-92. Now that this language design effort has completed, and the SQL3 standards bodies are integrating constructs from TSQL2 into that language, it seems appropriate to consider TSQL3, which was initially envisioned to be an object-oriented extension of SQL3 incorporating time.

This panel considered the following questions related to this issue.

- Are new temporal constructs even necessary, or do the existing object-oriented constructs in SQL3 provide sufficient functionality?

- Do we have sufficient implementation experience in temporal object-oriented database management systems to define a standard temporal object-oriented query language?

- TSQL2 has at its core a few "big ideas", including the separation of representational data models from a single conceptual data model and the use of restructuring. What big ideas should guide the design of TSQL3?

- Is SQL3 a sufficiently stable base on which to define TSQL3? What time frame for the definition of TSQL3 is appropriate?

- What organizational structure should be put into place?

- What are the important design parameters for TSQL3?

  - Should TSQL3 be temporally grouped complete?
  - Should objects or attributes be versioned?
  - Should transaction time be linear or branching?
  - How should schema evolution interact with schema versioning?

PANEL
The State-of-the-Art in Temporal Data Management: Perspectives from the Research and Financial Applications Communities

Panel Chair: James Clifford, New York University

Part I: Current State of Temporal Data Management Infrastructure
Panelists:
Christian Jensen, University of Aalborg
Richard T. Snodgrass, University of Arizona
Michael H. Böhlen, University of Arizona

In the first part of the panel, several well-known researchers from the temporal database field discussed ongoing efforts to create an infrastructure to support temporal data management. What infrastructure now exists, or should exist soon?

Specific aspects of the infrastructure that were addressed included:

The Temporal Database Glossary What has been the impact of the previous glossary? There are some 26 terms in the nextGlos.tex file. Should a new version be initiated? If so, which areas should be emphasized?

The TSQL2 Language Design The current status on this language was discussed, including the ongoing efforts at standardization.

Implementations of Temporal DBMS Existing implementations of temporal database management systems were summarized.

Part II: Current State of Temporal Data Management in Financial Applications
Panelists:
Hasan Dewan, Morgan Stanley
Duri Schmidt, Union Bank of Switzerland

In the second part of the panel, several practitioners from the financial community discussed the current practices in the field, from their individual (and corporate) perspectives. They addressed both the potential benefits and problems inherent in the current directions being taken by the research community.

Specific aspects of temporal data management in financial applications that were be addressed included:

- What are the temporal data management needs of applications in this area?

- What are the state-of-the-art industrial practices in place today for temporal data management in this application community?

- What input can practitioners in this application area provide to database researchers in the area regarding temporal data modeling and temporal data management capabilities for future DBMS development?

- What aspects of TSQL2 appear to be useful in this application area?

- What shortcomings does TSQL2 appear to have with respect to the needs of this community?

Author Index

Published in 1990–93

User Workshop, Oxford 1989, Proceedings of the Fourth Annual Z User Meeting, Oxford, 15 December 1989
J. E. Nicholls (Ed.)

Formal Methods for Trustworthy Computer Systems (FM89), Halifax, Canada, 23–27 July 1989
Dan Craigen (Editor) and Karen Summerskill (Assistant Editor)

Security and Persistence, Proceedings of the International Workshop on Computer Architectures to Support Security and Persistence of Information, Bremen, West Germany, 8–11 May 1990
John Rosenberg and J. Leslie Keedy (Eds)

Women into Computing: Selected Papers 1988–1990
Gillian Lovegrove and Barbara Segal (Eds)

3rd Refinement Workshop (organised by BCS-FACS, and sponsored by IBM UK Laboratories, Hursley Park and the Programming Research Group, University of Oxford), Hursley Park, 9–11 January 1990
Carroll Morgan and J. C. P. Woodcock (Eds)

Designing Correct Circuits, Workshop jointly organised by the Universities of Oxford and Glasgow, Oxford, 26–28 September 1990
Geraint Jones and Mary Sheeran (Eds)

Functional Programming, Glasgow 1990
Proceedings of the 1990 Glasgow Workshop on Functional Programming, Ullapool, Scotland, 13–15 August 1990
Simon L. Peyton Jones, Graham Hutton and Carsten Kehler Holst (Eds)

4th Refinement Workshop, Proceedings of the 4th Refinement Workshop, organised by BCS-FACS, Cambridge, 9–11 January 1991
Joseph M. Morris and Roger C. Shaw (Eds)

AI and Cognitive Science '90, University of Ulster at Jordanstown, 20–21 September 1990
Michael F. McTear and Norman Creaney (Eds)

Software Re-use, Utrecht 1989, Proceedings of the Software Re-use Workshop, Utrecht, The Netherlands, 23–24 November 1989
Liesbeth Dusink and Patrick Hall (Eds)

Z User Workshop, 1990, Proceedings of the Fifth Annual Z User Meeting, Oxford, 17–18 December 1990
J.E. Nicholls (Ed.)

IV Higher Order Workshop, Banff 1990
Proceedings of the IV Higher Order Workshop, Banff, Alberta, Canada, 10–14 September 1990
Graham Birtwistle (Ed.)

ALPUK91, Proceedings of the 3rd UK Annual Conference on Logic Programming, Edinburgh, 10–12 April 1991
Geraint A.Wiggins, Chris Mellish and Tim Duncan (Eds)

Specifications of Database Systems
International Workshop on Specifications of Database Systems, Glasgow, 3–5 July 1991
David J. Harper and Moira C. Norrie (Eds)

7th UK Computer and Telecommunications Performance Engineering Workshop
Edinburgh, 22–23 July 1991
J. Hillston, P.J.B. King and R.J. Pooley (Eds)

Logic Program Synthesis and Transformation
Proceedings of LOPSTR 91, International Workshop on Logic Program Synthesis and Transformation, University of Manchester, 4–5 July 1991
T.P. Clement and K.-K. Lau (Eds)

Declarative Programming, Sasbachwalden 1991
PHOENIX Seminar and Workshop on Declarative Programming, Sasbachwalden, Black Forest, Germany, 18–22 November 1991
John Darlington and Roland Dietrich (Eds)

Building Interactive Systems: Architectures and Tools
Philip Gray and Roger Took (Eds)

Functional Programming, Glasgow 1991
Proceedings of the 1991 Glasgow Workshop on Functional Programming, Portree, Isle of Skye, 12–14 August 1991
Rogardt Heldal, Carsten Kehler Holst and Philip Wadler (Eds)

Object Orientation in Z
Susan Stepney, Rosalind Barden and David Cooper (Eds)

Code Generation – Concepts, Tools, Techniques
Proceedings of the International Workshop on Code Generation, Dagstuhl, Germany, 20–24 May 1991
Robert Giegerich and Susan L. Graham (Eds)

Z User Workshop, York 1991, Proceedings of the Sixth Annual Z User Meeting, York, 16–17 December 1991
J.E. Nicholls (Ed.)

Formal Aspects of Measurement
Proceedings of the BCS-FACS Workshop on Formal Aspects of Measurement, South Bank University, London, 5 May 1991
Tim Denvir, Ros Herman and R.W. Whitty (Eds)

AI and Cognitive Science '91 University College, Cork, 19–20 September 1991
Humphrey Sorensen (Ed.)

5th Refinement Workshop, Proceedings of the 5th Refinement Workshop, organised by BCS-FACS, London, 8–10 January 1992
Cliff B. Jones, Roger C. Shaw and Tim Denvir (Eds)

Algebraic Methodology and Software Technology (AMAST'91)
Proceedings of the Second International Conference on Algebraic Methodology and Software Technology, Iowa City, USA, 22–25 May 1991
M. Nivat, C. Rattray, T. Rus and G. Scollo (Eds)

ALPUK92, Proceedings of the 4th UK Conference on Logic Programming, London, 30 March–1 April 1992
Krysia Broda (Ed.)

Logic Program Synthesis and Transformation
Proceedings of LOPSTR 92, International Workshop on Logic Program Synthesis and Transformation, University of Manchester, 2–3 July 1992
Kung-Kiu Lau and Tim Clement (Eds)

NAPAW 92, Proceedings of the First North American Process Algebra Workshop, Stony Brook, New York, USA, 28 August 1992
S. Purushothaman and Amy Zwarico (Eds)

First International Workshop on Larch
Proceedings of the First International Workshop on Larch, Dedham, Massachusetts, USA, 13–15 July 1992
Ursula Martin and Jeannette M. Wing (Eds)

Persistent Object Systems
Proceedings of the Fifth International Workshop on Persistent Object Systems, San Miniato (Pisa), Italy, 1–4 September 1992
Antonio Albano and Ron Morrison (Eds)

Formal Methods in Databases and Software Engineering, Proceedings of the Workshop on Formal Methods in Databases and Software Engineering, Montreal, Canada, 15–16 May 1992
V.S. Alagar, Laks V.S. Lakshmanan and F. Sadri (Eds)

Modelling Database Dynamics
Selected Papers from the Fourth International Workshop on Foundations of Models and Languages for Data and Objects, Volkse, Germany, 19–22 October 1992
Udo W. Lipeck and Bernhard Thalheim (Eds)

14th Information Retrieval Colloquium
Proceedings of the BCS 14th Information Retrieval Colloquium, University of Lancaster, 13–14 April 1992
Tony McEnery and Chris Paice (Eds)

Functional Programming, Glasgow 1992
Proceedings of the 1992 Glasgow Workshop on Functional Programming, Ayr, Scotland, 6–8 July 1992
John Launchbury and Patrick Sansom (Eds)

Z User Workshop, London 1992
Proceedings of the Seventh Annual Z User Meeting, London, 14–15 December 1992
J.P. Bowen and J.E. Nicholls (Eds)

Interfaces to Database Systems (IDS92)
Proceedings of the First International Workshop on Interfaces to Database Systems, Glasgow, 1–3 July 1992
Richard Cooper (Ed.)

AI and Cognitive Science '92
University of Limerick, 10–11 September 1992
Kevin Ryan and Richard F.E. Sutcliffe (Eds)

Theory and Formal Methods 1993
Proceedings of the First Imperial College Department of Computing Workshop on Theory and Formal Methods, Isle of Thorns Conference Centre, Chelwood Gate, Sussex, UK, 29–31 March 1993
Geoffrey Burn, Simon Gay and Mark Ryan (Eds)

Algebraic Methodology and Software Technology (AMAST'93)
Proceedings of the Third International Conference on Algebraic Methodology and Software Technology, University of Twente, Enschede, The Netherlands, 21–25 June 1993
M. Nivat, C. Rattray, T. Rus and G. Scollo (Eds)

Logic Program Synthesis and Transformation
Proceedings of LOPSTR 93, International Workshop on Logic Program Synthesis and Transformation, Louvain-la-Neuve, Belgium, 7–9 July 1993
Yves Deville (Ed.)

Database Programming Languages (DBPL-4)
Proceedings of the Fourth International Workshop on Database Programming Languages – Object Models and Languages, Manhattan, New York City, USA, 30 August–1 September 1993
Catriel Beeri, Atsushi Ohori and Dennis E. Shasha (Eds)

Music Education: An Artificial Intelligence Approach, Proceedings of a Workshop held as part of AI-ED 93, World Conference on Artificial Intelligence in Education, Edinburgh, Scotland, 25 August 1993
Matt Smith, Alan Smaill and Geraint A. Wiggins (Eds)